DAVID BUSCH'S
DJI Mini 3/ Mini 3 Pro

GUIDE TO
DRONE PHOTOGRAPHY

DAVID D. BUSCH

**David Busch's DJI Mini 3/Mini 3 Pro
Guide to Drone Photography**
David D. Busch

Project Manager: Jenny Davidson
Layout: Bill Hartman
Cover Design: Mike Tanamachi
Indexer: Valerie Haynes Perry
Proofreader: Mike Beady

ISBN: 979-8-88814-132-8
1st Edition (1st printing, February 2024)

© 2024 David D. Busch

All images © David D. Busch unless otherwise noted

Rocky Nook, Inc.
1010 B Street, Suite 350
San Rafael, CA 94901
USA
www.rockynook.com

Distributed in the UK and Europe by Publishers Group UK
Distributed in the U.S. and all other territories by Publishers Group West

Library of Congress Control Number: 2023937139

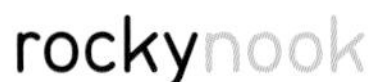

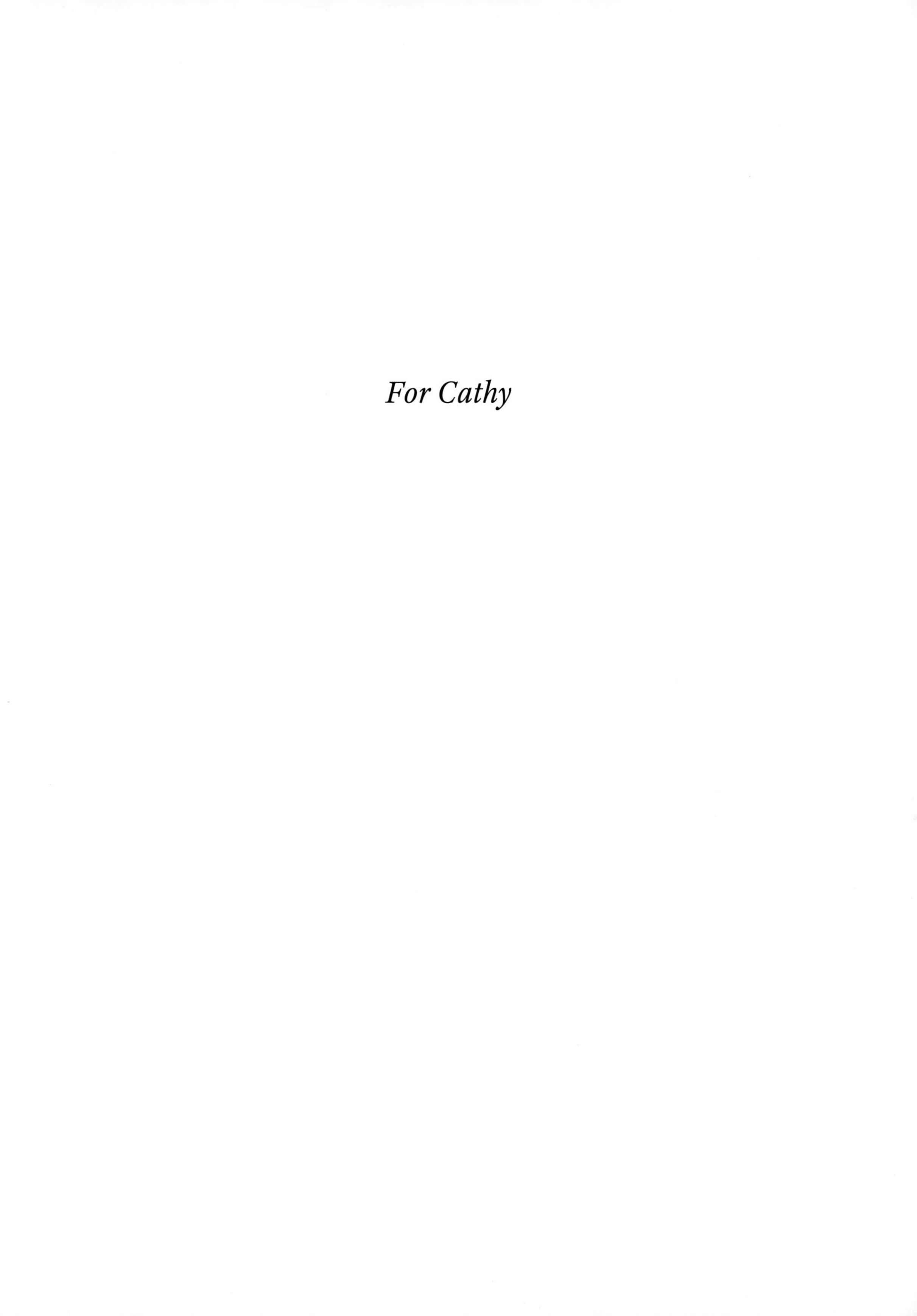

For Cathy

Acknowledgments

Thanks to everyone at Rocky Nook, including Scott Cowlin, managing director and publisher, for the freedom to let me explore the amazing still photography and video capabilities of the DJI Mini 3 and Mini 3 Pro in depth. I couldn't do it without my veteran production team, supervised by my project manager, Jenny Davidson. Also, thanks to Bill Hartman, layout; Valerie Hayes Perry, indexing; Mike Beady, proofreading; Mike Tanamachi, cover design; and my agent, Carole Jelen, who has the amazing ability to keep both publishers and authors happy.

Special thanks go to technical editor Don Burkholder. He was an accomplished professional photographer even before he got his commercial pilot's license decades ago, and insights from his experience with drone photography were invaluable. I also want to thank veteran shooter Kolman Rosenberg, a consummate photojournalist who also applies his skills to a broad range of other types of photography, including compelling images from his DJI aircraft. You can see more of his work at www.kolmanphotos.com. Finally, I was lucky enough to receive some very useful tips from another commercial photographer and drone pilot, Rick Murray, who contributed some of the best example images you'll find in this book. You'll find some inspirational shots at www.memoriesbymurray.com.

About the Author

With more than 3 million books in print, **David D. Busch** is the world's #1 best-selling camera guide author. Always quick to adopt the latest digital imaging technology, his foray into aerial photography was prompted by the emergence of affordable, highly capable Unmanned Aerial Vehicles (UAVs) suitable for hobbyists and small businesses from companies like Shenzhen DJI Sciences and Technologies Ltd. (DJI).

Busch has written dozens of hugely successful guidebooks for digital cameras, scanners, and image-editing software, including the all-time #1 bestsellers for several different camera models, as well as many popular books devoted to photographic techniques. As a roving photojournalist for more than 20 years, he illustrated his books, magazine articles, and newspaper reports with award-winning images. He's operated his own commercial studio, suffocated in formal dress while shooting weddings, and shot sports for a daily newspaper and an upstate New York college. His photos and articles have appeared in *Popular Photography, Rangefinder, Professional Photographer*, and hundreds of other publications. He's also reviewed dozens of digital cameras for CNet and other CBS publications.

When About.com named its top five books on Beginning Digital Photography, debuting at the #1 and #2 slots were Busch's *Digital Photography All-In-One Desk Reference for Dummies* and *Mastering Digital Photography*. Busch has had as many as 18 books listed in the Top 100 of Amazon.com's Digital Photography Bestseller list—simultaneously! Busch's 300-plus other published books include bestsellers like *Digital SLR Cameras and Photography for Dummies*.

Busch is a member of the Cleveland Photographic Society (www.clevelandphoto.org), which has operated continuously since 1887.

Visit his website at http://www.dslrguides.com, or https://www.facebook.com/DavidBuschGuides/ on Facebook.

Contents

CHAPTER 6

Mastering Still Photography   117

CHAPTER 7

Keys to Great Photos   157

CHAPTER 8

Shooting Video   189

CHAPTER 9

Menu Reference   227

Preface

*D*avid Busch's *DJI Mini 3/Mini 3 Pro Guide to Drone Photography* is your comprehensive resource and reference guide to capturing high-quality photographic still images and high-definition video with the DJI Mini 3 and Mini 3 Pro aircraft. These affordable, easy-to-fly drones are taking off all over the United States and worldwide. Photo and video enthusiasts as young as 16 can capture compelling images and video for personal use, social media, and YouTube channels. This drone-specific guidebook from David Busch—the world's #1 selling camera guide author—will lead you through registration, pre-flight prep, and mastery of every feature in a concise, fun, and straight-forward way.

Filled with detailed how-to steps, and full-color illustrations, *David Busch's DJI Mini 3/Mini 3 Pro Guide to Drone Photography* explores the drones' capabilities in depth, from understanding the FAA rules and regulations, to taking your first photos and videos. You'll learn how to perform basic aerial moves and use the Mini 3/Mini 3 Pro's built-in flight tools, including QuickShots, MasterShots, Focus Track, and Panoramas. With best-selling photographer and mentor David Busch as your guide, you'll quickly have full creative mastery of your drone's capabilities, whether you're shooting on the job, as an advanced enthusiast, or are just out for fun. Start building your knowledge and confidence with the DJI Mini 3 and Mini 3 Pro today.

Introduction

Recreational drones began life as a new, fun way to fly model aircraft. Radio-controlled airplanes fascinated early flyers simply from the ability to send a heavier-than-air flying machine skyward and conduct aerial maneuvers that tested the skills and imagination of the Earth-bound pilot. Cameras and photography came much, much later.

The current surge in interest in drones stems from several factors. First and foremost, while DJI produces high-end drones used for a mapping, surveying, and agriculture, it also has pioneered affordable *prosumer* aircraft (at around $2,000) as well as downright inexpensive ($1,000 or less) drones like the Mini 3 and Mini 3 Pro for enthusiasts and recreational flyers. Today, just about anyone who is serious about photography can get a full-functioned flying photo platform for about the price of an entry-level camera body or an interchangeable lens.

Although the cost of entry is relatively low, drones can be easily accessorized to fine-tune and expand their capabilities. Because of the market dominance of DJI, these tools are available from the company itself as well as many third-party sources. Everything from landing gear extensions and propeller guards to inexpensive anti-collision lights and clip-on wide-angle accessories are available. Polarizers, variable neutral-density filters, lens hoods for the camera's gimbal, and sunshields for your remote's screen are all offered.

Why You Need This Book

I get it. You can find information about just about any aspect of drone operation from videos. Indeed, online resources have become somewhat essential because DJI's own manuals for these most-affordable drones provide only the most basic information within the roughly 70-page guides provided for the Mini 3 Pro and Mini 3. You have to pore over these booklets just to figure out what your drone's features are, with little guidance provided on how to actually use them.

Videos are a convenient way to go beyond what DJI includes in its manuals. The company itself offers a variety of video tutorials, available from the Academy icon within the DJI Fly app on the controller. (See figure below.)

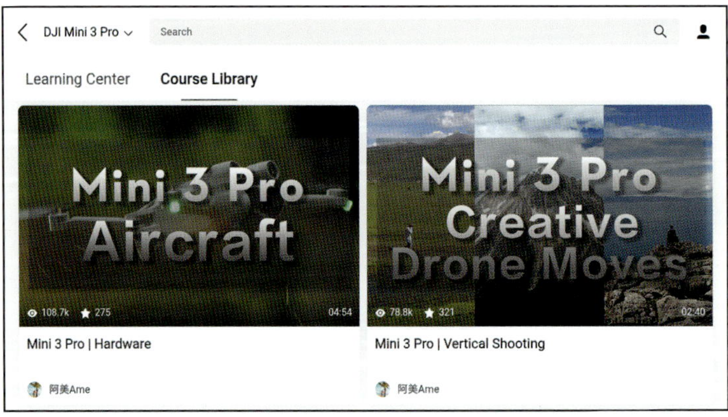

In addition, there are thousands of YouTube videos, including many that are specific to the actual Mini 3/Mini 3 Pro you own. They will tell you how to set up a new drone, successfully plan and execute your first flight, and navigate the confusing maze of regulations, restrictions, and guidelines offered by the FAA, DJI, and common sense. Individual features are also covered.

Videos are not too bad when you need an overview, but can be time-consuming, and are less useful when you need/want to know one specific thing. Watching a 10-minute video just to figure out one obscure feature is not a good use of time. Humans absorb information by reading much more quickly than by listening to the narration of lengthy videos. With a book like this one you can use the index or skim through text to rapidly locate the exact explanation or how-to you need.

Reliance on video tutorials that teach flight operations has meant that, until now, there have been no dedicated model-specific *drone photography* guides. In order to take the best aerial photos you need to know more than how to manipulate all the remote control's buttons and dials, or memorize the rules about where you can or cannot fly. Whether you're a new photographer trying to master a drone's capabilities, or a veteran pilot looking to improve their images, a book that relates the capabilities of a sophisticated tool like the Mini 3/Mini 3 Pro is the fastest way to bring everything together.

Who Am I?

After spending many years as the world's most successful unknown author, I've become slightly less obscure in the past few years, thanks to a horde of camera guidebooks and other photographically oriented tomes I've written. You may have seen my photography articles in the late, lamented *Popular Photography, Rangefinder, Professional Photographer,* and dozens of other photographic publications. But, first, and foremost, I'm a photojournalist and made my living in the field until I began devoting most of my time to writing books. Although I love writing, I'm happiest when I'm out taking pictures, either at ground level or from an aerial perch. That's why I divide my time between writing books and taking photographs of my favorite subjects, which includes covered bridges, sunsets, and landscapes of ocean shorelines.

Like all my digital photography books, this one was written by someone with an incurable photography bug. I've worked as a sports photographer for an Ohio newspaper and for an upstate New York college. I've operated my own commercial studio and photo lab, cranking out product shots on demand and then printing a few hundred glossy 8 × 10s on a tight deadline for a press kit. I've served as a photo-posing instructor for a modeling agency. People have actually paid me to shoot their weddings and immortalize them with portraits. I even prepared press kits and articles on photography as a PR consultant for a formerly dominant (and now vestigial) Rochester, NY company. My trials and travails with imaging and computer technology have made their way into print in book form an alarming number of times, including hundreds of volumes on photographic topics. I teach classes and have branched out into online training courses.

Like you, I love photography for its own merits, and I view drone technology as just another tool to help me get the images I see in my mind's eye. But, also like you, I had to master this technology before I could apply it to my work. This book is the result of what I've learned, and I hope it will help you master your DJI Mini 3 or Mini 3 Pro.

I'd like to ask a special favor: let me know what you think of this book. If you have any recommendations about how I can make it better, visit my website at www.dslrguides.com, click on the E-Mail Me tab, and send your comments, suggestions on topics that should be explained in more detail, or, especially, any typos. (The latter will be compiled as they are received on the Errata page you'll also find on my website.) I really value your ideas and appreciate it when you take the time to tell me what you think! Some of the content of the book you hold in your hands came from suggestions I received from readers like yourself. If you found this book especially useful, tell others about it. Visit http://www.amazon.com/dp/B0C37XKGYY and leave a positive review. Your feedback is what spurs me to make each one of these books better than the last, and if enough of you like what I've done, Rocky Nook may be moved to ask me to follow up with a new book the next time DJI introduces one of its aerial photographic innovations. Thanks!

Your Mini 3/Mini 3 Pro Flight Plan

1

In many respects, it's difficult to believe that affordable recreational and commercial drone photography has reached its current level of popularity in just the last decade. Yet, here we are, with fully featured aerial photographic platforms like the DJI Mini 3 and Mini 3 Pro available for about the same expenditure that still-photography enthusiasts readily pay for an accessory lens or high-end electronic flash. Making the transition from Earth-bound camera operator to aerial photographer has never been easier or more affordable. But although the recent proliferation of drones has been breathtaking in speed and scope, the aircraft we use today are actually the product of a long process of evolution.

As you might guess, quadcopters like your Mini 3 and Mini 3 Pro evolved in a circuitous way from the first radio-controlled model airplanes, pioneered by 21-year-old twins Walt and Bill Good in 1937. They added remote control to their 8-foot gasoline-powered plane, paving the way for much lighter, more agile model aircraft. The hobby really took off, so to speak, in the early 2000s, as technology brought significant improvements in cost, weight, performance, electronics, and battery power. It didn't take long for these breakthroughs to appear in today's versatile drone aircraft.

Frank Wang, a graduate of the Hong Kong University of Science and Technology, began developing innovative quadcopters in 2006, and by 2013, the company he founded—DJI—had eclipsed French drone manufacturer Parrot with the introduction of the iconic DJI Phantom 1. RC airplane aficionados were attracted to the hobby for the joy of building and flying their model aircraft, and the hovering ability of drones introduced a new enticement: a steady platform that could be used for still photography and movie shooting.

Recreational drones were transformed from a flying machine that could take pictures into an enthusiast camera that could also fly. Many Mini 3/Mini 3 Pro owners can take justified pride in being able to call themselves pilots, but a large number of us think of ourselves, foremost, as photographers. For those who moved into the drone world from photography, the Mini 3 and Mini 3 Pro are, in a sense, the world's most versatile tripod.

Shenzhen DJI Sciences and Technologies Ltd. (more commonly known by its trade name DJI) has worked hard to provide highly automated, easy-to-use consumer versions of the drone technology that has made the company the world leader in the music, television, and motion-picture industries. Yes, there are some skills you need to acquire, and, yes, there are some regulations you need to learn and abide by; but this book will provide you with everything you need to know to use your Mini 3/Mini 3 Pro from registration, pre-flight prep, and mastery of every feature in a concise, fun, and straightforward way.

Crafting Your Flight Plan

One of the challenges of writing a guidebook like this is satisfying the needs of both veteran drone pilots coming from other UAS platforms as well as less-experienced would-be pilots hoping to take their photographic experience to new heights. Moreover, in addition to long-time drone flyers and fledgling newbies, the audience for this book will include a broad spectrum of Mini 3/Mini 3 Pro owners with experience levels somewhere in between. Many of you are dedicated photo enthusiasts, while others are still trying to master photographic basics. Even in these days of digital publishing, it's not practical to write a single book that concentrates on the needs and interests of just one of these factions.

Even so, whether you're an experienced drone pilot/photographer or starting from a more modest level of photographic expertise (or somewhere in the middle), I plan to provide you with advice that will prove useful. Veterans can skim through material they already know, realizing that everyone was a beginner once. Beginners can learn about the features and concepts they need at their own pace. Note that the title of this book includes the phrase "Mini 3/Mini 3 Pro Guide to Drone Photography." My goal was to make it more than just an operations manual for these two aircraft; the aim here is to help DJI pilots *of any experience level* improve their skills at both flying and capturing images. Consider this a dual-purpose handbook for the features and capabilities of your Mini 3 or Mini 3 Pro drone, as well as a guide to mastery of photographic techniques with drone aircraft.

The important thing to remember is that you don't have to read this book cover to cover in chapter order. I organized the material to give you what you need to understand regulations and take flight safely, but you should feel free to read (or study) the information you need, as you need it. In this chapter, I'm going to help you craft your own plan for learning everything you must know to enjoy the photographic capabilities of your DJI Mini 3 and Mini 3 Pro to their fullest.

Your Drone Mastery Syllabus

As I noted earlier, I recognize that readers of this book will have varying levels of experience and expertise in both drone operation and photographic concepts/techniques. This section describes what is covered in each chapter and includes my recommendation for how those at various levels approach them.

Chapter 1: Your Mini 3/Mini 3 Pro Flight Plan

No need to be circular; you're already here, reading this chapter that provides an overview of the book's intent and an outline of what is covered. Beginners will find these sections useful in planning how to approach learning about their new drone and prioritizing which parts of the book to study before actually attempting any ambitious aerial activities. With conventional cameras, inexperience generally results in nothing worse than a series of bad or unusable photographs. Drone photography, in contrast, has the opportunity for multiple unpleasant (or disastrous) outcomes. Too little knowledge *can* be a dangerous thing.

For those who are experienced pilots looking to familiarize themselves with their latest drone, skimming the recommendations that follow will be helpful in planning which of the remaining eight chapters of this book you want to explore next.

Chapter 2: Meet Your Mini 3/Mini 3 Pro

This chapter is a comprehensive guide to each of the components and features found in the DJI Mini 3 and Mini 3 Pro aircraft. Beginners will find the "Your Out-of-Box Experience" section useful, as it describes each of the items included with both drones and typical Fly More Combos, along with the purpose of each. There are quite a few individual pieces and optional accessories to learn about, and I'll provide descriptions of them all.

More experienced pilots may want skim through the unboxing checklist and begin with the "Mini 3/Mini 3 Pro Roadmap" section. Beginners and veterans alike will find detailed views of the drones with callouts pinpointing each important part or component. Also included in this chapter is a discussion of the differences between the Mini 3 and Mini 3 Pro; most of them are slight, but some are important to consider—such as the Rear Vision System found in the Mini 3 Pro, but not in the Mini 3, which lacks its sibling's robust collision avoidance system.

Chapter 3: Safety and Regulations

True beginners absolutely should, if possible, *study* this chapter before attempting their first flight. Drone operation—most particularly *in which areas you are permitted to fly*—is quite strictly regulated; you need to understand the basics (and more) to avoid committing an infraction or crime, at best, and, at worst, to avoid damaging your drone or harming other humans or property. The "Getting Legal" section will help you understand registration (if required for your drone), controlled and uncontrolled airspaces, and specific limitations.

Neophytes and veteran drone flyers alike will want to study (or review) this chapter's introduction to obstacle avoidance, drone sensor systems, flight range, and flight modes, with an emphasis on safe flying. All these are explained in more detail in later chapters, so a quick study is recommended.

Chapter 4: Getting Flight Ready

Right out of the box your Mini 3 or Mini 3 Pro drone needs a certain amount of setup. This chapter explains some of the vagaries of the lithium ion batteries your drone uses, the differences between the basic Intelligent Flight and Intelligent Flight Pro batteries, and how to charge them. Beginners will learn some important facts about using these batteries.

Experienced pilots probably only need to review the battery section, plus the descriptions of recommended apps. This book does not go into detail on using any software other than the DJI Fly controller app, in any case. Also included in this chapter is information about propellers and installing them, along with a comparison of the features of the three remote controls currently available.

Chapter 5: Your First Flight

By the time you get to this chapter, beginners will be ready for their first flight and more practiced flyers will be impatient. The drone must be activated with DJI before flying, and while this process is now pretty much automatic, beginners will want to learn how and why activation is performed.

Next up is a preflight checklist of steps to take before actually taking off. Beginners will want to memorize this or print out a copy of the recommendations to avoid overlooking anything; these steps will be second nature to veterans. The section on finding a suitable location for take-offs and landings includes descriptions of limitations within National Parks and Federal lands, State Parks, and other public areas.

You'll find a section on mastering your remote's operating controls, including selecting from Normal, Sport, Cine/Tripod, and ATTI modes. You'll also see reminders on checking airspace, dealing with authorizations for flying in particular airspaces, instructions for launching, an introduction to capturing stills and movies, gimbal manipulation, and aerial navigation. Pay special attention to the extensive section on returning your drone for a safe landing. Beginners should study these sections; experienced pilots may just want to quickly review the material.

MANUAL MANEUVERS

This chapter includes instructions on conducting simple maneuvers that can be done manually, such as circles, figure eights, and orbit flights. More advanced techniques, such as dolly shots and flybys, are located in Chapter 8, for two reasons.

First, and most importantly, I think beginners should concentrate on learning how to get their drone in the air, to take a few pictures or video clips, practice the simple routines described in Chapter 5, and then return safely. However, neophytes are completely free to move to the more sophisticated drills any time they want if they feel they are ready. Just because I don't explain how to perform these maneuvers right off the bat does not mean you can't skip ahead to Chapter 8 to study more sophisticated routines when you want to spread your wings (so to speak).

My second reason for describing advanced maneuvers in Chapter 8 is that they are most useful for video shooting, where the camera's movement relative to the subject matter is part of the creative process.

Chapter 6: Mastering Still Photography

As I've noted, this book is intended to be more than a manual for operating the DJI Mini or Mini 3 Pro drones. Getting them up in the air and flying around is just half the fun. Many of you are photography enthusiasts looking to elevate (so to speak) your creative techniques using aerial platforms. Others have different interests, such as capturing video or just flying for its own sake. This chapter (and the next) will help both groups become better still photographers by providing a thorough grounding in the photographic potential of the Mini and Mini 3 aircraft. You'll want to read it even if you're an experienced shooter, and especially if you are a pilot just learning about photography.

You'll learn how to use the drone's Auto and Pro Mode options for taking stills; explore the finer points of exposure, including dynamic range, histograms, and white balance; deal with noise; use bracketing; and create high dynamic range (HDR) images. You'll also find information on focusing and the use of filters.

Chapter 7: Keys to Great Photos

This chapter is devoted to describing the most important principles of compelling photographs as they apply to still photography from using a drone. Many of the concepts apply equally to video shooting, as well. You'll learn to use your drone as the world's most versatile "tripod" platform, working with perspective, centers of interest, and composition. Incorporating a sense of movement, shooting at twilight and at night, and other aspects are all covered. Because even basic photographic principles are affected by your Mini 3 or Min 3 Pro's viewpoint, experienced enthusiasts and snap-shooters alike will find something useful here.

Chapter 8: Introduction to Shooting Video

The DJI Mini 3 and DJI Mini 3 Pro are capable of high-quality video 4K and Full HD movies, plus slow-motion video. They provide a high degree of manual and automatic control and include impressive, programmed shots that can produce compelling cinematic effects. While complex video techniques and editing are beyond the scope of this book, in this chapter you'll find everything you know to get started.

You'll learn about resolution, frame rates, coding formats, and profiles, along with the special considerations needed for an aerial camera that has a fixed focal length and non-adjustable aperture. You'll be able to continue practicing smooth maneuvers such as circles, figure eights, and orbits, and you'll learn about new maneuvers, such as flyovers, flybys, and flythroughs. Practice elevator, banking, and chase sequences and various Intelligent Flight Modes available for your particular drone.

If you're most interested in still photography, this chapter will let you add video to your repertoire. Those who plan to do more extensive video work can use this introduction to jump start their movie-shooting efforts.

Chapter 9: Menu Reference

This chapter provides a ready reference to the five individual menu tabs in the System Settings screen of the DJI Fly app. Each entry in the Safety, Control, Camera, Transmission, and About menus is explained, along with all the options. You'll find these descriptions useful as you begin to master all the flight options of your Mini 3 or Mini 3 Pro, and then return to this chapter from time to time for reference when you need to refresh your knowledge when it's time to adjust or recalibrate a particular feature.

Next Up

The next chapter introduces you to all the features and capabilities of your DJI Mini 3 or Mini 3 Pro, including a visual roadmap of the key components of each drone. I'll also explain the key differences between the two. Both beginners and veteran pilots alike will need to review this chapter before flying, although experienced drone operators will probably get up to speed quickly using the information included.

Meet Your Mini 3/Mini 3 Pro

2

Unless you already have previous experience flying a drone, or are a licensed pilot, making your first flight with your Mini 3 or Mini 3 Pro can be a bit daunting. That's especially true for enthusiast photographers and videographers, because mastering the use of an unmanned aircraft requires a whole new skill set. You may already know quite a bit about photography—how to achieve correct exposure, how to change your perspective with interchangeable lenses, and how (and when) to use a tripod to provide a rock-steady platform for your camera.

Now you're tasked with capturing stills and video with a camera mounted on a platform that needs to be navigated safely through the air, has a non-interchangeable 24mm (equivalent field of view) lens with a fixed f/1.7 aperture, uses a motorized camera mount called a gimbal to point the camera, and relies on inboard electronics for image stabilization. Oh, and all the adjustments must be made from a remote control you hold in your hands while your camera soars hundreds of feet away within your line of sight. You "see" what the camera sees through a screen on the remote.

Don't panic! Camera drones have come a long way since they were first adapted for commercial use in the 1950s. Today, they are often called Unmanned Aerial Vehicles (UAV) if you're referring just to the drone itself, or, perhaps, more accurately as Unmanned Aircraft Systems (UAS), which encompasses the drone, the controller, and the communications link between them. The terms are often used interchangeably. The important thing is that drones have made enormous strides in capabilities and ease of use in just the last few years. Indeed, you should be able to unpack your drone and get it ready to fly with nothing more than the guidance provided in the next couple chapters.

Your Out-of-Box Experience

Your Mini 3 or Mini 3 Pro comes in an attractive box filled with stuff. The aircraft can be purchased in a number of configurations, starting with just the basic drone, battery, charger, propellers, and cables. The starter configuration can include a radio controller, or, if you already have one (say, from a previous drone), and have purchased the drone only, no controller at all.

Unless you have previously owned a compatible aircraft that uses the same batteries or accessories, there is little incentive to buying your UAS in this bare-bones configuration. The smarter and more economic choice is to get one of the Fly More Combos, or, with the Mini 3 Pro, the separately available Fly More Kit. Each includes additional Intelligent Flight batteries, a case, extra propellers, a two-way charging hub, and a remote. Trust me, you *will* need extra batteries.

Another excellent choice is the Fly More Combo/Kit purchased with the DJI Care Refresh package. The latter is a protection plan that provides coverage in case of accidental damage, natural wear, and, the ultimate catastrophe known as a "fly-away." (Yes, that's exactly what it sounds like.) Don't worry, your drone has a plethora of built-in features, including obstacle avoidance and a versatile series of "return-to-home" protocols that will retrieve your aircraft automatically when control is lost.

Of course, nothing is foolproof, given the wide range of events that can happen, so DJI Care Refresh is often a good idea. Your drone comes with a Limited 1-Year Warranty (excluding propellers), and there is a Limited 1-Year/200-Charge Cycle Warranty on flight batteries. As I write this, the Mini 3 Pro (only) is available in a Fly More Kit Plus that includes two of the higher capacity Intelligent Flight Plus batteries, which provide up to 94 minutes of additional flight time. Other packages may be available by the time this book is published.

In my personal experience, DJI provides excellent customer service in the United States. I've needed service twice, once for a controller problem and later with a motor failure. In both cases, DJI paid for shipping in both directions, and I had my replacement one week later, door-to-door.

Depending on which configuration or combo you opted for, you'll receive some or most of the items described next in a numbered list that corresponds to the number labels in Figure 2.1:

1. **Shoulder bag.** This padded bag has a compartment to stow your folded drone with propellers attached, and separate areas to store the standard controller and two or three extra batteries. There's an outside zippered pocket you can use to keep items you may not need during a particular session, such as neutral-density filters, spare propellers, or control sticks. You could stuff your Small UAS Certificate of Registration and a copy of your TRUST (The Recreational UAS Safety Test) Completion Certificate or your Part 107 pilot certification there, too. (I'll tell you more about those later on.)

   My recommendation: I find this soft-sided bag provides sufficient protection and holds everything I need for most outings. When traveling, especially by air, you may prefer one of the many available hard-shell cases available from third parties, such as Pelican.

2. **Low-noise propellers.** Sets of propellers come in two different types: Type A, marked with a raised ridge near the center hub, and the other, Type B, with no ridge (see Figure 2.2). The Type-A props should be attached to marked arms, and the Type-B props to the unmarked arms. I'll show you how to correctly mount the propellers in Chapter 4. Each type rotates in the opposite direction from the other to provide stability in flight. A set of screws used to attach the propellers is supplied with each pair, using the screwdriver that is furnished with the aircraft, or, preferably, a more robust third-party PH0 Phillips-head screwdriver with a larger, easier-to-grip handle.

   My recommendation: Your quadcopter uses four of these, and you'll eventually need more (at $9 a set). When new, they are dynamically balanced, but with continued use they'll eventually perform less well, and some damage during flight is inevitable. I've managed to crash my drone into tree branches more than once, and am still amazed at how little damage can occur to the drone and its props during a tumble down to the ground. But it's still a good idea to change propellers from time to time to maintain reliable, quiet performance.

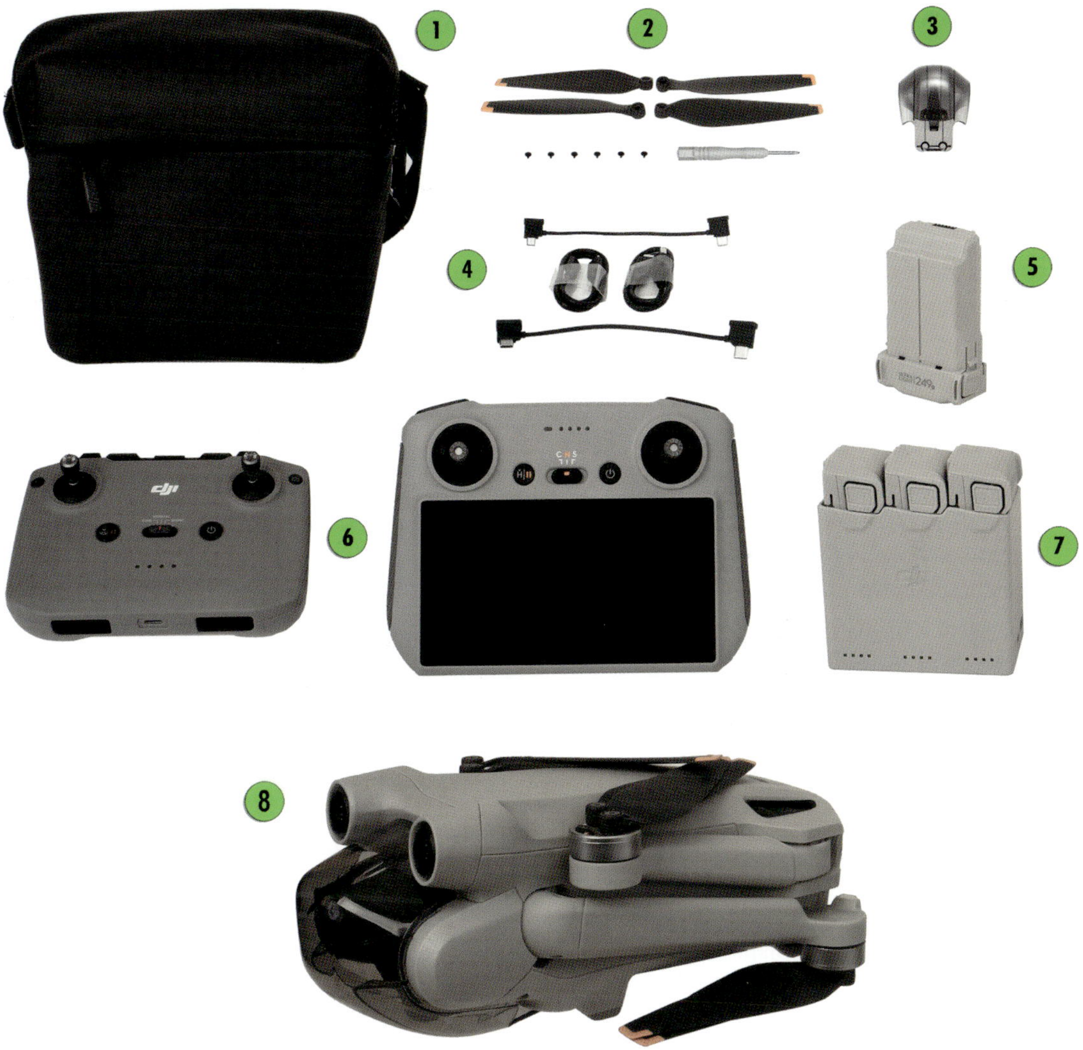

Figure 2.1 Major components and accessories.

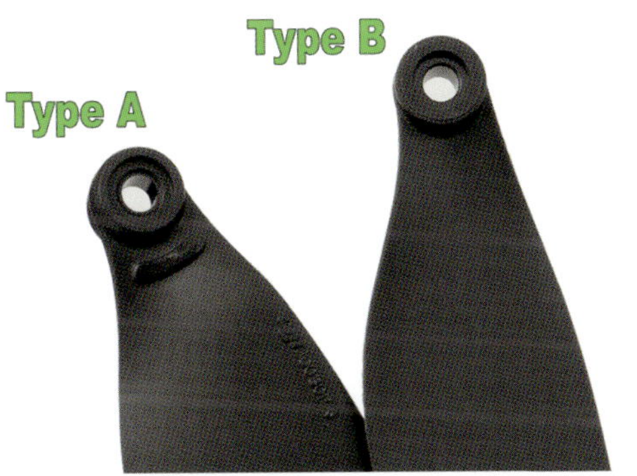

Figure 2.2 Type-A and Type-B propellers rotate in opposite directions.

3. **Gimbal protector.** This shield protects the sensitive gimbal/camera mount from damage during transport, or any time the drone is not being flown.

   My recommendation: Don't be misled by the fact that it's transparent (in order to make it easier to see the orientation of the gimbal when the protector is being re-attached). You won't be using it during flight; it must be removed when the Mini 3 or Mini 3 Pro is powered up to allow the gimbal to move freely.

4. **USB Type-C cables.** Cables with USB Type-C connectors used to link the drone or remote controller for battery charging or data/image transfer are included. In addition, the RC-N1 RC remote controller is furnished with its own set of cables used to connect that controller to your smartphone or tablet. These are six-inch cables with a USB Type C connector on one end that plugs into your remote controller, and a connector on the other end to connect to your Android or iOS device. Three of these cables are supplied, with Lightning, Standard Micro USB, and USB-C connectors to fit your phone or tablet.

   My recommendation: The cable used for your smart device stores within the RC-N1 remote controller, so you're not likely to lose one. Replacements are about $10 each. You won't need a longer remote cable unless you plan to use a tablet with one of the third-party tablet mounts or extension brackets available that require one.

5. **Intelligent Flight Battery/Plus (BWX162-2453-7.38/BWX162-3850-7.38).** Your drone's motors and all its electrical components (including the gimbal and camera) are powered by the Lithium-Ion battery that fits inside the aircraft's body. When fully charged, the basic Intelligent Flight Battery's 2,453 mAh (milliAmpere hour) capacity provides up to 34 minutes of flight time with DJI Mini 3 Pro or 38 minutes of flight with the lighter Mini 3. The Intelligent Flight Battery Plus offers 3,850 mAh of juice, giving you up to 47 minutes of flight time with DJI Mini 3 Pro, or 51 minutes with DJI Mini 3.

   My recommendation: In practical terms, you'll want to stay aloft for six or seven minutes *less* than the maximum time to allow for last-minute maneuvers and a safe return to origin with a bit of power to spare. As the name suggests, these are *intelligent* batteries with advanced overcharging, current, and temperature protection, and a hibernation mode, as I'll describe shortly.

   The more batteries you have on hand, the better. Treat them with care; Lithium-Ion batteries are not your grandfather's NiCad cells in multiple ways. I'll have recommendations for getting the most from your Intelligent Flight batteries at the beginning of Chapter 4.

6. **Remote controllers.** The DJI Mini 3 Pro and Mini 3 are both compatible with the DJI RC-N1 remote controller shown at center far left in the figure, and the DJI RC remote seen to its right. These are the standard remotes furnished with the various Fly More Combos. The Mini 3 Pro is also compatible with the DJI RC Pro controller, a $1,000 plus device I'll describe in Chapter 4.

   These remotes use long-range transmission technology to allow controlling your Mini 3/Mini 3 Pro and camera gimbal while receiving nearly real-time video at distances far beyond the permissible visual line of sight (VLOS) separation drones are limited to. As a recreational pilot, you'll (hopefully) never be far from your drone, as you must maintain line-of-sight status at all times. But the remote controller's robust range means that your controller-to-drone link will be more reliable at the distances you do encounter.

My recommendation: As shown in the figure, the controllers include a pair of joystick-like control sticks which can be removed and then stored in notches on the underside or back of the controller itself, plus a spare pair. It never hurts to have another replacement set (about $10). "Extended" control sticks and other options are available from third parties. I'll tell you more about the controllers and their use later in this chapter.

7. **Battery Charging Hub (CHX162-30).** This handy hub accepts three Intelligent Flight batteries at once so they can be recharged one after another. When charged batteries are docked, it can also be used as a power brick to use the juice in your Intelligent Flight batteries to recharge/power your phone or other devices.

   My recommendation: I always use the hub to recharge my batteries at home, and only do the single-battery thing when using my car charger or a third-party USB charger while out in the field or traveling. I'll tell you more about recharging your drone's batteries later in this chapter.

8. **DJI Mini 3 Pro/Mini 3 drone.** The DJI Mini 3 Pro is shown in the figure folded up for transport with the gimbal protector in place. The Mini 3 looks similar. I'll explain the differences later in this chapter.

The items listed above are by no means all of the essentials you need to take flight. Even if you spring for a Fly More Combo, you'll find that several additional accessories are more or less non-optional. One glaring omission is the lack of any sort of charger to rejuvenate your Intelligent Flight batteries between sorties. The Battery Charging Hub and USB Type-C cable needed to connect it to a power source are of little use if you don't have a charger to supply the necessary current. Your batteries are best charged using a USB-C Power Delivery (PD) charger with 30W or greater output—your smartphone charger generally won't cut it. Fortunately, DJI itself offers a pretty good one for about $19.

Here's an overview of some of the things you should consider adding to your equipment list. When shopping, make sure the item is compatible with your models; some items designed for other DJI aircraft cannot be used with your drone, and some accessories for each are not compatible with the other.

■ **USB charger.** As I noted above, no charger is provided with your drone, so you'll need one.

   My recommendation: Any Power Delivery (PD) charger with 30W output will work, and because so many people already have one for charging their laptops and other devices, DJI did not include one with your Mini 3 or Mini 3 Pro. I wanted one I could dedicate for drone usage, so I got the small but mighty DJI Fast Charger PD-30, a bargain at $19. You can connect it to the USB-C port on your drone to charge the battery while it's still in the aircraft or plug it into the Battery Charging Hub to revive three Intelligent Flight batteries in sequence. It will charge the basic battery in about 64 minutes, and the Intelligent Flight Battery Plus in around 101 minutes.

- **Memory card and reader.** You'll need to purchase a microSDXC memory card, available in sizes from 32GB and up, as one is not included. While the Mini 3 Pro contains a small amount of internal memory (1.2GB), the Mini 3 has none at all. Adding a card provides essential on-board storage, and, when used with a card reader, offers a convenient way to transfer your still photos and videos to your computer.

  My recommendation: Memory cards are cheap, so you should have several, each at least 64GB to 128GB in size. Any fast Class 10 card should do; as I write this, DJI drones use UHS I rather than the newer UHS II protocol. Each microSDXC card is usually furnished with an adapter that allows using the card with any SD card reader.

- **Landing pad.** A variety of third parties offer landing pads, often about 30 inches in diameter, but available with widths of as much as eight feet. They're generally orange, marked with an H (just like real helipads), often foldable, and sometimes waterproof. You might not need a pad on solid surfaces, but I recommend using one in dusty, grassy, or rocky areas, especially for the Mini 3 Pro, which lacks the Mini 3's front legs.

  My recommendation: These pads make landings easier and safer. You can make your own out of cardboard, but there are so many available for less than $20 that you can easily justify splurging.

- **Control sticks.** If you detach your control sticks for storage, you might want a spare pair if you're prone to losing things. Third parties also offer "extended" control sticks that are length-adjustable to suit your preference.

  My recommendation: Extra or adjustable sticks are not essential, so obtaining them is strictly a personal choice.

- **Tablet mount.** The adjustable bracket for the standard RC-N1 remote controller furnished with some Mini 3/Mini 3 Pro packages can accommodate Android or iOS smartphones measuring $3.4 \times 7 \times .4$ inches. If you want to use a tablet, such as an iPad, you'll need an extender or add-on tablet mount.

  My recommendation: I do like using the larger screen of my iPad Air 2 (no relation to the DJI Air 2 drone!), although it makes for a bulky controller. The $60 tablet mount available from DJI is the most solid and easy to use, but third parties offer serviceable models priced at $10 to $20 that can accommodate tablets up to 12 inches wide. (Which means the 12.9-inch iPad Pro will not fit.)

- **Monitor hood.** Because most of our flying is done outdoors and in the daytime, it should come as no surprise that bright sunlight can make the monitor screen difficult to see. DJI and third parties make hoods that fit the standard RC-N1 remote controller, the DJI RC, and DJI RC Pro at prices from about $18 to $30.

  My recommendation: This inexpensive add-on is a good value if you find you often have trouble seeing your phone's screen.

- **Optional controller.** There are three common controllers compatible with the Mini 3 and Mini 3 Pro. Both aircraft are often sold bundled with the RC-N1 as the standard controller, which is used with your smartphone or tablet connected to provide a viewing screen. You can also purchase the deluxe DJI RC Pro controller (which, as I write this, is compatible with the Mini 3 Pro only) or the less-expensive DJI RC controller.

My recommendation: The self-contained controllers with a screen don't require using your smart device and are more convenient to use because of their bright built-in display. They're more durable, and especially useful for those who own multiple drones because they are compatible with many different aircraft. I like the RC Pro for my Mini 3 Pro because it has an HDMI port so you can output what you're seeing to an external monitor for large-screen viewing by others, and has four programmable buttons.

You'll find a detailed description of the three available remote controllers and their functions in Chapter 4.

By this time you've probably noticed a trend: DJI worked very, very hard to make the Mini 3 and Mini 3 Pro friendly for both newcomers and experienced pilots who wanted a small, easy-to-use drone. They've cut costs in some areas to keep the price affordable (without sacrificing quality or important features), and designed both drones to be as light as possible. The 248/249-gram weight (roughly 8.4 ounces) of the drones with the basic Intelligent Flight battery means that recreational flyers don't even have to register their aircraft with the FAA. (If you use the Intelligent Flight Battery Plus, the drone's weight increases to about 290 grams and *does* require registration.) The lack of heft also means that your Mini 3/Mini 3 Pro can remain aloft for a longer period of time without needing to return to home for a new battery.

The cost-cutting and weight reduction means that some features had to be omitted from the Mini 3 and Mini 3 Pro, but you still have the option of springing for some additional accessories that can come in handy, especially if you're shooting video or want to fly at night. Four of them are shown in Figure 2.3.

1. **Extended landing gear/skids.** The Mini 3 has stubby legs on the front propeller arms to keep the nose of the drone (and its delicate camera gimbal) high and dry. For the heavier Mini 3 Pro, DJI left those legs off entirely. If you use a landing pad, or are certain you will be able to land on a relatively flat surface without a lot of grass, rocks, or other obstacles, you should have no problems. I've landed both drones on my well-trimmed lawn many times. However, several third parties offer extended landing gear and skids that attach to the bottom of your drone, providing additional clearance when landing in taller grass, gravel, and other uneven surfaces. (See Figure 2.3, upper left.)

   My recommendation: These are useful, but, again, add a tiny bit of weight to the drone. If you plan to keep the weight of your Mini below the 255-gram threshold to avoid the need to register it, you'll be reluctant to add even a small amount of weight. If you expect such conditions, a better choice might be a landing pad that you purchase or make yourself. But if you're going to register your drone anyway, your only weight concern is a tiny reduction in flight time, and you might consider that a small price to pay for the extra clearance add-on gear/skids provide.

2. **LED lights.** If you fly your drone at night, in addition to the other rules you need to follow, you absolutely *must* have a flashing strobe light visible for at least three miles that meets the FAA rules for night flying. There are hefty fines and other less-pleasant consequences for not complying.

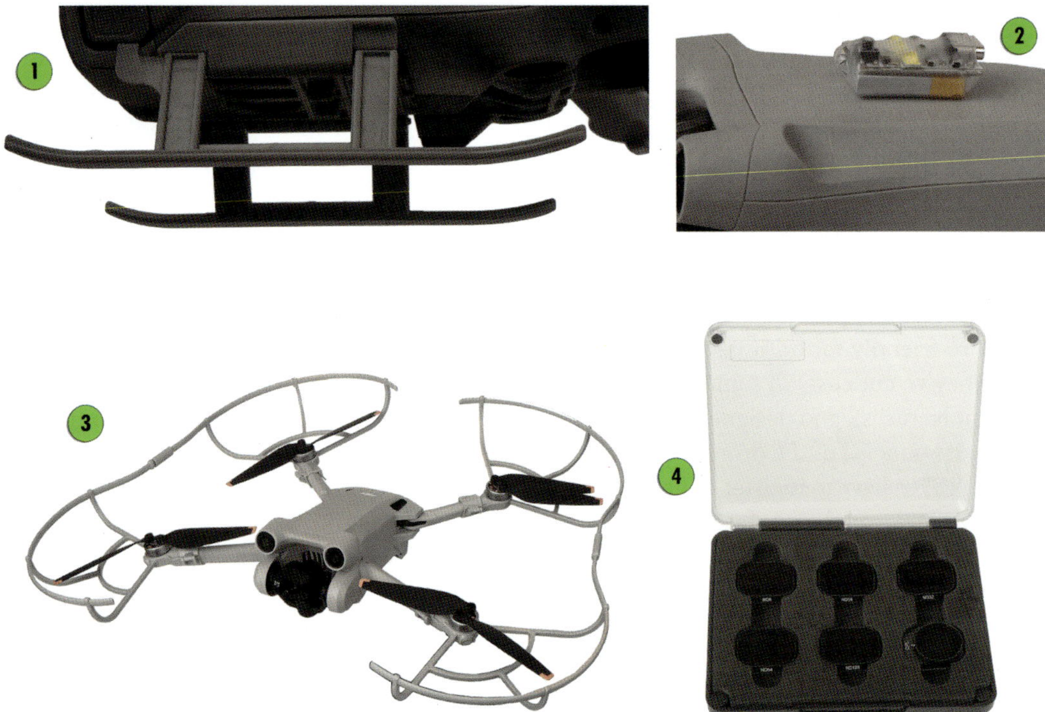

Figure 2.3 Useful accessories.

My recommendation: A variety of options are available from third parties, but for compact drones like the Mini 3 and Mini 3 Pro, you'll want a feather-light device. Figure 2.3, upper right, shows the VIFLY Drone Strobe Light I use. It weighs just six grams and attaches to my Mini 3 aircraft using industrial-strength Velcro tabs. Its battery will last up to four hours. The highly regarded Firehouse Arc V is another excellent option.

3. **Propeller guards.** These protectors quickly snap onto the drone around the lower motor housings, and shield the propellers and motor during collisions with hard objects. (See Figure 2.3, lower left.) Some are accompanied by propeller holders that strap the props tightly to the drone when it's folded for storage.

My recommendation: These guards add a small amount of weight to your drone, which can have a minor effect on flight time and push you over the weight threshold for registration. If you use the shoulder bag, they must be removed and stored separately. Like most pilots, I tend to not use them for routine flights, especially if I know I won't be flying or landing my drone anywhere near rocks or other obstructions. If you fly your drone indoors for fun or for specific applications (real-estate photographers frequently do indoor "fly throughs" of properties), they're more useful. Properly equipped, your drone can theoretically bounce off walls and fly indoors without endangering people or pets. (That's no excuse to be careless, however, because propeller guards aren't foolproof.)

4. Filters. There are many different camera attachments for the Mini 3 and/or Mini 3 Pro. They include polarizers (to reduce reflections and enrich colors), wide-angle modifiers (to expand the field of view to a whopping 111 degrees instead of 82 degrees), and anamorphic lenses (to allow "squeezed" frames to be expanded to a Panavision-like wide-screen look).

The most common attachments are neutral-density filters, which reduce the amount of light reaching the sensor by a measurement in increments called "stops." Each stop reduces the amount of light by one half, allowing you to use a shutter speed of double the length at the same lens aperture and ISO sensitivity setting (say, 1/125th second instead of 1/250th second). I'll explain exposure settings in more detail later in this book. (See Figure 2.3, lower right.)

My recommendation: As I write this, DJI offers only a set of three ND16, ND64, and ND256 filters, which produce 4, 6, and 8 stops of light reduction, respectively. Third-party vendors may bundle different combinations, such as ND4, ND8, ND16, and ND32 filters (reducing the light by 2, 3, 4, and 5 stops, respectively), or ND64, ND128, ND256, and ND512 filters (6, 7, 8, and 9 stops), which means that under very bright beach or snowy conditions, you could use a shutter speed as low as 1/8th second at ISO 100. The other attachments mentioned are available from a wide variety of sources, and I'll tell you more about them in Chapter 8.

SHUTTER SPEEDS AND VIDEO

Veteran still photographers know that higher shutter speeds help freeze action, and they often use the highest shutter speeds possible while adjusting sensor sensitivity (ISO) to allow working with a desired aperture size. Your drone is a different breed of cat: unlike a conventional still camera, it has a fixed f/1.7 lens. The only way to adjust exposure is by changing the ISO sensitivity or switching to a different shutter speed.

That complicates video capture, because the best video images require using a shutter speed in the 1/125th-second to 1/30th-second range, for reasons I'll get into later. (Don't worry: your drone uses electronic image stabilization to counter erratic movement in flight; *subject* movement is apt to be less of a concern.) As I'll explain in Chapter 8, ND filters give you great flexibility in choosing an ISO sensitivity setting and shutter speed for the best results for both still and video photography.

Mini 3/Mini 3 Pro Roadmap

When you first slip the drone out of its bag, you'll unfold the booms that contain the motors and indicator lights. Move the top booms outward toward the rear of the aircraft, and then unfold the bottom booms downward and toward the front of the drone. (It doesn't really matter which order you use.)

On the front of the drone, you'll find a clear plastic gimbal protector that shields the gimbal and camera. Carefully pull it forward to detach it, and be sure to replace it when transporting the drone between flights. While the gimbal itself is quite robust, a hard knock can damage it or misalign it. I'll show you how to recalibrate a wayward gimbal later in this book, but it's a good idea to treat this component with the respect it deserves. **Note:** *As I noted earlier, the gimbal protector should not be mounted on the drone when the aircraft is powered up or in flight.*

Initially, you'll want to remove the yellow-accented stickers found on various places, such as the battery, USB port, memory card slot, and other locations. Don't forget the foam rubber piece inserted behind the gimbal to hold it steady during shipping. I'll show you how to install the propellers later in this chapter. The Mini 3 and Mini 3 Pro are physically very similar, with a few external differences (the Mini 3 has landing "legs" in front, and the Mini 3 Pro does not, for example). I'll explain the key distinctions later in this chapter. While I'll use the Mini 3 Pro for most of my descriptions, they will also apply to the basic Mini model. I'll point out any differences in operation as we go along.

The visual roadmap that follows provides multiple views of the aircraft from different angles. I'm going to provide an overview of each component here. You'll learn more about how to work with each of them later in this book.

- **USB port.** Located on the rear of the aircraft is a standard USB Type-C port (see Figure 2.4, left). It is used to connect to a power source so the Intelligent Flight battery can be charged internally. You can also link the drone to a computer to exchange information and download photos. The Mini 3 Pro's 1.2GB of internal storage will appear on your desktop as a disk drive (the Mini 3 has no internal storage); if a microSD card has been installed, it will appear as a separate disk drive. You can transfer files from the aircraft to your computer over the USB connection. Transferring images through the USB connection can be more convenient than removing the memory card and inserting it into a card reader.

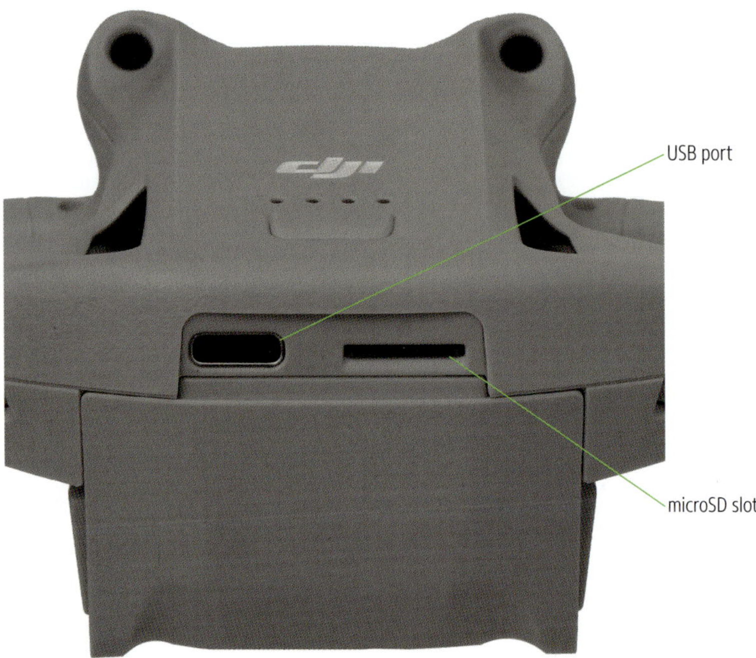

Figure 2.4 USB port and microSD card slot.

- **microSD slot.** Located to the right of the USB port, this slot accepts any microSD card. (See Figure 2.4, right.) DJI recommends using a UHS-I Speed Grade 3 card, which supports a minimum sustained write speed of at least 30MB/second, needed for recording 4K Ultra HD video (the Mini 3 Pro has an additional 5.4K video mode). Although SD card speed nomenclature has changed several times, the only thing you need to look for is the number 3 inside a U "bucket" ("U3") symbol. If your card has a "U1" symbol or is an older card marked Class 2, Class 4, or Class 6, it is too slow for 4K video. **Note:** Your drone can *use* UHS II microSD cards, but it does not support the faster read and write speeds of these newest media. It's fine to use them, but there is no advantage in doing so.

- **Backward Vision System (Mini 3 Pro only).** Your drone has three different systems that allow it to locate and stabilize itself during flight, using visible light, infrared sensing, and GPS satellite data. The Backward sensors are shown in Figure 2.5.

- **Power button.** Press the power button, seen in Figure 2.5, once to check battery level, and then press again, holding for two seconds, to turn the battery on or off.

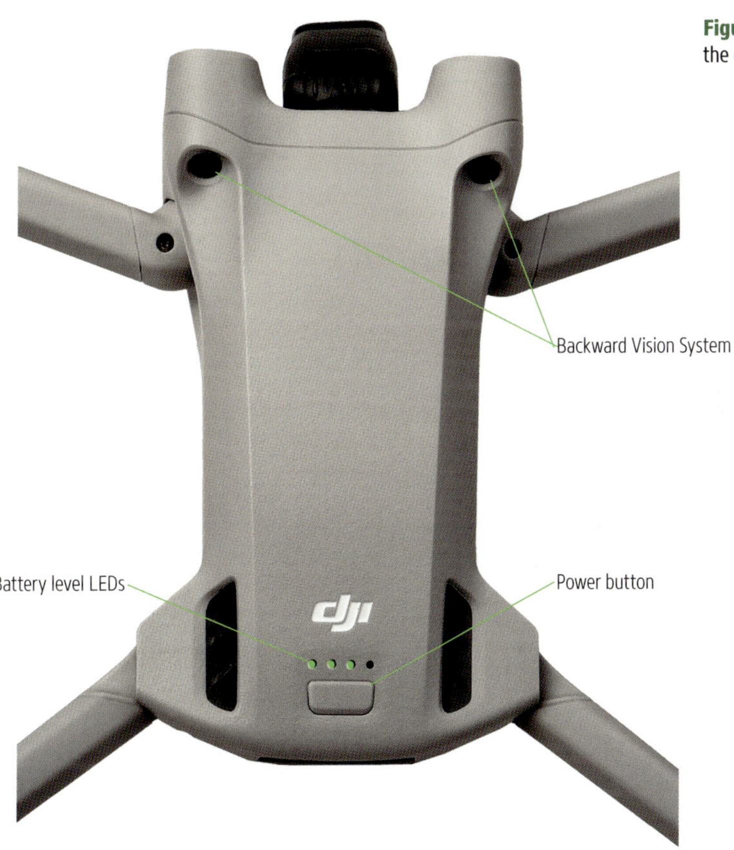

Figure 2.5 Top view of the drone.

- **Battery level LEDs.** Four LEDs underneath the power button illuminate to indicate the amount of charge. (See Figure 2.5.)
- **Battery buckle.** Buckles located on the left and right side of the aircraft can be pressed to release the battery when you need to replace it with a fresh power source. (See Figure 2.6.)
- **Forward Vision System.** In Figure 2.7, you can see the pair of front-facing sensors used for the Forward Vision System.
- **Air vents.** Air vents allow releasing the heat built up by the electronics within the drone, especially by the battery, which can become quite warm during a typical flight.
- **Gimbal and camera.** Also shown in Figure 2.7 are the drone's swiveling camera and the three-axis gimbal mechanism that stabilizes and aims the camera during flight as you capture still photographs and video.

Figure 2.6 Side view of the drone.

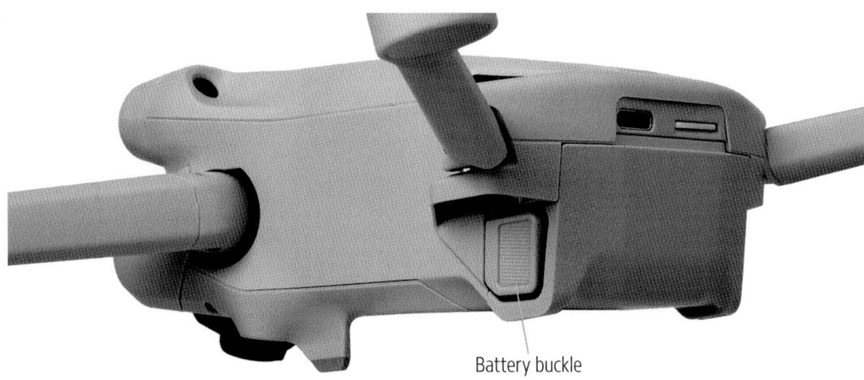

Figure 2.7 Front view of the drone.

- **Infrared Sensing System.** Figure 2.8 shows a pair of 3D infrared sensors on the Mini 3 Pro that help the drone navigate within its surroundings when GPS navigation is unavailable. The IR sensors on the Mini 3 are slightly smaller, and located in roughly the same position.

- **Downward Vision System.** Also shown in Figure 2.8 are the dual downward-pointing sensors of the vision system of the Mini 3 Pro, which helps the drone maintain a hover position more precisely, and are particularly useful when flying indoors. The Mini 3 has only a single, smaller downward sensor, located between the two infrared sensors.

- **Propellers.** Your drone uses two different propeller configurations; each pair rotates in the opposite direction from the other to counter the side-to-side rotation (yaw) each produces, preventing the aircraft from spinning. With four props, the craft can be balanced in several ways, with four points of variable thrust that enable the drone to maintain its position in the air and hover smoothly. The system is much simpler than that found in helicopters, which must vary the pitch (angle) of its rotors to provide control. (See Figure 2.9.)

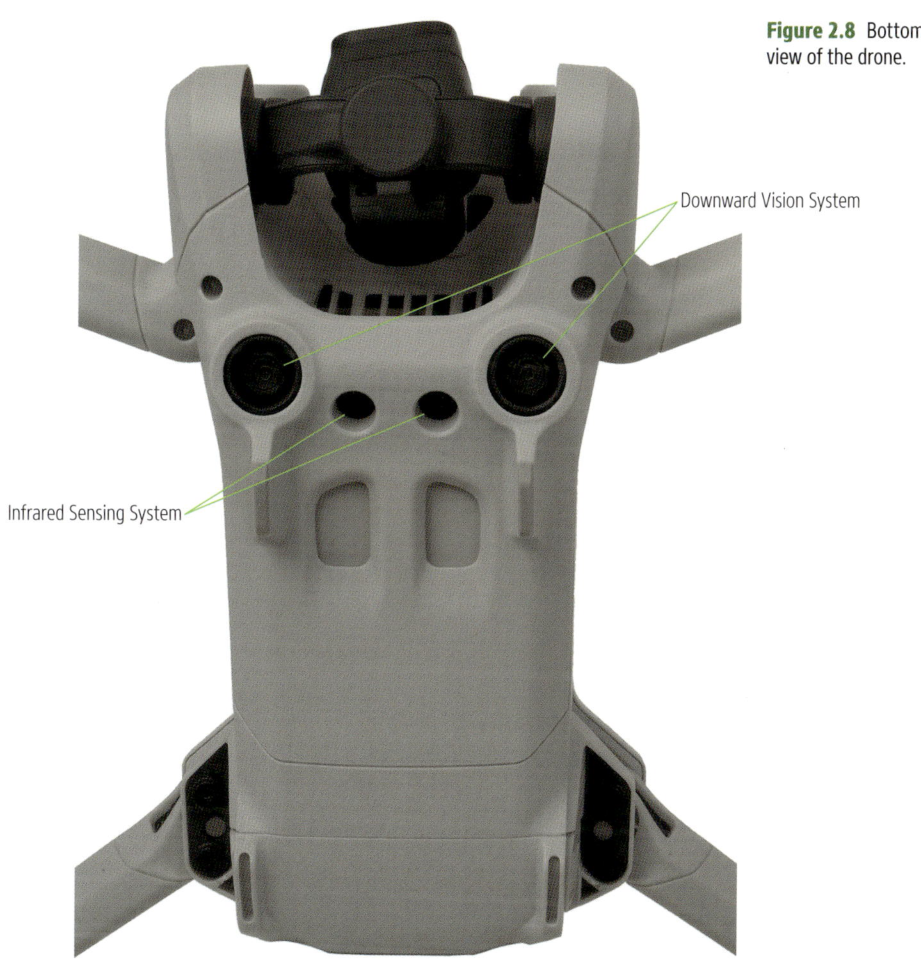

Figure 2.8 Bottom view of the drone.

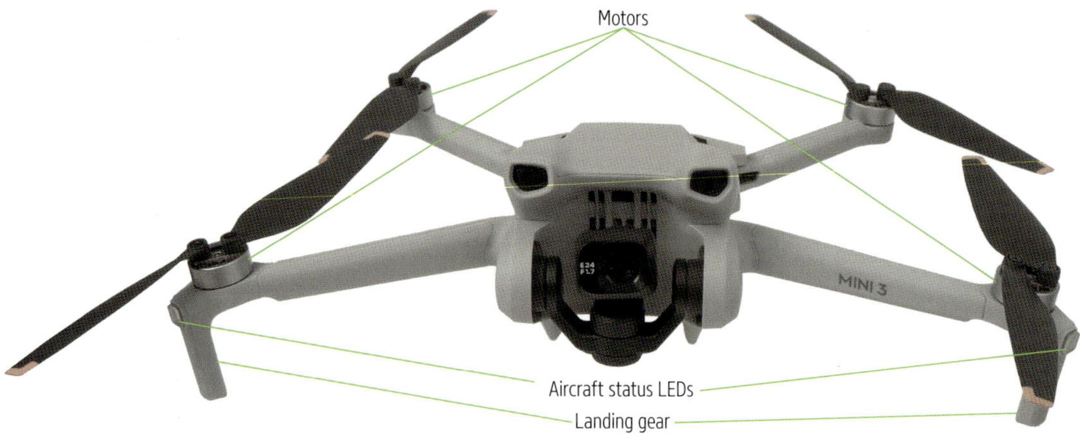

Figure 2.9 Status lights and motors.

- **Motors.** Also shown in Figure 2.9 are the four electrical motors that power the aircraft, located at the end of the fold-out arms that extend from the sides of the Mini 3/Mini 3 Pro.

- **Aircraft status LEDs.** These LEDs are found at the ends of the front arms. They will blink or glow solidly in red, yellow, or green to indicate the aircraft's current status during warm-up or when there are error conditions. I'll explain the different indicators in Chapter 4. Once the motors start, the LEDs will blink green, indicating normal operation.

- **Landing gears (Mini 3 only).** These legs are located below the status LEDs at the front of the aircraft, elevating that end slightly to keep the sensitive gimbal from contacting the landing surface.

Key Features and Differences

As I've been noting throughout this chapter, the DJI Mini 3 and Mini 3 Pro are externally very similar in terms of components, size, and weight. Most of the visible differences are almost irrelevant; the Mini 3 Pro at 249 grams with the standard battery is only one gram heftier than the more basic Mini 3. The most notable difference is the addition of two forward- and two backward-facing optical proximity sensors on the Mini 3 Pro in addition to a downward-facing pair, giving it the useful capability of being able to detect objects/hazards in front of or behind the drone as well as below. The Mini 3 has only a single downward-facing optical sensor.

This section provides a quick overview of the most important differences between the two aircraft. I'll provide more detail about how these differences affect operation of your drone in relevant parts of the book. Other than the exceptions I'll mention, you can generally treat the two as if they were otherwise identical. Both include some very cool features not available in all drones, such as the True Vertical Shooting mode in which the camera is able to rotate a full 90 degrees to capture vertical-format images, without the need to digitally crop them. (Users of TikTok, Instagram Stories, and other social media using a 9:16 aspect ratio take heed.) The Mini 3 and Mini 3 Pro gimbal also offers a wider rotation range for low-angle shots than was available with previous Mini models.

Those who are heavily into first-person view (FPV) flying, particularly for drone racing or exciting flythroughs, will be pleased to know that the Mini 3 Pro is compatible with DJI goggles and the DJI RC Motion 2 controller, a hand-held device that allows complex flight maneuvers with great accuracy and more dynamic movement.

Still Image Quality

The Mini 3 Pro and Mini 3 both rely on upgraded 1/1.3-inch CMOS sensors, measuring 9.8mm × 7.3mm with an effective maximum resolution of 48MP. The sensors provide a 4:3 aspect ratio and are much smaller than the typical 24mm × 36mm sensor with 3:2 proportions found in conventional full-frame still cameras, as seen in Figure 2.10, upper left. If you like, you can alternatively capture still photos using the 16:9 proportions always used for high-definition video instead.

All sensors "see" only black and white, and provide color information thanks to red, green, and blue filters placed over them. Figure 2.11 left, shows a section of a sensor with the typical layout of filters, called a Bayer array, named after Kodak scientist Bryce Bayer, who invented it. Half of the photosites are green sensitive (because human eyes are most responsive to green light), and one quarter of the photosites are each assigned to red and blue. The sensor is a true 48MP *black-and-white* imager, but covered by a *Quad Bayer* filter array, in which adjacent pixels are assigned the same color, as shown at right in Figure 2.11.

Figure 2.10 Sensor size comparison.

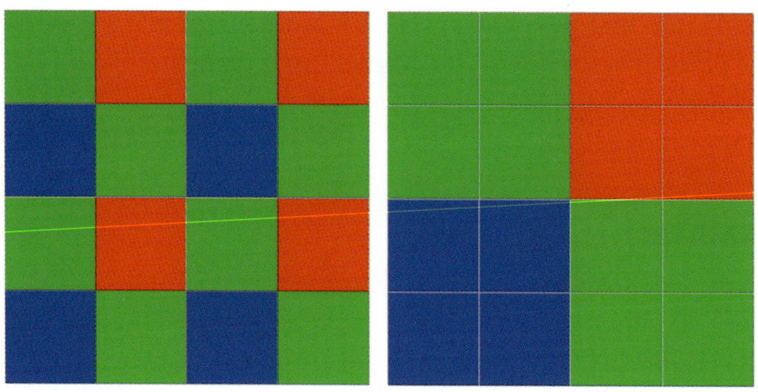

Figure 2.11 Conventional Bayer array (left), Quad Bayer array (right).

The advantage of the Quad Bayer filter pattern is that in low light, the four photo diodes behind each color patch can be combined to act as a single, larger pixel to produce a 12MP image with lower noise. Under better lighting conditions, the four pixels behind each patch can be re-interpreted to simulate an image as if each patch had a conventional Bayer arrangement with a 48MP sensor.

So, even though there are 48MP worth of photodiodes available, the *color* resolution is actually just 12MP. The sensor's electronics use a special algorithm to interpret this information as it creates the final "48MP" image. Effectively, the sensor is able to see slight differences in *detail* between pixels behind the same color square, but cannot detect any *color* differences. So, while the sensor is *effectively* a 48MP sensor, you're not capturing a true full-color 48MP image.

However, both the Mini 3 Pro and Mini 3 have improved image quality over previous models in the Mini lineup, because, whether capturing 48MP or 12MP images, they both boast pixels that are much larger than those found in sensors of the previous Mini aircraft. The upgrade from the 1/2.3-inch sensor of the previous DJI Mini models to the new 1/1.3-inch sensor was a significant enhancement, with roughly 2.5 times as much light-sensitive area. The larger photosites are able to capture more light, which translates into better/higher ISO performance and improved low-light capabilities.

For example, the Mini 3 Pro offers Auto ISO and manual adjustment in the range of ISO 100 to 6400 for both video and still photo capture. The Mini 3 lacks automatic ISO settings, but sensitivity can be set manually from ISO 100 to ISO 3200 for video and stills.

Added Zoom

Neither the Mini 3 nor Mini 3 Pro have an optical zoom lens to provide adjustments in the field of view. Their cameras have fixed focal length lenses with a wide-angle perspective equivalent to a full-frame camera's 24mm with a fixed f/1.7 aperture. Depth-of-field (the range of sharp focus) extends from 39 in./1m to infinity. You generally won't be capturing images at a distance of one meter or less, so effectively, every still photo or video you capture should have an acceptable range of sharp focus.

The increased pixel size makes a digital "zooming" feature possible. The Mini 3 and Mini 3 Pro can simulate an optical zoom by enlarging a cropped area of the sensor to fill the frame. While this cropping reduces the resolution and image quality of the area captured, it does allow zooming in to produce an enlarged image from the same aerial position.

The ability to vary the camera's field of view through zooming is most important in video shooting. Still photos can easily be cropped in an image editor to provide the desired perspective. With video, what you see is generally what you get. Instead of optical zooming, the drone is capable of enlarging portions of the frame digitally to simulate various zoom factors while capturing video. Zooming is performed either by pressing and holding a "zoom" icon on the controller screen or by using a custom button held down while rotating the gimbal dial on the controller. I'll show you how to do this in more detail in Chapter 7. Typical maximum zoom ratios are shown in Figure 2.12.

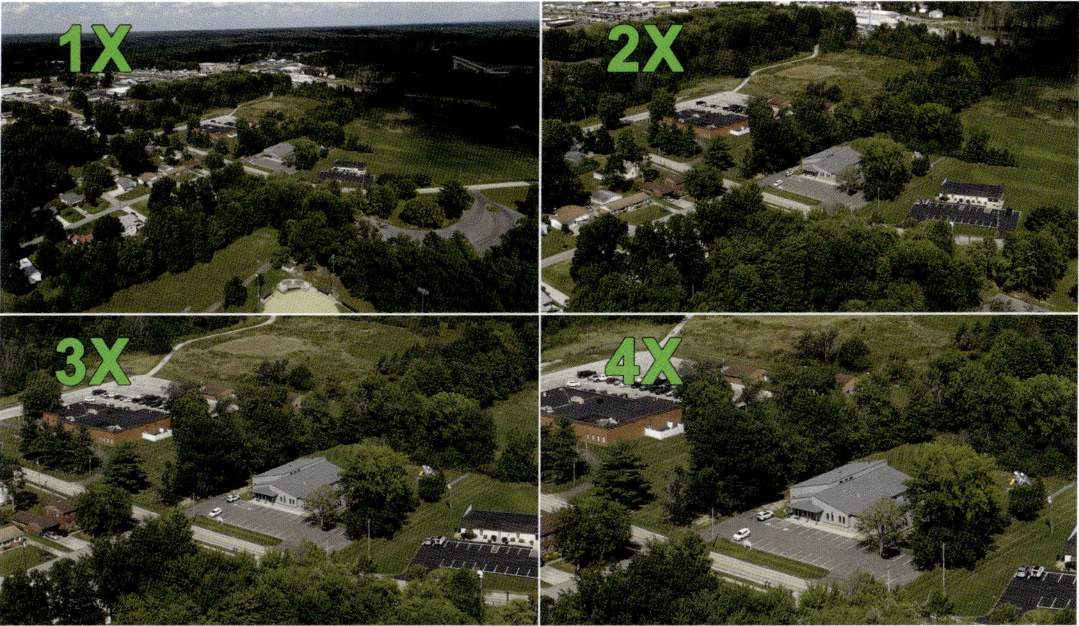

Figure 2.12 Zoom factors.

Image Quality Enhancements

Both drones support JPEG and Adobe Digital Negative (DNG/RAW) capture for stills. Your drone also uses image stabilization to counter the inevitable movement during flight. The gimbal-mounted camera can account for motion along three axes: tilt, roll, and pan. (See Figure 2.13.) I'll discuss image quality features in more detail in Chapter 6.

Figure 2.13 Image stabilization.

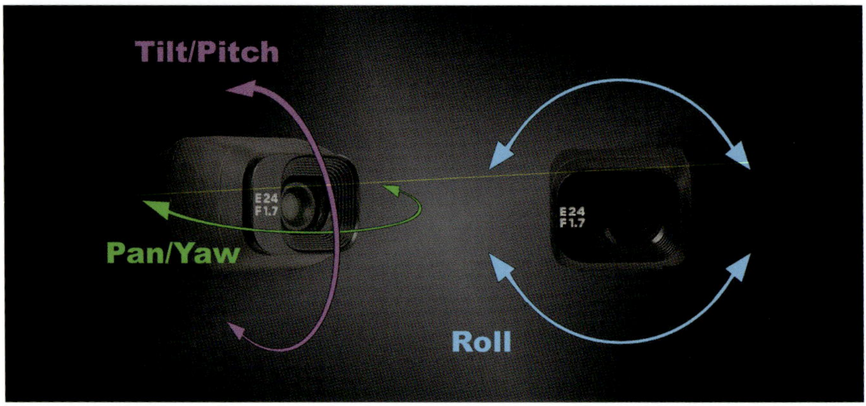

Shooting Modes

Both of these drones include a selection of smart shooting modes, including QuickShots, and (with the Mini 3 Pro) MasterShots. Here's an overview of the options available for both, as well as several more offered for the Mini 3 Pro only:

- **Dronie.** The aircraft flies backward and ascends, with the camera locked on the subject.
- **Circle.** The aircraft circles around the subject.
- **Helix.** The aircraft rises and spirals around the subject.
- **Rocket.** The aircraft rises rapidly with the camera pointing downward.
- **Boomerang.** The aircraft flies around the subject in an oval path, rising as it flies away from its starting points and descending as it returns.
- **Asteroid (Mini 3 Pro only).** The aircraft flies backward and upward, captures multiple images, and then returns to the starting point. The video is created automatically. It starts with a panorama at the highest position and then documents the descent and return.
- **Panorama.** In addition to QuickShots, both drones have a Panorama feature.
- **MasterShots (Mini 3 Pro only).** Select a subject, and the drone will execute a sequence of impressive maneuvers, and then generate a professional-looking brief cinematic video.
- **FocusTrack (Mini 3 Pro only).** These are three modes that allow tracking and following a subject during video capture. Spotlight 2.0: Keeps the subject in frame during manually controlled flight. Point of Interest 3.0: Circles the subject in a prescribed flight radius and speed. ActiveTrack 4.0: Offers options to track the subject at a constant distance, or, tracking at a constant angle and distance beside the subject.

Flight Performance

The Mini 3 Pro and Mini 3 both use DJI's OcuSync technology, giving them stronger resistance against signal interference and automatic adjustments between two frequencies. The Mini 3 Pro includes the updated O3 transmission system, giving it a transmission range of 5 miles/8 kilometers, while the Mini 3 uses OcuSync 2 (O2) with a transmission range of 3.7 miles/6 kilometers. Both drones use DJI's Advanced Pilot Assistance Systems (APAS) 4.0, which automatically detects and finds a safer path around obstacles during flight.

Video Features

Both drones have robust video capabilities and can capture 2.7K and Full HD at the common frame rates of 24, 25/30, 48, and 50/60 frames per second. The Mini 3 Pro can also capture 4K video at those frame rates, but the Mini 3 is limited to 24 and 25/30 fps at 4K. As you'll learn, the 25/30 and 50/60 fps rates apply to the PAL and NTSC video standards, respectively. PAL is used in Europe, most of Asia, Oceania, and Africa, and parts of South America. NTSC is used in North America, Central America, parts of South America, and in Japan, South Korea, and some other countries. The Mini 3 Pro can transfer video to the memory card at up to 150 Mbps, while the Mini 3 is limited to 100 Mbps. The Mini has an HDR video mode available at 24 and 25/30 fps rates, while the Mini 3 Pro has a Full HD slow-motion mode capable of shooting 120 fps.

The Mini 3 Pro also has D-Cinelike Color mode, which provides more visual information to offer you richer color and additional flexibility when editing. I'll explain how to use this mode in Chapter 8.

Next Up

In the next chapter, I'm going to introduce you to the technologies and techniques you need to know to operate your drone safely, with special emphasis on obstacle avoidance and sound takeoff/landing procedures. You'll also learn about the Mini 3 and Mini 3 Pro's sophisticated Intelligent Flight modes. I'll also explain the requirements and restrictions you need to follow to fly legally. New drone owners should absorb everything in this chapter before they attempt to fly for the first time. Veteran pilots may want to skim through and review to make sure they understand the differences between the Mini 3 Pro and Mini 3 and other drones they have operated.

Flying Safely and Legally 3

If you're a photography enthusiast with experience operating a conventional still or video camera, the first thing you may do when you get your hands on a new piece of gear is take it out and put it through its paces. The tendency is to want to see what your equipment can do right off the bat, and resort to the manual only *after* you've discovered that certain operations aren't quite as intuitive as you'd thought, or that you'll need some help understanding all the options of a particular feature. With conventional cameras there are few limits on where or when you can take pictures, within the restrictions of privacy and private property rights.

So, serious photographers can venture out with a new camera and experiment freely to discover their gear's capabilities even before cracking open a manual for the first time. While trial and error isn't the best way to learn how to work with a camera, a surprising number of photo enthusiasts choose that route, at least for their initial sessions with a new piece of equipment.

Alas, a hit-or-miss approach is *not* a good way to learn about drone photography, as you will very likely experience more hits than misses, and when your aircraft is flying 100 feet above the ground, any close encounters of the wrong kind will be unpleasant—and costly. Moreover, it's easy for a beginner to encounter some legal roadblocks if you don't understand the regulations that control drone operation.

This chapter is an essential introduction to the technologies that help your drone fly productively and safely, along with a summary of the rules you need to be aware of and follow to meet regulatory standards. Even though, as a recreational pilot, you don't need official FAA Part 107 certification to enjoy your hobby, and may not be required to register your drone, you still must be aware of and comply with limitations imposed on all flights, regardless of whether they are intended for commercial applications.

Obstacle Avoidance

As you begin operating your aircraft, you'll quickly become aware of the importance of obstacle avoidance. Much of the time, your chief concern will be evading trees, or, if your altitude is low enough, buildings, towers, and other structures. Common sense can be your best friend. Trees most commonly are under 40 feet in height, with some reaching up to 70 or even 100 feet. Only the tallest firs, sequoias, pines, and redwoods stretch above 200 feet. So, if you want to capture some autumn colors, send your drone up 100 feet or more in a forested area and you should be able to shoot to your heart's content. (See Figure 3.1.)

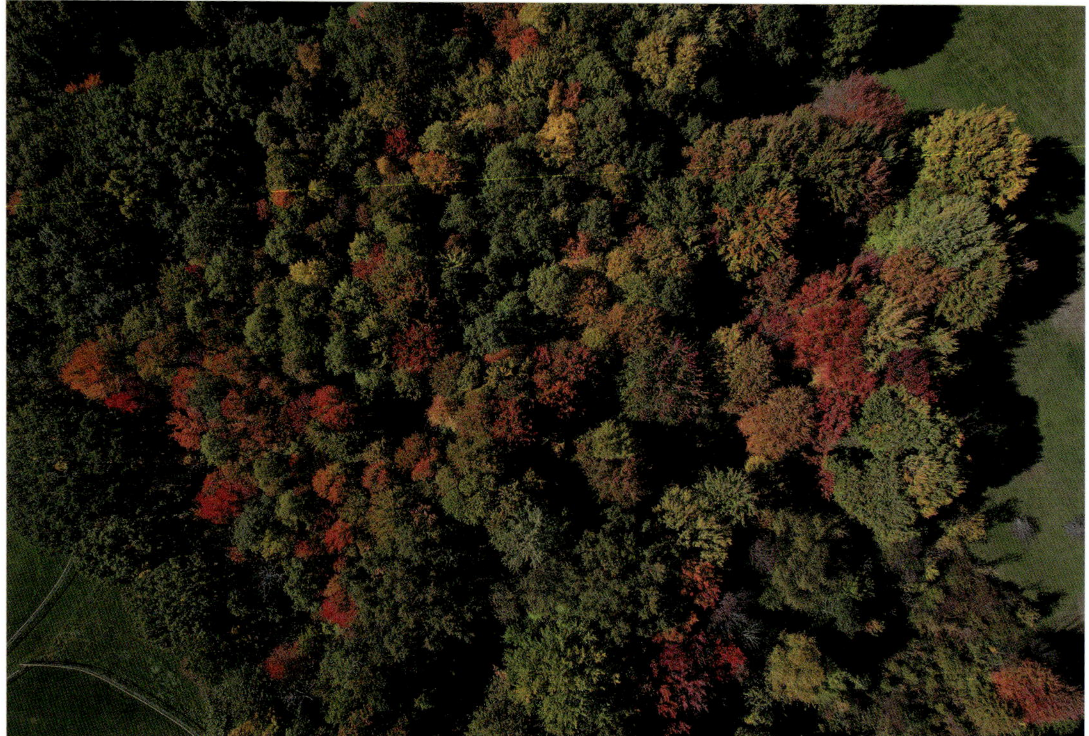

Figure 3.1 Above a couple hundred feet, you won't be colliding with trees.

However, in other aerial environments, you may find you have to avoid other drones, or, in worst-case scenarios, piloted aircraft. Incidents of the latter type should be rare to the point of non-existence. As a recreational flyer, you must keep your Mini 3/Mini 3 Pro below 400 feet above ground level at all times. The DJI Fly app that you use to control your drone will let you know when you approach your altitude limit with a helpful message on the screen like the one shown in Figure 3.2. Your Height indicator, shown at the bottom of the figure in the telemetrics area, will turn red when you reach your maximum altitude.

The DJI Fly app you'll use to operate your drone can be configured to issue this warning at an altitude *lower* than 400 feet, if you like, and also can let you know when your drone flies further than a defined distance from the controller. (See Figure 3.3.) I'll show you how to make maximum altitude and distance settings using DJI Fly in Chapter 4.

Most of the time, a maximum altitude of 400 feet will keep you out of the airspace used by piloted aircraft—as long as you are operating within the airspace allowed for drones. I'll explain the various classes of airspace later in this chapter. Except when necessary for takeoff and landing, piloted aircraft are prohibited from flying lower than 1,000 feet over any congested area of a city, town, or settlement, or over any open-air assembly of persons. They also must maintain an altitude of 1,000 feet above the highest obstacle within a horizontal radius of 2,000 feet of the aircraft. Outside those areas, piloted craft must maintain an altitude of 500 feet above the surface, or no closer than 500 feet to any person, vessel, vehicle, or structure, except over open water or sparsely populated areas.

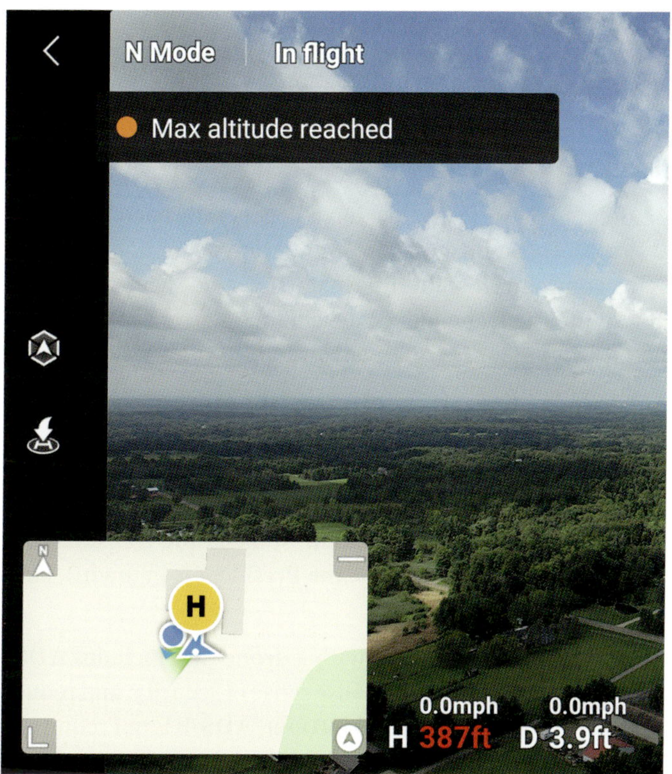

Figure 3.2 Maximum altitude warning.

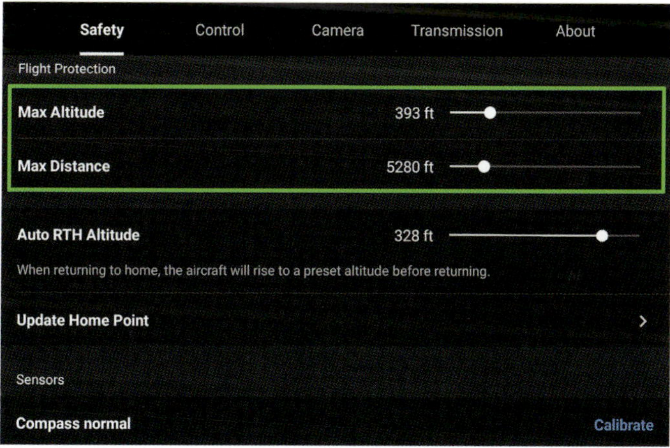

Figure 3.3 You can specify maximum altitude and distance parameters.

So, the 400-foot limit imposed on you should be safe enough in most instances, assuming your flight is within legal airspaces. Note that there are exceptions for helicopters, powered parachutes, or weight-shift-control aircraft (such as hang gliders), which can and do fly below 400 feet.

BOLO (Be On the Lookout)

While BOLO is a law-enforcement term a layperson will generally encounter only on TV cop shows, DJI Mini 3 and Mini 3 Pro pilots should keep the semi-acronym in mind when flying. That's because these drones both lack a common, if sometimes controversial, feature found in many other DJI aircraft called ADS-B (Automatic Dependent Surveillance-Broadcast) technology. In drones that have it, the system (potentially) identifies manned aircraft in the area and notifies the remote pilot to either land or yield the right of way.

ADS-B has two modes: ADS-B Out (the aircraft's transponder sends information packets containing data such as aircraft identification, position, altitude, and velocity approximately once per second while airborne) and ADS-B In (the device is able to receive that information). In the United States the ADS-B system is enhanced with other capabilities, including transmission of information on weather, temporary flight restrictions (TFR; say, the President is in town!), and Notice to Air Missions (NOTAM).

The controversy stems from the fact that even with a drone that includes ADS-B, not all manned aircraft are identified, which can give the pilot a false sense of security, and reduced awareness. Note that not all piloted aircraft are required to use ADS-B Out. ADS-B is not required in the low altitudes where most drones typically operate. Their use is mandated depending on the type of airspace, and there are exceptions, especially for military aircraft, helicopters, and low-altitude operations including agricultural spraying, emergency response flights, search and rescue, or aerial news coverage.

Since the Mini 3 and Mini 3 Pro lack the feature entirely, it's important that you be on the lookout constantly while flying, maintaining visual line-of-sight with your drone, and monitoring your surroundings using your eyes and ears to locate and identify any aircraft or hazards in your vicinity. You should also check for NOTAMs using software installed on your smart device or controller. I'll describe some recommended apps later.

APAS 4.0

The Mini 3 Pro includes a system called Advanced Pilot Assistance System (APAS), which uses the drone's proximity sensors that face forward, behind, and underneath the aircraft for advanced obstacle avoidance. (The Mini 3 has only a downward-facing sensor and does not include APAS.) Obstacles are most often approached from the front or rear, so there are no sensors looking to the sides or above the drone. The downward-pointing sensors of the vision system are supplemented by a pair of 3D infrared sensors on the bottom surface that help the drone navigate within its surroundings when GPS navigation is unavailable.

The information from the sensors is processed by the Mini 3 Pro's upgraded APAS 4.0 software. The feature is available only when the Obstacle Avoidance Action entry in the System > Safety menu is set to Bypass. When enabled, the drone responds to your commands, but APAS detects obstacles in its path and automatically calculates a route to avoid them by flying above, below, or to the left or right. If there is no safe path, the drone will stop and hover in place until it receives a new command.

APAS is designed to operate when the drone is moving forward or backward; it is not used during left, right, or upward movements. *That's because, as I noted, the Mini 3 Pro does not have sensors facing upward or to either side.* When Obstacle Avoidance Action is set to Bypass, an additional entry appears in the Safety menu: Disable Sideways Flight. If you activate the option, the Mini 3 Pro will ignore left/right joystick movement and will fly only in forward/backward directions. This capability is especially useful when flying through hazardous areas to avoid accidentally hitting trees or structures located to either side of the drone.

APAS is available when flying manually in Normal and Cine modes. It functions best when the Downward Vision System is available, GNSS signals are strong, and conditions are neither excessively bright nor dark. APAS may be less effective as the drone approaches its flight limits. APAS 4.0 is not available while using Intelligent Flight modes (described shortly) or when video is at high resolutions (4K, 48/50/60 fps; 2K, 48/50/60 fps; or FHD at 120 fps).

Flight Time/Distance

Keeping a drone aloft takes a lot of juice. The on-board camera, positional sensors, GPS, and controller circuitry all drain the battery. But most of the demand comes from the quartet of motors that keep the propellers rotating to provide the lift and thrust needed to counter the forces of drag and gravity during flight. All that power comes from the Intelligent Flight batteries, which also account for a hefty portion of your drone's weight.

The standard battery weighs roughly 2.8 ounces/80.5 grams, which is about one-third of the roughly 250-gram/8-ounce take-off weight of both the Mini 3 and Mini 3 Pro. Substitute the heavier Intelligent Flight Battery Plus and each of these aircraft will weigh about 290 grams/10.2 ounces, and the more powerful battery then accounts for about 42 percent of the drone's weight.

Table 3.1 shows the approximate maximum flight times, hovering times, and distances your drone can expect to travel using each type of battery. All these figures assume flight at a specified speed, under windless conditions; flying faster or slower will affect flight times. In addition, flights into the wind decrease flight time/distance, and flying with a tail wind increases both.

Your controller will display the remaining available flight time on the screen, and most pilots start thinking about having the drone return to home at about the 5-to-6-minute mark anyway. Note that actual flight times also depend heavily on weather conditions and the direction of the winds.

TABLE 3.1 Maximum Flight/Hover Times/Distances

	MINI 3 PRO INTELLIGENT FLIGHT BATTERY	MINI 3 PRO INTELLIGENT FLIGHT BATTERY +	MINI 3 INTELLIGENT FLIGHT BATTERY	MINI 3 INTELLIGENT FLIGHT BATTERY +
Maximum Flight Time: 13.4 mph/21.6 kph	34 minutes	47 minutes	38 minutes	51 minutes
Maximum Hover Time	30 minutes	40 minutes	33 minutes	44 minutes
Maximum Distance: 26.8 mph/43.2 kph	11.2 mi/18 km	15.5 mi/25 km	11.2 mi/18 km	15.5 mi/25 km

Range

It's easy to be confused by the transmission range specifications of your Mini 3/Mini 3 Pro's controller, as the ratings indicate distances measured in kilometers, and recreational drone pilots would not be operating their aircraft beyond a visual line of sight with a much smaller range. However, strong signals are still beneficial even if you're not planning a cross-country voyage. A robust radio signal provides connection stability and a superior transmission link between your drone and your controller even when objects, such as tall buildings, potentially interfere with your signal. Interruptions can be annoying when you're streaming video, and risky when you lose control of your aircraft. (Don't worry; your aircraft has built-in return-to-home [RTH] features that come into play when that happens, as I'll explain in Chapter 5.)

Ranges given are calculated using two different transmission specification systems. In the United States and Canada, the drone will use the FCC-approved system. In most other countries, a less-powerful transmission system in compliance with Conformitè Européenne (CE) requirements is used. (China and Japan have their own separate certification requirements.)

The relevant long-range transmission technologies built into the remote controllers used by the drones are called OcuSync 2.0 for the Mini 3 and OcuSync 3.0 (also called O3) for the Mini 3 Pro. OcuSync 2.0 uses two antennas, while the more potent OcuSync 3.0 uses four. Both systems provide a decent transmission range. The Mini 3's OcuSync 2.0 offers a range of 6.2 mi/10 km (FCC) and 3.7 mi/6 km (CE). With the Mini 3 Pro, you can expect a transmission range of up to 7.5 mi/12 km (FCC) and 5 mi/8 km (CE). Live view streaming is available at up to 1080p (Full HD) resolution with the Mini 3 Pro, and a lower resolution 720p (Standard HD) streaming with the Mini 3.

Flight Modes

The Mini 3 and Mini 3 Pro both have Normal, Sport, and Tripod/Cine (N, S, T/C) flight modes, selectable using a Flight Mode switch on the controller, plus a fourth mode, Attitude (ATTI), that the drone may shift into automatically when vision systems or the GNSS signal for GPS location is weak, or the internal compass experiences interference.

Your flight modes are:

- **Normal.** You'll be using Normal mode most of the time. Operation is different for each drone:

  Mini 3 Pro. The Mini 3 Pro uses Forward, Backward, and Downward Vision Systems, plus Infrared Sensing and/or GNSS geolocation (if the signal is strong) to orient and stabilize its flight. Obstacle sensing and avoidance is used. Top speed (without benefit of tailwinds) is 22.3 mph/36 kph.

  Mini 3. The Mini 3 has only a Downward Vision System, plus Infrared Sensing and/or GNSS geolocation to navigate. Because there are no front- or back-pointing vision sensors to provide the same obstacle avoidance features of the Mini 3 Pro, you'll need to use extra caution when flying. The top speed is the same as that of the Mini 3 Pro.

- **Sport.** This mode is optimized for responsiveness to the controls, fast movements, and agility. DJI says the Mini 3 uses its Downward Vision System and GNSS for navigation. Because the drone is more responsive to small control stick adjustments, you should be more careful in directing your aircraft in this mode. Obstacle sensing and automatic avoidance is disabled, and a slightly higher maximum flight speed is available. Top speed for both models in this mode is a brisk 42 mph/68 kph. Because of the faster motion in Sport mode, the minimum distance for braking is 98 feet/30 meters.

- **Tripod/Cine.** This mode is given the Tripod label on some older controllers used, and Cine on newer controllers. Performance is similar to that of Normal mode, but the top speed is limited to roughly 14 mph/22 kph to provide more stable flight that's desirable when capturing video.

- **ATTI.** When the drone's vision systems are unavailable or the compass or GNSS signal cannot be used, the aircraft will shift into Attitude, which you can consider Manual for all intents and purposes. In earlier drones it could be selected manually, but now is only invoked automatically as required. Automatic positioning systems are not available, so your drone will be unable to maintain a stable hover, and can lose altitude or drift sideways if you don't make corrections. The most common reason ATTI is invoked is proximity to a strong source of signal interference, or flying under an overhead obstacle, such as a canopy of trees. You'll use ATTI mode if you're operating your aircraft indoors, too. Once GPS stabilization is lost, you'll need to take over quickly.

One speed metric that is sometimes overlooked by beginners is the speed at which the drone can ascend and descend, which can be especially important when you need to bring your aircraft down quickly, say, to avoid an overhead obstacle. In Sport mode, the Mini 3 Pro can ascend and descend at rates of about 11 mph/18 kph. The Mini 3 can fly upward at the same 11 mph/18 kph rate, but takes longer to descend at 7.5 mph/12 kph. Ascent and descent speeds are slower in Normal and Tripod/Cine modes.

Intelligent Flight Modes

Both drones also boast an array of QuickShot Intelligent Flight modes that provide automatic cinematic video clips. The Mini 3 Pro adds FocusTrack modes, which allow the drone to maintain focus while the drone and its subjects are in motion. These include Point of Interest, which commands the drone to "orbit" moving objects such as vehicles or people, and Spotlight, which centers and locks the camera on a subject. The Mini 3 Pro uses an upgraded Active Track 4.0 feature with improved accuracy. Panorama modes are also considered Intelligent Flight modes. The Intelligent Flight modes are explained in detail in Chapter 8.

The Mini 3 Pro includes these two groups of Intelligent Flight modes:

- **FocusTrack:**
  - Point of Interest
  - Spotlight
  - Active Track

- **Hyperlapse:**
  - Free
  - Course Lock
  - Circle
  - Waypoint

Both the Mini 3 and Mini 3 Pro offer automated QuickShots modes:

- **QuickShots:**
  - Dronie
  - Rocket
  - Circle
  - Helix
  - Boomerang
  - Asteroid (Mini 3 Pro only)

One significant upgrade provided by the Mini 3 Pro is the addition of a new MasterShots mode. Just select a subject, choose a template you like, and the aircraft will automatically keep that subject in the center of the frame while executing a series of maneuvers and a variety of automated routines, including Rocket, Circle, Helix, and Asteroid. The app can stitch together a video of the best shots, add background music and titles, and create an FHD (1080p) clip. I'll cover MasterShots in detail in Chapter 8.

Getting Legal

You're not a lawyer. You don't play one on TV. You don't consult one every time you operate your Mini 3 or Mini 3 Pro. Even so, within and outside of the United States, there are certain rules that apply to drone pilots, and you're required to obey them. So, it's your responsibility to learn what you can do as a recreational flyer, a task that's made more complicated by the fact that the rules change from time to time. (I'll address one of the newest of them, the FAA Remote ID requirement, later.) The shifting sands of regulation in the USA are the result of the fairly recent introduction of hobby drone use to this country; drones have been used recreationally in other countries, particularly the United Kingdom, for much longer. Consequently, it's taken a long time for the governing body—the Federal Aviation Administration—to recognize the need for regulation, and to formulate the relevant rules.

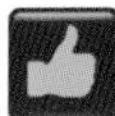 **TIP** I'm going to provide you with an overview of the things I learned, but I can't guarantee—especially given how the rules and their interpretation have changed—that every possible thing you might need to know is covered. I'm going to explain requirements in the United States only; if you live elsewhere or are a U.S. resident and want to operate your drone outside your home country, the rules are different.

In addition, this book covers recreational users only; the requirements for what is called 14 CFR Part 107 certification are much more rigorous. For certification, a pilot must:

- Be at least 16 years old.
- Be able to read, speak, write, and understand English.
- Be in a physical and mental condition to safely fly a drone.
- Pass the initial aeronautical knowledge exam: "Unmanned Aircraft General—Small (UAG)."

The qualification test has 60 questions, and you must answer 70 percent of them (42 questions) correctly to qualify. There are many available guidebooks and practice guides for those who want to take the next step and qualify to fly their drones for profit.

A Visit to Acronymland

The rules for operating unmanned aircraft systems (UAS) weighing less than 55 pounds in the National Airspace System (NAS) are contained in the Code of Federal Regulations (CFR) as 14 CFR Part 107, also called the Small UAS Rule. Those who want to fly drones for recreation must follow a subset of those regulations (a "carve out") with a basic set of requirements that qualifies as a limited statutory exception. I'll list those requirements shortly.

By National Airspace System, the FAA is referring to a broad network that encompasses airspaces over land and bodies of water that are either controlled (with strict rules governing what aircraft—both piloted and unmanned—can do) or uncontrolled. The NAS also includes, according to the FAA, "air navigation facilities, equipment, and services; airports and landing areas; aeronautical charts, information, and services; rules and regulations; procedures and technical information; and manpower and material."

To fly your drone under the Exception for Recreational Flyers you must follow these guidelines:

- **Current registration for any drone heavier than 250 grams.** Both the Mini 3 and Mini 3 Pro weigh less than 250 grams (about 8.8 ounces) with the standard Intelligent Flight battery, and *do not* need to be registered for recreational use. However, you must still adhere to all the other rules of drone operation, such as the requirement to fly no higher than 400 feet above ground level.

  If your Mini 3 or Mini 3 Pro uses the Intelligent Flight Battery Plus, or you have added any accessories, such as strobe lights, that increase the aircraft's weight above 250 grams, you'll need to register your drone. If you're a recreational flyer, you can receive a single registration number that can be used to identify all the drones you own, and it is valid for three years. The number must be affixed externally to the drone and easily visible (I use a Brother labelmaker.). The cost is $5. (Part 107 pilots must register each drone separately for $5 each.) I'll describe the registration process shortly.

- **Fly only for recreational purposes.** Recreational flight is flying as a hobby for personal enjoyment. Non-recreational flights are, contrary to popular assumption, not just those performed for a business or financial compensation. Activities done for goodwill or other non-monetary considerations can also be classified as non-recreational. The FAA website lists taking pictures of a high school football game or volunteering to use your drone for a non-profit organization as examples of non-recreational flight.

  That's not to say that the FAA will come after you if it's reported you used your drone to inspect your neighbor's roof when they put their house up for sale. But you need to know and abide by the rules using your own judgment. For example, you can operate your drone for profit legally in the presence of a Part 107–certified pilot who serves as remote Pilot in Charge (PIC) who is able to assume command if necessary.

- **Pass The Recreational UAS Safety Test.** The TRUST test is designed to ensure that you know all the basic rules that must be followed to fly recreationally. I'll tell you more about the TRUST test shortly.

- **Follow the safety guidelines of a community-based organization (CBO).** This one is a little tricky, because, as this is written, there are only a small number of approved CBOs (including the Academy of Model Aeronautics, First Person View Freedom Coalition, Flite Test Community Association, and STEM+C Inc.). I expect additional CBOs will be approved during the life of this book.

  In all cases, the intent is to direct recreational drone pilots to follow the *additional* safety guidelines of these types of organizations, such as drone or model airplane clubs (which frequently have their own designated flying fields). Until CBOs for drone aircraft become more widely recognized by the FAA, the agency requires you to adhere to its current safety guidelines, which are basically summed up by the remaining bullet points in this list.

- **Keep your drone within your visual line of sight.** You must keep your drone within the visual line of sight or use a visual observer who is co-located (physically next to) and in direct communication with you.

- **Give way and do not interfere with any manned aircraft.** Usually, you will not encounter any piloted aircraft in the airspace you are allowed to fly, but keep in mind there are exceptions, particularly for helicopters, which can and do land in areas other than actual airports.

- **Fly at or below 400 feet in controlled airspace and only with prior authorization.** This applies to both recreational drone pilots and Part 107–certified pilots who must receive authorization—not by contacting the FAA/air traffic controllers directly—through communication with LAANC (Low Altitude Authorization and Notification Capability) or DroneZone facilities.

- **Fly at or below 400 feet in uncontrolled airspace.** This restriction applies to you as a recreational drone user. You can view the classes of airspace and flying restrictions in your area using the B4UFLY app, available on smart devices, dedicated controllers, and on the web. I'll describe this app and other recommended utilities in Chapter 4.

- **Comply with all airspace restrictions.** Although you are generally permitted to fly within Class G airspaces if keeping below 400 feet above ground level, additional rules may apply to you, such as temporary flight restrictions (TFRs). The next section explains airspaces in more detail.

Airspaces Simplified

If you decide to move on from recreational flying to become Part-107 certified, you'll hear a lot more about airspace classification, particularly controlled airspaces, designated Class A–E. Commercial drone pilots may be able to fly within Classes B–E, with authorization (forget Class A: it *begins* at 18,000 feet above sea level and extends higher).

As a recreational flyer, you may not operate your drone within *any* controlled airspace without authorization from an FAA Approved LAANC UAS Service Supplier, and, as noted earlier, must fly no higher than 400 feet above the surface under any circumstances. It's useful to have a good understanding of airspaces, however, so you'll know exactly what your limitations are.

According to the FAA, there are two categories of airspace, regulatory and nonregulatory. Within these two categories, there are four types: controlled, uncontrolled, special use, and other airspace. The categories and types of airspace are dictated by the complexity or density of aircraft movements, nature of the operations conducted within the airspace, level of safety required, and national and public interest.

Note that in addition to the guidelines for controlled and uncontrolled airspaces, temporary flight restrictions (TFRs) may be issued through a Notice to Air Missions (NOTAM), formerly called Notice to Airmen. These messages include the effective time period of the restriction, the area, and altitudes affected, plus other information. As I'll explain in Chapter 5, you should access the FAA's B4UFLY app to determine whether you are located within an airspace where takeoff of your drone is permitted, and to determine if there are any TFRs in effect. (Say, the President is in town.) The app is available for both iOS and Android devices (see Figure 3.4) as well as on the web.

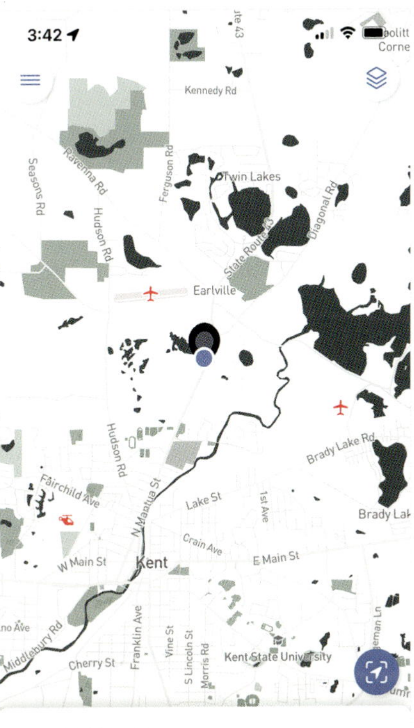

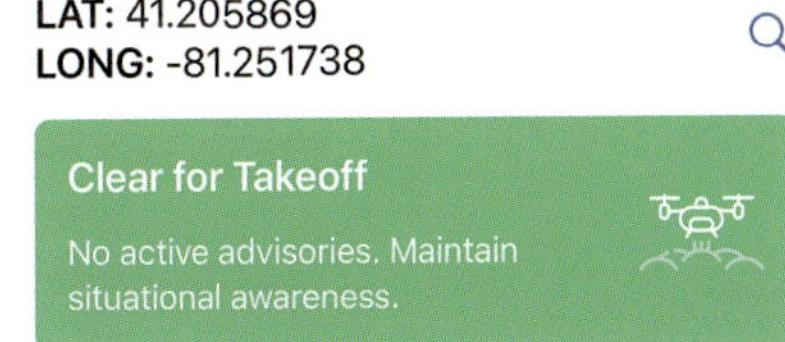

Figure 3.4 The B4UFLY app will display nearby airports and restrictions in effect.

Controlled Airspace

You can think of controlled airspace as areas within which air traffic control (ATC) service is provided. It covers areas around airports and other areas where aircraft travel. **Reminder:** You *must* obtain an authorization before flying in any Class B–E airspace. (Your drone is effectively unable to even *reach* Class A airspace, roughly 3.4 miles above sea level.)

- **Class A.** Generally refers to airspace at 18,000 feet above mean sea level (actually, the average height of the sea, accounting for tides) and higher, shown in red in Figure 3.5. This airspace extends over waters within 12 nautical miles of the coast of the 48 continuous states and Alaska.

- **Class B.** This is the airspace extending from the surface to 10,000 feet above sea level surrounding the USA's busiest airports, its lateral dimensions shaped like an inverted wedding cake, represented by the dark blue shape in the figure.

- **Class C.** This airspace extends from the surface to 4,000 feet above the airport elevation (charted using mean sea level), in the two-tiered shape shown in purple in Figure 3.5. Less busy than our larger airports, they will have an operational control tower, are serviced by radar approach control, and include instrument flight rules.

- **Class D.** A simple cylinder, shown at right in the figure, represents the Class D airspace from the surface to 2,500 feet above the airport elevation (charted in mean sea level), surrounding other airports with an operational control tower.

- **Class E.** This class encompasses all the controlled airspace not incorporated within the other four classes. It can begin at 700 feet *above ground level* (adjacent to Class B or Class C airspaces); at 1,200 feet *above ground level* in most other areas; or at the surface (around untowered airports with no instrument approach).

Airspace Simplified

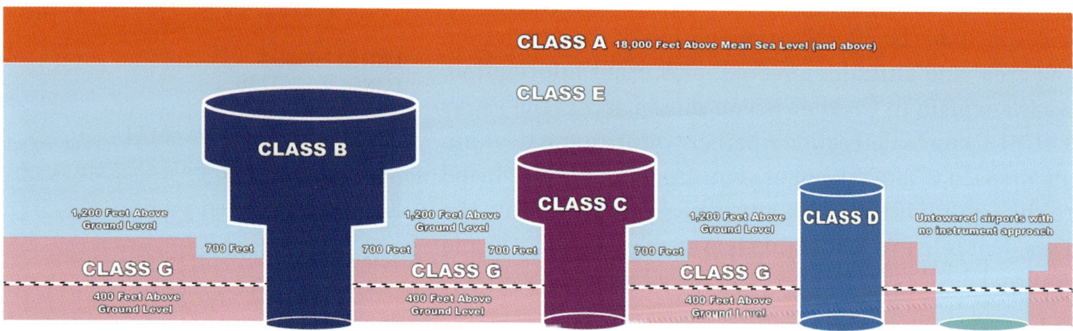

Figure 3.5 Simplified diagram of airspaces.

Uncontrolled Airspace

Most other regulatory airspaces fall within Class G, which is called uncontrolled airspace. Note that *uncontrolled* does not mean *nonregulated*; Class G airspaces are definitely subject to FAA rules. Nonregulated airspaces include military operations areas, warning areas, alert areas, and controlled firing areas.

Class G airspace is the least regulated of the airspaces, and is shown in pink in Figure 3.5. (There is no Class F in the United States.) It extends from the surface to the base of the overlying Class E airspace, but as a recreational pilot, you can go no higher than the first 400 feet above ground level within Class G. The FAA does not control air traffic within this airspace, but you need to watch out for other drones as well as aircraft, including helicopters, which may descend into this airspace.

Special-Use Airspace

This type of airspace is dedicated to areas in which certain activities must be confined, or where other limitations may be imposed on aircraft that are not part of those activities. They include prohibited areas, such as the National Mall in Washington, DC, where the White House and Congress are located, and restricted or warning areas where flights are affected by hazards. Alert areas, with a high volume of pilot training or unusual action, military operation areas, and controlled firing areas are other types of special airspaces.

The Recreational UAS Safety Test (TRUST)

The FAA really, really wants you to understand the rules before you fly. So, the organization has created The Recreational UAS Safety Test (TRUST) exam and asks you to carry proof that you've passed the free test when you're flying. You may take this test online through any of the FAA-approved test administrators.

This is not a difficult test; in fact, if you get a question wrong, you are supplied with the correct answer and invited to answer it again before proceeding. If you're not obstinate, you'll finish the test with a 100 percent score. The goal is to make sure you have been briefed on the rules and understand them. If you read through the Study Guide, you'll have a good understanding going in. The guide is shown in Figure 3.6, with the permission of Flying Legit, LLC, and may be copied and distributed without modification only.

After answering a series of multiple-choice questions like the one shown in Figure 3.7, you'll be able to download, save, and print your completion certificate, which looks like the facsimile seen in Figure 3.8. If you lose your certificate, you will need to re-take the test, as test administrators do not keep a record of your certificate. You must present a copy of your certificate if asked by law-enforcement officers. It never expires.

TRUST

The Recreational UAS Safety Test
Study Guide

Requirements

- **Recreational drone pilots may only fly for fun.** Do not fly for work, payment, or for a business.
- **Controlled Airspace** is usually found around airports, cities, and metropolitan areas. Most likely requires authorization through LAANC or FAADroneZone.
- **Uncontrolled Airspace** does *not* mean unregulated. Airspace closest to ground level and away from airports. Does not require authorization but does require compliance with all other rules including not flying over 400 feet above ground level.
- **Prior to flying your drone,** check with a *LAANC UAS Service Supplier* or the *B4UFLY* app to find out if the airspace you plan to fly in is restricted/needs authorization or is prohibited.
- **Temporary Flight Restriction (TFR)** can happen anytime/anywhere. Usually issued for events like Presidential/VIP visits, major sporting events, or for severe weather.

Preparation

- **The person flying the drone is responsible for all aspects of the flight,** including where it flies, how high it flies, and that all rules and regulations are followed.
- **Factors that can affect your ability to fly your drone safely include** distractions, drugs/medications, alcohol, sickness, health, stress, fatigue, weather conditions, and physical obstacles (power lines, trees, buildings, people, etc.).
- **Check your drone before and after each flight** to make sure it's working properly and there isn't any damage. Do not fly with a low power or damaged battery.

Safety

- **Community Based Organization (CBO)** safety guidelines must be followed when flying under the Exception for Recreational Flyers.
- **Maintaining Visual Line of Sight (VLOS)** helps avoid ground obstacles, bystanders, and manned aircraft. No binoculars, cameras, or other devices are allowed.
- **Using a visual observer** does not allow a recreational flyer to fly a drone beyond VLOS.
- **If you are using first-person-view (FPV) goggles** or looking at your control station for most of the flight, you must have a visual observer next to you and they must maintain VLOS of the drone.
- **Drones must give way to manned aircraft at all times during flight!**

Limitations

- **Before flying your drone for the first time,** you should read the manufacturer's safety information to learn about maximum altitude, weight, and flight distance; automated features; and battery duration, strength, and range.
- **Most common cause of drone incidents is a lost signal.** Know how your drone will respond.
- **Register your drone with the FAA** if it weighs 0.55 pounds (250 grams) or more. Registration number must be displayed on drone exterior.
- **Must provide proof of registration and TRUST course completion** upon request by law enforcement or FAA personnel.

Ready to Take TRUST?

Scan QR code with phone or visit
www.TrustFAA.com/enroll

Note: The term "drone" includes a variety of Unmanned Aircraft Systems such as RC airplanes, RC helicopters, and quadcopters. An unmanned aircraft is a component of an unmanned aircraft system (UAS). Defined by statute, an unmanned aircraft is an aircraft that is operated without the possibility of direct human intervention from within or on the aircraft (Public Law 112-95, Section 331(8)).

Figure 3.6 TRUST study guide.

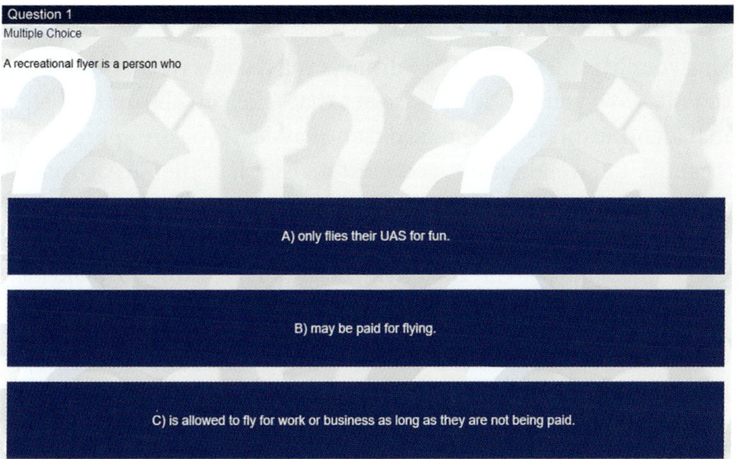

Figure 3.7 Answer a series of multiple-choice questions.

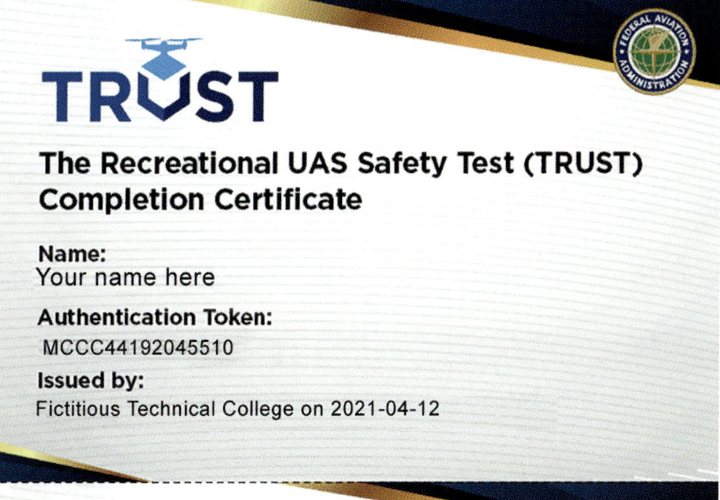

Figure 3.8 TRUST completion certificate.

How to Register Your Aircraft

I recommend registering your Mini 3 or Mini 3 Pro drone, even if yours weighs less than 0.55 pounds (250 grams). Doing so will allow you to add accessories that take you above the weight limit, and provide you with formal identification (and thus avoid any hassles if you are approached by authorities). If your aircraft is above the weight limit, you *must* register it at the FAA DroneZone website https://faadronezone.faa.gov. The process is easy, and is open to owners as young as 13 years old (anyone younger than that must have a person 13 years old or older register their drone). You must be a U.S. citizen or legal permanent resident; the FAA will issue a *recognition of ownership* certificate instead, rather than certificate of U.S. aircraft registration to foreign operators.

The fee is $5, and the registration number supplied is valid for three years. Recreational flyers can use the same registration number for all the drones they own; Part 107–certified pilots must receive an individual registration number for each drone they operate.

To register, you need:

- A physical address and mailing address (if different from your physical address).
- Your email address.
- Your phone number.
- The make and model of your drone, e.g., Mini 3 or Mini 3 Pro.
- Specific Remote ID serial number provided by the manufacturer. Yours is at the front edge of the battery compartment, next to the bar code, and visible once you remove the battery from the aircraft.
- Credit or debit card. I can assure you that you'll get your $5 worth of value from the FAA.

IMPORTANT NOTICE

There are a number of websites that masquerade as official Federal sites that will "register" your drone for you, at an inflated cost. They include add-ons, such as "official" required registration card and lanyards and stickers for your drone. The total for that package at one site I visited came to $50 plus $1.50 shipping. They do, in fact, pass along your information to the FAA so you end up registering your drone, but unless you want a fancy card and stickers, this service is not worth the money. You can print your own registration card at home, and use a permanent marker or label maker to apply the number to your drone. I prefer labels, because you can peel them off if you transfer your drone to someone else the next time you upgrade.

Remote ID Requirements

Although drones have been used for military and commercial purposes for decades, dating back to the '50s, their widespread use for recreation/hobbies and the latest commercial applications is relatively new. FAA regulations are still being developed and refined and are somewhat in a state of flux.

One of the most significant types of drone regulation is starting to take place, and should be in effect during the life of this book. It involves a new system of Remote Identification. The technology provides an integrated way for authorities to monitor airborne drones and their pilots. No, the government is not coming to take your drones away from you; rather, Remote ID (RID) will make it easier to ensure safe flights while protecting people and property on the ground, and airplanes and helicopters who share the same sky with drone aircraft. It may even open up new areas to drone pilots, such as night flying, or directly over people someday.

The new Remote ID rules first started going into effect on April 21, 2021, and have been phasing in ever since. The technology transmits the drone's position, altitude, and serial number by radio to receivers on the ground. The radio protocol must be one that can be received by common handheld devices (say, phones or tablets), such as Bluetooth or Wi-Fi. You will not be required to connect to a mobile network, pay a monthly fee, or store your flight data in a government database.

All *new* drones weighing more than 0.55 pounds/250 grams introduced after December 2022 are required to have this Remote ID functionality built in. All *existing* registered drone aircraft were required to include Remote ID after September 2023. DJI has stated its intention to make the technology available to owners of recent drones introduced before December 2022 as seamlessly as possible. As I write this, the Mini 3 Pro has already received FAA approval. It is expected that, for many other models, the upgrade to Remote ID will be accomplished through a software upgrade to the aircraft's firmware. The company says that since the FAA will allow drone pilots to satisfy Remote ID requirements with a separate add-on module, it anticipates even the oldest DJI drones, including those out of production, will be able to comply. DJI released the first firmware updates for its compatible drones in September, 2023. Currently, there are three ways drone pilots can meet the identification requirements of the Remote ID rule:

- **Operate a drone equipped with Remote ID built in.** These will broadcast identification and location information of the drone and control station automatically. The feature is activated in firmware, and once enabled cannot be turned off.
- **Operate a drone with an add-on Remote ID broadcast module.** This component will provide the drone's identification, location, and take-off information. The broadcast module is a device that can be attached to a drone or installed inside the drone. Persons operating a drone with a Remote ID broadcast module must be able to see their drone at all times during flight.
- **Operate without Remote ID equipment.** The government has established FAA-recognized identification areas (FRIAs) sponsored by community-based organizations or schools. These are often flying fields or other areas used specifically by aircraft hobbyists. FRIAs are the only locations unmanned aircraft (drones and radio-controlled airplanes) may operate without broadcasting Remote ID message elements. Drones without Remote ID must operate within visual line of sight and within the FRIA. Anyone can fly in these locations, but FRIAs can only be requested by community-based organizations and educational institutions.

Some drone flyers have been concerned that RID will enable bad actors to identify, locate, and harass legitimate UAS users through apps that show the location of a particular aircraft's remote control. Remote ID technology is still too new to know exactly what any unintended consequences may take place, but my guess is that we don't have to worry about marauding hordes of drone vigilantes just yet.

Next Up

In the next chapter, you'll find detailed instructions on how to prep your aircraft for its initial flight. Veteran users should just consider it a refresher to confirm that their own pre-flight checklist checks all the right boxes. New pilots will want to follow my recommendations carefully, as skipping any of the essential steps can be a real downer, in several senses of the word.

Getting Your Drone Flight-Ready

4

It's time to get your drone ready for your first flight. You'll need to charge the batteries, download the essential apps used prior to and during flight, install the propellers, and become familiar with your remote controller. You'll accomplish all of these items in this chapter. I'll show you how to activate your drone and make your first actual flight in Chapter 5.

Charge the Batteries

If your drone has been idle for more than a few days, you'll want to charge your Intelligent Flight batteries to their maximum before taking your aircraft out to fly. That's because, as a safety measure, your batteries automatically discharge when not used and, if you want to achieve the maximum flight time, they must be recharged not long before they are installed in your Mini 3/Mini 3 Pro.

There are two ways to charge your batteries. Up to three batteries can be charged, one after another, when installed in the charging hub connected to a power source, as shown at left in Figure 4.1. A single battery can be recharged while it is still in the aircraft itself when the power source is plugged into the USB Type-C port on the back of the drone, as shown at right in Figure 4.1.

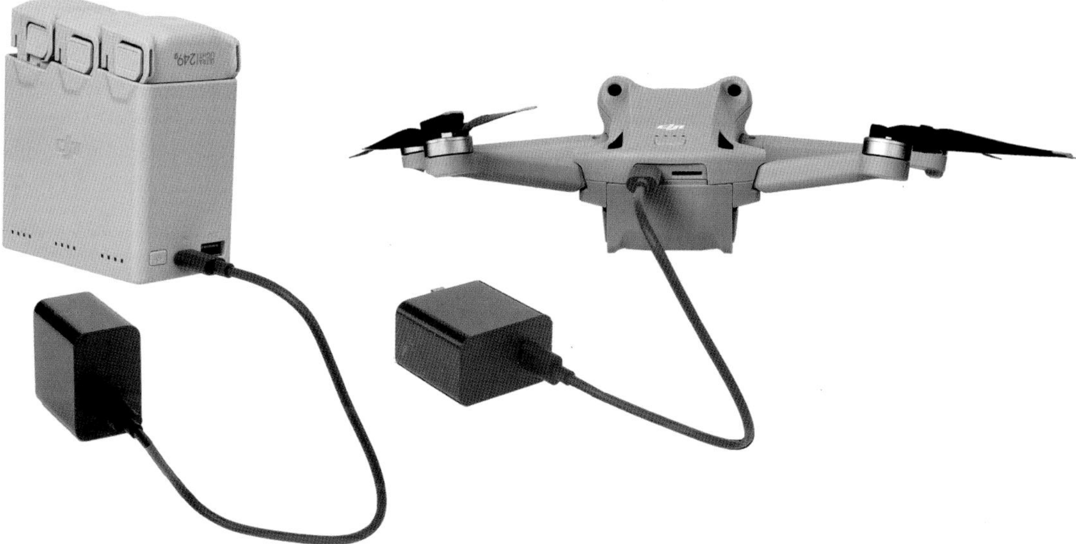

Figure 4.1 Charging the Intelligent Flight batteries and controller.

As I noted in Chapter 2, both the Mini 3 and Mini 3 Pro can use either the basic Intelligent Flight battery (a 7.38V, 2453 mAh [milliAmpere hour] unit), or the Intelligent Flight Battery Plus (a 7.38V, 3850 mAh device). Lightweight and powerful, they have some characteristics that benefit from the intelligent circuitry built into the batteries used in your drone. Your batteries require special care when charging, discharging, and during storage. They tend to swell when overheated (you should be careful when extracting a battery from your drone after a flight). The circuitry built into your Intelligent Flight batteries provides protection from the most common issues. If you handle your batteries with care, you should not have any problems, but some drone pilots keep their extra batteries in an inexpensive flame-retardant bag for extra protection.

The battery's "smarts" take an active role during charging. Temperature detection is built in, so charging is possible only when the temperature is in the 41–104 degrees Fahrenheit (5–40 degrees Celsius) range. As charging progresses, the voltages of the individual cells within the battery are automatically balanced. If excess voltage is detected, the battery stops charging. Charging ceases automatically if the temperature of the battery cells exceed 131 degrees Fahrenheit (55 degrees Celsius). This can sometimes happen if you try to recharge a battery immediately after a flight, when the battery is already quite warm from powering the motors. Very warm days can also contribute to elevated battery temperature. Charging stops when the battery is fully charged, or if a short circuit is detected.

When in use, your battery will switch to Hibernation mode after 20 minutes of inactivity. If the battery has been depleted to less than ten percent or battery cell voltage is lower than 3.0V, it switches to Hibernation mode to prevent over-discharge.

As mentioned, batteries can swell if stored for long periods fully charged, so your Intelligent Flight batteries automatically discharge to the 96 percent level when idle for one day, and then discharge to the 60 percent level (at its most stable so-called *storage voltage*) after five days. It's normal for the battery to feel warm to the touch during automatic discharge. So, it is safe to store your drone with a battery installed; just don't expect it to be fully juiced the next time you fly if you haven't recharged it recently. Discharging stops automatically to prevent depleting the battery when not in use. If you expect long idle periods, DJI recommends that you recharge every three months to maintain battery health, and when transporting batteries (say, when traveling), discharge to the 30 percent level. Just fly the drone until it reaches that point; it's guaranteed to take less than about 30 minutes!

Checking Battery Status

The easiest way to check the power level of the battery is to insert it into your drone and press the power button on the top surface (see Figure 4.2). The four LEDs located above the button will glow, flash, or remain dark for about three seconds in some combination that indicates the current power level. The LEDs are designated LED 1, LED 2, LED 3, and LED 4, starting from the left. When a battery is almost depleted, the LED 1 will flash, indicating that 0 to 13 percent power remains. You should not attempt to fly with a weak battery. Higher power levels are indicated by other LED displays, as shown in Figure 4.3. If LEDs 3 and 4 blink simultaneously without the power button being pressed when you insert the battery into the drone, a malfunction has occurred. Try removing the battery and reinserting securely; that may correct the problem. Otherwise, you may have a defective battery.

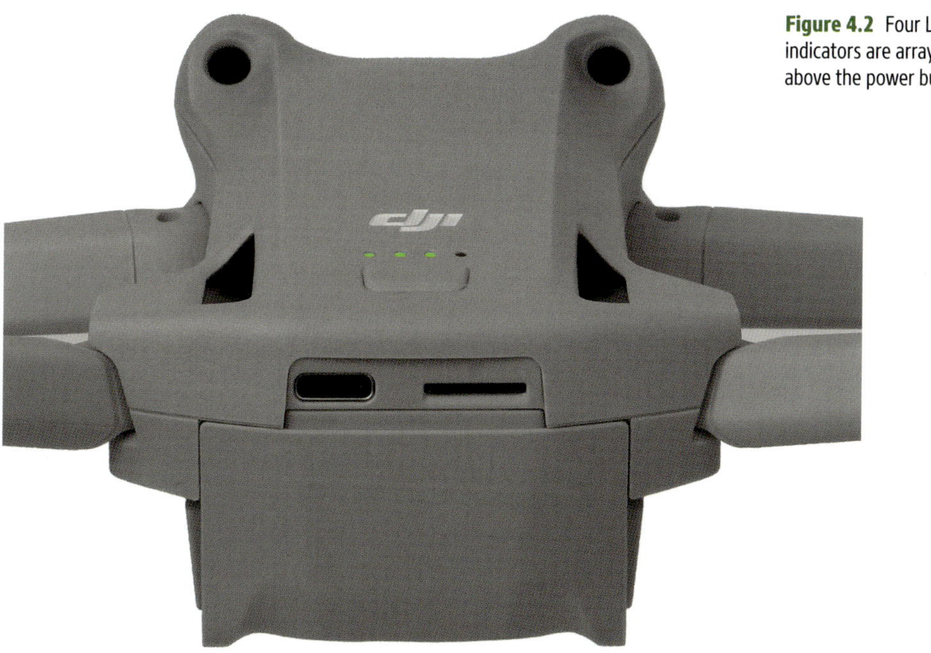

Figure 4.2 Four LED indicators are arrayed above the power button.

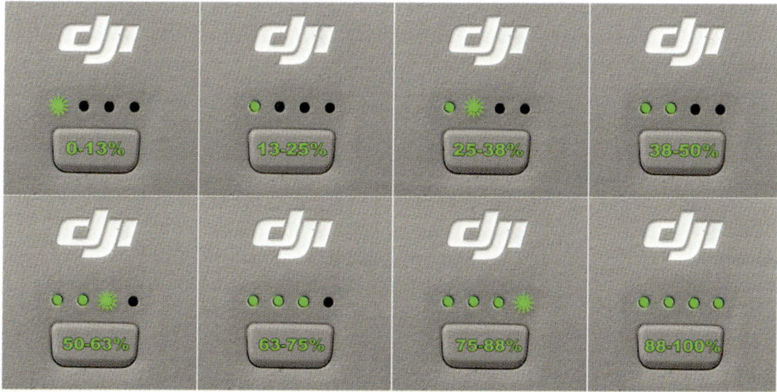

Figure 4.3 When you press the power button once, the battery status LEDs will flash for three seconds to indicate power level.

As I noted earlier, you should not charge Intelligent Flight batteries immediately after a flight, as they will probably be too warm. The recharging time will vary depending on which type of battery you are using, and how depleted it is. You can expect a charging time of about an hour with the basic Intelligent Flight battery and roughly 80 minutes with the Intelligent Flight Battery Plus. An upscale charger with 60 watts or more of output can reduce charging time significantly.

In-Drone Charging

An easy, no-fuss way to recharge your drone's battery is to connect the DJI 30W USB-C charger (or another USB Power Delivery charger) to the USB Type-C port on the back of the Mini 3 or Mini 3 Pro. The advantage of using in-drone charging is that you don't have to carry any extra gear other than a USB cable and the small USB PD charger. A key disadvantage is that you can't fly your drone while you are charging a battery; even if you have several fully charged batteries ready to go, if you elect to charge a depleted unit in the drone, you're grounded until charging is finished.

While charging is underway, the four LEDs on the top surface of the drone will flash, using a slightly different display than the battery status display described earlier. LEDs 1 and 2 will flash consecutively as the battery charges from 0 to 50 percent; LEDs 1, 2, and 3 will flash as charging proceeds from 50 to 75 percent; all four will flash as the charge reaches 75 to 100 percent. All four LEDs will glow steadily when the battery is fully charged. But if all four continue to blink, that indicates the battery is damaged. **Note:** The blinking frequency during charging varies, depending on the power output of the charger used. Rapid blinking indicates fast charging; if you're using a lower power connection (say, your cable is plugged into your computer instead of a USB PD charger), blinking will be slower.

Using the Charging Hub

It's usually more efficient to use the DJI Two-Way Charging Hub, which will allow you to charge up to three Intelligent Flight batteries, one after the other, as well as provide juice to external devices The hub includes the status LEDs, a function button, a USB-C IN power port that accepts incoming power, and a USB-A OUT port, as shown in Figure 4.4. When the hub has one or more batteries installed, it can be used in one of three ways.

- **Charge Intelligent Flight battery.** Insert up to three batteries in the available bays until they click into place. Then connect an external power source, such as the DJI 30W USB-C charger, to the USB-C IN power port. The battery with the highest power level will be charged first (a priority that gives you at least one fully charged battery the most quickly). When it is fully charged, the other batteries will be charged in sequence based on their relative power levels, too. The four status LEDs for each battery will flash as described earlier for in-drone charging, until the battery is fully charged, and its LEDs change to solid green.

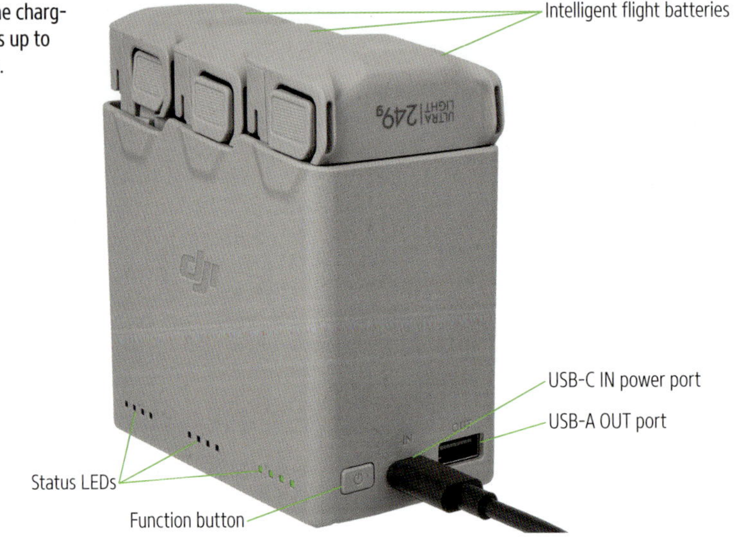

Figure 4.4 The charging hub accepts up to three batteries.

- **Power Bank mode.** If you have more Intelligent Flight batteries than you need for upcoming flights, you can use your extras as a bank to power or recharge other devices. For example, if your DJI RC-N1/RC-N2, DJI RC, or DJI RC Pro (currently compatible with the Mini 3 Pro only) is nearly dead, you can't fly, even if you have a plethora of fully charged flight batteries. Fortunately, you can connect a USB Type-A-to-USB-C cable into the USB-A OUT port of the hub, and recharge your controller, smartphone, tablet, or any other device that needs 5V, 2A DC current.

  The battery with the lowest power level will be discharged first, followed by the others in sequence according to their power levels. You can monitor the usage of the hub's batteries with the LED indicators. You may need to press the function button if charging does not begin immediately.

  I usually have at least three basic Intelligent Flight batteries and three Intelligent Flight Battery Plus units with me, so it is often practical to "sacrifice" the lower capacity basic batteries if I need to recharge something when power isn't available. In practice, though, if I am near my vehicle, I usually take advantage of my car's DC power to rejuvenate the controller, and don't need to resort to this.

- **Charge battery and external device.** If the hub is connected to an external power source through the USB-C IN power port, you can recharge *both* the Intelligent Flight batteries and your external device. The hub gives priority to the batteries, and will charge them first if an external device is connected. But if, say, charging your remote is more important, because you do have some fully charged batteries, you can manually switch priorities by pressing and holding the function button for about two seconds. The external device will then receive power until it is fully charged, or has been charging for four hours. (The hub may not be able to detect when a full charge is reached for some external devices, so it "assumes" the device is fully charged when four hours have elapsed.) After that, battery charging will resume.

  I like this mode when I need to charge batteries and my remote overnight. I can connect them all, then wake up with everything fully juiced.

Battery Protection

If an abnormal condition is detected during charging, LEDs 2, 3, or 4 may blink:

- **LED 2:** Two blinks per second indicates overcurrent; three blinks per second represents a short circuit.

- **LED 3:** Two blinks per second indicates overcharge; three blinks per second represents a charger with excessive voltage (probably a third-party charger).

- **LED 4:** Two blinks per second indicates the temperature is too low for charging; three blinks per second indicates the temperature is too high.

To resume charging, unplug the charger and substitute a different charger if necessary. If the temperature is too low or high, you don't need to unplug the battery; simply wait until the charging temperature has returned to normal. Charging will restart automatically.

Download the Apps

In order to fly your Mini 3/Mini 3 Pro, you'll need to have, at a minimum, three different applications. There are additional optional software utilities you can work with, but at a bare minimum you'll need one of the three main types of applications described in the next section. You can find the smart device versions in the iTunes App Store or Google Play Store, and, for access from a PC or Mac computer, on the web.

Pre-Flight Checklist Software

First on your list should be the free B4UFLY app furnished by the FAA, and provided in Android, iOS, and web versions. (See Figure 4.5.) Situational awareness is a crucial part of safe and productive drone flying, and B4UFLY (or one of the third-party alternatives) is essential. The app is especially useful for recreational pilots who aren't as familiar as they should be with airspace restraints, restrictions, and possible conflicts. It collects information and provides a "Clear For Takeoff" message when appropriate. When takeoff is allowed, you can fly with confidence, as long as you remain alert and maintain all common safety requirements.

The app lets you know that it's clear to fly and whether there are any Temporary Flight Restrictions (TFRs) or Notice to Air Missions (NOTAMs). It shows maps with information about controlled airspace, airports, national parks, military training routes, and other restrictions. Although it defaults to your current position, you can search for other locations to see if it is safe to fly there. You can submit data for consideration in updating the FAA's database about local rules, location of private property or critical infrastructure, and other information. You can file Low Altitude Authorization and Notification Capability (LAANC) requests for authorization to fly in controlled airspaces, and access links to additional FAA drone resources, including regulatory information.

There are additional pre-flight tools available from third parties that you might want to try out as your experience builds, all available in iOS and Android versions. They include Open Sky (see Figure 4.6, left). It's a free mobile app (with a companion web application) that provides notifications of when and where it's safe to fly, and automated airspace approvals. The best weather app is UAV Forecast, which provides accurate wind data (see Figure 4.6, center). There is a free version of Aloft Air Control (the company that developed the current version of B4UFLY for the FAA). (See Figure 4.6, right.) Aloft, (formerly Kittyhawk) has commercial drone and fleet management software as its primary product.

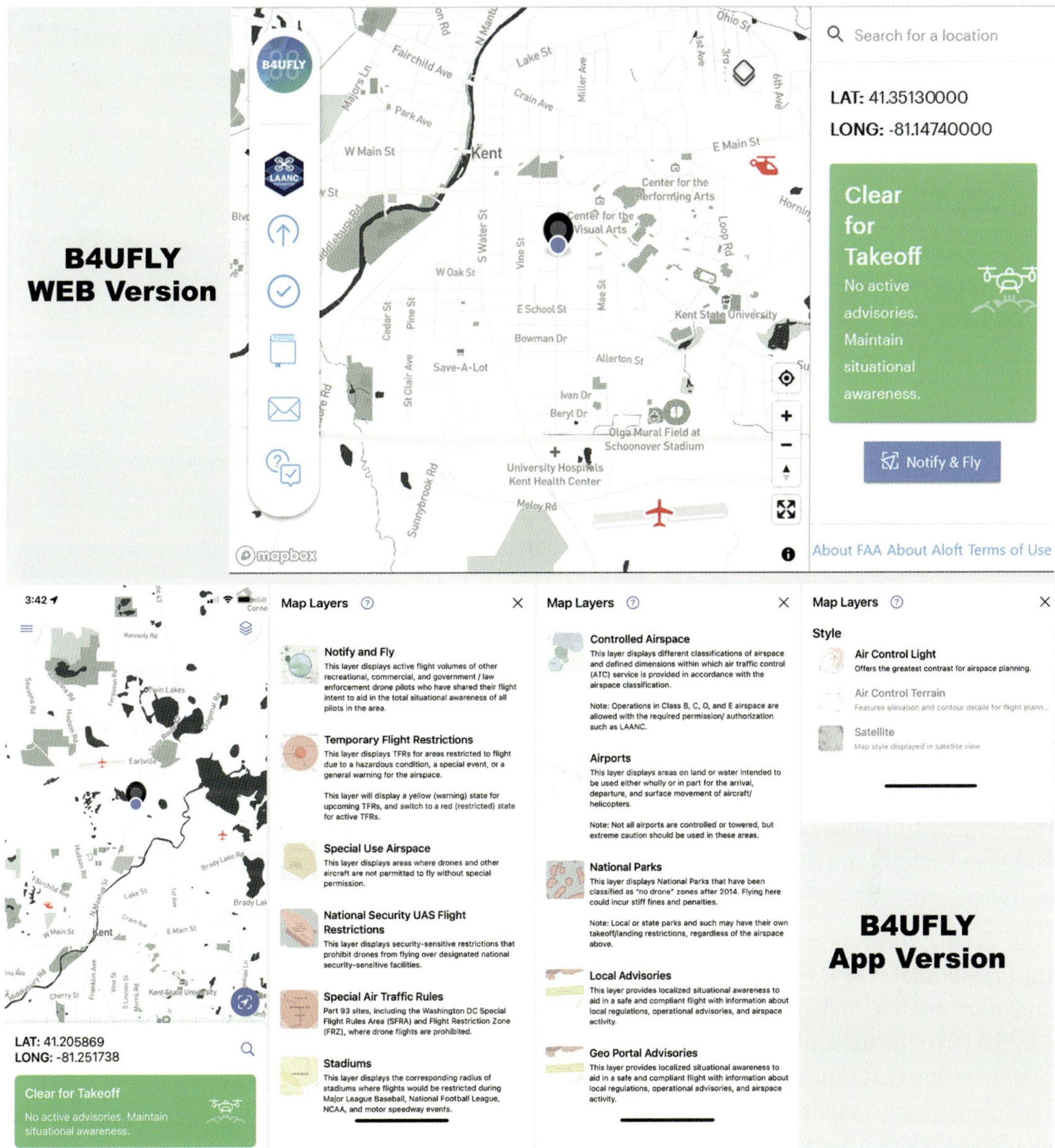

Figure 4.5 The FAA's B4UFLY is available on the web (top) and in app form for smart devices (bottom).

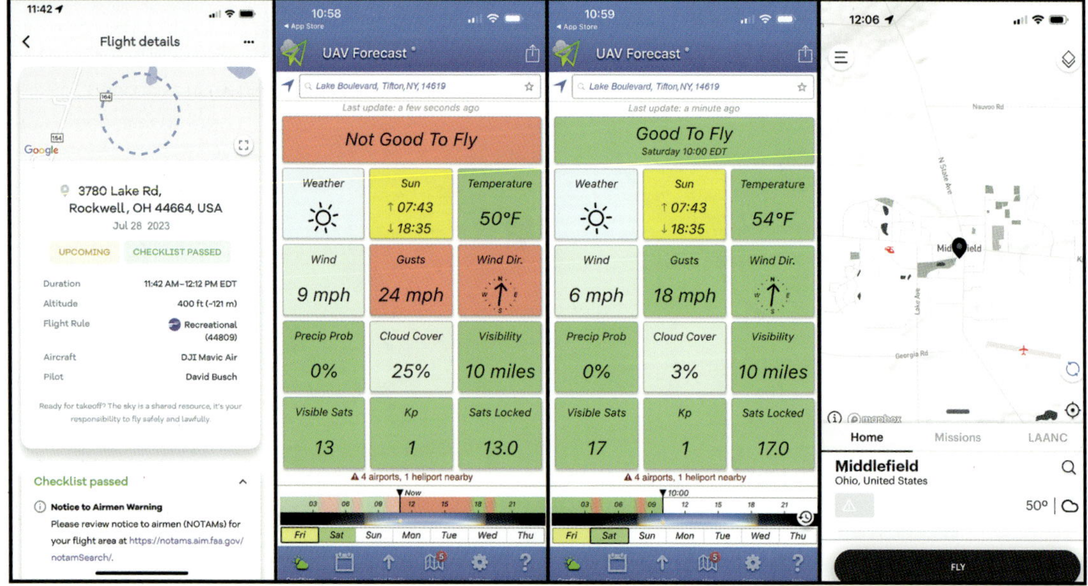

Figure 4.6 Open Sky (left); UAV Forecast (center two); and the free version of Aloft Air Control (right).

Drone Controller Application

At the heart of all your aerial antics is the controller program that runs on your Android or iOS smart device, or on your dedicated remote controller. You'll need it for takeoff, manual flying, using Intelligent Flight modes, and return to your home position when your flight is finished. It monitors the Mini 3/Mini 3 Pro's battery level and flight time remaining, provides information about altitude and speed, allows you to adjust exposure controls, and choose from the various still photo and video options.

Your default controller app should be DJI's own DJI Fly, shown in Figure 4.7. It effectively replaces the previous DJI Go 4, which was used with some earlier drones, such as several Phantom 4 models, and other models, including the original Mavic Air. Third parties have offered alternatives to DJI Go 4 in the past; the most popular being Litchi. It's not free—it has a one-time cost of $24.99. As I write this, a version that supports the Mini 3 or Mini 3 Pro has been teased, but not released. I've not tried Litchi out on any of these drones, so I can't offer any advice other than to make sure you've explored all of DJI Fly's rich feature set before you begin looking for other apps.

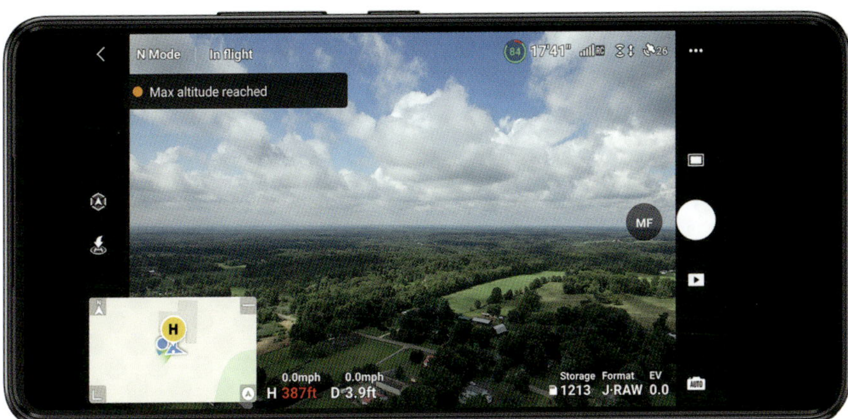

Figure 4.7 DJI Fly provides control of your drone from your smart device or dedicated remote controller.

DJI Assistant 2 (Consumer Drone Series)

The third must-have application is DJI Assistant 2 (Consumer Drone Series). You can download this free Windows and Mac application. **Note:** Do not download DJI Assistant 2 for Mavic! It is for earlier models and is not compatible with the DJI Mini 3 or Mini 3 Pro. This version of DJI Assistant 2 has a wide variety of features.

The basic screens, shown in Figure 4.8, allow you to connect to your drone, monitor and apply firmware updates, and access flight logs. From time to time your Mini 3 Pro drone's gimbal will need to be recalibrated, using a facility shown in Figure 4.9. You can export the data that the app collects to a file on your computer. All data available can be exported, or only the most current data, in either compressed or uncompressed form. (See Figure 4.10.)

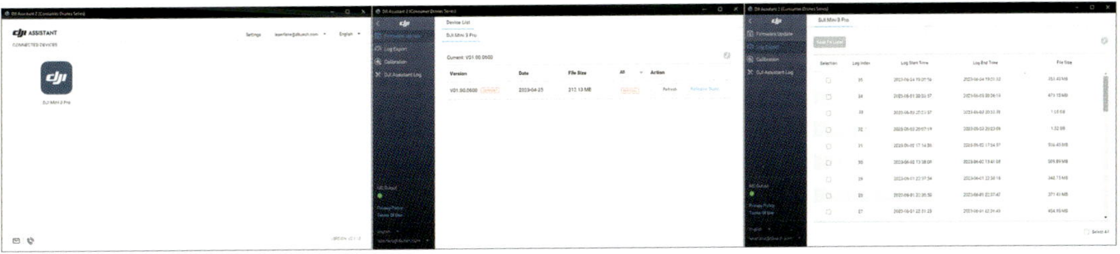

Figure 4.8 Connected devices (left); Firmware Update (center); Log Export (right).

Figure 4.9 Gimbal calibration.

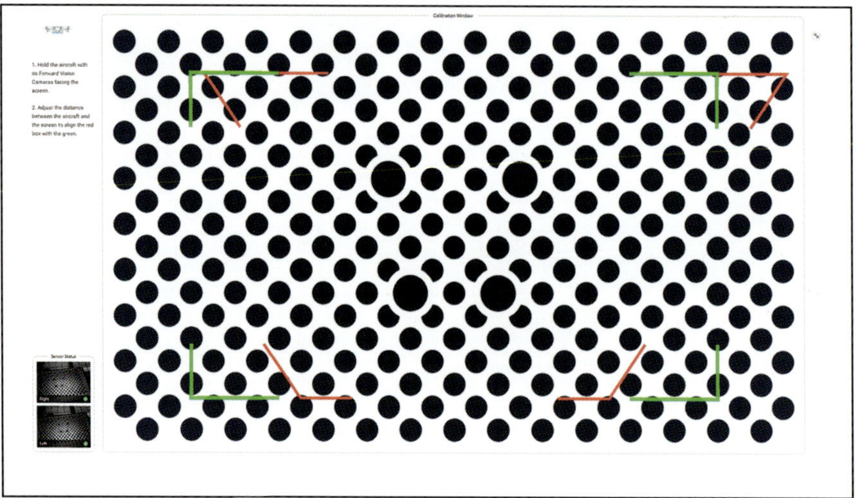

Figure 4.10 DJI Assistant Log exporter.

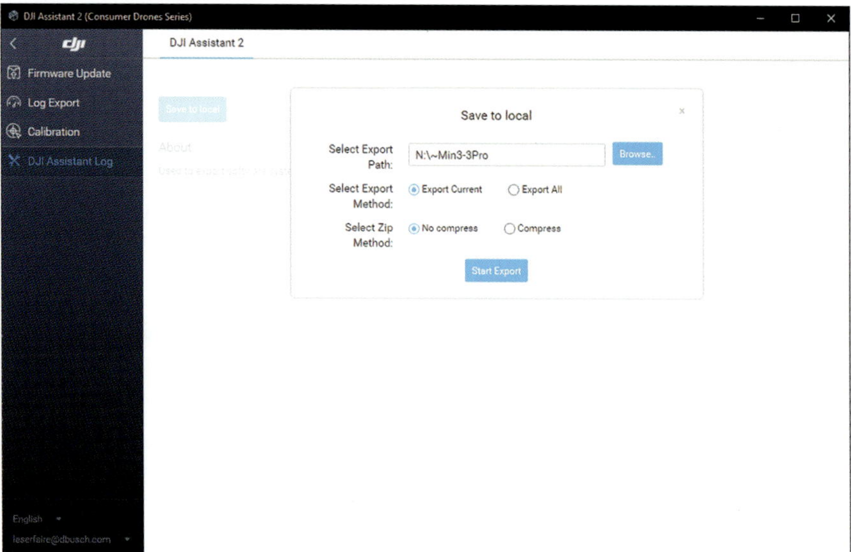

Install the Propellers

Your drone uses pairs of propellers of two different varieties, Type A, marked with a ridge near the hub, and Type B, which has no such marker. (See Figure 4.11, left.) The arms of the drone have matching markers, which are very faint, but enhanced at upper right in Figure 4.11 for better visibility. To save weight, DJI has used propellers that must be attached with tiny Philips screws, using a small screwdriver supplied with the drone. Those who expect to change propellers often will definitely want to purchase a sturdier third-party PH0 Phillips-head screwdriver with a larger handle. You should always make sure that the screws are tightly fastened after installation, and it's a good idea to double check to make sure they haven't loosened before each flight.

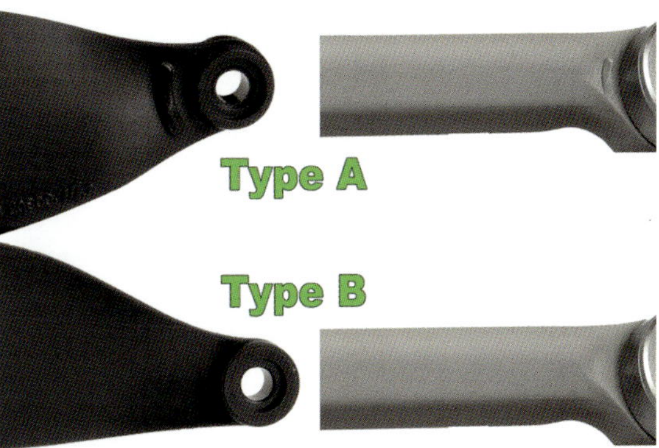

Figure 4.11 There are two different types of propellers, mounted on their respective marked or unmarked motor hubs.

In all cases, your propellers are designed to spin in opposite directions, which keeps the drone from tending to spin around rapidly. (Techies call this *conservation of angular momentum*.) When the four rotors spin at the same speed, the net torque is zero. The front left and rear right (front port/rear starboard for you former Navy types) rotors spin one way, while the front right and rear left (front starboard/rear port) spin the other way.

Your Mini 3/Mini 3 Pro moves in the air by changing the power applied to the rotors in various combinations, which you can visualize using Figure 4.12:

- **Ascend/Descend.** The drone moves up and down, gaining or losing altitude, by increasing or decreasing the speed of the rotors, as seen at right in the figure. You can move the drone up or down and adjust the speed of ascent or descent by pressing the left stick on the remote controller forward or back. (This assumes you're using the default Mode 2; other control arrangements are also available.) **Tip:** When you move the left and right control sticks, the farther you push the stick from the center position, the faster the movement. I'll explain use of the remote controller later in this chapter.

- **Roll.** Roll is produced when an aircraft rotates around its front-to-back axis, as indicated by the blue arrows at right in the figure. Roll is applied by slowing all the motors on one side and/or speeding up those on the other. Because the thrust is now slightly sideways, a *slight* amount of roll moves it left or right. You wouldn't want your drone to roll drastically, as it cannot fly upside down (this isn't *Top Gun*!). Move the remote controller's right stick to the left or right to move your drone horizontally in those directions.

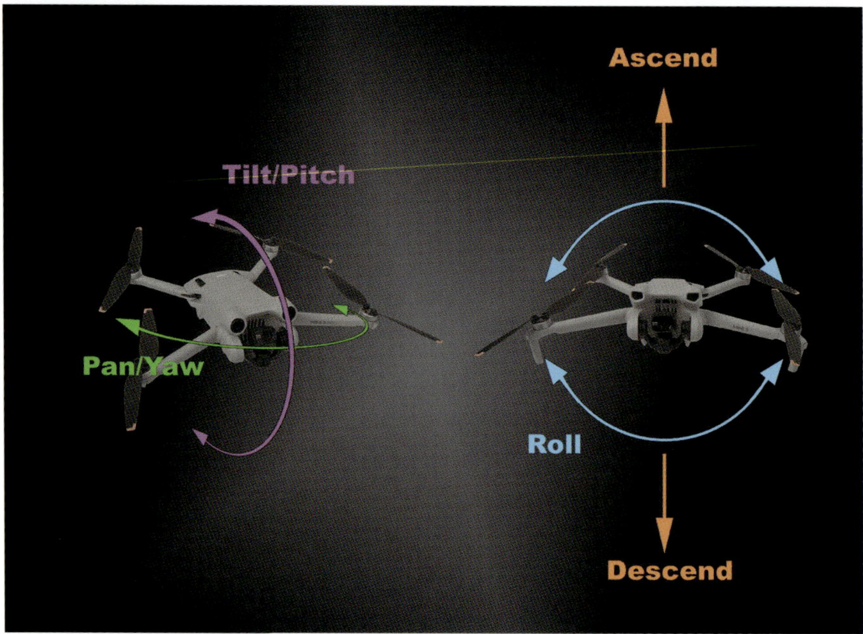

- **Panning/Yaw.** DJI sometimes calls side-to-side rotation through the top-to-bottom axis "pan," but "yaw" is the more common term. Your drone executes this maneuver by creating a difference in rotational speed between pairs of opposite-rotating rotors. Remember that I said the four propellers spin at the same speed to prevent spin and conserve angular momentum? Panning takes advantage of this to produce torque that will rotate the drone clockwise or counterclockwise. Just move the left stick on the remote controller to the left to rotate counterclockwise, and to the right to rotate clockwise (in Mode 2).
- **Tilt/Pitch.** This type of movement is used to produce forward and backward motion. When the front rotors spin at normal speed while the rear rotors spin faster, torque around the side-to-side axis is produced and the "nose" of the drone tilts downward slightly as the aircraft moves forward. When the front props are spinning faster than those in back, the rear dips and the drone moves backward. Press the right stick forward or back to move your drone in those directions.

Become Familiar with Your Remote Controller

While this book was being written, the DJI RC-N1 remote controller was the standard remote most often used with both the Mini 3 and Mini 3 Pro. (See Figure 4.13.) However, DJI is in the process of replacing it as its "basic" controller with the new RC-N2, introduced at the same time as the Mavic Air 3. Currently, the only other controller compatible with *both* models (at this time) is the DJI RC controller, which can be purchased as part of a bundle, or available separately for about $300. The RC controller, too, is being replaced by a new model, the RC 2.

The Mini 3 Pro can also be used with the pricey DJI RC Pro controller. This section will provide an introduction to your controller options, and provide some background on the important role these electronic devices play in the operation of your drone.

How a Remote Controller Works

A drone remote controller (sometimes referred to as a radio transmitter or radio controller) is a device the pilot holds in their hands to make the drone do the pilot's bidding. It operates by sending a radio signal to a receiver on the aircraft which interprets the incoming commands with its onboard flight controller electronics. Remote controls for small, unmanned aircraft aren't new, dating back to hydrogen-filled model airships flown in auditoriums as novelty entertainment in the late 19th Century.

While flying modern radio-controlled model airplanes requires certain skills, they often involve controlling just a single motor and various control surfaces of the aircraft. The pilot can easily use the throttle on their controller to adjust the power supplied to the motor, and use the elevators, rudders, ailerons, or flaps (depending on the particular aircraft) to adjust the direction and rates of climb and descent. Multi-rotor drones have raised the stakes to a whole new level.

It would be virtually impossible for a remote pilot to control the throttles of multiple rotors simultaneously, as balancing each motor with the others would be a nightmare. So, drone controllers use advanced flight controller electronics to keep the drone stable in the air and provide the right amount of power to each motor to maintain steady flight in the desired direction.

Controllers are generally of two types, those that include an integrated screen, like the DJI RC Pro or DJI RC, and those that use the screen of your smartphone or tablet to display drone software applications and the live view transmitted from the drone during flight, such as the DJI RC-N1/RC-N2. The screens can display useful preflight information from apps like B4UFLY, as well as menus used to make adjustments to your drone's operation, view still images and videos you've captured, and other information.

During flight, the controller adjusts roll, pitch, and yaw movements of the drone in the air (moving it left, right, forward, backward, and rotationally) and speed, using the throttle (the harder you push the control stick in a certain direction, the faster it moves as the propellers' revolutions per minute increase). Other features may include the ability to post photos and video directly to the internet, or HDMI output to monitors.

Whether you have a controller with a built-in screen or use your smart device as a display, one thing you'll quickly discover is that very sunny days can make your screen difficult to see clearly. Sometimes you can find a shady place to stand or sit, but your best bet may be to add a sun hood or screen. I prefer the kind that fold up compactly and have a compartment so I can leave the joysticks attached and ready to go when I pack up. They are available from a variety of sources. (See Figure 4.13.)

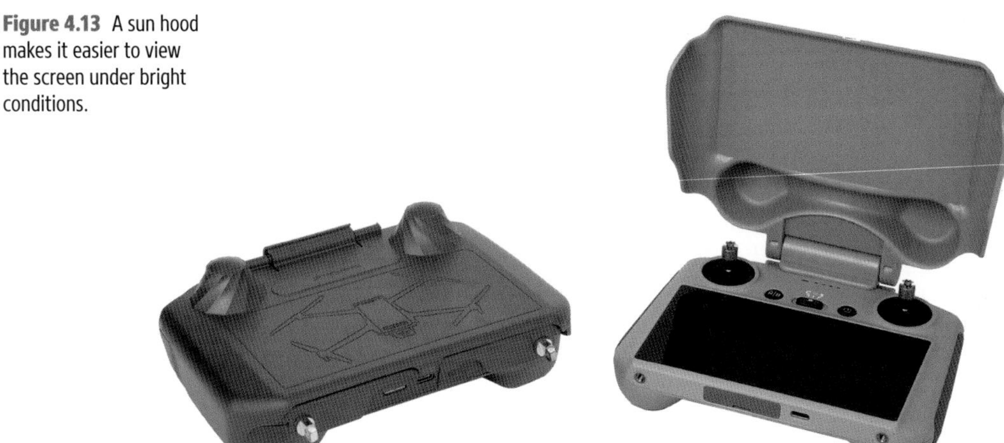

Figure 4.13 A sun hood makes it easier to view the screen under bright conditions.

Your Remote Controller Options

As I noted, your controller options for the Mini 3 or Mini 3 Pro include the DJI RC-N1/RC-N2 (which use your phone/tablet device screen), the DJI RC-series, and, for the Mini 3 Pro only, the DJI RC Pro. I'm going to emphasize use of the original RC-N1 controller in this book, as I expect most readers will be using it, at least to start. The functions, buttons, and dials of the other controllers are very similar, so once you've mastered the standard controller, migrating to one of the more advanced controller options should be easy.

If you own the Mini 3 Pro and decide to upgrade, choosing between the DJI RC and DJI RC Pro may seem easy on the surface: the DJI RC costs $309 while the RC Pro commands a hefty $1,200 price tag. However, there is more to the story, especially if you already own the RC Pro (as I did). Here's an overview of the key aspects:

- **Brighter screen.** The RC Pro's screen is rated at 1,000 nits while the RC (and RC 2) screen is not quite as bright at 700 nits, and therefore less easy to see outdoors under bright sunlight, which, by coincidence, happens to be the precise environment under which you may quite frequently be using your drone. *Nit* is a slang term for *candela per square meter*, and used instead of the equally murky term *lumens* (unless you happen to work often with light sources). You don't really need to know anything more about nits, other than the cheaper DJI RC-series screen isn't quite as bright outdoors. That viewing problem can be easily solved by the simple expedient of buying/making a hood to shield the screen from direct sunlight.

- **No internet.** Neither controller has built-in internet connectivity, so if you want to download maps or other aids to the controller, you need to either do it at home where the controller can connect to your Wi-Fi or activate your smartphone's hot-spot capability onsite.

- **Built-in memory.** Both controllers run the Android operating system. The RC Pro has 32GB of auxiliary memory and can be supplemented with a microSD memory card, so you can download a variety of third-party programs to your controller. The DJI RC has 8GB of internal auxiliary memory (upgraded to 32GB with the RC 2) augmented by a memory card slot.

- **Range.** The RC Pro has two radio transmitters and four receivers; the original RC has just one transmitter and two receivers, with the RC 2 boasting two transmitters and four receivers. You'd think that the more expensive controller's robust radio components would lead to greater reliability and range. Theoretically, it should, but multiple users have tested this and report that, in practice, they each have very similar performance, with a range of roughly 10 kilometers. I tend to adhere quite strictly to the line-of-sight regulations, and so haven't tested this personally, but I'm willing to accept the findings of pilots who are more daring and adventurous than I.

- **Weight.** The more advanced RC Pro weighs 680 grams (about 24 ounces), while the RC tips the kitchen scale at 385 grams (roughly 14 ounces). You'll have your clammy fingers wrapped around your controller for up to 34 minutes at a time, so it's theoretically possible that the ten extra ounces of the RC Pro controller can become a burden—but I doubt it. However, it is proportionally a bit heavier than the cheaper model if that matters to you.

- **Battery life.** The RC Pro includes a 5,000 mAh battery, good for three hours of use, on average, while the more affordable RC can wring up to four hours from its 5,500 mAh battery. If you plan some lengthy flights and have enough Intelligent Flight batteries to accommodate such excursions, a power pack and USB Type-C cable, or a car charger, may be a valuable accessory. However, you'd really need quite a few drone batteries to fly for more than four hours in one session (allowing an extra safety margin to make sure your drone doesn't lose power before it returns to home). So, it's not likely you'll need to use a controller for more than four hours any time.

- **HDMI.** The RC Pro has a mini-HDMI port for outputting to an external monitor or recorder, and the RC does not.

- **Buy now, save later.** Even if you don't need all the features of the RC Pro now, if you upgrade to a more advanced DJI drone in the future you won't have to purchase an additional remote controller. A hefty price tag is less painful when amortized over a series of aircraft that can share a single "deluxe" remote.

I'm going to compare the three controllers in more detail in the following sections.

DJI RC-N1 Remote Controller

The standard controller is affordable because it uses the screen and processing power of your personal smartphone or tablet to augment its own built-in electronics. In use, your device is mounted to a bracket built into the RC-N1 controller and linked using one of three included cables, as shown in Figure 4.14. The six-inch cables have a USB Type-C connector on one end that plugs into your remote controller, and a Lightning, Standard Micro-USB, or USB-C connector on the other. One of these should be compatible with your Android or iOS device.

To attach your mobile device to the controller, lift the spring-loaded device clamp to reveal the slots for the connector cable, as shown at left in Figure 4.15. The end of the cable with an icon plugs into the USB-C port on the controller, while the other end can be removed from its dummy slot (no electronics are there) and plugged into your smart device, as seen at right in the figure. When the device is in position, release the clamp so the smartphone or tablet is firmly mounted to the controller. Finally, remove the control sticks from the storage slots in the bottom edge of the controller and screw them in.

Figure 4.14 The RC-N1 remote controller uses your smart device's screen and electronics.

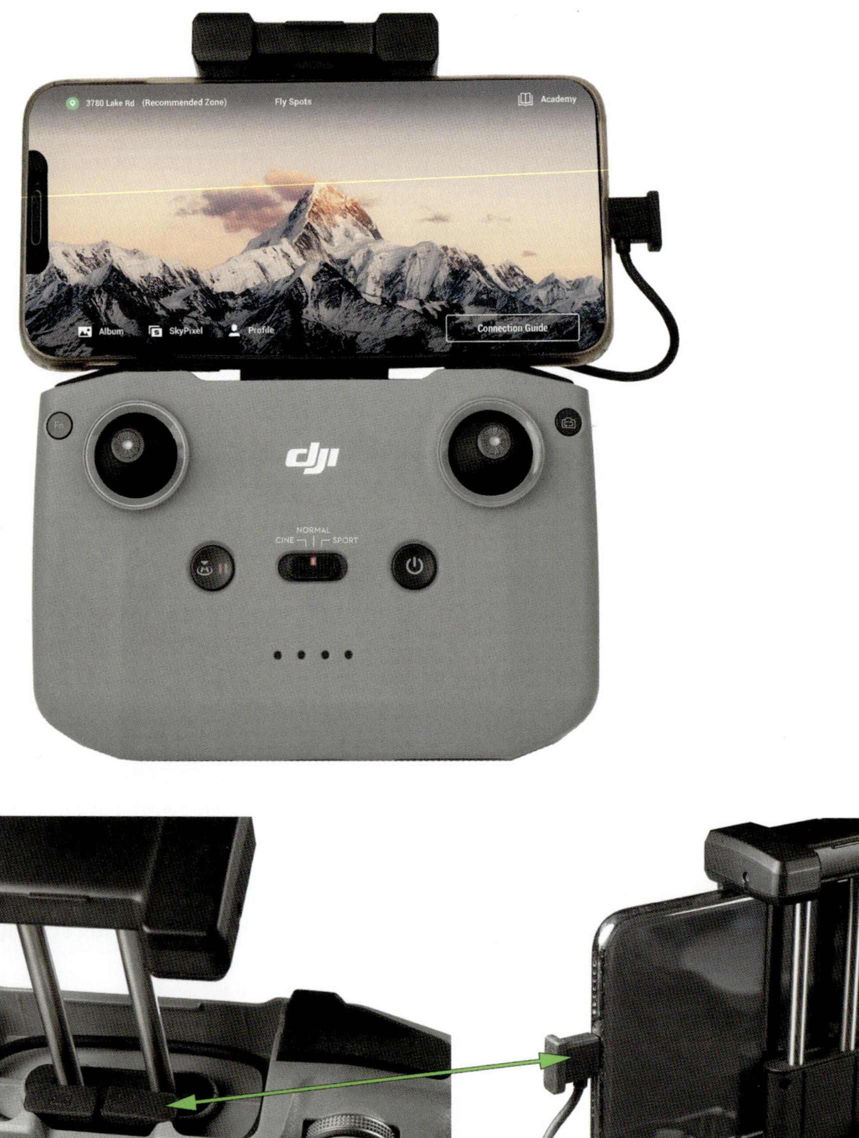

Figure 4.15 The connector cables are stored under the retracted mobile device clamp (left) and plug into your smart device (right).

Working with Tablets

The adjustable bracket of the standard remote controller can accommodate Android or iOS smartphones measuring 3.4 × 7 × .4 inches. If you want to use a tablet, you'll need an extender or add-on tablet mount and, possibly, a cable longer than the ones supplied with the RC-N1. As I mentioned in Chapter 1, mounts for most tablets are available for $10 to $60 from DJI and third parties. Figure 4.16 shows the Hanatora RC-N1 remote controller 4.7-to-12.9-inch tablet holder mount that I use with my Amazon Fire tablet.

Note that DJI Fly and other essential apps are *not* available from the Fire's Amazon App store. However, it is possible to change the settings of many recent Fire tablets to add the Google Play store to the tablet, and to allow downloading other apps from the Silk browser (such as DJI Fly, which is no longer available from Google Play).

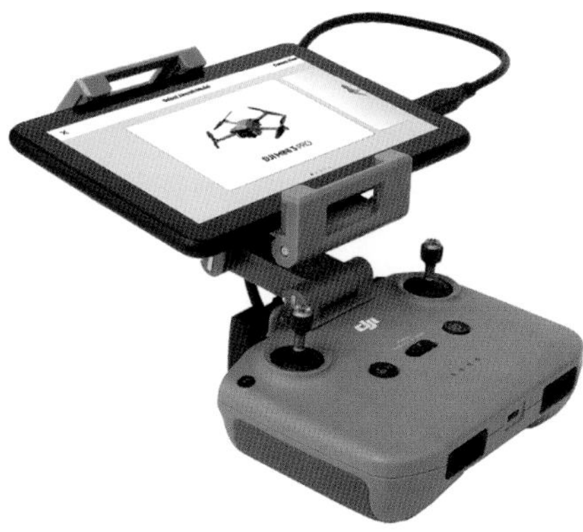

Figure 4.16 Tablets can be attached using an accessory mount.

You're usually better off using a tablet that officially supports DJI Fly, including many Samsung Galaxy and Huawei models. However, if you already own a Fire tablet, you can use Google to locate instructions for enabling downloads from sources other than the Amazon App store.

Taking Control of the RC-N1 Remote

Familiarize yourself with the control dials, buttons, and switches on the standard controller. I'll explain their use in more detail when you take off for your first flight in Chapter 5. The major components, as seen in Figure 4.17, are these:

- **Power button.** Press this button once to view the Battery Level status LEDs. Press and hold to turn the controller on or off.
- **Battery level LEDs.** These four LEDs illuminate to indicate the amount of power remaining in the controller.
- **Flight mode switch.** Your drone operates in three flight modes selectable using this switch: Sport (optimized for agility and speed, with obstacle sensing disabled); Normal (GPS and vision/infrared sensors used); Cine/Tripod (speed limited to promote stability for longer exposures).
- **Flight Pause/Return to Home (RTH) button.** This is another dual-purpose button. If you press it once, the drone will brake and hover in place, say, if you spot an obstacle or want to pause for a moment. The feature works only when the GNSS (GPS) and Vision systems are available. Press and hold down the button to start the Return to Home sequence. Press and hold again to cancel RTH.
- **Control sticks.** These are removable sticks you use to adjust movements of your drone in flight, ascending, descending, rotating, and moving in various directions. The functions of the two sticks can be customized using the DJI Fly app, as I mentioned in Chapter 1. There are three preprogrammed modes, with the default being Mode 2 (left stick up/down, turn left/right; right stick forward/backward, move left/right). This mode is pretty much the standard default among drone aircraft in general; it's not DJI-specific terminology.

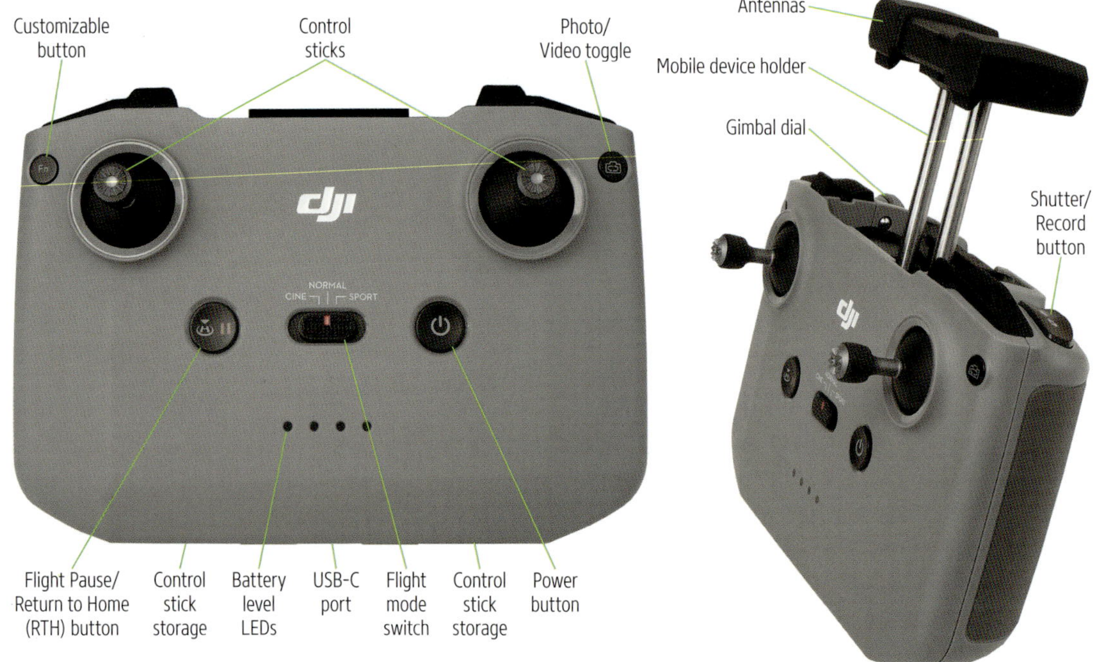

Figure 4.17 Components of the RC-N1 remote controller.

- **Customizable button.** This button can be assigned various functions. The default actions in still photo mode are Auxiliary bottom light on/off (one press) and Recenter gimbal/turn gimbal down (two presses). You can redefine these functions in the DJI Fly app.

- **Photo/Video toggle.** Switches between photo and video modes each time it is pressed.

- **Mobile device holder.** This is the frame that holds your smart device in place. As I mentioned earlier, the frame accepts devices up to 3.4 × 7 × .4 inches.

- **Antennas.** The drone's apparatus for radiating or receiving electromagnetic signals are located here.

- **Gimbal dial.** This dial controls the amount of tilt of the Mini 3/Mini 3 Pro's camera. In video mode, with the Mini 3 Pro (only), you can rotate this dial to zoom while holding down the customizable button.

- **Shutter/Record button.** Press this button once in still photo mode to take a picture, or to start/stop video recording in movie mode. (You can also tap the shutter release icon that appears on the right side of the DJI Fly screen.)

- **USB-C port (on bottom edge).** This port can be used for charging and connecting the remote control to a computer.

- **Control stick storage slots (on bottom edge).** A pair of slots provide a convenient place to store your control sticks.

- **Speaker (not shown).** A speaker that emits sounds during operation is located on the back of the controller.

DJI RC Remote Controller

The big benefit of the DJI RC remote controller is that it includes a built-in 5.5-inch touchscreen. Since it weighs the same as the RC-N1, about 13.7 ounces/390 grams, the RC remote is actually *lighter* than the RC-N1 + smartphone/tablet combination. It's available separately for about $309. I compared its features with the DJI RC Pro controller in the "Your Remote Controller Options" section earlier in this chapter.

The DJI RC remote controller is shown in Figure 4.18. Its form factor is a combination of the RC-N1 and RC Pro, and the available buttons, dials, and controls are a mix of both, so I won't describe them

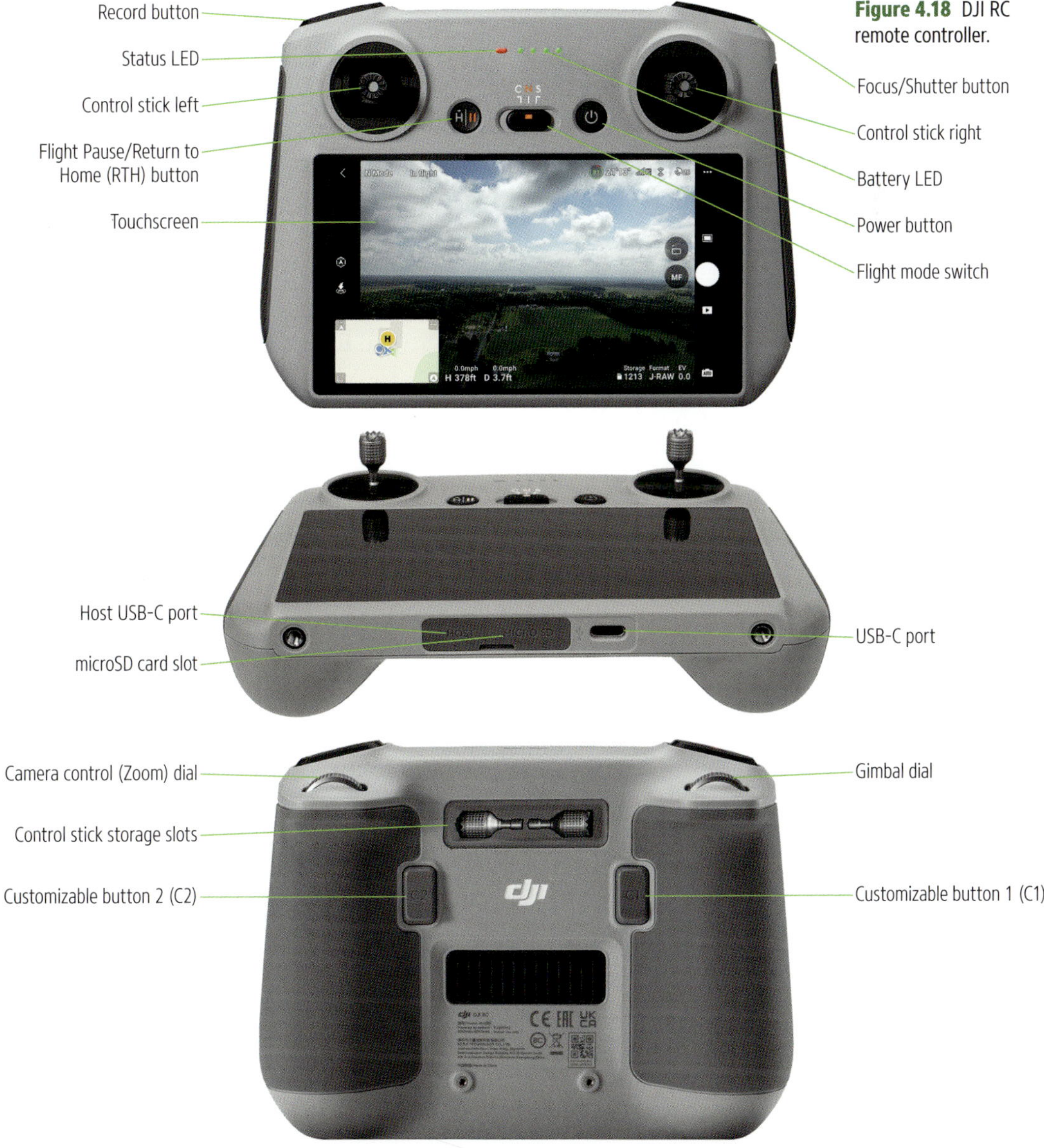

Figure 4.18 DJI RC remote controller.

in detail separately. Not shown in the figure are a pair of speakers located in the center of the top panel.

This controller lacks external antennas, but boasts a 5.5-inch, 1920 × 1080–pixel screen like the RC Pro, along with O3 transmission protocols (and O3+ for higher-end drones that support it). You might wonder about the second USB-C port located under the cover that protects the microSD card slot. DJI refers to it as a "host" port, and, currently, it is used to connect a DJI Cellular Dongle, which adds cellular communications to the RC remote. At the time I am writing this, cell service for this controller is available only in China though a subscription. Whether it may become available elsewhere remains to be seen.

An upgraded DJI RC 2 remote controller was introduced along with the Mavic Air 3 as this book was being written. It's very similar to the original RC remote, with the addition of external antennas like those found on the DJI RC Pro remote controller described next, and without the "host" port.

DJI RC Pro Remote Controller

The RC Pro controller, which is fully compatible with the Mini 3 Pro, but not the Mini 3, has buttons, dials, and switches that are similar to those of the RC-N1 and RC-N2 units. However, some dual-purpose controls on the RC-N1/RC-N2 get a dedicated button on the RC Pro, plus there are some new components. Figure 4.19 shows each of the controls, and I'll describe them next, not repeating the information listed above that applies to both the RC Pro and RC-N1/RC-N2 controllers.

- **Antennas.** These more powerful antennas need to be flipped up to use, and for optimal transmission, should be oriented so that they are facing toward the drone and the angle between the back of the controller is 180 or 270 degrees.
- **Power button.** Same as the RC-N1/RC-N2 and RC remotes.
- **Battery level LEDs.** These are located at the top edge of the RC Pro controller.
- **Flight mode switch.** Same as the RC-N1 and RC remotes.
- **Flight Pause button.** This is a separate button on the RC Pro controller, and not combined with Return to Home, like its counterpart on the RC-N1 and RC remotes.
- **Return to Home (RTH) button.** A separate button, but the RTH function is the same as its equivalent RC-N1.
- **Control sticks.** Slightly fancier sticks, but functionally the same.
- **Back button.** Located in the same position as the Customizable button of the RC-N1, this button has multiple functions. Within an app, it can be pressed once to return to the previous screen, and pressed twice to return to the home screen of the app. It serves as a sort of control key when you hold it down and then press another button to invoke a particular function. For example, hold the back button down and press the Focus/Shutter button to capture a shot of the current LCD screen.
- **5D button.** Press to gain access to advanced controls.
- **Focus/Shutter button.** Press to initiate focus or to capture a photo.

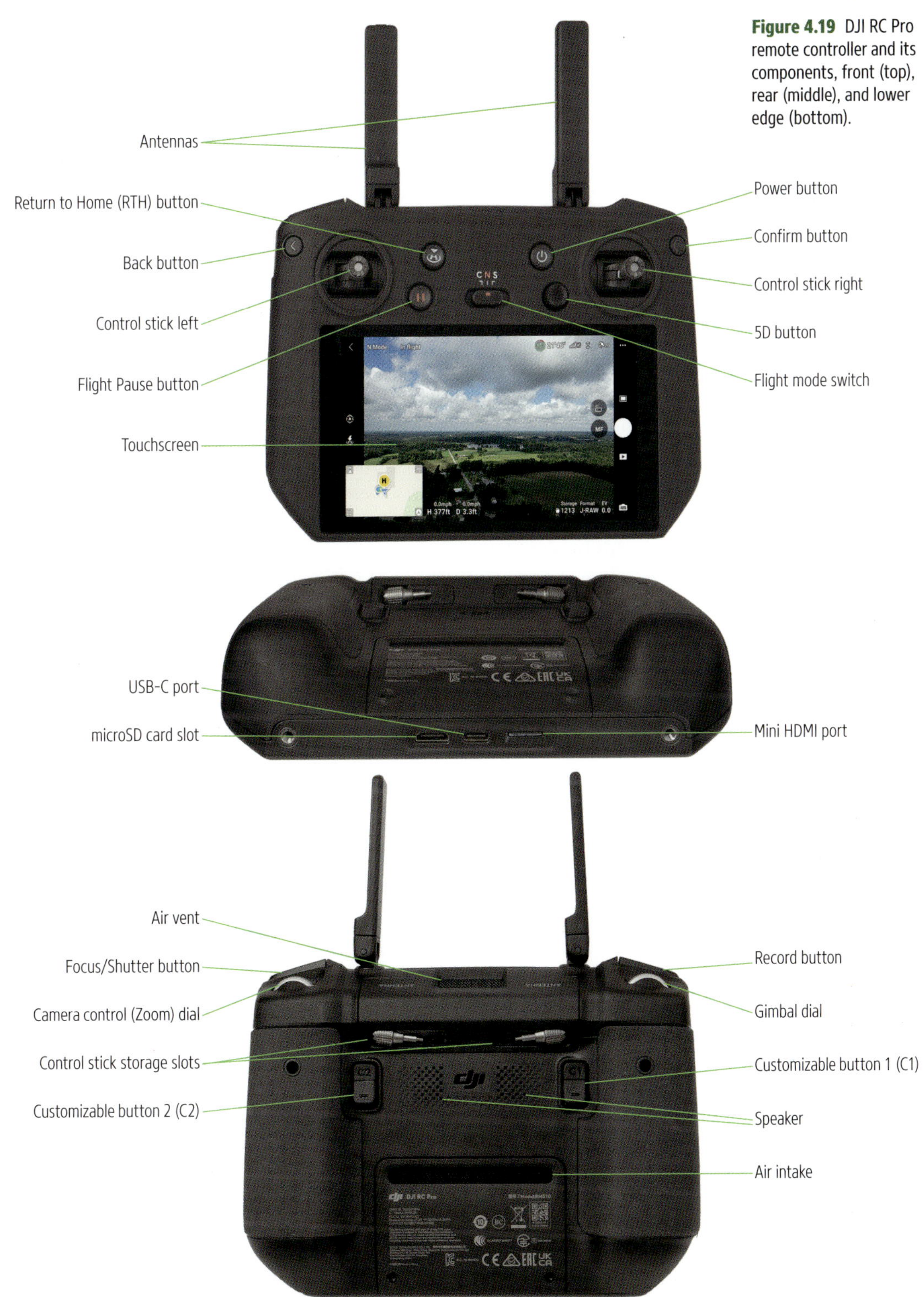

Figure 4.19 DJI RC Pro remote controller and its components, front (top), rear (middle), and lower edge (bottom).

- **Confirm button.** This is the Enter/Return button when using menus. Press it once to confirm a selection. As I write this, the button has no function when using the DJI Fly app, but the company has indicated that a future firmware update will allow it to be used as a customizable C3 button.

- **Touchscreen.** Using taps and other gestures on this screen you can navigate among various options.

- **microSD card slot.** Insert a memory card here to increase the available storage of the controller. **Note:** It can be difficult to get the card to "seat" in the slot as it does not click into place until pushed all the way in. I frequently have to resort to shoving with a fingernail or small jewelers' screwdriver to insert/remove the card. This is apparently a design defect and not an equipment failure. I returned the first RC Pro controller I received to DJI because of the difficulty I was having inserting the card. They cheerfully (and swiftly—one week door-to-door) replaced my controller with a spanking new one that performed in exactly the same way. Other RC Pro owners had warned me that the reluctant memory card slot was typical, but I felt that mine must surely behave worse than the norm, at least until my replacement controller arrived.

- **USB-C port.** You can recharge the controller using a USB-C cable connected to a power source. If the cable is plugged into your computer, you can access the controller's storage as if it were a removable disk drive. I used it as a quick way to retrieve screenshots of the controller's menus and displays while writing this book.

- **Mini HDMI port.** You can direct video to an external device for display or recording using a cable with a Mini HDMI (Type C) connector on the end that plugs into the controller.

- **Gimbal dial.** Controls the amount of tilt of the Mini 3/Mini 3 Pro's camera.

- **Record button.** Press once to start or stop video recording.

- **Camera control (Zoom) dial.** In video mode, with the Mini 3 Pro, you can rotate this dial to zoom. Note that this dial is not present on the RC-N1 controller, which performs video zooming with the left/gimbal dial instead. If you happen to use both controllers, it's easy to forget that the RC Pro zoom dial is located on the back-right panel, rather than left.

- **Air vent.** Dissipates heat build-up in the controller during operation. Be careful not to block this opening.

- **Control stick storage slots.** Your control sticks fit into these slots when not in use.

- **Customizable button 1 (C1).** As with the RC-N1 controller, the default function of this button is to toggle between recentering the gimbal and pointing it downward. The DJI Fly app can be used to redefine its behavior to some other function.

- **Speaker.** Beeps, audible warnings, and other sounds emanate from this speaker.

- **Customizable button 2 (C2).** The default behavior is to turn the Auxiliary Bottom Light of the drone on or off with a single press. You can redefine its behavior in the DJI Fly app.

- **Air intake.** Air circulating through the controller enters here. As with the vent, you should avoid blocking this opening.

DJI RC-N2 and RC 2 Remote Controllers

These two new remote controllers, introduced at the same time as the Mavic Air 3, were not available for testing while this book was being written. Visually, they are very similar to the older models, except for the external antennas added to the RC 2. Here are the main changes for each:

- For the DJI RC-N2:
  - **A new antenna design for better performance.** Like its predecessor the RC-N1, the new version has two antennas and two receivers, but now includes a pair of transmitters, instead of just one.
  - **Faster charging.** DJI says the remote control can be fully charged in just 3.5 hours instead of 4; however, battery life is listed as 2.5 hours rather than the published 4-hour time for the older version.
  - **Support for OcuSync 4.0 (O4).** The new remote controller supports the upgraded O4 transmission offered by compatible drones, like the Mavic Air 3. However, it is backward compatible with drones using O3.
  - **New processor chip.** Better, faster processing during flight.
  - **Support for enhanced image transmission module.** It is able to transmit 1080p video with compatible drones.
- For the DJI RC 2:
  - **New antenna design.** The RC 2 has double the number of antennas, receivers, and transmitters of its predecessor, with four antennas/receivers, and two transmitters. There are two built-in and two external antennas for enhanced signal strength.
  - **Increased storage.** It has 32GB of internal memory.
  - **Upgraded CPU and GPU performance.** A new processor provides smoother operation and more intuitive control during flights.
  - **Faster charging.** Fully charges in 1.5 hours like its predecessor, but the increased number of receivers and transmitters reduces battery life from four hours to three.
  - **Support for OcuSync 4.0 (O4).** The RC 2 also supports the upgraded O4 transmission offered by compatible drones, using 2.4GHz, 5.1GHz, and 5.8GHz frequency bands with a longer maximum range. However, it is backward compatible with drones using O3 and O3+.

Next Up

If you're just starting out with drone photography, the next chapter will guide you through getting your Mini 3 or Mini 3 Pro safely aloft for the first time, show you how to navigate through the skies smoothly, perform simple aerial maneuvers, and return your drone to its takeoff location. Again, veteran flyers may want to skim this chapter as a review, but new pilots will find everything they need for a successful first flight.

Your First Flight 5

I've been writing guidebooks like this one for almost 20 years, and I've found that there are a significant number of readers who can't resist jumping ahead to a chapter like this one, eager to spread their wings (or, in this case, propellers), and, to mangle metaphors, hit the ground running with their shiny new photography tool. If you've skipped earlier chapters, I urge you to proceed with caution as you work your way through the following sections. And, if you *haven't* skipped the chapters, I also urge you to proceed with caution, as well.

That's because, unlike most photographic equipment you may be used to, newbie errors committed while using a drone won't just result in blurry, poorly composed, or improperly exposed photos. Despite all the smarts and failsafes built into your aircraft, carelessness can change an enjoyable photo excursion into a crashing disappointment. It's important to keep in mind that more than your drone is at stake: personal injury, property damage, as well as legal and financial issues can result from a lack of preparation and caution. Fortunately, my job is to do everything I can to help you enjoy success from your very first flight, so, don't hesitate to review the suggestions found in the first four chapters if you find you have a question.

Activate Your Drone

Activation is required before you can use your drone, its remote controller, and batteries. It's a good idea to perform this step before you leave your home base to begin your flight. Activation, firmware updates, and downloading of maps requires a reliable Wi-Fi connection. Although activation of the aircraft and controller is done only once, firmware updates happen fairly frequently. Some are *mandatory* to the extent that the DJI Fly app will not allow your drone to take off until the update is installed. It can be extremely frustrating to arrive at the site where you plan to fly, only to discover that your aircraft is effectively disabled until you've installed a software update. Your smart device's internet connection or Wi-Fi hotspot may not be available or reliable every single time, so it's always best to check for firmware updates *before* you leave for a flight.

Activation is the first step, and it begins with setting up an account with DJI. I've found the easiest way to do that is by registering ahead of time on a computer by navigating to https://www.dji.com/. There, click on the Profile icon in the upper-right corner of the screen and choose Register, as shown at left in Figure 5.1. Enter your email address, specify a password, agree to the privacy/terms-of-use provisions, and, once you've verified that you are not now, nor have ever been, a card-carrying automaton, your account will be created. (See Figure 5.1, right.)

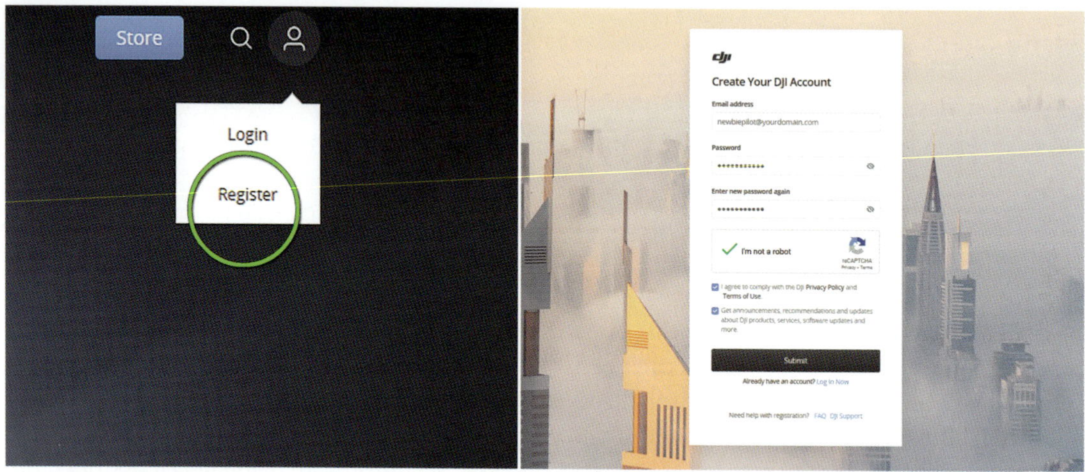

Figure 5.1 Create an account at the DJI website.

To activate, first assemble your aircraft by attaching the control sticks to your remote control (and connect your smart device if using the standard RC-N1 controller), as described in Chapter 3. Unfold your drone. Remember that the front motor/prop booms are pulled downward and toward the front of the drone first, and the rear booms pulled toward the back after that. (Do in the reverse order when repacking the aircraft for transport.) Attach the propellers if you have not already done so.

Next, energize the remote control by pressing the power button once, then again, holding it down for two seconds so it will turn on. Perform the same short press/long press sequence on the power button on the top surface of your Mini 3/Mini 3 Pro to bring the aircraft to life. I always power up the remote and drone in that order by habit, dating back to when it wasn't a good idea to have a drone powered up with no remote ready to control it. These days you don't have to worry about your aircraft doing anything undesirable prior to connection, but it's still a good plan to turn the controller on first.

When the remote is on, the DJI Fly app should launch itself automatically, assuming you have already installed it on your smart device. (The DJI Fly app is preinstalled in the RC Pro and RC controllers.) If you have *not* already installed the DJI Fly app, this is a good example of why skipping Chapters 1 to 4 is not the most efficient procedure. The first screen you'll see will ask you to activate/register your equipment with DJI. Follow the screen prompts, entering the email address and password you used when you signed up with DJI as suggested earlier. You can also register now, if necessary.

Once activated, you may see a notification of the availability of a firmware update appear in the upper-left corner of the DJI Fly app, as seen in Figure 5.2, upper left. Tap the Update label and follow the prompts and progress displays, seen at upper right and lower left in the figure. You'll be informed when the update is complete (see Figure 5.2, lower right). Firmware activation may be required for the aircraft itself, the controller, and batteries.

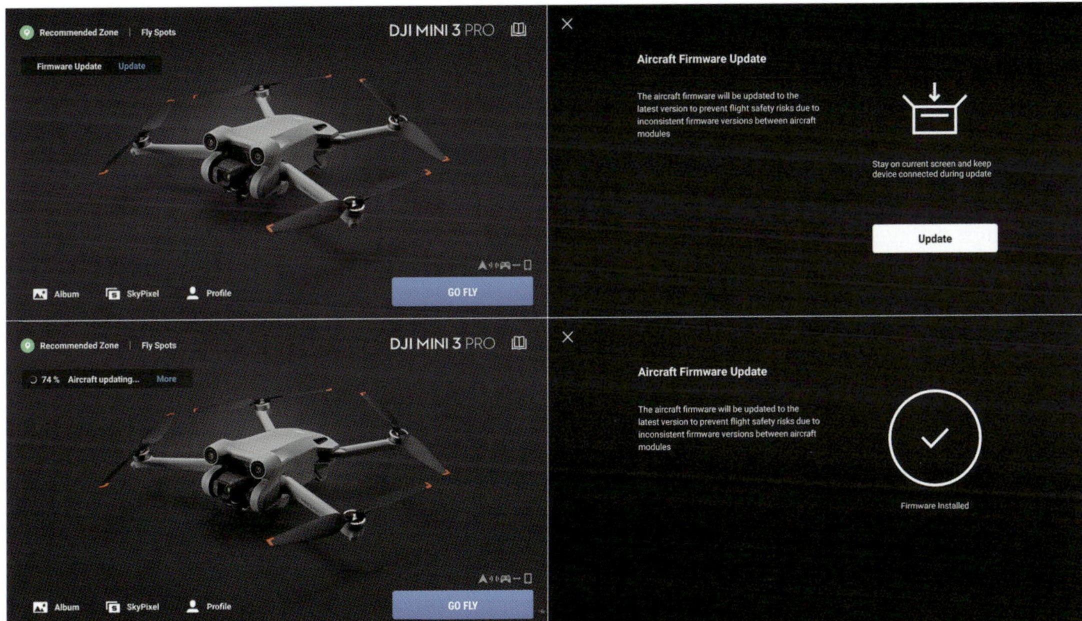

Figure 5.2 Installing a firmware update.

Preflight Checklist

Once your gear has been activated and all recommended firmware updates installed, you're ready for your first flight. You'll want to perform a preflight checklist to double-check that you and your aircraft are ready to go. Here's a list that I follow:

- **Check propellers.** Examine your drone's propellers, making sure that none of them are chipped, cracked, or show any damage, and that they are mounted on the motor hub that matches their mark (or lack thereof). Your propellers are carefully balanced to ensure stability in flight, and any damage can affect the quality of the still or video images the drone produces or, in the worst cases, result in failures that can end in a crash.

- **Battery charge.** Press the power button to check its charge level. You'll want to maximize your flight time, and ensure your drone will have enough juice to return to home safely before you take off. Now is the time to check your *other* batteries to make sure your spares are also fully charged. Most outings last more than the 31 to 34 minutes a single battery may allow, so it's good to know ahead of time whether you have enough extra batteries to continue flying when your first one has pooped out.

- **Battery condition.** Look for cracks, swelling, puffiness, or any other physical indication that the battery has seen better days. Lithium-ion batteries heat up as they dispense energy and, despite the built-in safeguards, can be damaged.

- **Fuselage and gimbal.** Check the body of the drone and the gimbal-mounted camera for damage.

- **Extra storage.** Have a microSD card of sufficient capacity and transfer speed installed. Video uses a lot more storage than stills, with 4K movies being the most demanding. Make sure you have enough storage available for your planned flight.

- **Weather conditions.** Even though weather may be sunny and mild now, it may change. I always check the weather app on my smartphone to see if rain, storms, or wind conditions are on the horizon (so to speak). UAV Forecast, available for both iOS and Android, provides a good profile of wind speeds at various altitudes. You may find that winds may be calm at ground level, but gusts that are more than the aircraft can handle are raging aloft.

- **"Ground truth" check.** Maps and apps don't tell you everything you need to know about your flight area. Remote sensing technology using satellites or aircraft uses visual *ground truth checks* to confirm that what you see is what you got. It's a good idea for drone pilots to visually check your surroundings, as well, so you know where obstacles such as trees, utility towers, buildings, and other hazards may be ahead of time. You may very well spot some things that aren't detected by your drone's sensors or apps, or which aren't readily visible from the aircraft's camera during flight.

- **Mission plan.** What do I hope to accomplish with this flight? Are there specific shots or video clips I want to shoot? Or, do I just want to get up in the air and see what looks good? Any planning you do *now,* before you take off, means less time expending battery power in the air deciding what to do next, and can result in a safer flight.

- **Physical and mental well-being.** It's a good idea to remain mindful of your own condition, as flying a drone requires alertness and a degree of concentration. Did you get enough sleep last night? Are you in a good mood and not distracted? Do you take a medication that might interfere with your responses? We tend to exclude ourselves from the flight-worthy equation, but our own well-being nevertheless deserves attention.

- **Good to go?** The last step will be to use the B4UFLY app to see if you are cleared to fly and make sure you have the permissions, authorizations, and certification required to take off in this area. As a recreational flyer, you won't often require any special clearances and will be using uncontrolled airspace. The B4UFLY app will inform you of any NOTAMs or other restrictions and let you know that it's okay to take off.

Finding Suitable Locations for Take-off/Landing

One of the most engaging parts of drone flying is locating places to fly your aircraft. You'll want a place that is visually interesting and accessible, with minimal obstacles or hazards to make safe take-offs and landings challenging. You'll want favorable weather conditions, too. Your flight must take place in uncontrolled airspaces, or controlled air spaces in which you have authorization to fly. You'll need to maintain line-of-sight requirements, and consider having an observer with you to help track your drone visually. An ideal location won't cause problems with other legalities, such as flying over people. Even with all these considerations, finding places to put your Mini 3 or Mini 3 Pro through its paces can be a lot of fun. Here are some suggestions.

Your Backyard

Those of you who don't live in an apartment, condominium, townhouse, on a boat, or in a cave may have an excellent site for the initial flight of your Mini 3 or Mini 3 Pro. If you're lucky enough to have a backyard and friendly neighbors, your own property may be the best location from which to do your first exploration of your drone's capabilities.

I'm lucky enough to live just outside the city limits of a small town, in a house on 1.65 acres with a cornfield as my neighbor on the east, and separated from my congenial neighbors on the west by a stand of 40-foot-tall pine trees. They can't even hear my drone take off, just like I don't know when their band (F.O.G.) is practicing in their basement. I've done a lot of drone testing (and experienced my first crashes into the pine trees as a newbie) at home for years.

If you have the opportunity to perform your first flights on your own property, you'll enjoy the freedom of using your drone any time you want, at the spur of the moment, with ready access to resources (your home computer, Wi-Fi system, AC power to charge batteries, and so forth) you might not have out in the field. When I was getting ready for my own first flights, I noticed an old saucer sled in the garage and took it out to act as my very first take-off/landing pad.

Of course, your backyard isn't limited to drone-training purposes. You can record a backyard party (don't fly directly above your guests), check out the condition of your home's roof, enjoy a bird's-eye view of your abode and property, shoot video selfies (called "dronies"), or capture footage for your next homemade action movie. Just remember that privacy laws still apply. Your neighbors may have told you they won't be disrupted by your drone flights, but they still wouldn't appreciate you taking pictures through their windows. (It's not legal.)

Near the Water

As you gain confidence with your drone, you'll be less apprehensive about using it in more adventurous locations, especially those near bodies of water. It can be chilling the first time you send your aircraft out to sea to snag an offshore image like the one shown in Figure 5.3, but an unintentional water landing is no more likely than a crash into an onshore obstacle. There are many water-oriented locations that are great for drone photography. For example, many beach towns still allow drone use in and around boardwalks.

Lighthouses, especially historic beacons, are perfect subjects for your aircraft's camera. Many are located right on the shore, or built on a hill near the shore, giving your drone a spectacular view with an engaging backdrop. You'll find dozens in your area if you live near a coast, and, for those inland, a visit to the east or west coast of the United States or any of the states bordering the Gulf of Mexico are worth the trip. There are dozens of lighthouses adjacent to the Great Lakes, too.

When shooting near water, you do need to pay attention to wind (just like pilots of any other type of aircraft). Gusts at the shore of large lakes can be strong at certain times of day, and of less concern at others. Breezes are generally present because the land and water heat up and cool at different rates, and the difference in temperatures in adjacent areas creates the wind. Your drone is powerful enough to handle a great deal of air movement, whether it's caused by the drone's motion as it navigates the sky, or by Mother Nature while the aircraft hovers. (See "Wind Resistance" later in this chapter.)

Smaller bodies of water and rivers are likely to be more friendly for drone flight and can make excellent subjects. Just remember that a river may cross into Class B airspace when near a seaport or airport and you'll need to request Low Altitude Authorization and Notification Capability (LAANC) permission, as mentioned in Chapter 3.

Figure 5.3 Offshore photography provides a unique point of view.

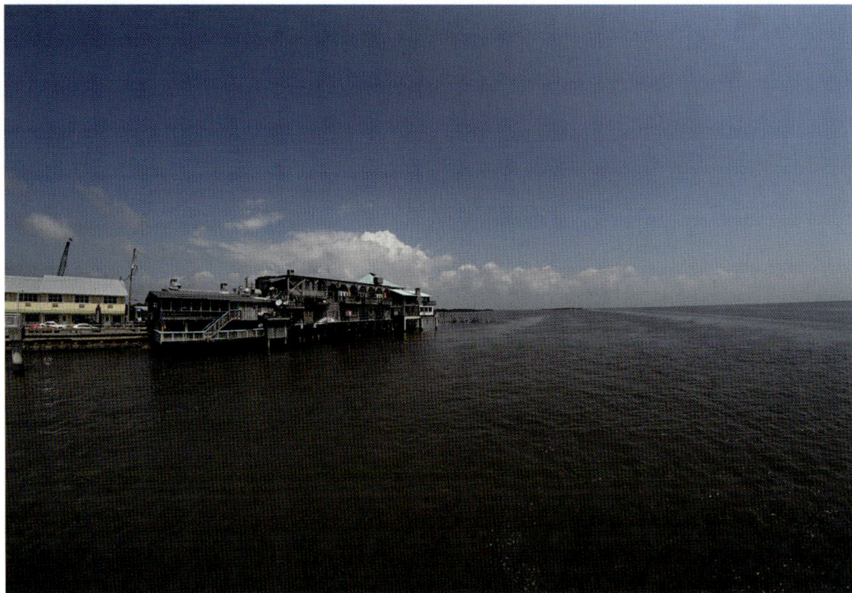

National Parks and Federal Lands (No-No! and Maybe)

The rules are very clear when it comes to areas administered by the National Parks Service (NPS). Don't even *think* about trying to fly your drone in any National Park in the United States without permission. The prohibition also includes National Monuments, National Recreation Areas, National Historic Sites, National Seashores, National Memorials, and other areas administered by the NPS.

As of August 20, 2014, launching, landing, or operating an unmanned aircraft from or on all lands and waters administered by the National Park Service (NPS) is prohibited. By "unmanned aircraft" the NPS means a device that is used or intended to be used for flight in the air, including model airplanes, quadcopters, or drones that are used for any purpose, including for recreation or commerce. Unless you're Ken Burns working on a documentary or conducting scientific research, don't expect to easily get written approval from the park superintendent to bypass this restriction. Violations can result in up to six months of time in jail plus a fine of up to $5,000.

You'll want to be careful when flying adjacent to National Parks and related areas, so you don't wander into forbidden space. Drone operators have tried to bypass the restrictions by taking off from private property, but regulations covering wildlife disturbance and the need to keep your drone within visual line of sight makes the attempt to circumvent the rules risky. The B4UFLY app will clearly warn you about any NPS lands in your vicinity, so it's fairly difficult to accidentally violate the regulations. (See Figure 5.4.)

The rules are not as clear-cut when it comes to federal lands administered by other federal agencies, such as the Forest Service and Bureau of Land Management (BLM). Your drone may be allowed in some national forests and in some Bureau of Land Management areas that aren't designated as wilderness. You still need to follow guidelines like these:

- Never fly over or in close proximity to any fire operation, which may disrupt aerial firefighting operations and create hazardous situations.

- Avoid Forest Service aircraft flying at low altitudes to perform natural resource management. The local Ranger District Office can provide information about scheduled flights in the area.

- Do not fly over congressionally designated wilderness areas or primitive areas.

- Do not fly over or near wildlife. Intentional disturbance of animals during breeding, nesting, rearing of young, or other critical life history functions is not allowed unless approved as research or management.

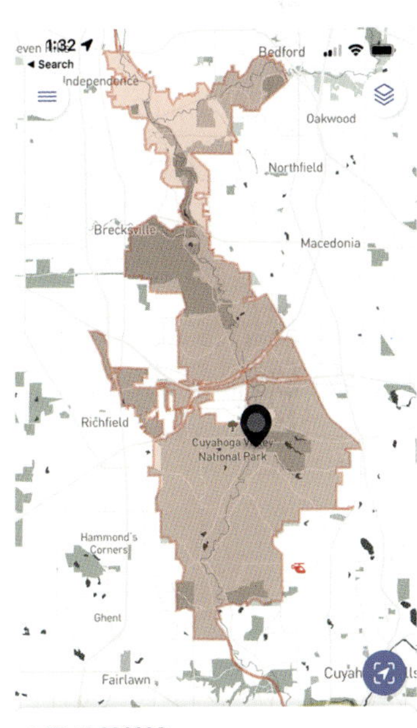

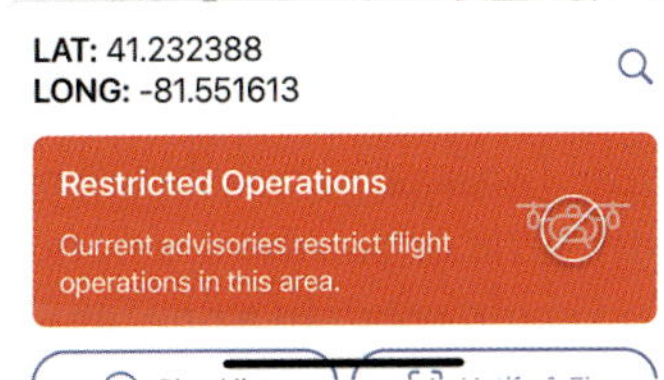

Figure 5.4 B4UFLY will warn you about prohibited areas.

- Follow state wildlife and fish agency regulations on the use of your drone to search for or detect wildlife and fish.
- Launch the drone more than 100 meters (328 feet) from wildlife to avoid disturbing them. Do not approach animals or birds while flying.

State Parks

You'll find that the use of drones in state parks varies from state to state, so you'll need to look into the regulations for your particular area. I escape my frigid home state each winter to take photographs for my books in various locations in Florida, a state which has some of the best state parks I've ever encountered. Many of them have modest admission fees (which provide the funding that makes these parks outstanding), so I purchase an annual pass each year. Although I enjoy capturing the birds, wildlife, and scenery in these parks with my still cameras, drone photography in any of them is forbidden.

Back home, however, there are no specific laws forbidding flying over state parks. However, each park has the right to establish and enforce its own rules. They can ban take-offs or landings inside the park, or restrict the areas in which you fly. All of them have park rangers cruising around at regular intervals, and I've never had a problem, at least with drones. (I've been reprimanded about not having a sufficient number of life vests for an inflatable watercraft I was about to launch.) Other drone pilots I've talked to have been advised to not fly in certain locations. If a state you wish to fly in does not have an overall ban against drones in its parks, you should be good to go if there are no signs at the entrance to the park that mention drone aircraft.

Other Parks and Public Areas

In general, many areas have no restrictions on drone flights, while others have had to enact regulations due to increased unmanned aircraft use in their areas. In general, you are allowed to fly your drone in public areas, such as public parks, if you adhere to the limitations and the restrictions set by the FAA regarding drone flight. But just don't assume that your local parks are free to use for your flights. Do some research to see what your state and local governments allow regarding drones. For example, Cleveland, Ohio has an outstanding network of metro parks, but only three specific areas are designated for drone usage, all of them large, open fields. However, I've successfully taken photos in many public parks, at schools, and a variety of other areas throughout my state and in others. I'm careful not to fly over people or be a nuisance to others enjoying the area.

Even if a location is a public space, if a disaster or event requiring emergency response personnel unfolds, the area may be automatically assigned Temporary Flight Restrictions (TFR), sometimes with little or no advance notice. In that case, drones are not allowed to enter that airspace. A violation could result in a fine, or worse, and interfere with efforts to save life.

Special Events

You may be tempted to emulate the Goodyear Blimp to get a bird's-eye view of a sporting contest, stadium concert, or an exciting NASCAR race. However, as a recreational drone user, it is illegal for you to fly your drone near one of those locations, generally from one hour before it begins to one hour after its conclusion. Even so, it can be fun to capture an image of your favorite venue at other times, when no spectators or workers are present, as seen in Figure 5.5.

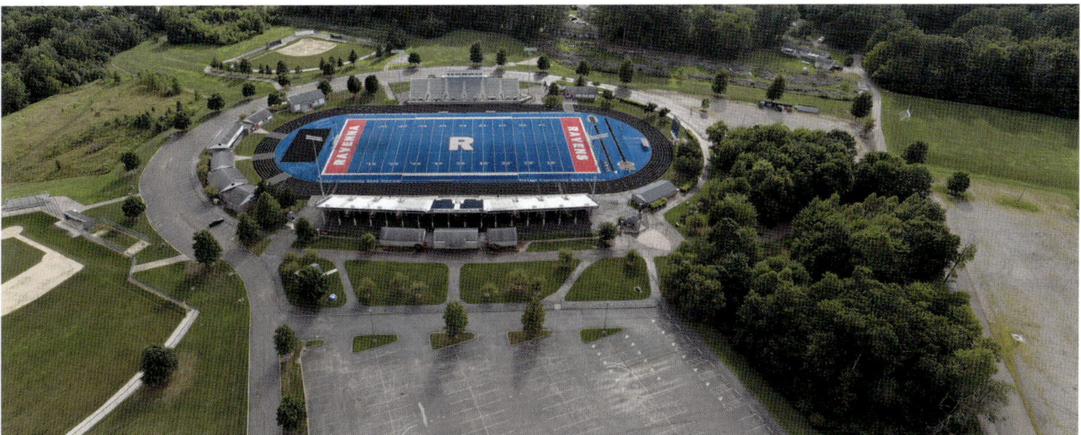

Figure 5.5 Shooting a typical stadium.

Mastering the Controls

Nothing is more exciting than seeing your drone take flight for the first time and watching it ascend skyward to become a buzzing tiny dot above you. It's time to take that step, send your aircraft aloft, and capture your first aerial images. The following sections will get you airborne.

Choosing a Flight Mode

Your Mini 3/Mini 3 Pro has four different flight modes, three of which, Normal, Sport, and Cine/Tripod, are selectable using a switch on the controller. (See Figure 5.6.) The fourth, ATTI, is selected automatically when all of the conditions required for one of the three Standard modes is not available. The next sections provide an overview of these flight modes.

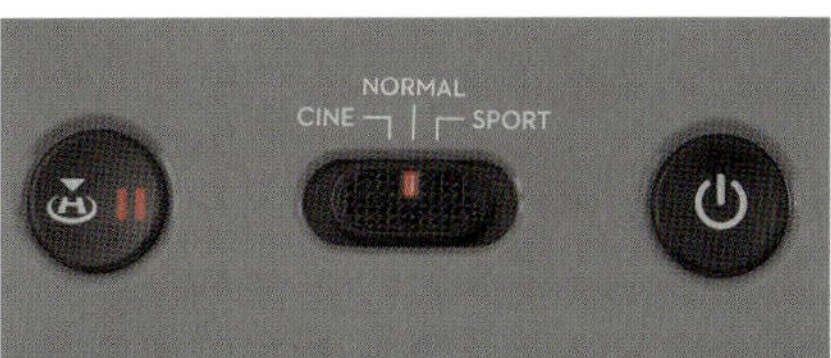

Figure 5.6 Choose a flight mode.

Normal Mode

N-mode, the center position of the three-way sliding Flight Mode switch on the controller, is the default mode of your drone, and will be the one you will spend the most time using. I highly recommend using N-mode for your first flight and suggest you don't experiment with one of the more specialized flight modes until you've had experience flying your aircraft at its default settings.

This mode is optimized for a broad range of flight types. It deploys its full complement of tools to orient and stabilize its flight. GNSS (Global Navigation Satellite System) is used when satellite signals are strong enough, working in tandem with the drone's vision system, to provide robust obstacle sensing and avoidance. The vision system includes pairs of forward, backward, and downward sensors, plus, with the Mini 3 Pro, two upward sensors. Two 3D infrared modules provide additional sensing that's particularly useful when landing or flying indoors (where geolocation may not be available). In N-mode, the top speed (without benefit of tailwinds) is 22.3 mph/36 kph for both the Mini 3 and Mini 3 Pro.

Sport Mode

If N-mode gives you Tesla-like object-avoidance features, then S-mode is the NASCAR of drone photography. It relies heavily on the skills of the pilot to direct and navigate. Only GNSS is used for positioning and orientation, and automatic obstacle sensing and avoidance is disabled, so you'll need to remain alert and fully in command of your aircraft's movement.

The advantage of S-mode is that, freed from its obstacle avoidance tether, the drone is agile and more responsive to small control stick adjustments, and has a slightly higher maximum speed of 42 mph/68 kph. Because of the faster motion in Sport mode, the minimum distance for braking is 98 feet/30 meters.

Here are some things to think about before tackling Sport mode:

- **Master your controls.** When maneuvering your drone in S-mode, you frequently won't have time to stop and think about which control stick to move next, or in what direction. Your controls should be second nature to you, and you should understand how the drone responds to adjustments. You'll need to know how quickly the drone can stop and how rapidly it turns, ascends, and descends. You must know how to handle radio interference, signal loss, and unexpected gusts of wind.

- **Monitor battery levels.** S-mode depletes your batteries much more quickly, generally due to the increase in flying speed, as well as the rapid ascents and descents typical of many Sport mode maneuvers. Consider using your newest, most robust Intelligent Flight batteries to extend the time you can remain aloft, and then monitor the remaining flight time on your controller's display.

- **Obstacle avoidance.** In S-mode, all obstacle avoidance features are disabled, because it's unlikely the aircraft's systems could react in time given the increased responsiveness and speed. Obstacle avoidance isn't perfect even in N-mode and the demands of Sport mode reduce the feature's efficacy considerably. So, pay extra attention to your surroundings so you can identify and evaluate hazards visually and compensate to protect your drone from damage while preserving the safety of living creatures within your flight zone.

- **Adjust Return to Home settings.** Your drone's Return to Home (RTH) function still operates in S-mode, *but obstacle avoidance doesn't.* You can initiate RTH manually, or the drone will automatically activate the feature should your battery reach low or critical levels. However, automatic RTH won't avoid potential hazards as it returns. When returning, the drone will first ascend to an altitude you specify before making its way back to its home location. It's a good idea to make sure this altitude is appropriate for your current environment before takeoff, and then, once RTH has commenced, monitor your drone's position to ensure it can land without interference.

- **Choose your environment.** S-mode is best used in open places with few hazards to worry about while using the enhanced speeds and responsiveness of this mode. In addition to obstacles, you should be extra aware of any wind and weather conditions that might affect your flight.

Cine/Tripod Mode

Depending on the age of your controller, this position on the mode switch may be labeled either C (for Cine) or T (for Tripod). The two modes are quite similar. Tripod mode allows adjusting the maximum speed of the drone. In Cine mode, performance is comparable to Normal mode, but the top speed of the drone is limited to 11 mph/18 kph, which gives you more of a consistent, stable flight needed for video capture.

This cinematic mode, as you might expect from its name, is especially useful for capturing video. Braking distance is longer and smoother; if you don't use a control stick after a flight maneuver, the drone will slow down before stopping, rather than stopping immediately. When rotating the drone left or right, the yaw movement maximum speed is reduced, producing a smoother pan.

ATTI Mode

Earlier DJI drones had a user-selectable ATTI (Attitude) mode, but now it's automatically selected when the drone is unable to use its vision systems, compass, or GNSS signal. This Attitude mode is equivalent to manual control and must be used when automatic positioning systems are not available. You'll need to manipulate the controls yourself to maintain a stable hover, and constant altitude and position. ATTI is most often invoked when the drone is experiencing a strong source of signal interference, or flying under an overhead obstacle. ATTI mode kicks in indoors, too. Once GPS stabilization is lost, you'll be fully in charge of the aircraft's flight, and should take control quickly.

Checking Airspace

One of the last things you should do before actually taking flight is to check to see if it is legal to fly in the airspace you plan to use, and, if necessary, obtain the required authorizations to operate in a particular area. As I mentioned, your best friend is the FAA's B4UFLY app for iOS and Android. Other airspace apps are available, including Aloft Air Control (formerly Aloft and Kittyhawk), which is offered by the same company that produced B4UFLY for the FAA.

B4UFLY provides a succinct screen like the one in Figure 5.7, telling you that you're clear for takeoff along with any advisories for your area. Other functions are available if you scroll down, as seen in Figure 5.8:

- **Additional information.** If you scroll down, you can view additional information, such as nearby airports or hospitals (which may have a heliport) and their distance from you. (See Figure 5.8, upper left.)

- **Submit Data.** At the bottom of the same screen is a tab used to submit data for your current location. Those updates are generally made only by authoritative agencies sharing verifiable ground rules and advisories. However, the app states that submitters can include drone operators, concerned citizens, property owners, or government agencies.

- **Checklist.** This feature simply displays reminders about FAA registration, drone labeling requirements, and the Trust and Safety Test (TRUST), with links to the appropriate sites.

- **Notify & Fly.** You can "file" a flight plan using this facility, starting with the screen shown at upper right in Figure 5.8. You can then enter the type of flight (Recreational, Commercial, Government, or First Responder) (see Figure 5.8, lower left), and, finally, share your flight with other users of the app. (See Figure 5.8, lower right.)

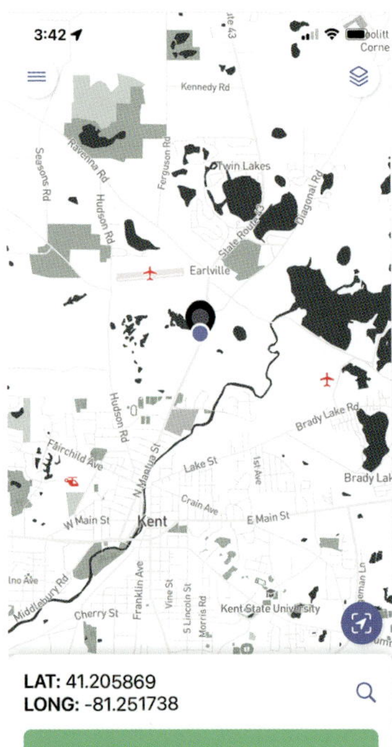
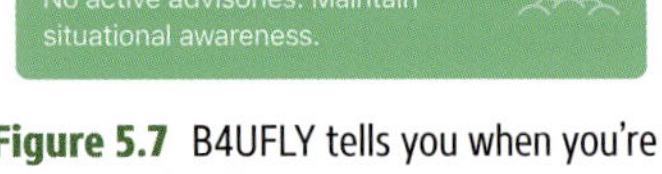

Figure 5.7 B4UFLY tells you when you're clear for takeoff.

You'll switch to the DJI Fly app before taking off. Even before you fly, the app will display a minimap, as seen at left in Figure 5.9. If you find the minimap intrusive, you can tap the L-shaped icon in the lower-left corner to reduce it to an icon, shown at right in the figure. I'll explain how to use the on-screen maps shortly. You should know that tapping on the minimap will enlarge it to full size, as seen in Figure 5.10. The screen will display a map of your local area, with the drone's Home Point and location indicated by an H icon and blue arrow. The drone camera's live view will be reduced to a thumbnail, as seen at lower left in Figure 5.10. Within the full-size map, you can use two fingers to zoom in and out. As you zoom out, the wider area shown on the full map will display any restricted areas, shaded blue, gray, yellow, and orange in the figure. You can review the restrictions in the map and then zoom back into your local area before you take off.

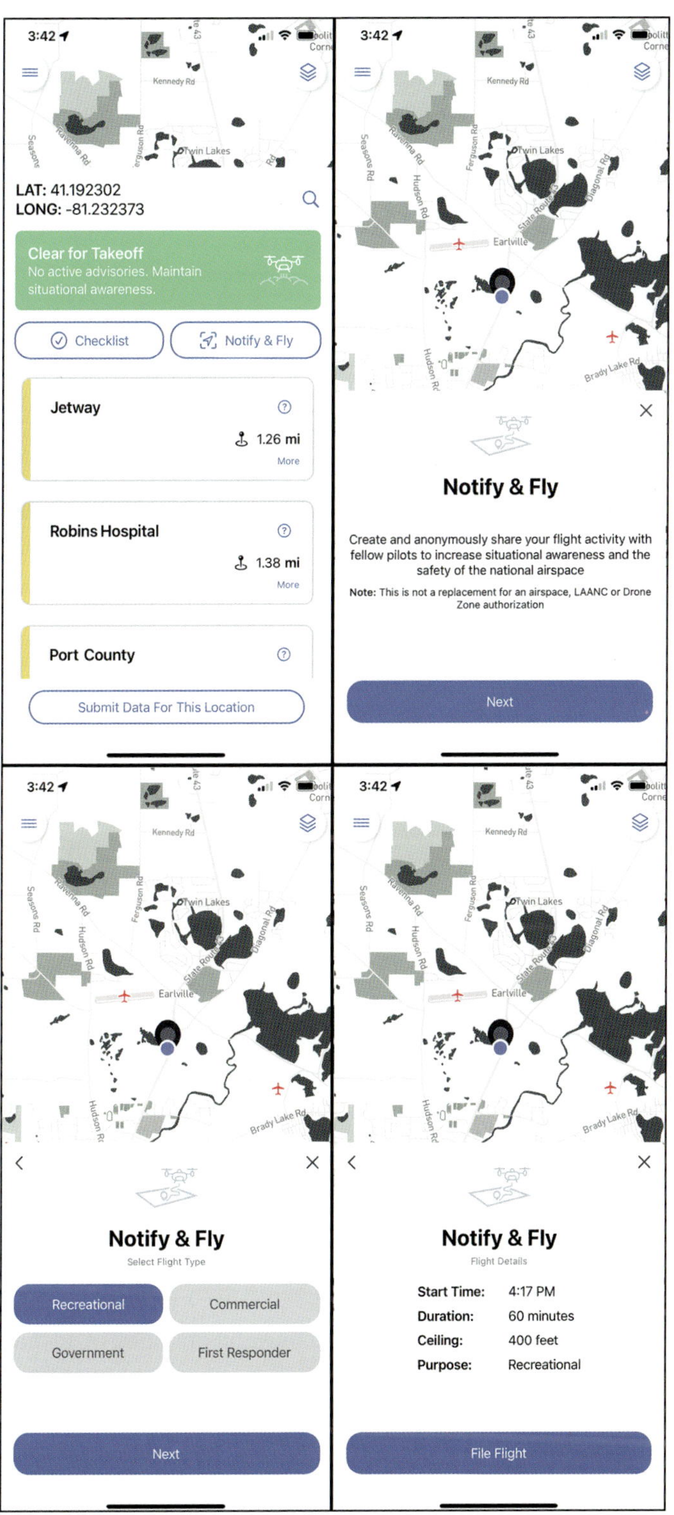

Figure 5.8 Additional information (upper left). Filing a notification of your flight plans (upper right and lower left/right).

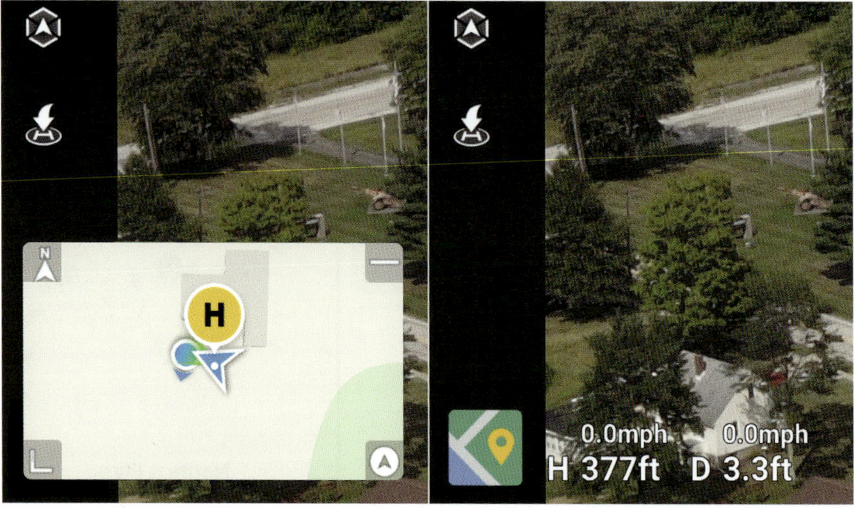

Figure 5.9 Minimap (left) and map icon (right).

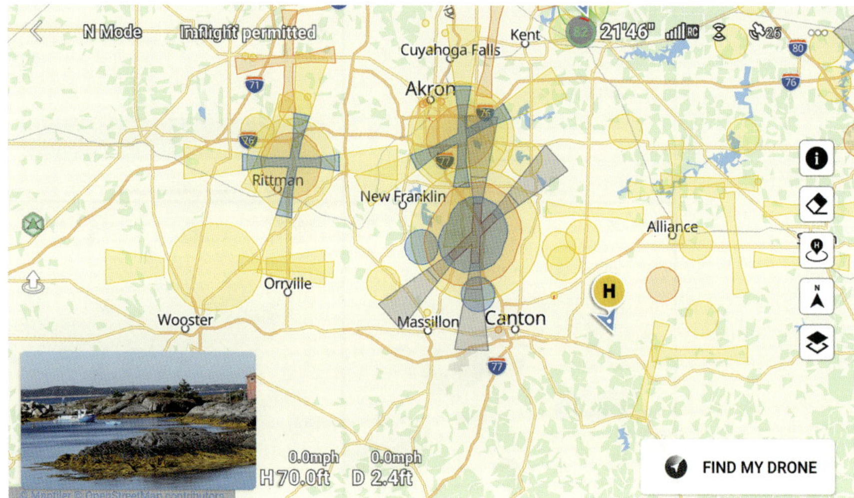

Figure 5.10 Zoom out from the full-size map to see restricted zones in your area.

LAANC and Geofencing

Up until this point I've emphasized the importance of understanding controlled and uncontrolled airspace. Recreational drone users will do most of their flights within uncontrolled airspaces. However, non–Part 107–certified pilots *are* allowed to fly under 400 feet in controlled areas near airports *if they receive an airspace authorization from the FAA* before they fly.

In order to operate in these air spaces, authorization must be obtained in advance, using a system set up by the FAA called Low Altitude Authorization and Notification Capability (LAANC). Fortunately, LAANC is a system that's not that difficult to navigate. Prior to LAANC, drone pilots needed to submit a request to the FAA DroneZone website, and wait from seven days to several months to receive authorization. Using Aloft Air Control, or one of several different alternative apps, it is now possible to get that authorization in near real time. Authorizations are available from 726 airports nationwide. If the airport you want to fly near is not on the LAANC list, you can use the manual process at the FAA's DroneZone site.

When using the utility, you'll need to enter the location where you want to fly, date, time, duration of the flight, planned altitude, and whether you'll be flying under commercial or recreational exceptions. (See Figure 5.11, left.) Scroll down to view the advisories (shown in Figure 5.11, center), and then proceed. If you receive your authorization (see Figure 5.11, right), you can review your information and submit to log your flight. Alternatively, you may receive a notice that your pre-check failed, and you were denied, or that conditional approval is available.

LAANC requests are cross-checked against multiple data sources, including UAS Facility Maps, Special-Use Airspace Data, Airports and Airspace Classes, and includes Temporary Flight Restrictions (TFRs) and Notices to Air Missions (NOTAMS). However, it is still your responsibility to check weather conditions and check for restrictions at the time you fly.

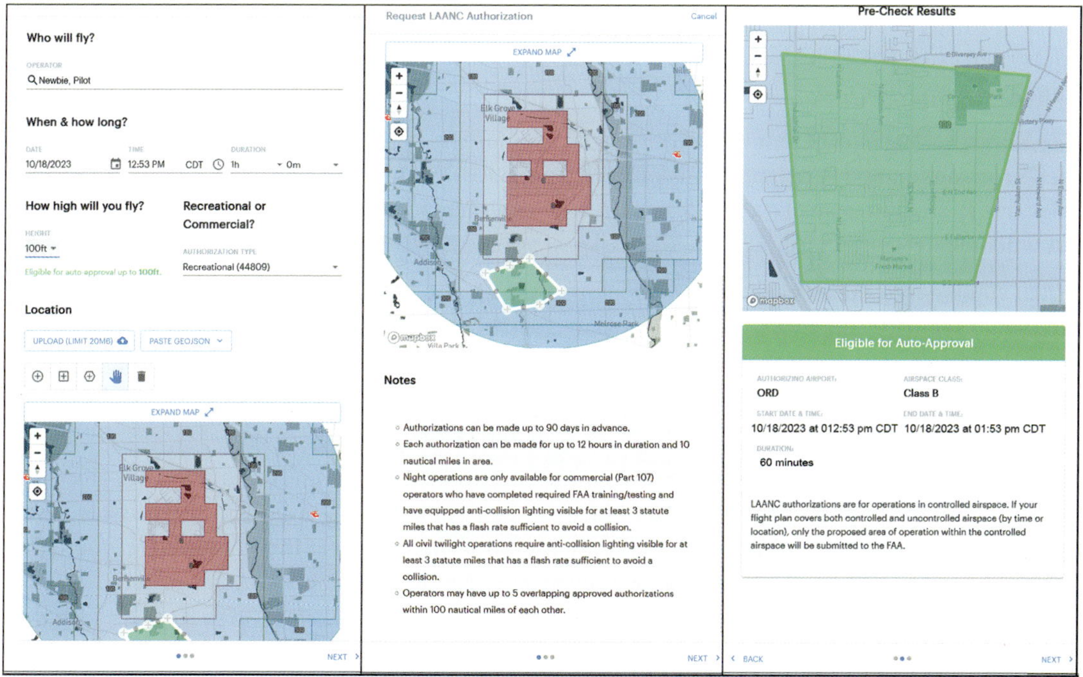

Figure 5.11 Using Aloft Air Control's access to LAANC authorizations.

Geofencing

However, LAANC is not the only obstacle governing where you can and cannot fly your drone. DJI has decided that further protection is needed. The company obviously has a vested interest in making sure drones are used wisely without becoming annoying nuisances and subject to even more restrictions than those already in place. So, DJI has embedded in the firmware of its drones a system called geofencing, which effectively locks you out of flying in forbidden zones. In effect, even if you intend to blatantly ignore flight restrictions, your drone may refuse to comply. You'll need to use DJI's own system to unlock the virtual fence with permission and proof of authorization.

Geofencing in itself is not new or proprietary to DJI. The term refers to an invisible barrier set up around a particular geographic area, large or small, and used by software or firmware to define the borders of operation for a device or utility. A geofence can trigger a signal in your dog's collar when he tries to wander outside the confines of your yard. Organizations may use a geofence to determine whether its vehicles remain within an assigned perimeter. Geofencing is even used by marketers to serve up targeted ads on your smart device.

In terms of drones, a geofence is useful for preventing a remotely controlled aircraft from accidentally or intentionally entering a restricted or unsafe airspace. DJI's Geospatial Environment Online (GEO) provides updated guidance about areas where flight may be limited due to regulations or safety concerns. DJI's Flysafe website is your tool to view and unlock the areas on the company's Geo Zone map.

Geo Zones belong in different categories, including borders between countries, sensitive locations such as prisons and power plants, and controlled airspaces. Some areas may have temporary restrictions due to stadium sports events, forest fires, or emergencies. Some zones may not be restricted, but will include warnings about potential risks.

When you log into the website (https://dji.com/flysafe), you can view the defined zones at various safety and security risk levels, and, if necessary (and allowed), unlock them so you will be able to cross the virtual fence into them. You can discover which places are entirely safe for flight, or you may discover your flight involves low-risk zones that can be easily unlocked. Those assigned higher risks require submitting credentials to guarantee compliance.

DJI's Geo Zones will prevent you from flying into certain zones, or even from taking off. However, those with verified DJI accounts can temporarily unlock some of those areas. So, your first step will be to make sure you have a registered account with DJI. When you visit the Flysafe page, you'll find some videos on safe operations and one on how to unlock a Geo Zone. When you click on Geo Zone map, you'll be shown a map of your current location and the restricted zones in that area, along with a code describing what each colored area on the map represents. (See Figure 5.12.) You can click on the map to enlarge it to full screen. (See Figure 5.13.) You can choose whether it shows Restricted, Altitude, and Authorization Zones, or click boxes next to Warning Zones and Enhanced Warning Zones to view even more details. (See Figure 5.14.)

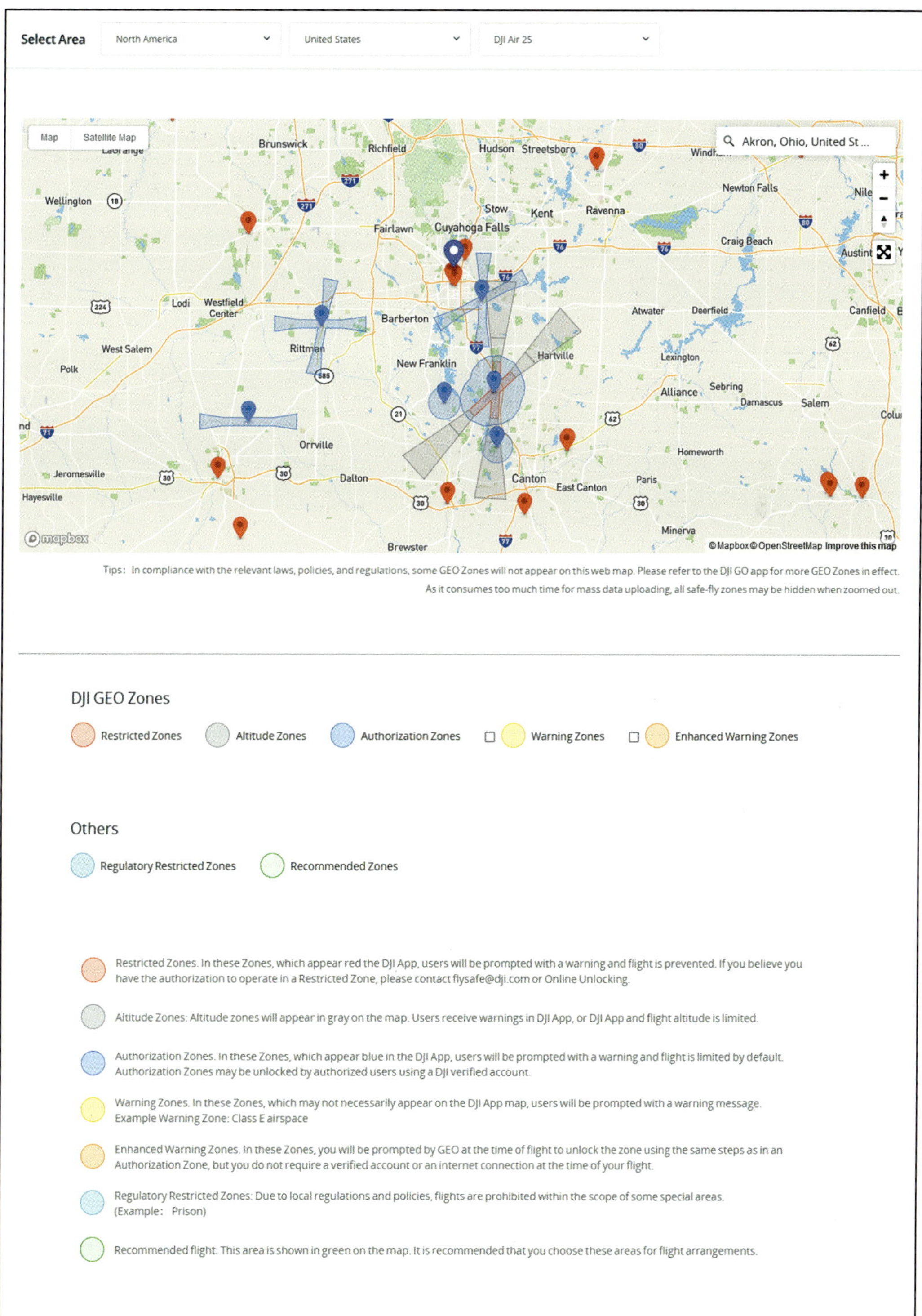

Figure 5.12 Viewing the Geo Zone map.

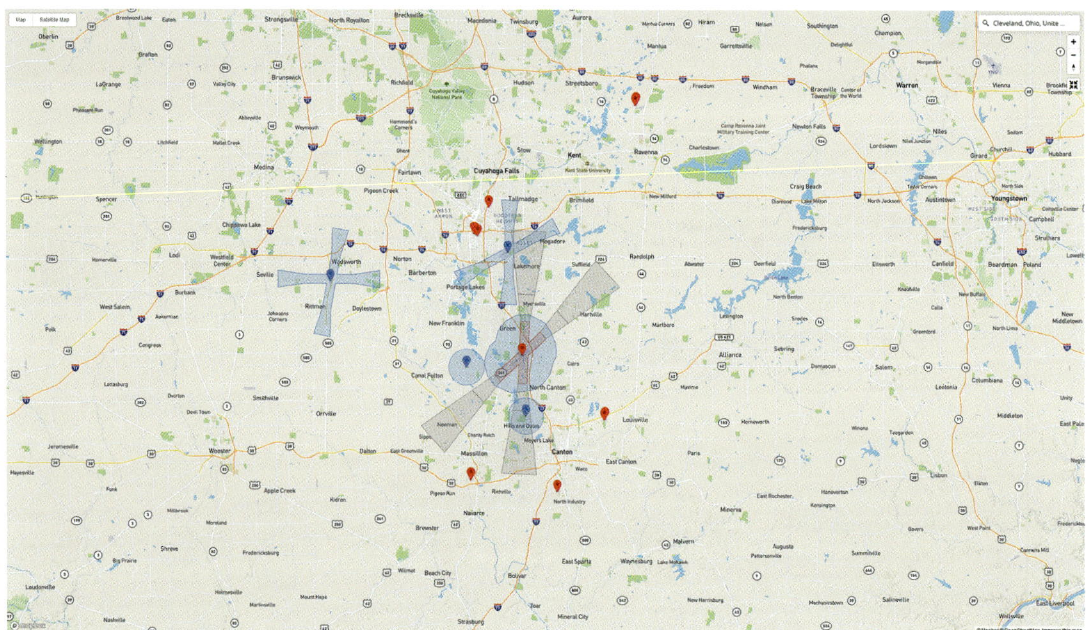

Figure 5.13 The Geo Zone map can be enlarged to full screen.

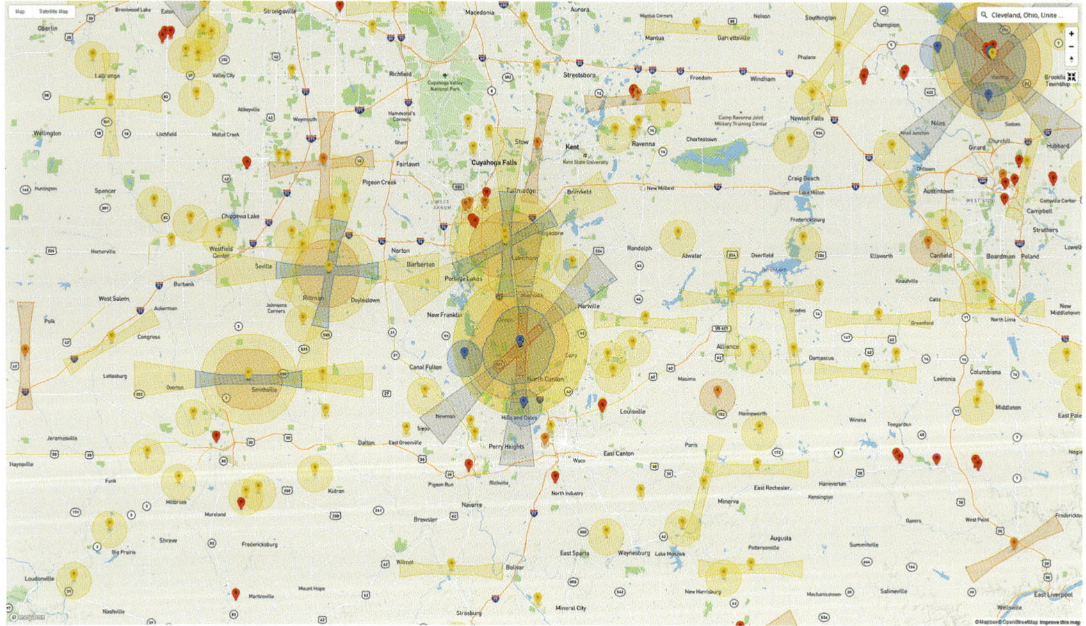

Figure 5.14 Extra Warning Zones can be displayed.

The key zones are these:

- **Restricted Zones.** These areas are shown in light red and represent air space in which you cannot fly.
- **Altitude Zones.** Shaded in gray, these areas indicate that the height of your planned flight may be regulated.
- **Authorization Zones.** Blue represents areas that require FAA permission to enter, using LAANC, Aloft Air Control, or another app.
- **Warning Zones.** Yellow-shaded areas can be flown through without LAANC authorization, but the DJI Fly app will give you an on-screen warning.
- **Enhanced Warning Zones.** These amber areas don't require LAANC authorization, but have been locked by DJI's GEO fencing. You'll need to use GEO's procedure to unlock them.

If you encounter a GEO zone that you need to unlock, you can do so by following these steps:

1. **Sign in.** On your computer, log into your previously created DJI account.
2. **Access Unlock.** Scroll down the page and click on Unlock a Zone. If this is your first time attempting to unlock a zone, you'll be asked to fill out an Authentication Application to set up a personal account, organization account, or permitted organization account. You'll need to supply information about yourself; your drone, including remote controller serial number; DJI account email; and other data.
3. **Click New Unlock Request.** At the Unlock page, you'll see a list of all your previous requests. When you click on New Unlock Request, you'll need to confirm responsibility on a disclaimer page.
4. **Choose Custom or Zone Unlocking.** Custom Unlocking requires specifying just the area planned for your flight. Zone Unlocking gains access to the entire Warning Zone. Click Confirm.
5. **Drone/Pilot information.** In either case, you'll need to fill in your drone and pilot information if you haven't done it already in Step 2.
6. **Access map.** In the search bar, type in the location you want to unlock.
7a. **Specify area (Custom Unlock).** Simply draw a circle around the area to be unlocked, provide the altitude you will fly to, your reason for wanting to unlock the zone, and the time and date of the flight. Click Submit.
7b. **Specify area (Zone Unlock).** On the map, click within the zone you want to unlock, specifying the date, time, and reason for wanting to unlock the zone. You may be asked to upload proof of authorization. Click Submit.
8. **View results.** You will receive an Unlock notice or denial. If approved, you'll receive an email with an approval number, along with a link to unlock your aircraft. The link will provide you with instructions for unlocking with your specific DJI drone model and controller.
9. **Go fly.** You are free to take off and land within the unlocked zone.

Launching

Once you've assembled and checked your drone and deemed it ready for flight, checked to see that there are no restrictions, and then selected a flight mode, you should be good to go. The next step at your flight location will be to launch your drone skyward. Just follow these steps:

1. **Determine launching "pad."** Set your drone down on a flat, relatively smooth surface such that the aircraft can sit level with nothing that can interfere with the movement of the gimbal, such as tall grass. This is particularly important with the Mini 3 and Mini 3 Pro, which have minimal landing gear/areas on their underside. If you're tempted to use, say, the hood or top of your vehicle, keep in mind that the steel panels can interfere with the aircraft's compass, so you're usually better off with an alternative site. (You should avoid proximity to large metal objects whenever recalibrating your compass, too.)

   You can also launch from the pavement in parking lots, or a designated landing pad you carry with you. A wide range of pads are available commercially, and I keep the one shown in Figure 5.15 in the trunk of my car. But when at home I most often use an old saucer sled that resides under our carport.

   Note: You may see videos of drone pilots launching their aircraft while holding it or resting it in the palm of their hand. Some even land the drone by catching it. This showboating looks cool and can be impressive, but is not a good idea, and could cause injury to the pilot or, even worse, damage to the drone or gimbal.

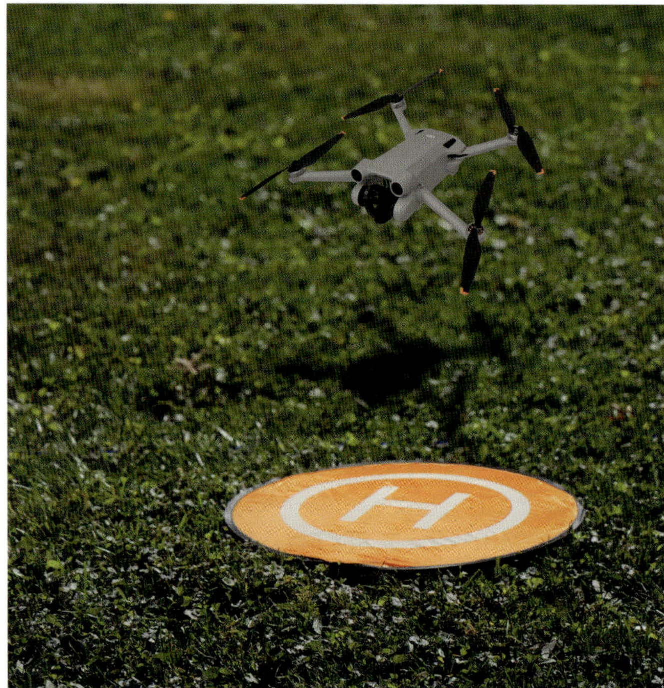

Figure 5.15 Launch from a suitable flat surface.

2. **Power up drone and controller.** Press the power button on each once, then hold down for about two seconds to turn them on. The DJI Fly app on your device should launch automatically, but if it doesn't you can do so manually. On the RC-N1 controller, a screen like the one shown at upper left in Figure 5.16 appears. With the DJI RC and RC Pro controllers a DJI Fly icon will appear on the home screen. You can tap it to launch the DJI app as required.

3. **Select aircraft.** The first time you use a controller with your drone, you will need to tap the Connection Guide icon in the first screen, then choose DJI Mini 3 or DJI Mini 3 Pro to command the app to look for your aircraft. (See Figure 5.16, upper center.) You'll be reminded to set up the aircraft properly while the app searches. (See Figure 5.16, upper right.)

   Note: On subsequent flights, the paired controller and drone should connect automatically without the need for Step 3.

4. **Await all clear.** When the controller and drone are connected, a screen appears. (See Figure 5.16, lower left.) The app will notify you "Takeoff Permitted" if all is clear, or provide advisories if it is not. The status LEDs on the aircraft will blink green indicating the Home Point has been recorded, and you'll hear a voice message confirming it.

5. **Take off.** Tap the Takeoff icon (it's the yellow oval with upward-pointing arrow) to produce the Auto Take Off panel. Press and hold the center of the Take Off circle until the Auto Take Off commences. The ring around the circumference of the circle will gradually turn green during the countdown for takeoff. You can tap the X at right in the panel to abort during the countdown.

   Manual takeoff: You can also take flight manually simply by gently pressing the left control stick forward.

6. **Flight begins.** The drone ascends to a height of 1.2 meters (about 4 feet) and updates the home position used during automatic Return to Home. (See Figure 5.16, lower center.)

7. **You're aloft!** You're ready to begin your flight. You'll notice a map located in the lower-left corner of the controller's screen. You can tap it to enlarge the map to fill the screen and reduce the camera view to the map's former footprint. (See Figure 5.16, lower right.) Tapping the small camera view restores it to full screen.

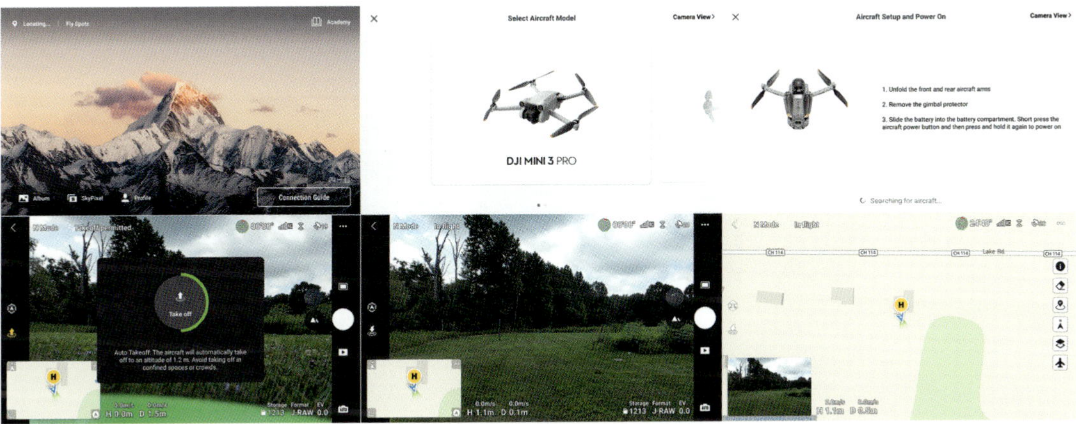

Figure 5.16 Connecting the drone with the controller (top row); taking off (bottom row).

STARTING/STOPPING MOTORS

- **Starting:** You can manually start the motors of your Mini 3/Mini 3 Pro. To start the propellers spinning, press both control sticks to the bottom inner or outer corners as shown at top in Figure 5.17. Release the sticks once the motors start.

- **Stopping:** The recommended method is to push and hold the left stick down, as seen at center in Figure 5.17. The motors will stop after about three seconds. You should do this *after* the drone has landed, naturally. Otherwise the aircraft will crash.

- **Emergency stop:** You will rarely need to stop the drone's motors instantly. The most likely scenario would be to halt an out-of-control aircraft in mid-air to avoid a serious collision with a person, another drone, or some other object, when conventional braking won't be fast enough. When the motors stop, the drone will immediately crash. The emergency stop stick command is shown at bottom in Figure 5.17.

Figure 5.17 Manually stopping and starting the drone's motors.

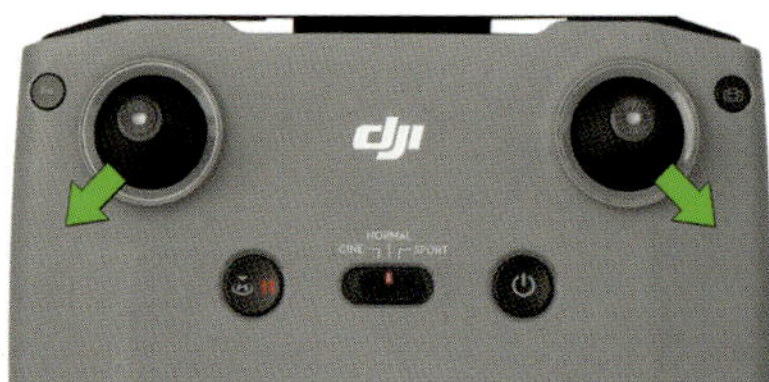
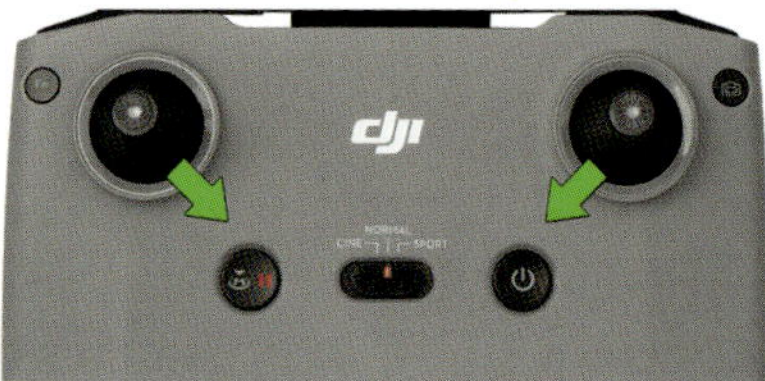

Start Motors

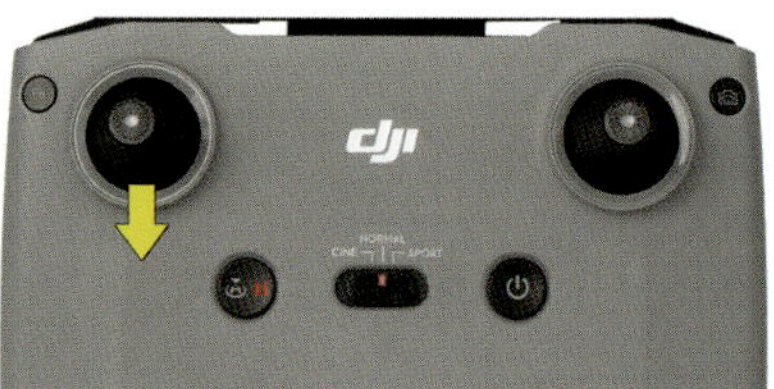

Motors stop after 3 seconds

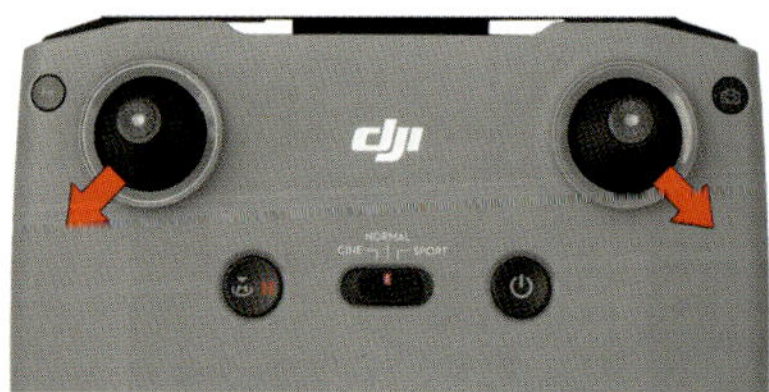
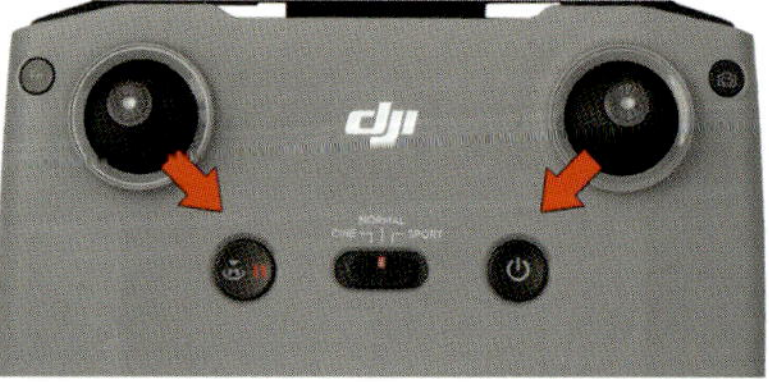

Motors stop immediately

Controlling Your Drone

Unless you're a private pilot or a fan of computer aircraft "trainer" software like Microsoft Flight Simulator, you're probably intimidated when you're shown the (relatively) simple array of gauges, instruments, switches, and controls found in light aircraft, and flabbergasted by the hundreds of components on the flight deck of a commercial aircraft like the Boeing 767. Fortunately, your Mini 3/Mini 3 Pro has far fewer controls to monitor while flying, although you'll discover quite a few *options* hidden away among the major controls.

Now that your drone is hovering overhead, it's a good time to review the controls at your disposal. I trust you've read the earlier chapters thoroughly *before* heading out to the airfield, so you're already fairly comfortable with the location of the physical controls on your radio controller. If you need a review, there are detailed photos of the DJI RC-N1, DJI RC, and DJI RC pro in Figures 4.16, 4.17, and 4.18 in Chapter 4. (The new RC-N2 and DJI RC 2 operate exactly the same as their predecessors.) For this recap, I'm going to use the RC-N1 as an example.

Using the Control Sticks

Learning to use the control sticks individually and in concert is the key to precise navigation of your Mini 3/Mini 3 Pro. As I mentioned in Chapter 4, all DJI controllers are programmed to use Mode 2 adjustments by default, with the left stick controlling up and down motion when pressed forward and backward, and horizontal rotation (yaw) by pushing left and right. The right stick can be pressed forward and back to move in those directions (from the perspective of the front of the drone), or to "slide" horizontally left and right when pushed in those directions. Figure 5.18 provides a visual reference. Mode 2 is not proprietary to DJI, of course; it is more or less a standard mode used by drones and controllers from other manufacturers.

The farther you press a given stick in any direction, the greater the speed with which the drone carries out your command. That's why you should be careful about your enthusiasm if you really don't want abrupt/fast movements. That's especially true when you want to capture smooth video, or are flying amidst a significant number of hazards. Pressing any stick diagonally produces a combination

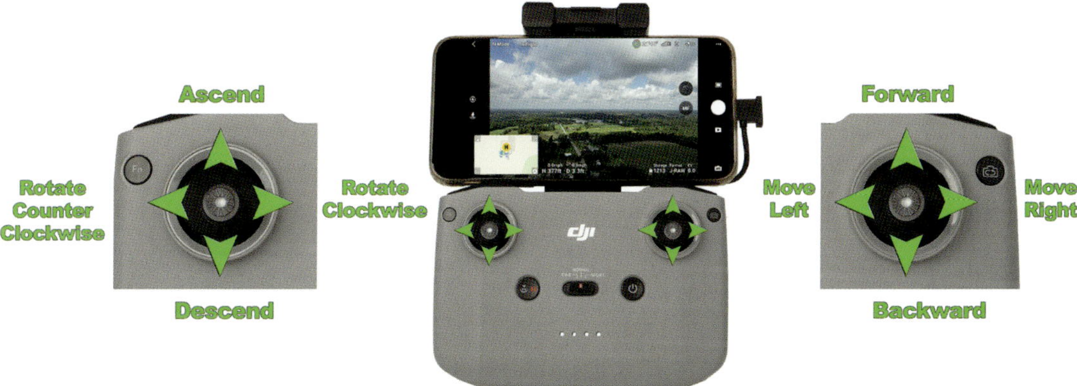

Figure 5.18 Using the control sticks.

of the two types of movement controlled by that stick: you can ascend (or descend) while rotating, or move forward/backward at an angle. If you release a control stick it returns to its centered position and if you want to halt motion quickly you can press the Pause/Return to Home button located to the left of the Flight Mode switch.

You'll want to master the use of each control stick so you can direct your drone to fly on the exact paths you want, smoothly, and without encountering other objects. As you'll learn, the drone's obstacle avoidance feature is good, but not perfect. I'll run you through some common, simple maneuvers later in this chapter.

- **Left stick: Forward/Back = Ascend/Descend.** All four motors increase or decrease speed equally as you push the stick forward or back, lifting your drone upward, or allowing it to reduce altitude, respectively. If you want the aircraft to rise or descend while maintaining the same horizontal viewing angle, be careful to orient the stick straight ahead or straight back. Even small motions in the diagonal direction can cause the drone to rotate slightly. With practice, you'll be able to do this smoothly.

- **Left stick: Side to Side = Panning/Yaw.** As I noted, DJI sometimes calls horizontal rotation through the top-to-bottom axis "pan," but "yaw" is the more common term. When you press the stick from side to side, motors in opposing corners rotate at different speeds, using the differential in torque to allow the drone to spin. Just move the left stick to the left to rotate counterclockwise, and to the right to rotate clockwise.

- **Right stick: Forward/Back.** Pressing the right stick toward the front of the controller moves the drone forward, relative to the front of the aircraft. Moving it toward the back of the controller sends the drone in the reverse direction. This movement results from the rear motors spinning faster or slower than those in front, causing the nose or rear of the drone to dip down while moving forward or backward (respectively).

- **Right stick: Side to Side = Move Left/Right.** Horizontal movement within the same plane (so to speak) is produced when the motors on one side both rotate faster than those on the other side. The aircraft "rolls" slightly as it slides in the direction of the lower side. Move the remote controller's right stick to the left or right to move your drone horizontally in those directions. Although some drones are capable of rolling completely over, yours is not. Trust me, that's a good thing.

Using the DJI Fly Control Screen

The heart of the Mini 3/Mini 3 Pro's flight options are accessible from a screen similar to the one shown in Figure 5.19.

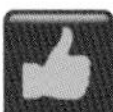

NOTE The screen displays of the Mini 3 and Mini 3 Pro sometimes are slightly different. Most of the screen shots in this book were taken while operating the Mini 3 Pro. If there are major differences between the two drones, I try to show an example of the Mini 3 screen as well. If the differences are minor, I may not include a supplementary figure, trusting that Mini 3 owners can easily find and use the counterpart functions on their drone.

Your options are:

- **Flight mode.** This indicator shows the current setting of the Cine/Tripod/Normal/Sport switch.

- **System Status bar.** This text screen displays several different status messages, such as Take Off Permitted, Flight Altitude Restricted, Take Off with Caution (no GPS), or, when aloft, In Flight. You should heed any warnings shown prior to takeoff.

- **Battery information.** This indicator displays the percentage of battery power remaining and an estimate of the available flight time, in minutes and seconds. The flight time display will show 00'00" until takeoff, and once shown will update during the flight. Tap the Battery Information icons to see additional time estimates, including Until RTH, Until Forced Landing, and Until Battery Depleted.

- **Video downlink signal strength.** Icons show the relative strength of the video downlink connection between the drone and the remote controller. Tap its icon to see a text readout, e.g., Strong RC Signal.

- **Vision Systems status.** Shows when the Vision Systems are active and available.

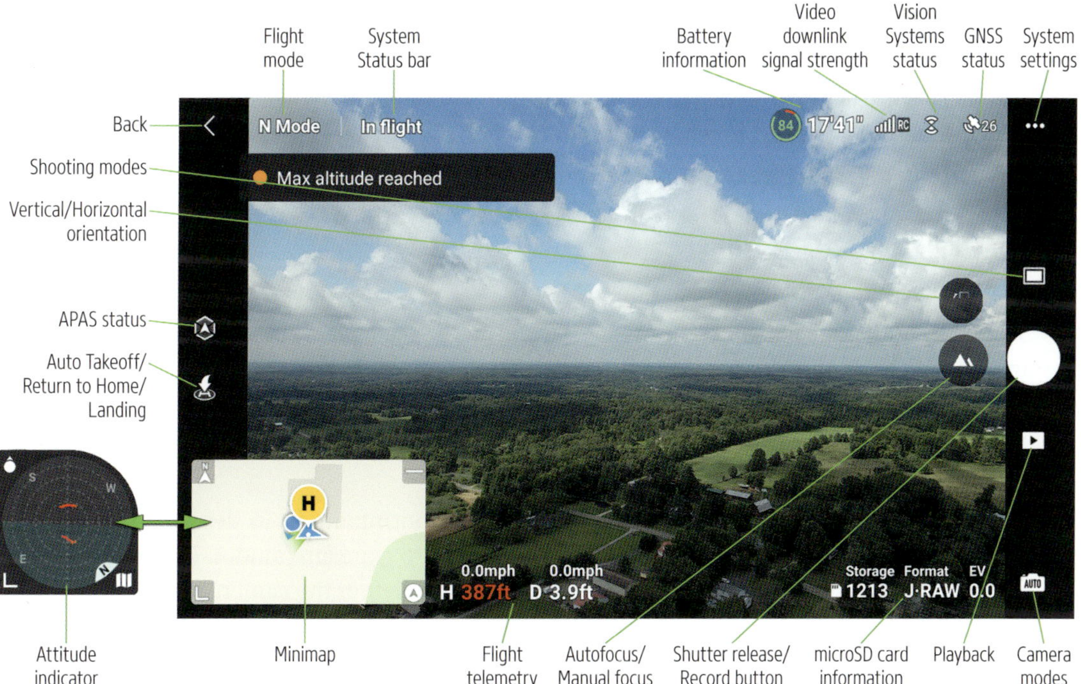

Figure 5.19 The DJI Fly screen when the drone is connected to the remote controller.

- **GNSS status.** Displays the current GNSS/GPS signal strength and the number of satellites linked. When the icon is white, the signal is strong, and the drone's Home Point can be updated. If satellite signals aren't strong, which may be the case in congested areas or buildings, or other obstructions block signals, you can wait a minute or two, then ascend to about 100 feet and hover until additional satellites are acquired. At that point, the Home Point data can be reset.

- **System settings.** Tap the three dots representing System Settings, and a tabbed menu with five headings appears: Safety, Control, Camera, Transmission, and About. (See Figure 5.20.) I'll explain all the options within these tabs in Chapter 7.

- **Autofocus/Manual focus.** Tap to switch between autofocus (AF label) mode and Manual focus ("mountain" icon).

- **Vertical/Horizontal orientation.** Rotates the gimbal camera 90 degrees to switch between vertical (Portrait) and horizontal (Landscape) shooting modes.

- **Shooting modes.** Tap this icon to produce a menu similar to the one shown in Figure 5.21, which allows you to select one of the available shooting modes (which will be explained in detail in Chapter 6):
  - **Photo:** Single, 48MP, Smart Photo, AEB, Burst, Timed Shot.
  - **Video:** Normal, Slow Motion.
  - **Master Shots (Mini 3 Pro only):** Master Shots operates automatically, although you can adjust the length of the sequence and choose one of the canned templates.
  - **Pano:** Sphere, 180 Degrees (Mini 3 Pro only), Wide Angle, Vertical.
  - **Quickshots:** Dronie, Circle, Helix, Rocket, Boomerang (Mini 3/Mini 3 Pro), Asteroid (Mini 3 Pro only).
  - **Hyperlapse:** Free, Circle, Course Lock, Waypoints.

- **Shutter release/Record button.** You can tap this button to take a photo or start/stop video recording. I tend to use the physical button located on the top-right edge of the controller, but the virtual button is here if you want it.

- **Playback.** Tap this button to activate Playback mode so you can review and export captured videos and still photos. (See Figure 5.22.)

- **Camera modes.** When you've selected Photo as your shooting mode, as described earlier, you can tap this camera icon to toggle between Auto and Pro exposure modes. In Auto mode, the current EV exposure adjustment will be displayed to the left of the camera icon. In Pro mode, the shutter speed, f/stop, ISO setting, and EV are displayed. You can tap that display to make adjustments for any of them, except for aperture, which is fixed at f/1.7 and shown for informational purposes only.

- **microSD card information.** Shows the remaining number of photos you can take in Photo mode, or the available movie recording time in video mode. Tap the icon to view the total capacity in gigabytes for storing internally or on any microSD card that has been inserted in the drone.

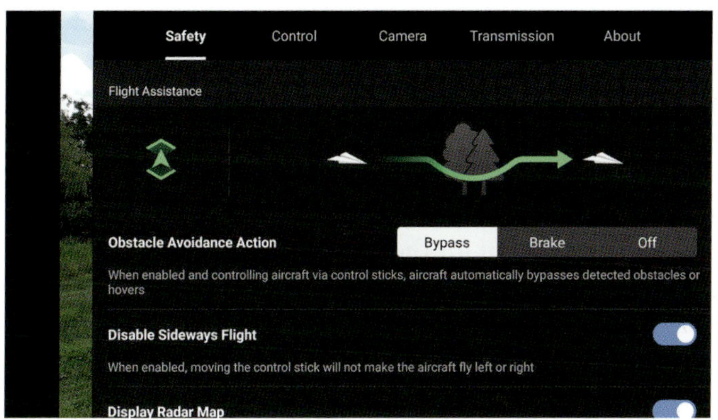

Figure 5.20 System Settings.

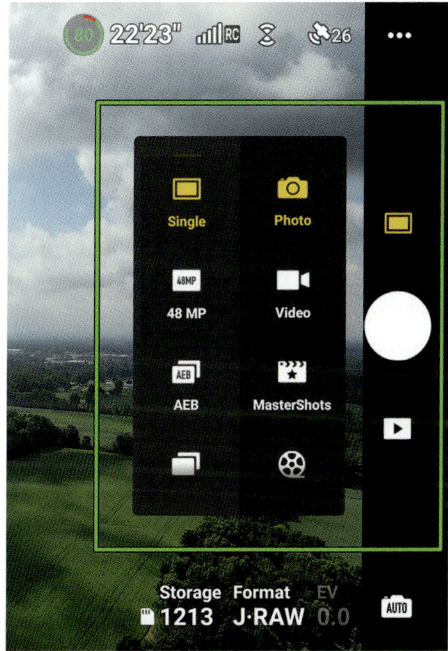

Figure 5.21 Shooting modes.

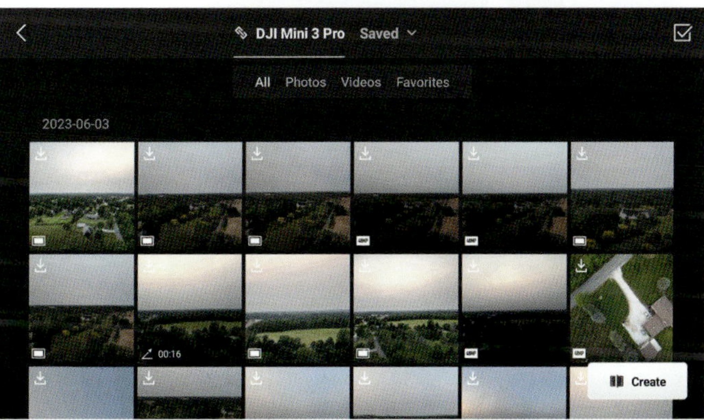

Figure 5.22 Playback mode.

- **Flight telemetry.** You'll be using this readout frequently while your drone is aloft, as it provides several key pieces of information.
  - **Height from the Home Point.** The indicator marked H shows the current altitude of your aircraft, helping you keep track of how high the drone is above your current surroundings. It's very useful if you want to shoot from the same altitude on different occasions. For example, when I am taking construction progress photos, I always launch from the same takeoff point, and then ascend to the altitudes used for the most recent shots, say, 100 feet, 200 feet, or some other elevation. **Note:** The readout will turn red when you've reached your maximum altitude, accompanying a voice reminder and the Max Altitude Reached text shown earlier in Figure 5.19.
  - **Distance from Home Point.** When your drone is directly overhead, this will display 0.0 feet, and change to reflect any horizontal movement away from that point. When returning to home, this indicator is a good way of knowing when the drone is directly above you again and descending.
  - **Horizontal/Vertical Speed.** The two numbers above the Height and Distance indicators show the speed of the aircraft.
- **Attitude indicator (Mini 3 Pro only).** You can cycle between this display and the minimap (described next), or view a full-screen version of the map. I'll show you how shortly. The Attitude (*not* Altitude) indicator is shown in Figure 5.23. It includes icons that show the position and orientation of the aircraft, the remote controller, and current Home Point, relative to the points of the compass shown along the icon's periphery, and the tilt angle of the drone. Before takeoff, they will all be clustered together; after takeoff they will separate and may be viewed on the minimap.

  You can tap the L symbol at lower left in the figure to collapse the Attitude indicator to a thumbnail icon, or the Map symbol at right to switch to the minimap.
- **Minimap.** The relative location of the drone, controller, and Home Point are seen on this small map that's inset in the lower-left corner of the screen when you are *not* using the Attitude indicator. The map is useful for keeping track of where the aircraft is located during its flight. I introduced you to this useful display earlier in Figure 5.9.

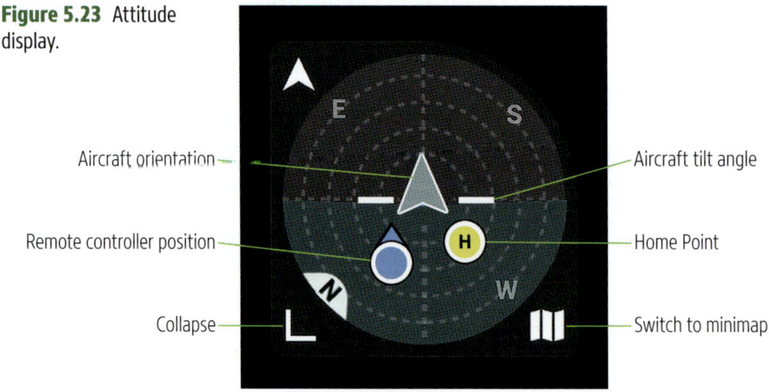

Figure 5.23 Attitude display.

- **Full-screen map.** If you want to see a full-screen version, tap the minimap and the map will expand, as shown at right in Figure 5.24. The aircraft's view is reduced to a small inset, as seen in the figure, so you can still monitor what the camera is seeing. The full-screen map has map layers.

- **Auto Takeoff/Return to Home/Landing.** This icon provides functions for takeoff, landing, and returning your drone to its Home Point. Tap the icon and when the function activation screen appears (the one for Takeoff is shown), press and hold your finger in the circle until the DJI Fly app responds. The drone will then takeoff, return to home, or land, as appropriate.

- **APAS status.** Shows the current APAS status (Mini 3 Pro only). The icon will be red if APAS is not functioning, or green if all is well.

- **Back.** Tap this button to back out of menu operations. The DJI RC Pro remote controller has a physical Back button you can use instead.

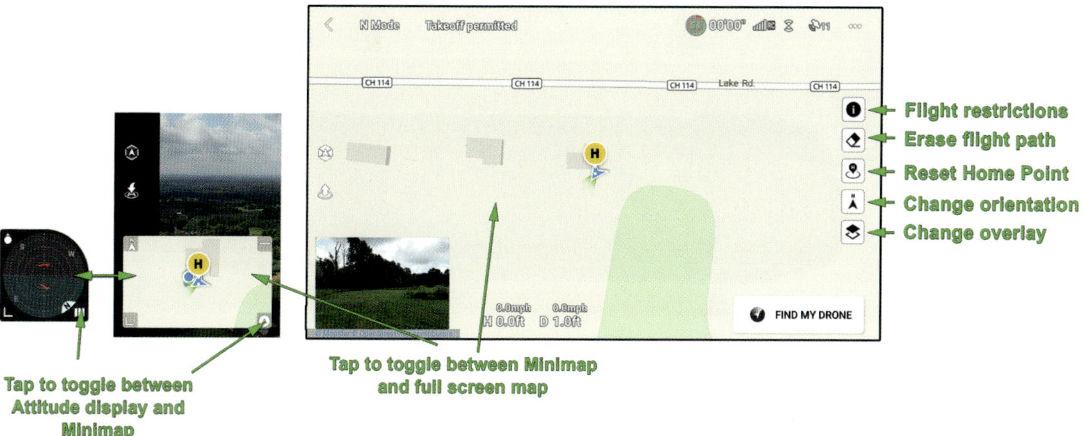

Figure 5.24 Cycling among the Attitude display, minimap, and full-screen map.

Capturing Still Photos and Movies

Once you are comfortable navigating your Mini 3/Mini 3 Pro in the air, it's time to begin taking images. Your aerial camera, despite its tiny size, is remarkably versatile and capable of impressive imagery. But for your first flight, you can use its automated features to capture stills and videos using just a few controls. Once you've reached a location with some interesting subject matter, just follow these steps to take your initial still photos and videos:

1. **Fly to your location.** You've learned how to ascend, descend, fly forward or back, and rotate your drone. Take off and maneuver your drone to the location where you want to take a photo, ascending or descending to the desired height, and rotating the aircraft in the required direction.

2. **Adjust viewing angle.** When the drone is in place, you'll want to adjust its viewing angle upward or downward to frame the subject you want to capture. Rotate the gimbal dial, located on the left side of the top edge of the controller to adjust the shooting angle. Figure 5.25 shows the position of the gimbal dial with the DJI RC-N1, DJI RC, and DJI RC Pro.

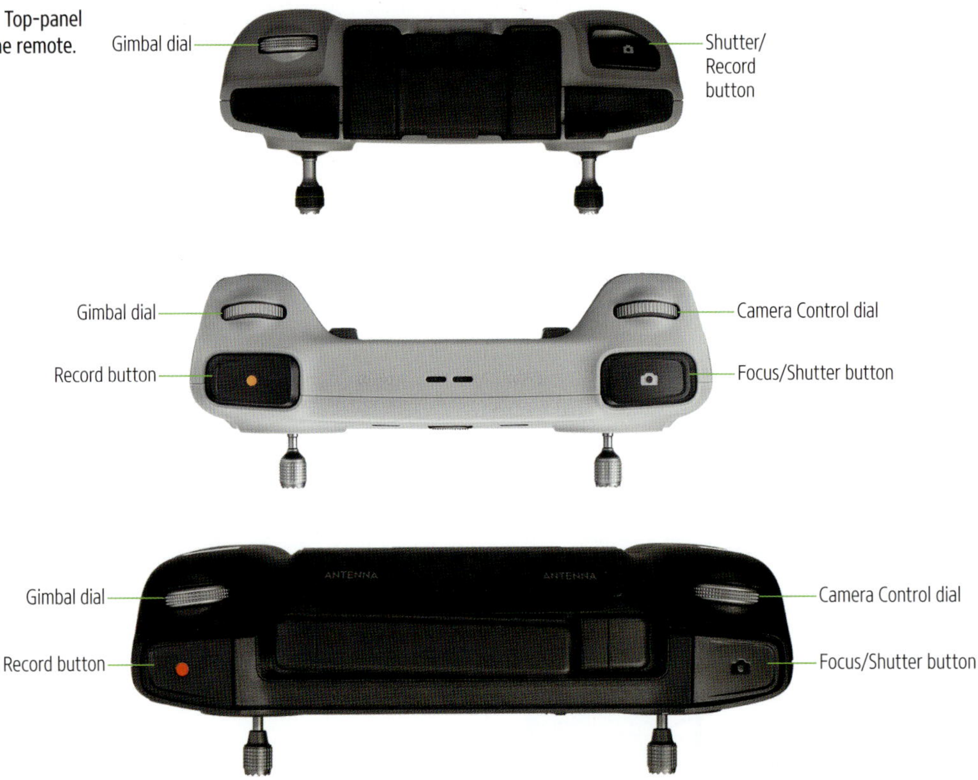

Figure 5.25 Top-panel controls on the remote.

You can also use camera view by pressing down on the screen until an adjustment bar appears. You can drag the bar up and down to control tilt of the camera with your finger. I'll explain more about how to use the gimbal shortly.

3. **Choose your shooting mode.** Tap the Shooting mode icon shown earlier in Figure 5.19. A menu will pop up like the one seen in Figure 5.26. The right-hand column displays the various shooting modes, including Photo, Video, MasterShots (Mini 3 Pro only), QuickShots, Hyperlapse, and Panorama. I'll explain each of these in more detail in Chapter 8.

4. **Select shot option.** The left-hand column will display the options for the type of shot you've chosen. The figure shows Photo options, which include Single, 48MP, Smart, AEB (auto exposure bracketing), Burst, and Timed Shot.

5. **Specify camera mode.** You can allow the drone to choose the appropriate exposure settings for you in Auto mode, or you can specify shutter speed, ISO sensitivity, and exposure compensation

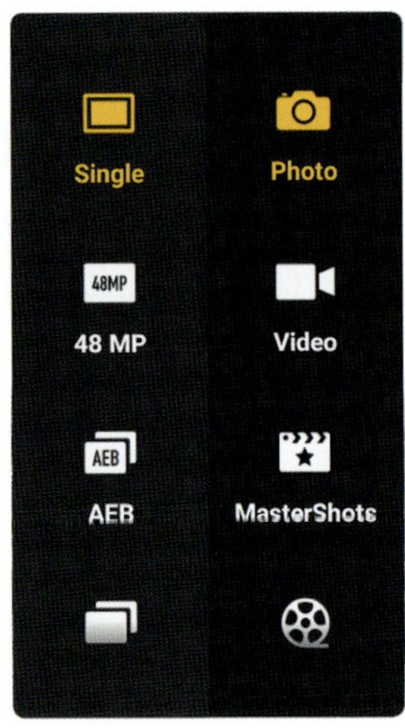

Figure 5.26 Shooting menu.

yourself in Pro mode. For your first stills or movies, I recommend sticking with Auto mode. Check out the Camera Mode icon in the lower-right corner of the screen (refer to Figure 5.19, if necessary, for its location) and, if necessary, tap it to switch from Pro mode to Auto mode. I'll explain Pro mode in detail in Chapter 6.

6. **Capture image/movie.** You can tap the shutter button icon on the screen, or press the relevant button on the top surface of the controller. With the RC-N1, that would be the Shutter/Record button seen in Figure 5.25. The RC and RC Pro controllers have separate Movie Record buttons on the left side for video, and Focus/Shutter buttons on the right side, also seen in Figure 5.25. Don't worry about focus; with the lens' wide-angle perspective and likely distance between the drone and its subject, virtually everything will be in focus. However, given the fixed f/1.7 aperture, depth-of-field may sometimes be insufficient for low-level panoramas or close-in views of subjects with distant backgrounds, and you'll need to manually focus.

7. **Hurry up and wait.** A progress indicator arc will cycle around the shutter button icon screen while the still image or movie is being captured. You are locked out of taking another picture until the process is finished and the icon turns green again.

Changing Viewing Angle with the Gimbal

The Mini 3/Mini 3 Pro drone's gimbal can move in three directions, and does so automatically when stabilizing an image, or to automatically provide a first-person view (FPV) during flight, as I'll describe shortly. The gimbal can also be adjusted electronically by you, as the pilot, to change the view of the aircraft's camera. Just tap the screen until the scales shown in Figure 5.27 appear. You can drag upward or horizontally with your finger to tilt or pan the gimbal's view. The gimbal has a specific range of movement limited by the drone's software (it is mechanically capable of an even greater range that isn't particularly useful).

Here is the adjustable range of movement:

- **Tilt.** The gimbal can be tilted from horizontal (with the camera looking straight ahead) downward 90 degrees (so the camera can display what is directly under the aircraft). The gimbal can be tilted upward by up to 60 degrees.

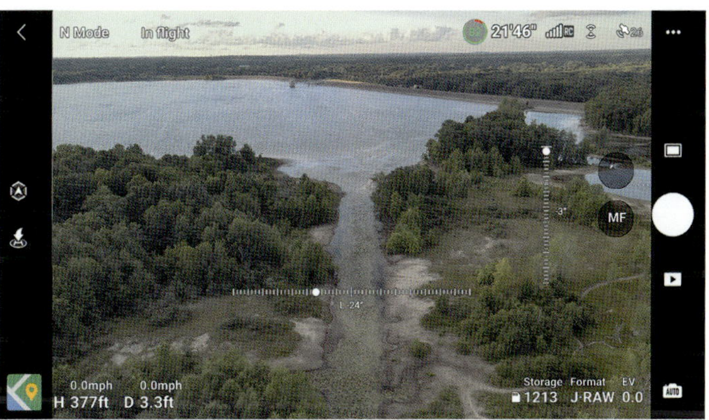

Figure 5.27 Drag up or horizontally to change the gimbal's view.

- **Yaw/Pan.** The drone uses this side-to-side rotation as it stabilizes the image in flight, or performs other functions, such as shooting a series of images from different angles to produce the frames stitched together to create a panorama. This movement is limited to plus or minus 80 degrees horizontally.

- **Roll.** The gimbal can roll independently of the aircraft during flight for image stabilization purposes, or to provide a first-person view. The gimbal will also roll to –90 degrees when you switch to Portrait mode for vertical shots, and back to 0 degrees when you switch to Landscape mode. You cannot adjust roll manually.

Adjusting the Gimbal

There are basic kinds of adjustments you can apply to the gimbal's operation. You can access these parameters by tapping the Settings icon, represented by three dots in the upper-right corner of the screen. The Settings screen has five tabs: Safety, Control, Camera, Transmission, and About. I'll describe the settings in each of them later in this book. For now, tap the Control tab to view the screen shown in Figure 5.28.

Here are your gimbal adjustments:

- **Gimbal mode.** The gimbal has two operational modes:
  - **Follow mode.** During flight, the gimbal adjusts so that the camera's view remains constant as the aircraft rolls slightly while moving. In effect, the horizon remains level while you are seeing the live view or capturing images/video, as seen at left in Figure 5.29. You'll be using this mode virtually all of the time.
  - **FPV mode.** The gimbal synchronizes the camera's view with the orientation of the camera, providing a first-person view. Your live view appears as if you were riding onboard the aircraft yourself. When the drone pivots while changing direction, your view changes to match. (See Figure 5.29, right.) This mode is used in drone racing with drones that are compatible with FPV goggles. At the time this was written, only the Mini 3 Pro officially supports FPV goggles.

Figure 5.28 Basic gimbal adjustments.

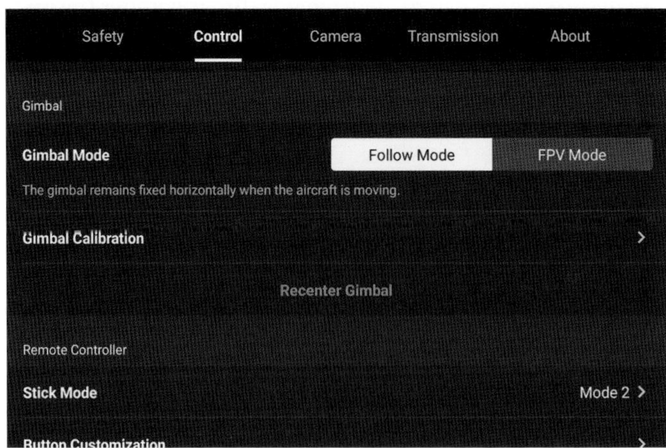

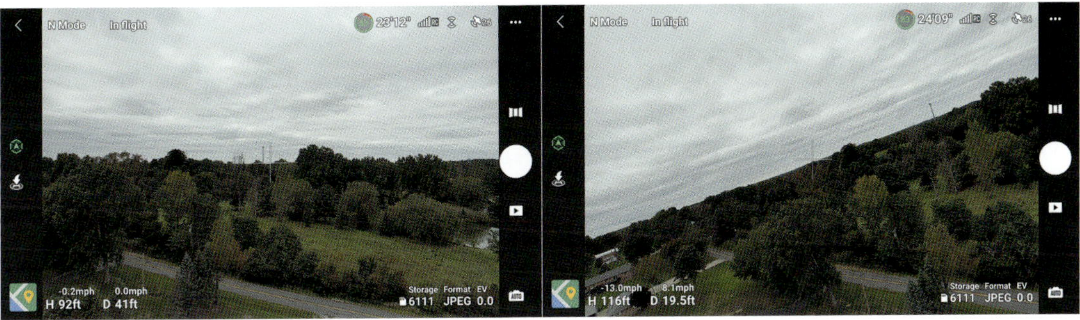

Figure 5.29 Follow mode view (left); First-person view (right).

- **Gimbal calibration.** From time to time, you may need to recalibrate your gimbal so that its orientation coincides with the orientation of the aircraft, i.e., when the drone is level, the gimbal should be level, too.
- **Recenter gimbal.** This command allows you to recenter the gimbal when needed. Just tap the Recenter Gimbal label shown earlier at the bottom of Figure 5.28. You can also recenter the gimbal by pressing a custom button. With the RC-N1 remote, press the Fn button twice. The C1 button on the RC and RC Pro remotes perform the same function.

As you might guess, the gimbal is a high-precision device and should be treated with respect. Here are some aspects to keep in mind:

- **Don't obstruct the gimbal's movement when the aircraft is powered up.** Be sure to remove the transparent gimbal protector before turning the drone on. When you set the drone on its launch site, make sure there are no objects (including grass or weeds) that would interfere with the gimbal as it orients itself on power up.
- **Use the gimbal protector between flights.** When power is off, it is okay to reorient the gimbal manually so it is centered when you put the protector on. Always keep the protector mounted between flights and when transporting your drone.
- **Protection mode.** If the gimbal is obstructed on its launch pad, it may go into protection mode, and you'll receive a message that the aircraft cannot take off. Turn the drone off and clear the obstruction before powering up again. Protection mode may be invoked if the aircraft is on uneven ground, or the gimbal experiences an external jolt.
- **Heavy clouds, fog, and moisture.** A wet gimbal may not operate, but should work fine when dried out. Dust or sand are also not a friend of your drone.
- **Collisions.** Any sort of collision or impact may damage the gimbal enough to require repair, or produce abnormal operation. DJI drones are fairly robust, however. One of my earliest flights with my Mini 3 resulted in a crash into the top branches of a maple tree, causing the drone to tumble down through the boughs to a rough landing on the ground. The aircraft has operated perfectly since then, with only a few grass stains to show for it. (Lesson learned: don't experiment with a QuickShot video at too low an altitude; side-to-side obstacle avoidance in that mode is not available.)
- **Recalibrate.** If recalibration of the gimbal is necessary, you'll be led step-by-step through the procedure, which isn't difficult.

Aerial Navigation

With a conventional piloted aircraft, a human being is onboard during flight and is able to visually monitor the surrounding airspace and use a variety of instruments to precisely determine the craft's location and altitude in order to navigate from one place to another. With a UAV like the Mini 3/Mini 3 Pro, the remote operator must depend even more heavily on technology to plot a course; the visual "window" on the nearby sky is limited to the drone camera's adjustable, but limited view.

Your primary tool for navigating will be GNSS, short for Global Navigation Satellite System, which, up until now, I have sometimes referred to as GPS. Most of us are already familiar with GPS; many use GPS systems in our cars, wrist fitness bands, and depend on them to Find My Phone when we want to know the current location of our devices.

In truth, GNSS is the correct broad term that encompasses the full range of global satellite-based positioning, navigation, and timing (PNT) systems. The familiar GPS (Global Positioning System) technology developed by the United States is just one particular type of GNSS service. Others include Galileo, a project of the European Union; BeiDou, offered by China; and GLONASS (Global Navigation Satellite System, owned by Russia). All four are worldwide services that use a constellation of satellites, and your Mini 3/Mini 3 Pro is able to take advantage of all of them except GLONASS.

A drone must have at least four of those satellites in view to triangulate (quadrangulate?) its position with the most accuracy. Using GPS alone, it can access 30 different satellites; add in BeiDou or Galileo and the number of visible satellites more than doubles, increasing both speed and accuracy. The ability to use three systems means that, when using its GNSS capabilities, your drone probably has a better idea of where it is than you do.

Unfortunately, GNSS isn't always available. Satellite signals can be blocked by tall buildings, dense forests, or tunnels, and it's not always available in some areas as the satellites in low-Earth orbits (GPS) or higher orbits (Galileo) progress around the globe. In addition, while GNSS can report where your aircraft is flying, it can't tell you anything about trees, power lines, tall buildings, or other hazards, nor provide feedback on the surface where you're planning to land. In such cases, the Mini 3/Mini 3 Pro's vision and infrared sensor technologies are invaluable.

Wind Resistance

Image stabilization is a marvelous thing. My decades of experience taking pictures with still cameras, both hand-held and on tripods, makes the ability of drones like the Mini 3/Mini 3 Pro to capture sharp images at shutter speeds that are measured in seconds, rather than fractions of seconds, truly miraculous. It's even more remarkable when you consider that your aircraft's gimbal is also called on to automatically swivel at high precision when it captures complex panorama images that are then stitched together seamlessly to provide ultra-wide-angle rectilinear or spherical views of your subject.

The drone performs this magic while compensating for the movement of air that is always present. That's true whether the aircraft is flying forward, backward, sideways, or in combination, or hovering while being affected (or even buffeted) by the prevailing winds that are a continuing factor. As a result, the drone's wind resistance, or ability to maintain a desired position against a blowing wind, is important.

A drone's wind resistance is affected by several factors:

- **Weight.** Heavier drones offer better inertia for improved stability in strong winds.
- **Size.** If a weight increase comes in a larger form factor, a larger drone will have more surface area to catch the wind.
- **Shape.** A drone with a sleek aerodynamic shape will have lower drag coefficients, allowing them to move through the air—or have air move past them—more readily.
- **Power.** A more powerful motor can produce sufficient speed to counter the effects of wind, but potentially at the cost of some size and weight, chiefly from the need for a larger, heavier battery.
- **Hardware/software design.** Your drone includes an inertial measurement unit (IMU) that combines gyroscopes and accelerometers to provide data that can be used to calculate the aircraft's position and velocity. Its GPS chip increases the accuracy of those measurements. These hardware components work with the drone's software to make real-time corrections for shifts in position caused by the wind.

Even with your drone's wind-resistance capabilities, you'll quickly discover that a drone nevertheless can become unstable in high winds. Unexpected updrafts near mountains or high buildings can produce undesired and unexpected gains in altitude. Dust carried by the wind can compromise your drone's object-avoidance sensors. Strong winds can do more than give you shaky images and increased battery drain. Winds can directly or indirectly damage your drone.

DJI is kind enough to tell you, approximately, what kind of wind will be beyond your drone's ability to compensate efficiently. A quick glance at the specifications for your drone will reveal it is rated to resist wind traveling at 10 to 10.7 meters/second, which equates to roughly 38 kilometers per hour or 24 miles per hour. Unfortunately, actual wind speeds mean very little to the average non-pilot until they reach the levels seen in weather broadcasts that feature hapless reporters who are shown drenched while dodging flying stop signs during a hurricane. When you're on site and ready to fly your drone, you might need a smartphone app to tell you just how much breeze to expect. The free version of Aloft Air Control tells you the current speed of the wind, the direction it's coming from, and the variability of gusts. I've been using UAV Forecast lately, which provides a much better picture of the winds at various altitudes.

Fortunately, there is a helpful specification used to describe wind-speed resistance of drones called the Beaufort scale, with levels ranging from 0 (complete calm) to 12 (hurricane). Drone wind resistance is expressed using these levels, with the Mini 3 and Mini 3 Pro both assigned Level 5, which equates to winds from 19 to 24 miles per hour. (I've found that more of my readers can relate to "miles per hour" than "kilometers per hour" or even the knots used to designate air and maritime speeds.) The higher the Level number, the better a drone can perform in strong winds. A drone that can withstand Level 5 winds is better than one that can only handle Level 4 velocities.

The Beaufort scale is valuable because you can use visual cues, like those I list in Table 5.1, to estimate approximately how fast the wind may be blowing at your current location. It is not an exact or objective scale; it was developed to replace totally subjective, not very useful evaluations like, "Wow, it's blowing really hard!" Devised in 1805, it was originally expressed using descriptions of how the sea appeared under various conditions. Land-based descriptors ultimately came into use, and slightly more precise measurements of actual wind speeds in miles/kilometers per hour and knots were eventually applied. Today, the scale is most often used in the United States for weather purposes when issuing small craft advisories (Force 6 or 7), gale warnings (Force 8 or 9), storm warnings (Force 10 or 11), and hurricane-force wind warnings (Force 12).

TABLE 5.1 Judging Wind Force

FORCE	SPEED	DESCRIPTION	VISUAL CLUES
0	<1 mph	Calm	Smoke rises vertically
1	1–3 mph	Light air	Rising smoke moves in wind direction
2	4–7 mph	Light breeze	Wind felt on face and moves leaves
3	8–12 mph	Gentle breeze	Leaves and twigs affected
4	13–18 mph	Moderate breeze	Dust lifted from dry ground
5	19–24 mph	Fresh breeze	Small trees moved
6	25–31 mph	Strong breeze	Large branches sway
7	32–38 mph	Near gale	Walking against wind meets resistance
8	39–46 mph	Gale	Small branches broken
9	47–54 mph	Severe gale	Shingles detached from rooftops
10	55–63 mph	Storm	Trees can be blown down
11	64–72 mph	Violent storm	Widespread wind damage
12	>73 mph	Hurricane	Entire structures destroyed

Manual Maneuvers

Although your Mini 3 and Mini 3 Pro have powerful automated flight modes, including QuickShots and (with the Mini 3 Pro) MasterShots, as you develop it's a good idea to become proficient with the most common manual maneuvers first. The following sections will introduce you to the basic exercises you'll need to master to form the foundation of your video skill set. For consistency, all these exercises begin with the drone located at the bottom of the figure used as an illustration. I'll prep you on other, more complex maneuvers, including dolly shots, elevator sequences, and others in Chapter 8.

Box: Simple and Nose Forward

This is a great maneuver to practice once you've mastered flying in straight lines forward, backward, and to either side. After you've reached the desired altitude, you can execute the box pattern using only the right control stick. Press it to the right to move to the first corner of the box, pause, then press forward to the second corner. Then press left to the upper-left corner. Pull the stick back toward you to move the aircraft back, and finish by moving to the right to your original position. (See Figure 5.30.)

Next, repeat the box pattern, rotating the drone so its nose is always moving in the direction of travel. The maneuver is done in much the same way as the simple box, except that at each corner you'll need to press the left control stick to the left to rotate the drone 90 degrees. (See Figure 5.31.) Practice this until you are able to execute the pattern smoothly. It takes some getting used to, because when the drone is returning to you, its left/right directions are reversed from your own.

Circle: Simple and Nose Forward

Now you're going to earn your wings! To execute a simple circle in the counterclockwise direction shown in Figure 5.32, you'll need to use the right stick pressed evenly in a diagonal direction toward the right and forward so that the drone moves in an arc from the initial 6 o'clock position to the 3 o'clock position, then diagonally to the left and forward to reach 12 o'clock, before switching to press the right stick diagonally left/down and finishing with diagonally right/down to finish at your initial position. Practice doing large circles, then switch to smaller ones to refine your technique.

Keeping the nose of your drone facing in the direction of travel requires coordinating movement of the left stick left and right (to rotate; be sure to avoid any forward/backward motion, which changes the altitude) and the right diagonally stick forward/backward and left/right (to move around the

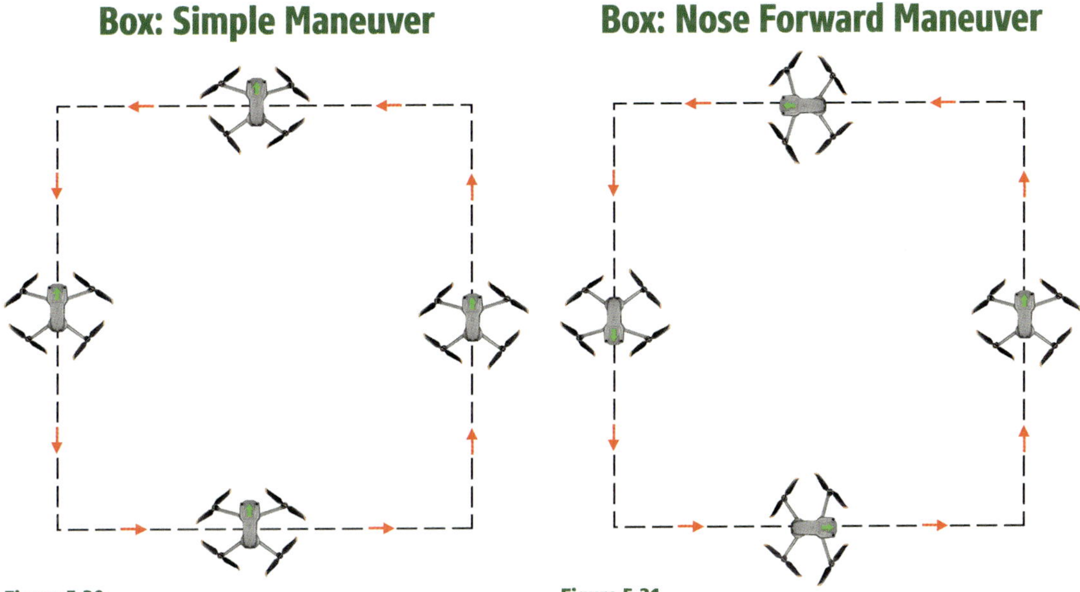

Figure 5.30   **Figure 5.31**

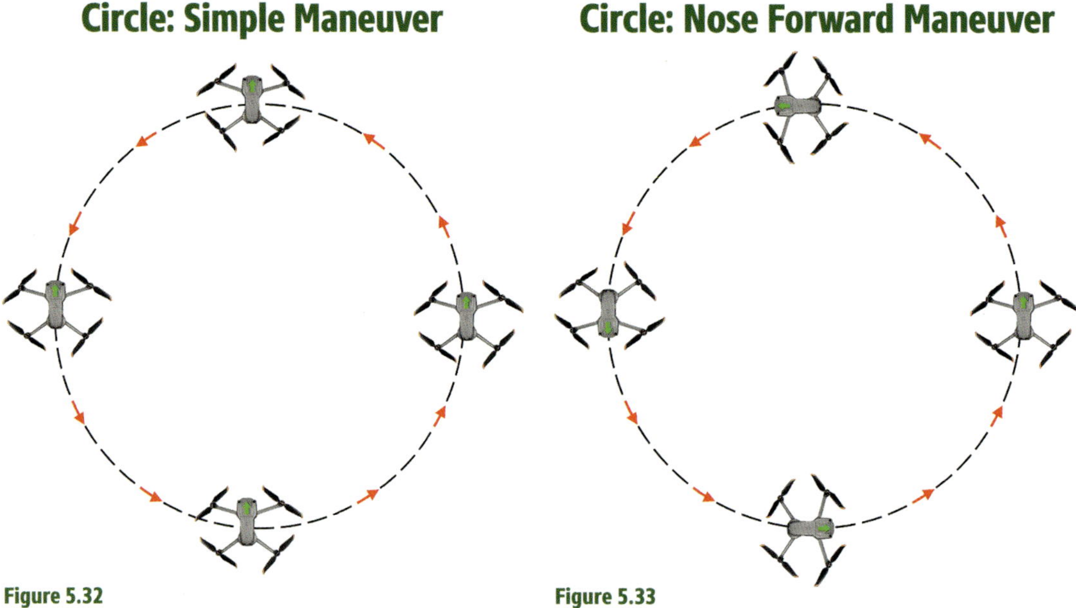

Figure 5.32   **Figure 5.33**

circle in a counterclockwise direction). (See Figure 5.33.) Once you've mastered both types of circles, you can try the same maneuvers going clockwise. Take your time. Moving both control sticks simultaneously takes some practice.

Figure 8: Simple and Nose Forward

There is method to all this madness! Once you've practiced your clockwise and counterclockwise circles, you'll be ready to demonstrate your mastery by combining them to create a figure-8 pattern. The key is to fly in two s-shaped arcs. A simple figure 8 can be accomplished by flying the first right-hand half circle as you did for the circle pattern above, then, when halfway, reversing your movements to create a left-facing half circle over the top to finish off an "s." Then, continue changing direction to create a reverse "s." (See Figure 5.34.)

Once you're comfortable doing a simple figure 8, you can work on mastering a more useful nose-forward figure 8. Once you can perform this maneuver smoothly and repeatedly, you can consider yourself competent in basic drone patterns. (See Figure 5.35.)

Orbit

Flying in an orbit pattern is much like completing a circle, except that the goal is to keep the nose facing toward the center, which will presumably be the subject of your video clip. The drone can perform this maneuver for you automatically, using the Orbit QuickShot, but it's useful to be able to perform it manually, as you can then make some creative choices about the aircraft's position during the flight.

Figure 8: Simple Maneuver

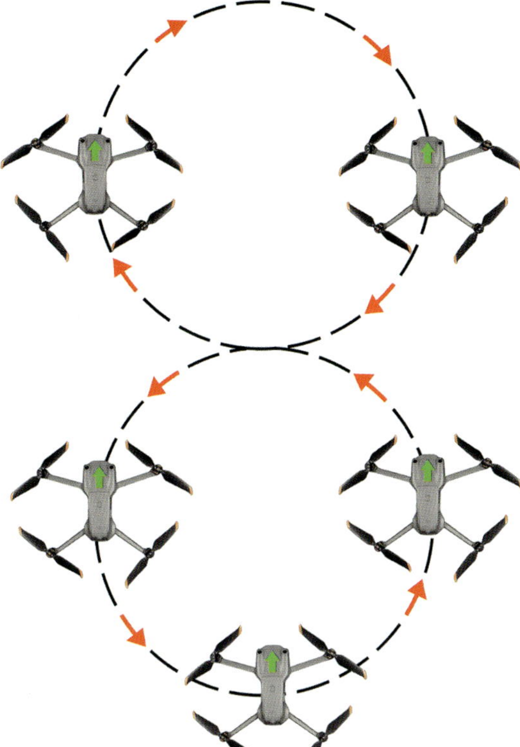

Figure 5.34

Figure 8: Nose Forward Maneuver

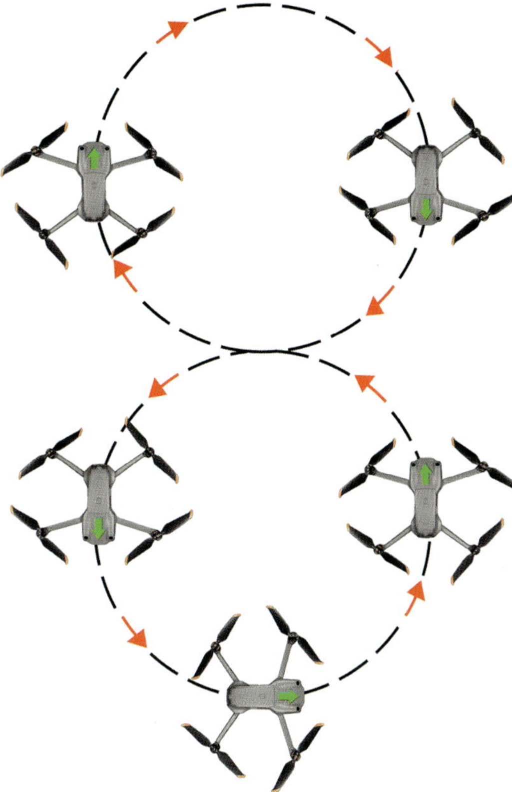

Figure 5.35

The object is to move around the circle smoothly and consistently, while keeping the subject in the center of the frame. You'll be working with the right stick to move the drone away from you and to first your right and then left (to reach the 12 o'clock position), and follow through bringing it back toward you while flying to the left and then to the right to return to the original position. The tricky part is pressing the left stick smoothly to the left to keep the drone rotating counterclockwise and facing the center. This is for a counterclockwise orbit; reverse the directions to fly the clockwise version. (See Figure 5.36.)

Orbit Maneuver

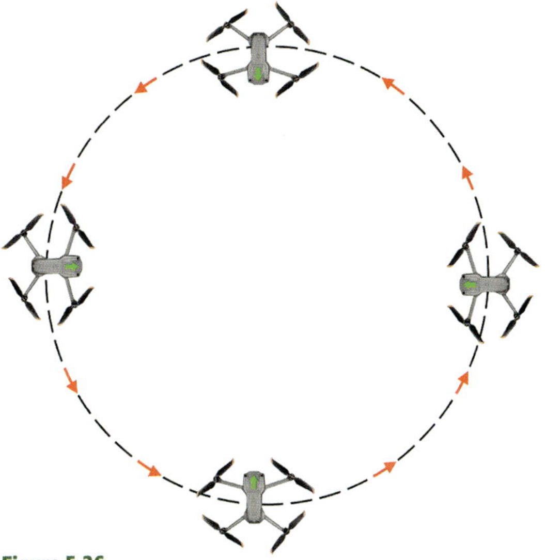

Figure 5.36

Bringing It All Back Home

Once you've successfully captured your first photos and/or videos, the final milestone will be to retrieve your drone, bringing it back from its maiden flight to a safe landing at its original location ("Home") or another spot of your choosing. It's actually quite easy to bring your aircraft back to you manually, and when I was first starting out, I liked to perform at least some of the final steps myself. I quickly learned to trust my aircraft's smarts and use the automatic Return to Home (RTH) feature most of the time. In this section, I'm going to show you how to avoid obstacles and achieve a smooth, safe landing, even under less-than-perfect conditions.

You'll be landing your drone when you reach one of several potential stages of your flight:

- **Mission complete.** You've accomplished the goals you set when the flight began, whether it was to test a particular feature, give yourself additional experience with your drone, or complete your aerial survey or photographic mission.

- **Environmental changes.** I often find myself performing an informal "abort" when unexpected weather appears, sometimes in the form of strong winds or rain. Smoky conditions can be found in park areas where fires occur, or controlled burns are staged. The latter are intentional fires used to remove dead or invasive plantlife, reduce insect populations, or even to prevent destructive wildfires.

- **Depleted battery.** Even if there are other aerial tasks you want to complete, it's prudent to land for a replacement battery when your current Intelligent Flight battery doesn't have enough juice remaining to finish your mission. I start thinking about returning when the DJI Fly indicators show five minutes or less flight time available.

- **Urgencies/Emergencies.** An unexpected Temporary Flight Restriction (TFR) in your area calls for immediate movement to a different area, or, more likely, just bringing your drone home. A nearby civil emergency requiring first responders may require retrieving recreational drones from the surrounding area.

- **Equipment malfunctions.** Losing a radio link to your drone won't happen frequently, but if you do experience communication problems or other equipment malfunctions, it's a good idea to land your drone and find out exactly what the problem is. Fortunately, your aircraft has built-in features that allow it to backtrack and/or land autonomously if you experience controller problems.

You can always retrieve and land your drone manually, directing the aircraft to fly from its current location to your position using the flight controls and the DJI Fly app's map feature to view icons representing the drone, its recent flight path, the Home Point, and the location of the controller (and yourself). Once the drone is directly overhead, you can use the gimbal dial to point the camera straight down, and monitor your descent visually until the aircraft is a dozen or so feet off the ground. You can then carefully descend to a safe landing in an area clear of obstacles and debris.

However, most of the time, the Mini 3/Mini 3 Pro's automatic Return to Home features will perform any or all of the necessary steps for you. The next sections will show you how to use your drone's three varieties of Return to Home: Smart RTH, Low-Battery RTH, and Failsafe RTH.

No Place Like Home

The automatic RTH modes bring the aircraft back to the last registered Home Point that was recorded by the geopositioning system, which includes the GNSS satellite signal and the drone's compass. By default, the Home Point is registered as the first location where the drone received an acceptable GNSS signal, which is indicated by the white "satellite" icon seen at upper right in Figure 5.37. The number of satellites available (in this case 26) are shown to the right of the icon. When the icon is red, as seen at lower right, the Home Point cannot be recorded.

During flight, the Home Point and your flight path so far can be viewed by tapping on the minimap to produce the full-screen map shown in Figure 5.38. The camera view will be reduced to a smaller thumbnail in the lower-left corner. With the full map you can view the location of the drone itself,

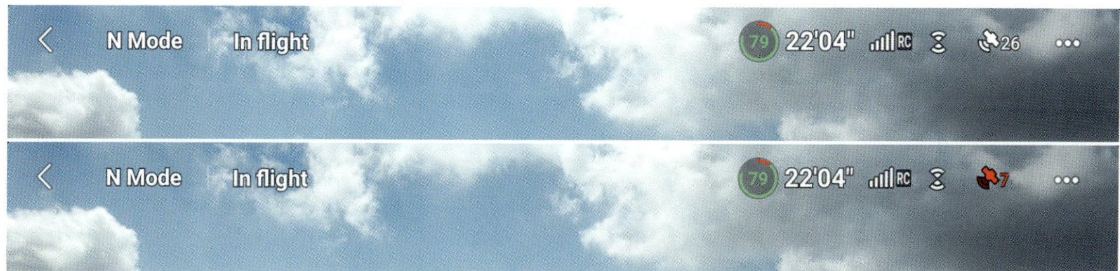

Figure 5.37 Automatic Return to Home is available when GNSS satellite signals are strong (top), but not when too few (or none) are linked to your drone (bottom).

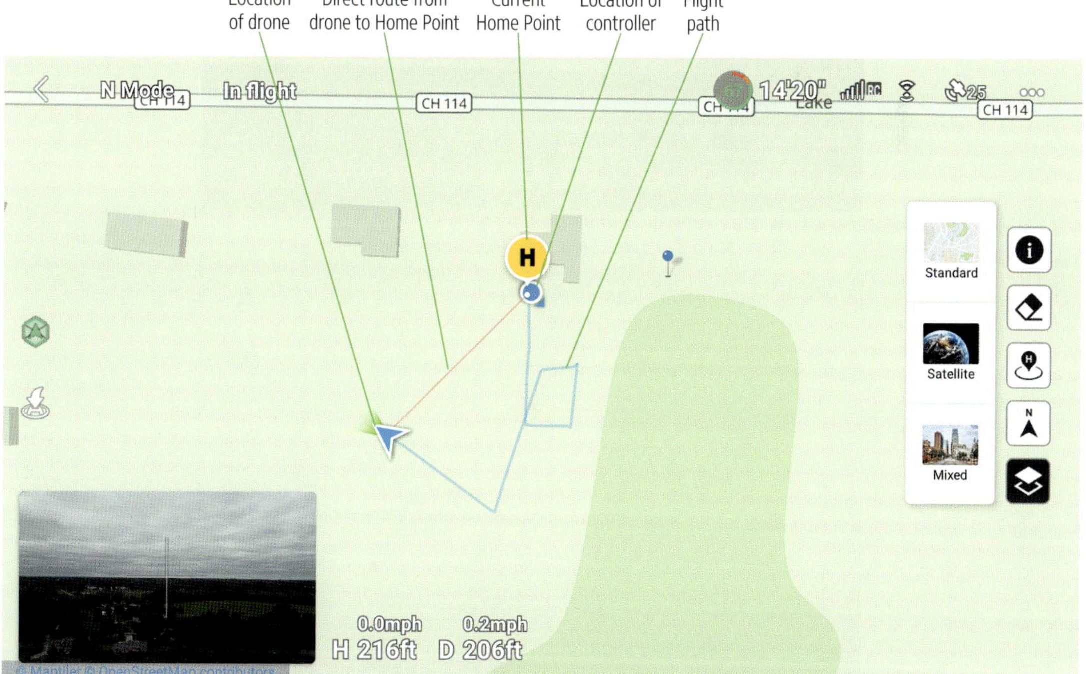

Figure 5.38 A full-screen map appears when you tap on the minimap.

the controller, current Home Point, and flight path information. Although the basic view is in map mode, you can change to a satellite view or combined map/satellite representation.

The Home Point can be set in several ways:

- **Automatically at takeoff.** When you use the automatic takeoff feature described earlier, the drone will ascend and record its location as the RTH position.
- **Using the map.** If you tap the minimap to enlarge it to full screen, you can tap the Home Point icon at right to reset it to the current drone location. Keep in mind that the new Home Point may *not* be located above a safe landing point, so you may have to perform the actual landing manually.
- **Safety menu.** Tap the Systems Settings trio of dots at the upper-right corner of the screen, then choose the Safety tab. Scroll down to Update Home Point, as shown in Figure 5.39, and access the setting screen seen in Figure 5.40. You can drag the Home Point to a new location. You might do this if you were yourself moving around and preferred to have the drone return to the position where you are currently, rather than your original spot. As noted, the new Home Point may not be above a safe landing point.

Figure 5.39 Resetting the Home Point in the Safety menu.

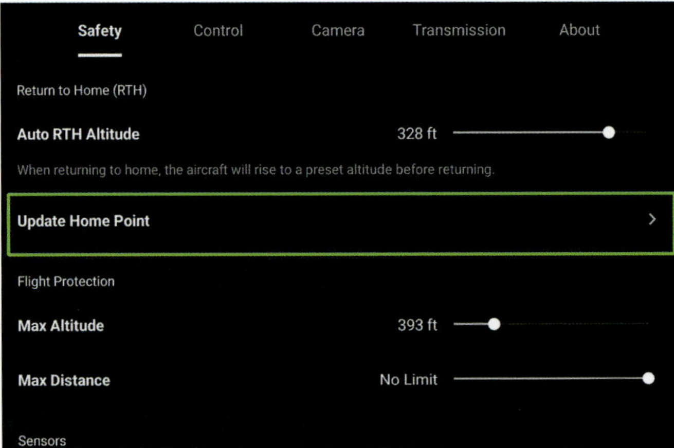

Figure 5.40 Drag the Home Point to a new location.

There are three additional related settings (also shown in Figure 5.39) you should update or check while browsing through the Safety tab:

- **Auto RTH Altitude.** This is an important safety feature. It tells the drone to ascend to a specified height *before* beginning the Return to Home sequence. That's because RTH does not retrace the drone's original flight path, which avoided any obstacles such as trees or structures. So, if the drone simply moves horizontally to a position above the original launching site, it may encounter intervening hazards. It's smarter to tell the aircraft to ascend to a known safe altitude before it begins returning.

  Of course, setting an altitude that is needlessly high will deplete the drone's battery more quickly. You can set the Auto RTH altitude to provide the safety margin you feel comfortable with, and can even adjust it before every flight if you want to. I generally set the preset altitude to about 250 feet, which is much higher than the forest canopies where I shoot (only giant redwoods and sequoias are taller).

- **Maximum Altitude.** You may want to limit how high your drone flies, as it can be difficult to maintain a visual line of site at the highest altitudes. In any case, your drone isn't permitted to fly higher than 400 feet above ground level, so you should set your maximum altitude below that.

- **Maximum Distance.** Again, your ability to keep your drone within your line of sight limits the horizontal distance you can cover. While it's likely that your remote controller can maintain contact with the aircraft for distances far beyond those you will encounter, the extra range is simply to ensure that you will be able to control the drone even if the signal is weak. You can specify a maximum distance or rely on your common sense to avoid sending your drone too far astray.

Smart RTH

If the GNSS signal is strong enough, you can use Smart RTH to return to the Home Point automatically. Just tap the RTH icon at left in the DJI Fly app, or press the RTH button on the remote control until you hear a beep. Then, the aircraft will begin its return using either Straight-Line RTH or Power-Saving RTH.

The Straight-Line procedure results in the drone flying horizontally until it is directly above the Home Point, then descending vertically to the Home Point, landing, and powering the motors down.

- **Home Point: Close.** If the drone is less than 5 meters/16 feet from the Home Point, the drone lands immediately, and the motors stop.

- **Home Point: Intermediate.** If the drone is 5 to 50 meters/16 to 164 feet away from the Home Point (Mini 3 Pro), the drone flies to the Home Point at its current altitude, lands, and the motors stop. If the current altitude is less than 2 meters/6.6 feet, the drone will ascend to 2 meters/6.6 feet and fly back to the Home Point.

- **Home Point: Distant.** If the drone is *further* than 50 meters/164 feet (Mini 3 Pro), the drone ascends to Auto RTH Altitude. If its current height is *higher* than Auto RTH Altitude, it remains at that altitude. In either case, the aircraft flies to the Home Point, lands, and the motors stop.

As long as the drone is more than 16 feet from the Home Point when RTH is initiated, you'll be given a choice of landing options.

Low-Battery RTH

Aerial daredevils (you know who you are) who tend to test the limits of their drones may accidentally (or intentionally) extend their flights to the point that the amount of battery power needed to safely return to home may be questionable. Fortunately, your Mini 3/Mini 3 Pro will intervene at an appropriate time and automatically initiate the Low-Battery RTH procedure. You'll receive a warning like the one shown in Figure 5.41.

If you don't respond to the warning within 10 seconds, the drone will automatically begin to return to the Home Point. However, if there isn't enough juice to return to the Home Point, the aircraft will land immediately from its current position. You cannot cancel this automatic landing, but you can use the remote controller to adjust the path of the drone during its forced landing.

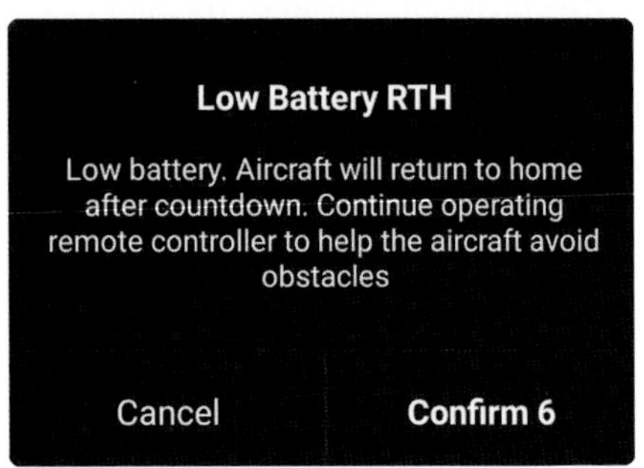

Figure 5.41 Low-Battery RTH will be triggered automatically when your Intelligent Flight battery is nearly depleted.

However, you can completely cancel a non-forced automatic return using the RTH/Flight Pause button. Just be aware that if you continue to fly the aircraft may not be able to land safely and will crash. Under most circumstances, you should allow the Low-Battery RTH feature to do its job.

Failsafe RTH

In general, you'll find the range of your DJI remote controller will be sufficient to maintain contact with your drone even if you wander beyond typical visual line-of-sight limits. Even so, adventurous fliers may lose contact with their drone from time to time, and signals can be lost from interference, especially if tall buildings or other structures intervene. I can say from experience that nothing causes panic quicker than losing control of your favorite aerial photography platform.

Fortunately, DJI has you covered. If the Home Point was successfully registered and your drone's compass is functioning properly, should the aircraft lose the remote controller signal for more than 11 seconds this Failsafe RTH will be triggered automatically. The procedure has multiple safeguards that integrate to land your drone as safely as possible.

First, the drone will retreat along its previous flight path for up to 164 feet and then enter the Straight Line RTH procedure as described above. The aircraft may regain radio contact as it does so. The return will proceed in one of three ways:

- **Home Point: Close.** If the drone is less than 50 meters/164 feet away, the drone flies back to the Home Point at the current altitude, lands, and the motors stop.

- **Home Point: Distant at lower altitude.** If the drone is *further than* 50 meters/164 feet, *and* the current altitude is *lower* than the preset Auto RTH Altitude, it will ascend to the specified height, fly to the Home Point, land, and the motors stop.
- **Home Point: Distant at higher altitude.** If the drone is *further than* 50 meters/164 feet, *and* the current altitude is *higher* than the preset RTH altitude you specified, the drone flies to the Home Point at its current altitude, lands, and the motors stop.

Managing Return to Home

Because the Return to Home procedures are automated, your drone takes control of certain functions, giving you limited override capabilities. Pausing or canceling the process, or making some adjustments to the flight may be your only options. If the drone enters a restricted GEO Zone during the return, it may descend until it exits that zone and then resume flight to the Home Point, or it may hover in place awaiting instructions from you.

Keep in mind that the aircraft will be unable to return to the Home Point if the GNSS signal is unavailable or weak. Should satellite contact be lost after RTH is initiated, the drone will hover in place for a period of time, giving you a chance to resume control, and then descend and land if you do not. Safe return may be affected by high wind speeds, too.

During an automated return, you cannot adjust the orientation of the aircraft or direction of flight. You can, however, use the remote controller to change the speed and altitude of the aircraft. If you need more control, say, because you want to perform the landing yourself, cancel the RTH by tapping the X icon on the screen. When RTH is initiated, you'll be offered choices of how to proceed (see Figure 5.42, top). If the drone detects an obstacle underneath it that makes the site unsuitable for landing, a warning to assume control will appear. (See Figure 5.42, bottom.) I'll describe landing protection in more detail shortly.

One trick to keep in mind is that you can *change* the Home Point, *even while the RTH procedure is underway.* Perhaps you forgot how far you've moved since your drone originally was sent aloft and realize you want to retrieve it at your new location. Just visit the Safety menu tab, as described earlier, and specify the new, more appropriate Home Point.

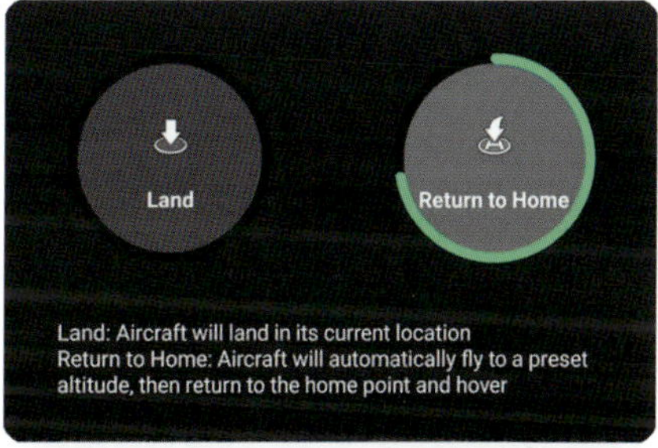

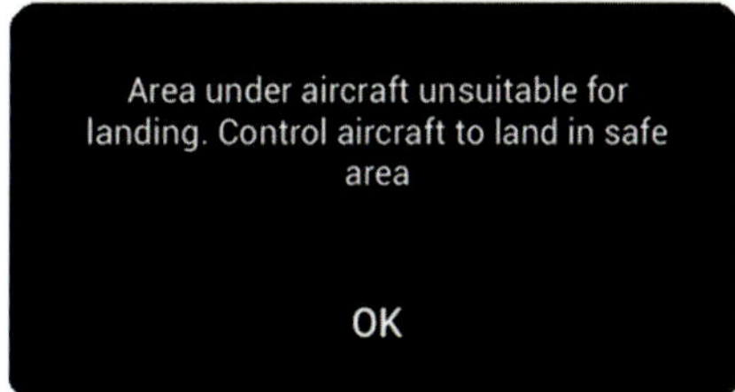

Figure 5.42 Landing options.

Obstacle Avoidance during RTH

As you might hope, your Mini 3 Pro (but not the Mini 3) uses its obstacle-avoidance capabilities to bypass hazards that it encounters during the Return to Home process, right up to, and including, landing. Here are some considerations to keep in mind:

- **Obstacles: Front/Rear.** The aircraft will brake to avoid a collision, and then reverse direction to a safe distance. If the drone was ascending when the obstacle was detected, it will then continue to ascend. If the drone was flying horizontally, it will ascend an additional 16 feet and then resume its former direction.
- **Obstacles: Below.** If a hazard is detected below the drone while descending, it will not proceed.
- **Obstacles: Side/Above.** Hazards located at either side of the drone or above it cannot be detected or avoided. You'll want to monitor the return to watch for these obstacles.

Landing Protection will be activated during Smart RTH, Low-Battery RTH, and Failsafe RTH. The drone's visual systems are disabled during the actual landing, so you should monitor the process yourself. During automated RTH, the following procedures are used:

- **Monitor Terrain.** The drone will monitor the terrain below and attempt to land only on a suitable surface. If the landing spot is not appropriate, the warning shown earlier in Figure 5.42 appears, giving you the opportunity to take over control.
- **Smart RTH.** The aircraft will carefully land. If Landing Protection is *not* available, a landing prompt will appear when the aircraft is within 20 inches of the ground. Pull down the left stick or tap the Auto Landing slider on the screen to land.
- **Low-Battery RTH/Failsafe RTH.** The drone will hover at about 6.5 feet and wait for you to confirm that it's safe to land by pulling down the left stick for one second or tapping the Auto Landing slider.

Transferring Photos and Movies

Unlike the casual snapshooter who ends up with April showers, May flowers, summer vacation photos, Thanksgiving dinner, and New Years' Eve celebrations—or maybe several years' worth of each—residing on their digital camera's memory card, as an enthusiast you're going to want to put your best aerial shots to good use. So transferring them from your drone to your computer or smartphone will be a must.

Fortunately, retrieving your drone's images and video clips is easy. However, there's one sticky point to be aware of. At the time I write this (and I hope DJI has a fix in the near future), it's not possible to apply a continuous numbering system that spans multiple cards or sessions, as you can with virtually every conventional digital camera. When you replace or format a card, your drone will start numbering over again at DJI_0001. So, you may need to copy each set of similarly numbered files into a separate folder to avoid duplicate numbering (at best), or overwriting existing files (at worst). Some image file transfer programs, such as Adobe Photoshop Elements Organizer, allow you to rename files as they are copied to your computer. (See Figure 5.43.) You can then use the day's date or another identifier to give each file a unique name.

When it comes to transferring files without a special transfer program, you have three alternatives available:

- **USB connection.** Plug a suitable USB Type-C cable into your drone's USB port, connect the other end to your computer, and the drone's internal storage and memory card (if installed) will appear on your desktop as another storage drive. You can drag and drop from your aircraft directly onto a folder on your computer.
- **Card reader.** If you've elected to store your stuff on a removable memory card you can simply remove the card and insert it into a compatible microSDXC card reader to copy onto your device.

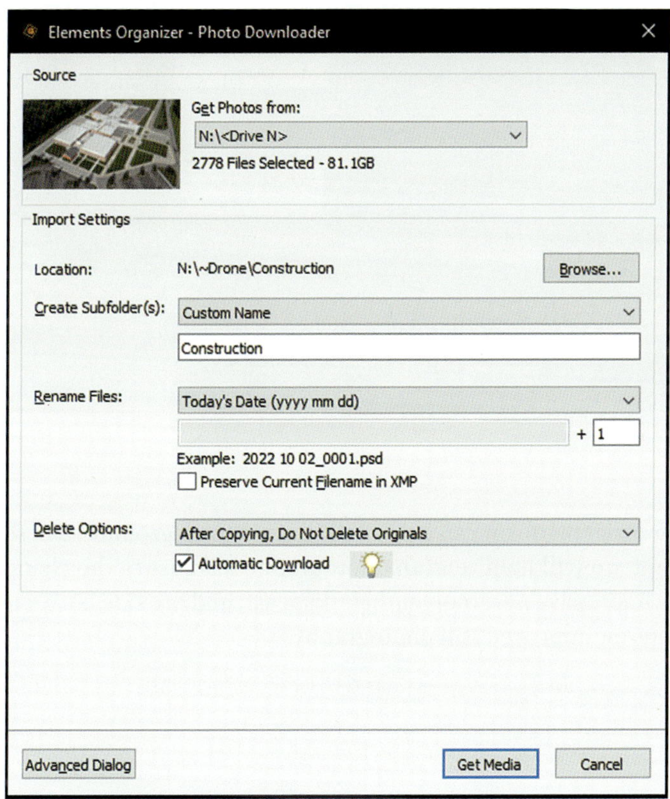

Figure 5.43 An image transfer program can rename files for you, avoiding duplicate names.

- **Direct upload to your smartphone or tablet.** You can direct the drone to upload a low-resolution version of your captures to your smartphone. I use this a lot, especially when I am working with the RC-N1 controller, which uses my iPhone as its screen. I can then share my work directly from my iPhone.

Within the DJI Fly app, tap on the System Settings trio of dots and navigate to the Camera tab. At the very bottom, you'll see a Cache When Recording switch, and a Max Video Cache Capacity entry below it. (See Figure 5.44.) Flip the switch on and choose the amount of storage you want to devote to this file cache. The DJI Fly app will transfer a low-resolution version of your files to your phone. The transfer is relatively slow—especially for video—and your drone and device must both be powered up and depleting their batteries, and the memory consumed by your cache can't be used for anything else.

You don't need to set a large cache size; when the available space is used up, older files will be deleted automatically to make room.

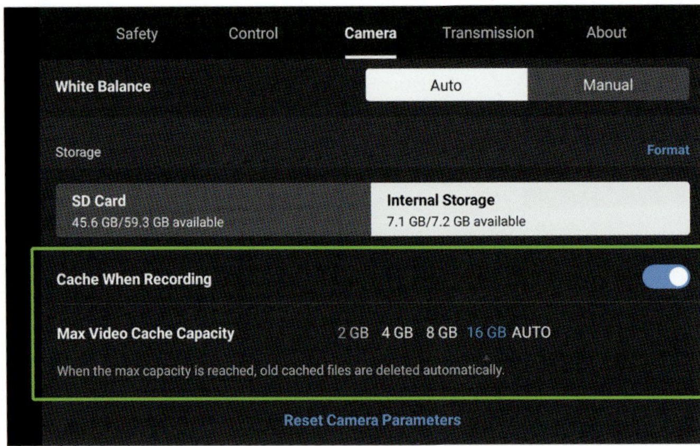

Figure 5.44 Your drone can create a cache backup of your files on your smart device.

Next Up

Photography from an aerial platform can be quite different from ground-level shooting with a traditional camera. Chapter 6 will help veteran photographers adjust to the changes, show budding photo enthusiasts the impressive new tools at their disposal, and provide both with a broad range of equipment-specific tips for improved still photography.

Mastering Still Photography | 6

Although much of this book is devoted to showing you how to use your drone's automated tools to take still photos and capture video with only minimal intervention, I'm going to devote a great deal of space to techniques for using your drone as a mobile camera, applying traditional photographic concepts to capture your creative vision. This chapter and the next will help you master your drone's Auto and Pro modes, so you can apply a full range of techniques to your photography. I'm going to include some photography basics for those who were avid pilots before they became aerial photographers. Those of you already well-versed in photography will also discover some things in this refresher that you might not have thought about from an aerial perspective.

I'm going to start out with the basics of exposure, DJI Mini style. Serious photographers will find that the typical Auto mode exposure settings—as determined by the camera's exposure meter and intelligence—need to be *adjusted* to account for your creative decisions or to fine-tune the image for special situations. For example, many times your main light source—usually the sun—may be within the frame or, at least behind the subject, whether it's a structure, trees, or something else. As a result, you'll end up with *backlighting*, which often results in an overexposed sky or other background and/or an underexposed subject. The drone's electronics recognize backlit situations nicely, and can properly base exposure on the main subject, producing a decent photo.

But what if you *want* to underexpose the subject, to produce a silhouette effect, as seen in Figure 6.1? You can use the Mini 3/Mini 3 Pro's EV adjustment to apply exposure compensation to override its

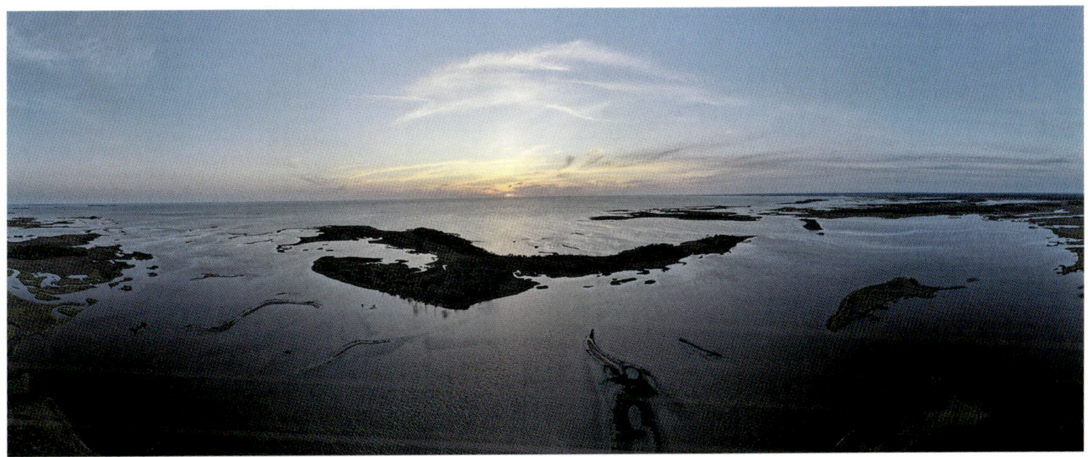

Figure 6.1 You may need to make exposure adjustments to get the silhouette or other effect you are looking for.

Auto exposure setting to get the look you want. The more you know about how to use your drone's camera, the more you'll run into situations where you want to creatively tweak the exposure to provide a different look than you'd get with a straight shot.

Your Basic Controls

In addition to the flight controls I've already described in the earlier chapters of this book (and the additional flight parameters I'll be discussing later on), your Mini 3/Mini 3 Pro has a certain number of capabilities that deal directly with still photography and video capture. They range from your file-format choices and storage options to autofocus/manual focus.

This chapter shows you the fundamentals of using the settings available with your Mini 3/Mini 3 Pro, so you'll be better equipped to override the defaults when you want to or need to. After all, correct exposure is one of the foundations of good photography, along with accurate focus and sharpness, appropriate color balance, freedom from unwanted noise and excessive contrast, as well as pleasing composition.

I'll be helping you with all of these. You have a great deal of control over each of them, although composition is entirely up to you. You must still frame the photograph to create an interesting arrangement of subject matter, but all the other parameters are basic functions of the camera. You can let your camera set them for you automatically, you can fine-tune how it applies its automatic settings, or you can make them yourself, manually. The amount of control you have over exposure, sensitivity (ISO settings), color balance, and other image parameters make the camera a versatile tool for creating images.

In the next few pages, I'm going to give you a grounding in the basics of exposure, either as an introduction or as a refresher course, depending on your current level of expertise. When you finish this chapter, you'll understand most of what you need to know to take creative photographs in a broad range of situations with the camera. As I said in the Introduction to this book, my aim is to provide a grounding in *drone photography*, rather than just provide a user's manual for a particular model DJI aircraft.

Auto Mode Options

When you tap on the Camera Mode icon at lower right in the screen to activate Auto mode, your choices are limited to those shown in the three screen variations illustrated in Figure 6.2. In all three, you can tap on the AF icon seen at upper right of each variation to switch from AF (autofocus) to MF (manual focus). I'll explain focus options later.

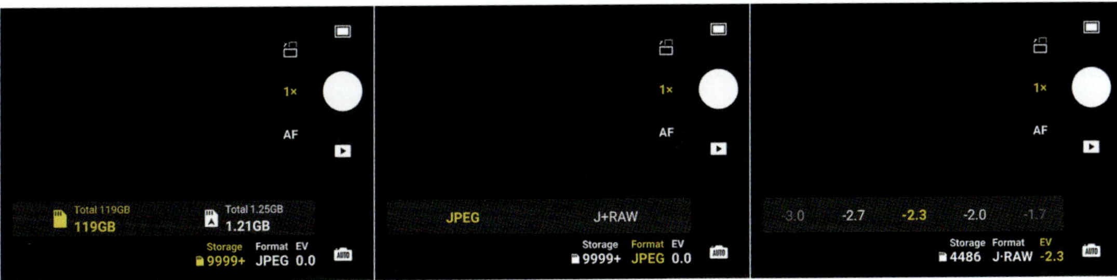

Figure 6.2 Storage (left), Format (center), and Exposure Value controls (right).

At the bottom-right corner of the screen are the three exposure controls available in Auto mode, labeled Storage, Format, and EV. When you tap on each of those labels, you gain access to the following adjustments:

- **Storage.** One or two icons shaped like an inverted microSDXC memory card appear. The Mini 3 Pro, which has 1.2GB of internal storage plus a microSDXC card slot, will display two icons if a memory card is present. The icon on the left represents the removable memory card, and does not appear if no card is present. The icon on the right represents the drone's internal storage, and it is overlaid with the same upward-pointing symbol that DJI uses to represent the drone itself in the map display (so you can easily tell them apart). See Figure 6.2, left, which shows the Mini 3 Pro screen. If no card is present, only the icon for the drone's memory will appear.

  Video clips, especially 4K movies, consume considerably more space than still photos, of course. If you expect to capture files totaling more than the Mini 3 Pro's 1.2GB of internal space, or want to be able to swap cards or transfer to your computer with a card reader, you'll definitely need to use a microSDXC card with sufficient capacity.

  The Mini 3 has no internal memory, so if no memory card is present, you will be unable to capture any photos, and no storage icon will be shown. A microSDXC card is mandatory for photography.

  The amount of total storage and available storage is shown next to each icon. The currently active storage location is highlighted in orange. You can tap the icon you want to use as the Mini 3 Pro's storage to switch between them. The total number of photos you can expect to take with the selected storage using the current format is displayed under the Storage label.

- **Format.** Click on the Format label, and the options shown in Figure 6.2, center, pop up. You can choose JPEG alone or both JPEG and RAW. As I'll explain shortly, JPEG files are the most compact, while RAW files allow more flexibility in post-processing. While saving both types simultaneously gives you the best of both worlds, storage is slower.

- **Exposure Value.** When you click the EV label, you're given the opportunity to add or subtract up to three stops of exposure, in one-third-stop increments, as seen in Figure 6.2, right. In effect, you're telling the drone to use slower or faster shutter speeds to increase or decrease the amount of light reaching the sensor. I'll explain exposure compensation shortly, too.

Pro Mode Options

When you tap on the Camera Mode icon at lower right in the screen to activate Pro mode, a much wider range of adjustments become available, giving you a greater degree of creative control. I've drawn a green box around the relevant labels in Figure 6.3 (the boxes do not appear on your screen). At center right is an AF label, which indicates that the camera is set for autofocus; tap it to switch to manual focus, in which case a "mountain" icon replaces the AF label. I'll explain the AF options later; for now I'm going to concentrate on the other camera settings within the three green boxes at the bottom of the screen in the figure. Here are the parameters available in the left-most box, shown in Figure 6.4, left:

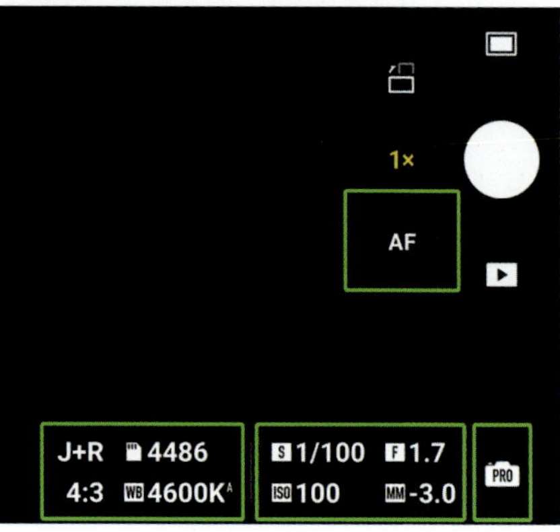

Figure 6.3 Pro mode options.

- **White balance.** You can trust your drone's electronics to select an appropriate white balance using the Auto setting. You'll find that works most of the time, particularly if you do most of your shooting outdoors in daylight. Alternatively, you can choose a color temperature manually (in Kelvin) from 2,400K to 10,000K. I'll explain white balance in more detail later.

- **Format.** This entry functions like its Auto mode counterpart. Choose JPEG alone or JPEG+RAW.

- **Size.** Choose 16:9 and your still images will be cropped and saved in the same aspect ratio (proportions) as your video clips. That can be useful if you intend to mix video and still photos in a presentation and want to retain the same look. Alternatively, you can choose to put the full image area of your sensor to work for your stills and select the 4:3 aspect ratio.

- **Storage.** In Pro mode, this option is used exactly as it is in Auto mode. One or two "SD card" icons appear, along with capacity information. With the Mini 3 Pro, you can tap either the internal storage icon (if available) or the external storage icon (if installed) to specify where files should be saved.

Figure 6.4 Camera adjustments (left) and Exposure adjustments (right).

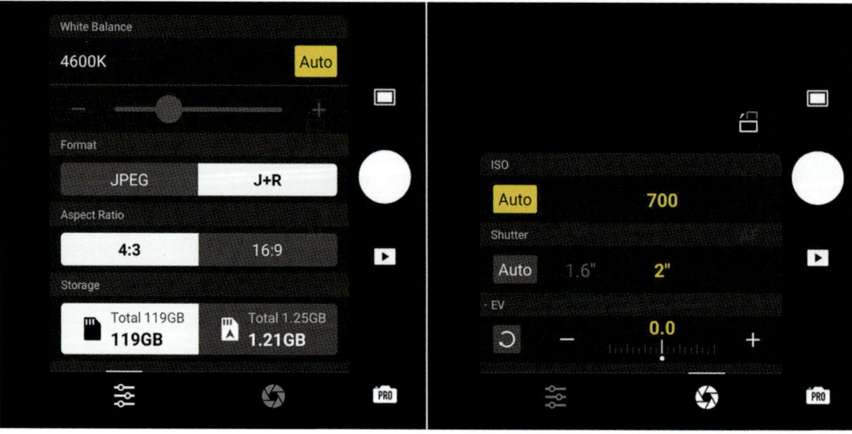

Exposure adjustments are available from the center box (highlighted in green in Figure 6.3), shown in Figure 6.4, right:

- **ISO setting.** Your Mini 3/Mini 3 Pro can calculate an appropriate ISO sensitivity given your selected or automatically chosen shutter speed when this is set to Auto. You can also specify a fixed ISO in the range ISO 100 to ISO 12800. There are some drawbacks to using higher ISO settings, including increased noise, as I'll explain later.

- **Shutter speed.** You can choose shutter speeds from 1/8000th second to 2 full seconds or allow the camera to select a speed for you by setting this to Auto. Believe it or not, your drone's stabilization features are effective at shutter speeds much longer than you, a mere human, would be able to hand-hold a conventional digital camera. Because the drone's camera has no adjustable aperture, you'll be using shutter speed, ISO, and, at times, neutral-density filters to achieve optimal exposure. As you'll learn, in video mode, shutter speed changes are used less and ND filters more because faster shutter speeds produce unwanted jerkiness in movies.

- **EV.** When either shutter speed or ISO are set to Auto, or when both are in Auto mode, you can override their settings by applying exposure compensation, expressed as EV (Exposure Value) changes. I'll explain EV in more detail later in this chapter.

These controls let you capture images in Pro mode that you could never take using your drone's Auto adjustments, especially when you take advantage of the additional processing capabilities an image editor can perform on the aircraft's RAW/DNG image files. Figure 6.5 is a panorama shot at dusk of the 2023 Freedom Festival at Drakes Creek Park in Hendersonville, Tennessee by photographer/writer Rick Murray. The basic image was exposed for 1/2000th second at f/1.7 and ISO 100, then fine-tuned in Adobe Lightroom and Photoshop to take advantage of the drone's already impressive dynamic range.

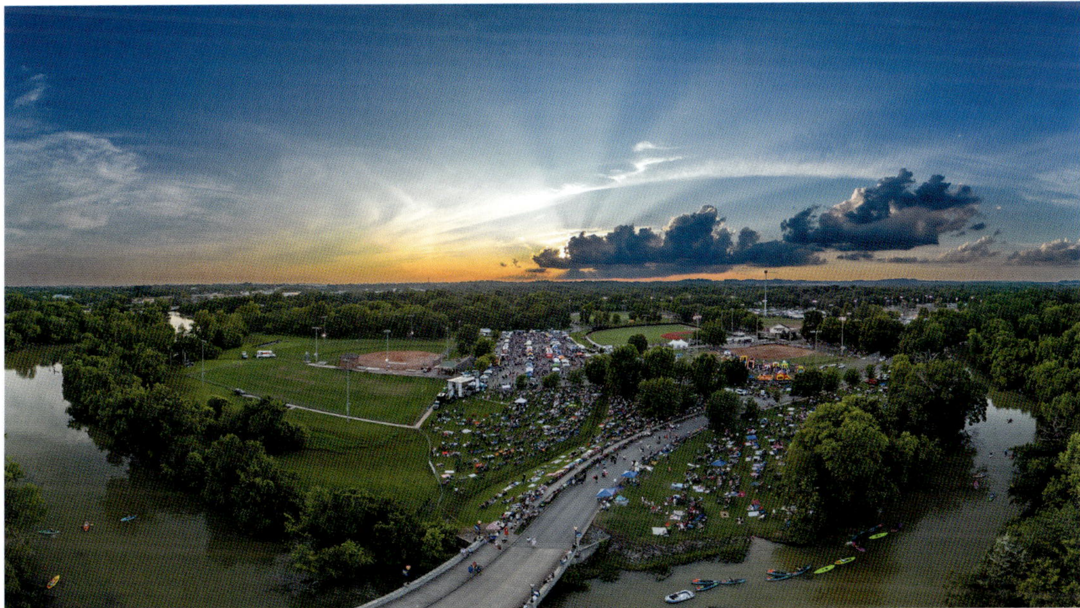

Figure 6.5 An impressive sunset image captured using the Pro exposure mode.

White Balance

As I noted above, you probably won't need to adjust white balance very often when shooting outdoors in daylight, as the drone's Auto White Balance (AWB) setting does a pretty good job of interpreting available light. You may want to choose a specific white balance setting to create a special effect at dawn or dusk, or in unusual situations where you'll be shooting under artificial light. If you have experience with conventional still photography or videography, you probably have a basic understanding of color balance.

White balance is important because various light sources produce illumination of different "colors," although sometimes we are not aware of the difference. Artificial illumination tends to be somewhat amber when using light bulbs that are not daylight balanced, while noonday light outdoors is close to white, and the light early and late in the day is somewhat red/yellow.

White balance is measured using a scale called color temperature. Color temperatures were assigned by heating a theoretical "black body radiator" (which doesn't reflect any light; all illumination comes from its radiance alone) and recording the spectrum of light it emitted at a given temperature in degrees Kelvin. So, daylight at noon has a color temperature in the 5,500- to 6,000-degree range. Indoor illumination is around 3,400 degrees. Hotter temperatures produce bluer images (think blue-white hot) while cooler temperatures produce redder images (think of a dull-red glowing ember). Because of human nature, though, bluer images are actually called "cool" (think wintry day) and redder images are called "warm" (think ruddy sunset), even though their color temperatures are reversed.

If a photo is taken under warm illumination with a sensor balanced for cooler daylight the image will appear much too red/yellow. An image exposed in daylight with the white balance set for warm artificial light will seem much too blue. These color casts may be too strong to remove in an image editor from JPEG files. Of course, if you shoot RAW photos with your drone in DNG format, you can later change the WB setting to the desired value in RAW converter software; this is a completely "non-destructive" process so full image quality will be maintained.

If you want to set a specific white balance based on color temperature, you can deactivate the Auto setting and choose a specific temperature, from 2,400K (a level that makes your image much bluer, to compensate for amber illumination) to 10,000K (a level that makes images much redder to correct for light that is extremely blue in color).

JPEG or JPEG+RAW?

Your Mini 3/Mini 3 Pro has the capability of saving its still image files in either JPEG or JPEG+RAW simultaneously. Both are standard formats that can be read by a wide variety of image-editing and processing software applications. Unlike Nikon, Canon, Sony, and most other makers of conventional digital cameras, DJI does not use a RAW format proprietary to the company. Drone's RAW files are saved in plain old Adobe DNG (Digital Negative Image) format, which can be loaded into your software and then saved in JPEG, TIF, PSD, or any other raster image format you like.

If you choose to tell your drone to save still images in JPEG, its digital image processing (DIP) chip will take the captured sensor data and convert it into a bitmap. In Single Shot mode, you'll end up with a 12MP, 4032 × 3024–pixel (Mini 3 Pro) or 4000 × 3000–pixel (Mini 3) image. Choose the 48MP mode, and either drone will deliver an image measuring 8064 × 6048 pixels. In any case, the exposure and other settings you specified are applied and their values embedded in the file's metadata, called EXIF (Exchangeable Image File Format). Most image editors and EXIF utilities can read this information should you later need to refer to it.

The EXIF data includes the camera maker, model number, serial number, image size, lens information, and exposure data. (See Figure 6.6, left.) The latitude, longitude, and altitude extracted from the GPS data is also available. (See Figure 6.6, center.) If, for some reason, you're curious, DJI also embeds data about the absolute altitude and relative altitude, and gimbal orientation. (See Figure 6.6, right.). The geographic coordinates are presented in degrees, minutes, and seconds.

GPS NOTES

During my recent trip from Chicago to California along historic Route 66, I didn't bother to take many notes as I photographed the sights from ground level with a Nikon Z9 and from the air with my Mini 3 Pro. Both record GPS data in their image files, and if I couldn't remember precisely where I took a particular photo (one New Mexico or Arizona mountain range looks pretty much like another), I could feed the data into a GPS coordinates converter app (they are available for both iOS and Android operating systems) and pinpoint the exact location quickly.

Your drone's RAW files are image files that have not yet had applied the settings specified at the time of exposure. You'll sometimes be told that RAW files are the "unprocessed" image information a camera produces before it's been modified. That's nonsense. RAW files are no more unprocessed than camera film is after it's been through the chemicals to produce a negative or transparency. A lot can happen in the developer that can affect the quality of a film image—positively and negatively—and, similarly, your digital image undergoes a significant amount of processing before it is saved as a RAW file.

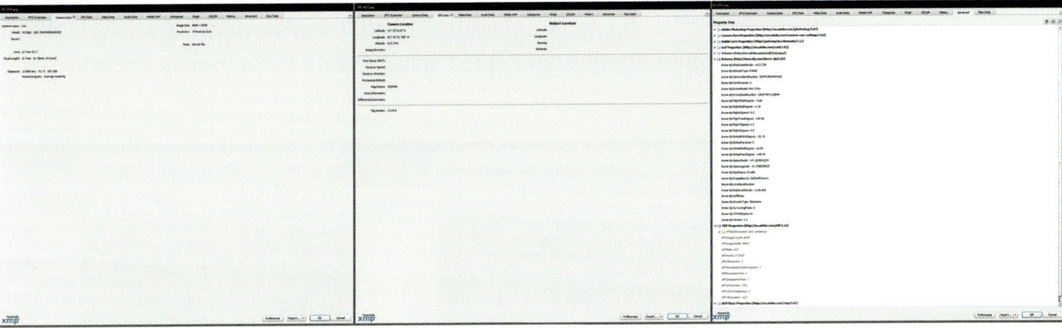

Figure 6.6 EXIF data from a typical JPEG file.

A RAW file is more like a film camera's processed negative. It contains the digitized sensor information with no compression, no sharpening, nor application of other settings. Your preferred settings are *stored* with the RAW file so they can be applied when the image is converted to a form compatible with your favorite image editor. However, using RAW conversion software you can override those settings and apply settings of your own. Figure 6.7 shows three of the panels available when converting a drone's DNG file in an image editor.

At left you can see an adjustment being made to white balance. Select Custom and you can tweak the Temperature slider to specify a different color temperature (actually, the blue/amber bias) and the Tint slider to adjust green/magenta bias. The same panel includes sliders for exposure, contrast, highlights, shadows, whites, blacks, clarity, vibrance, and saturation. The center panel histogram display has tools for adjusting the curve that controls shadows, highlights, and midtones separately. At right, you can see the sliders for enhancing sharpening and applying noise reduction. These capabilities are useful for those who are adept at (or want to master) image editing.

RAW exists because sometimes we want to have access to all the information captured by the camera before the camera's internal logic has processed it and converted the image to a standard file format like JPEG. RAW doesn't save as much storage space as JPEG. But what it does do is preserve the information captured by your camera after it's been converted from analog to digital form. Of course, the RAW format preserves the *settings* information.

So, why don't we always use RAW? Although some aerial photographers do save only in RAW format, it's more common to use RAW plus JPEG, or just shoot JPEG and avoid RAW altogether. That's because having only RAW files to work with can significantly slow down your workflow. While RAW is overwhelmingly helpful when an image needs to be fine-tuned, in other situations, working with a RAW file—when all you really need is a good-quality, untweaked image—consumes time that you may not want to waste. For example, RAW images take longer to store on the memory card, and require more post-processing effort, whether you elect to go with the default settings in force when the picture was taken, or just make minor adjustments.

JPEG was invented as a more compact file format that can store most of the information in a digital image, but in a much smaller size. JPEG predates most digital SLRs and was initially used to squeeze down files for transmission over slow dialup connections. Even if you were using an early dSLR with 1.3-megapixel files for news photography, you didn't want to send them back to the office over a modem (Google it) at 1,200 bps.

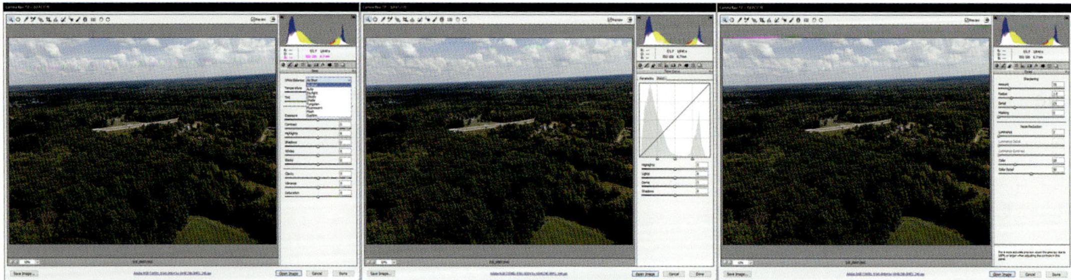

Figure 6.7 Some of the adjustments you can make to your drone's DNG/RAW files.

Getting a Handle on Exposure

If you've been using a conventional digital camera for a while, you know how important correct exposure is. In one sense, exposure is an even *more* important consideration with drone photography, because all the images and video you capture are not easily subject to retakes. If a scene or sequence is overexposed, underexposed, too contrasty, or plagued by flat lighting, once you've landed, it's virtually impossible to go back aloft and capture the exact same view with corrected settings. Even if you manage to return to the same coordinates, there are bound to be some differences. Greek philosopher Heraclitus of Ephesus was right: you can't step into the same river twice, or reproduce the same aerial perspective multiple times.

Fortunately, your Mini 3/Mini 3 Pro gives you a considerable amount of control over exposure, with tools that are probably familiar to you if you're a veteran digital photographer. You can select shutter speed, aperture, and ISO sensitivity, and use the drone's default averaging metering scheme or an optional "spot" mode (it's a rather large spot). There's a live histogram available to view so you can see exactly how the tones in your image are being captured. It's easy to bracket still photos to produce multiple images with slightly different exposure settings, too.

You don't cede control by opting for the drone's autoexposure system, either. As I mentioned earlier, you can override the AE setting by adding or subtracting exposure compensation in one-third-stop increments. I know some of you are experienced photographers, while others are still learning how to enjoy the photo features of their drone and need some grounding in fundamentals. So, consider the next sections as a refresher for the veterans and an introduction for newer drone photographers. It's always tricky serving the needs of a broad audience.

Basics of Exposure

In the most basic sense, exposure is all about light. Exposure can make or break your photo. Correct exposure brings out the detail in the areas you want to picture, whether you're trying to capture details of a construction site for aerial progress shots or detailing the range of colors in an overhead view of vibrant Fall foliage, providing the range of tones and colors you need to create the desired image.

Poor exposure can cloak important details in shadow or wash them out in glare-filled featureless expanses of white. However, getting the perfect exposure requires some intelligence—either that built into the drone's camera electronics or the smarts in your head—because digital sensors can't capture all the tones we can see. If the range of tones in an image is extensive, embracing both inky black shadows and bright highlights, we often must settle for an exposure that renders most of those tones—but not all—in a way that best suits the photo we want to produce.

If you're a photo enthusiast, you're probably aware of the traditional "exposure triangle" of *aperture* (quantity of light and light passed by the lens), *shutter speed* (the amount of time the shutter is open), and the *ISO sensitivity* of the sensor—all working proportionately and reciprocally to produce an exposure. The trio is itself affected by the amount of illumination that is available. So, if you double the amount of light, increase the aperture by one stop, make the shutter speed twice as long, or boost the ISO setting 2X, you'll get twice as much exposure. Similarly, you can increase any of these factors while decreasing one of the others by a similar amount to keep the same exposure. Of course, with your drone, only two of the three legs can be adjusted directly, as the aperture is fixed at f/1.7.

The traditional exposure triangle is shown in Figure 6.8.

Working with any of the three legs (aperture, shutter speed, or ISO sensitivity), involves trade-offs:

- **Aperture.** Larger f/stops (the smaller numbers, like f/1.7) provide less depth-of-field, while smaller f/stops (larger numbers, like f/11 or f/16) increase depth-of-field. As I noted, you don't have to worry about the effects of this leg of the triangle, since the Mini 3 and Mini 3 Pro do not have an adjustable physical aperture. Yes, you can *simulate* its effect on the exposure with neutral-density filters, but filters don't change depth-of-field.

- **Shutter speeds.** Shorter shutter speeds (like 1/250th or 1/500th second) do a better job of reducing the effects of camera/subject motion, while longer shutter speeds (such as 1/30th second) make that motion blur more likely.

- **ISO sensitivity.** Higher ISO settings increase the amount of visual noise and artifacts in your image, masking detail. Lower ISO settings reduce the effects of noise.

If you're a photo enthusiast who has experience with conventional still cameras, you might mourn the loss of the options when an adjustable aperture is available. Since you are *always* shooting at f/1.7, reducing the intensity of the light reaching the sensor with a neutral-density filter is inconvenient, and can't be done in mid-flight. You'll need to plan ahead or bring your drone back to home and mount the filter when needed.

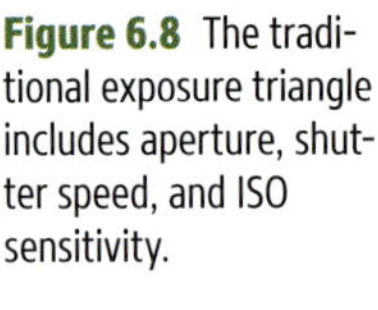

Figure 6.8 The traditional exposure triangle includes aperture, shutter speed, and ISO sensitivity.

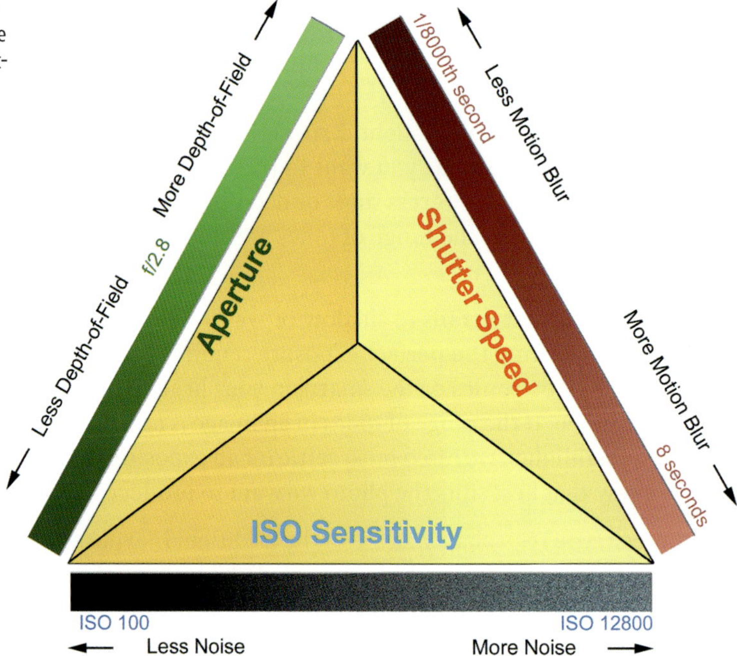

The fixed f/stop is a limitation, but at the same time it offers some advantages:

- **Faster shutter speeds.** Because the aperture is fixed at f/1.7, you'll be using motion-freezing faster shutter speeds for still photography, eliminating blur even beyond what the drone's image stabilization features can provide. At the *lowest* ISO setting, ISO 100, you'll probably be shooting at speeds in the 1/1250th-second range or faster, which will largely eliminate most blur from subject motion *and* from camera (drone) shake.

  Even so, note that brisk shutter speeds are not an advantage when shooting video. As I'll explain in Chapter 8, viewers are conditioned to see a small amount of blur as objects move from frame to frame, resulting in what is called a "cinematic" look. When individual frames are razor-sharp, however, the lack of transitional blur produces a hyper-realistic, jittery look, sometimes referred to as the "soap opera" effect that viewers find unsettling. For the best video quality, you'll want to use neutral-density filters to reduce the amount of light reaching the sensor and allowing shutter speeds no faster than twice the frame rate (60, 30, or 24 frames per second).

- **Depth-of-field.** The range of sharpness of an image (depth-of-field) changes as the aperture is adjusted. Relatively larger f/stops, such as f/1.7, produce less depth-of-field than smaller stops, such as f/8 or f/11. Because your drone's aperture never changes, the depth-of-field remains exactly the same shot to shot and video clip to video clip. In practice, that's more of an advantage for movie shooting, where unwanted changes in focus plane and depth-of-field may be distracting. I'll explain depth-of-field in more detail later.

- **Less diffraction.** Small f/stops cause some minimal sharpness lost due to a phenomenon called diffraction. "Small" is relative and is affected by the size of the sensor. I won't bore you with diffraction limitation formulas, but the bottom line is that with a sensor the size of the one found in the Mini 3 Pro, diffraction starts to affect the image at about f/5.6 and smaller (larger numbered) f/stops. The effect is gradual as the aperture is reduced. The good news is that at f/1.7, there should be no image loss from diffraction at all. In this sense, your drone's fixed f/stop is a very good thing.

Dynamic Range

Getting the perfect exposure can be tricky because your drone's sensor, like all image-capture devices, can't capture *all* the tones we can see. If the range of tones in an image is extensive, embracing both inky black shadows and bright highlights, the sensor may not be able to capture them all. Sometimes, we must settle for an exposure that renders *most* of those tones—but not all—in a way that best suits the image we want to produce. You'll often need to make choices about which details are important, and which are not, so that you can grab the tones that truly matter in your image. That's part of the creativity you bring to bear in realizing your photographic vision.

For example, look at three bracketed exposures presented at left in Figure 6.9. For the image at upper left, the darker areas and shadows are well exposed, but the brightest highlights—chiefly the sky—are seriously overexposed. The version at center left does a better job on the clouds, sea, and land, but the three are still unbalanced. At lower left, the sky looks great, but the land portions are much too dark. The camera's sensor simply can't capture detail in both dark areas and bright areas in a single shot.

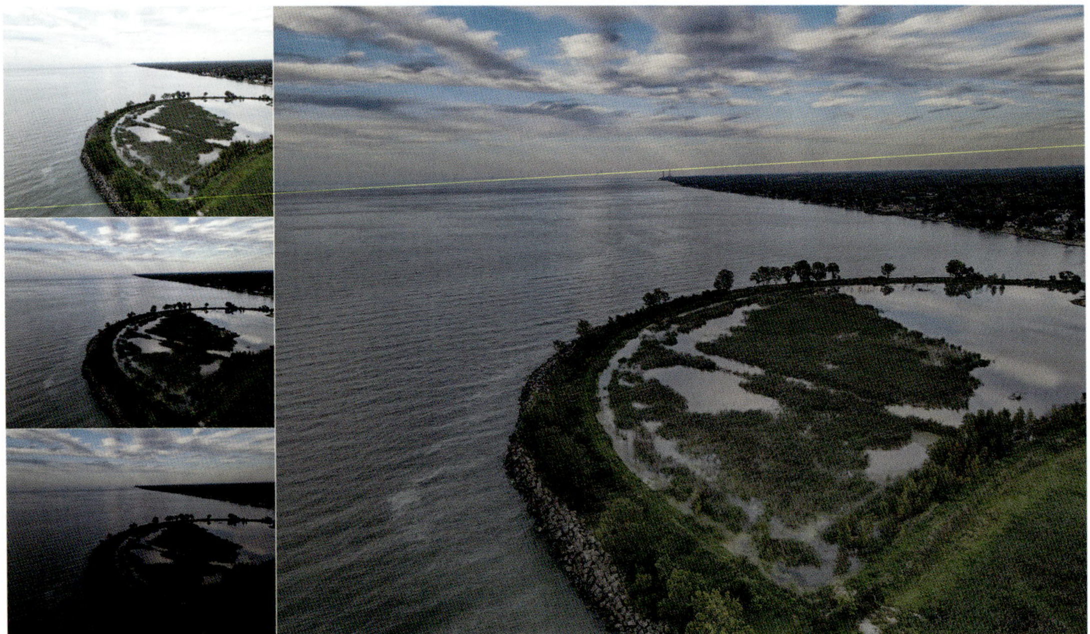

Figure 6.9 A set of bracketed exposures (left, top to bottom) that can be combined using HDR processing to produce the image seen at right.

With digital camera sensors, it's tricky to capture detail in both highlights and shadows in a single image, because the number of tones, the *dynamic range* of the sensor, is limited. That's one reason why it's a good idea to master using RAW format. However, the solution, in this case, was to resort to a technique called High Dynamic Range (HDR) photography. With HDR still images, multiple shots at different exposure settings are used to extract the best detail from each and combine them, resulting in an image like the one seen at right in Figure 6.9. You can capture a bracketed set of images taken at exposure increments you specify and combine them using an image editor such as Photoshop, or a specialized HDR tool like Photomatix. I'll explain exposure bracketing shortly.

Choosing an Exposure Mode

To calculate exposure automatically, you need to tell the camera *what* to measure (this is called the *metering mode*) and *what adjustments* should be used (ISO sensitivity, shutter speed, or both) to set the exposure. Together they provide your *exposure mode.*

If you're a conventional camera veteran, you know about metering modes. Digital cameras typically have three or more metering modes. The most sophisticated is Matrix/Evaluative mode, in which various parts of the scene are compared to determine what kind of scene it is and measure exposure from the most important subject. That's distinctly different from Averaging mode, in which the illumination of the entire frame is examined and exposure is based on the average brightness. Additional modes include Partial or Spot metering, in which all or most of the exposure is based on giving the most weight to measurements from a relatively small portion of the frame.

Your drone generally uses the Averaging mode by default. That's because aerial scenes often include important areas located throughout the frame rather than concentrated in one spot, which is typical with, say, portrait or macro close-up photo subjects that are common fodder for conventional digital cameras. So, Averaging works quite well most of the time.

If you do want to base your exposure on a certain subject within the frame, your drone offers a metering mode that DJI calls Spot, although it actually is more of a Partial metering scheme because the area measured is not the typical 3 to 5 percent of the frame used for traditional Spot metering. Because DJI feels you won't need Spot metering very often, it's activated on a per-capture basis:

- **Activate touch focus/spot metering.** Touch the controller screen with your finger on the area you want to meter. An icon like the one shown at left in Figure 6.10 appears as you hold your finger down on the screen.
- **Press to focus/meter.** As you press down, the drone will calculate the correct exposure and focus on the area within the square.
- **Adjust brightness.** A vertical line with the sun icon representing brightness will appear to the right of the focus/metering square. The "sun" will initially be in the center of the line. You can drag it upward or downward to adjust the exposure, producing a brighter image (drag upward) or darker image (drag downward). You are, in effect, changing the Exposure Value (EV) and applying exposure compensation.
- **Lock exposure.** Keep your finger in place until the Auto Exposure Locked indicator appears (see Figure 6.10, right).

As you might expect, because exposure is adjusted using only shutter speed and ISO sensitivity (plus ND filters), your drone doesn't have an exact counterpart to the Program Auto, Shutter-priority, and Aperture-priority modes you may be familiar with when using conventional still cameras. Next is a rundown on the choices you do have in Pro mode.

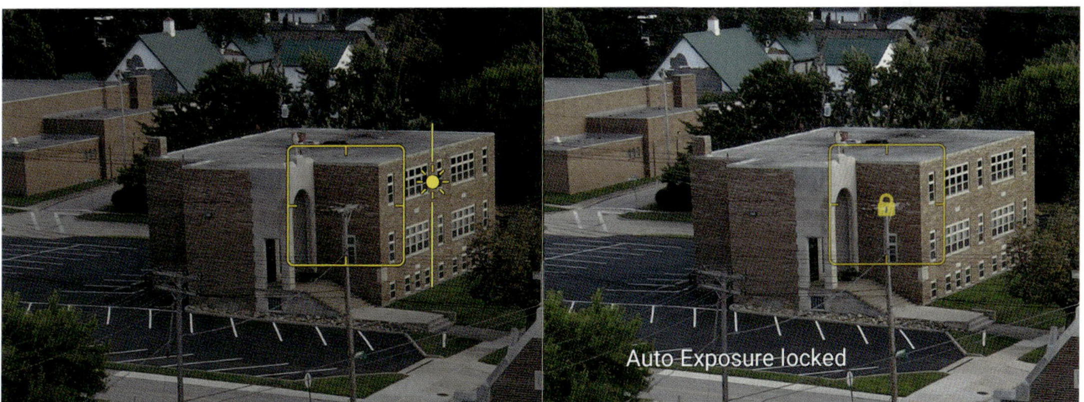

Figure 6.10 Focus and meter at a selected location (left); hold down to lock exposure (right).

Auto ISO/Auto Shutter Speed (Program Mode)

When you set both ISO and shutter speed to Auto mode, the drone will choose a shutter speed that will effectively counter any camera motion and typical subject motion, and then adjust the ISO to provide what it deems to be an appropriate sensitivity. This behavior is similar to what you get with the Program mode of digital cameras, except that dSLR and mirrorless cameras will adjust the aperture. The recommended exposure can be overridden if you want, using the EV adjustment described above. You'd use this mode:

- **When you're learning to use your Mini 3/Mini 3 Pro.** Set the camera to Auto ISO/Auto Shutter and you can concentrate on learning how to navigate and use your drone's photo and video options.
- **When you're in a hurry to get a grab shot.** The Mini 3/Mini 3 Pro drone camera will do a pretty good job of calculating an appropriate exposure for you, without any input from you.
- **When no special shutter speed or aperture settings are needed.** If your subject doesn't require special anti- or pro-blur techniques, and noise levels aren't important, use this mode as a general-purpose setting.

Auto ISO/Manual Shutter Speed (Shutter-Priority Mode)

You select a shutter speed, and the drone will choose an ISO sensitivity that will provide the correct exposure. This is similar to the S or Tv modes you may be used to. Perhaps you're shooting still photos of fast-moving subjects and you want to use the absolute fastest shutter speed available. In other cases, you might want to use a slow shutter speed to add some blur to a sports image that would be mundane if the action were completely frozen. Motor sports and track-and-field events particularly lend themselves to creative use of slower speeds. For example, if you were shooting stills of a motorcycle race (with permission, from a safe angle, not in a stadium nor above any spectators), your shots will have more excitement if the spinning wheels are slightly (or dramatically) blurry.

This Shutter-priority mode gives you some control over how much action-freezing capability your camera brings to bear in a particular situation:

- **To reduce blur from subject motion.** Set the shutter speed of the camera to a higher value to reduce the amount of blur from subjects that are moving. The exact speed will vary depending on how fast your subject is moving and how much blur is acceptable.
- **To add blur from subject motion.** There are times when you want a subject to blur, say, when shooting waterfalls with the camera set for a one- or two-second exposure.
- **To add blur from camera motion when *you* are moving.** Say your drone is following some running wildlife or humans. You might want to set the camera to take still shots at 1/60th second, so that the background will blur.
- **To reduce blur from camera motion when *you* are moving.** In other situations, the drone itself is in motion and you want to minimize the amount of blur caused by the motion of the camera.

Manual ISO/Auto Shutter Speed (Aperture-Priority Mode)

In this mode, you choose a fixed ISO sensitivity and allow the camera to adjust the shutter speed to arrive at an appropriate exposure. This option resembles the Aperture-priority mode you may have used with your dSLR or mirrorless digital camera, except that you don't get to *choose* the aperture, which is fixed at f/1.7, and the shutter speed is varied. ISO is locked at the setting you choose, which means that regardless of the shutter speed chosen by the drone, the noise levels and contrast that are dependent on ISO setting will remain consistent.

Manual ISO/Manual Shutter Speed (Manual Mode)

Part of being an experienced photographer comes from knowing when to rely on your camera's automation (Auto mode or Pro mode with Auto ISO, Auto Shutter Speed, or both) and when to set exposure manually. Still photography with drones in full manual mode can be tricky, though, because lighting conditions can change rapidly due to the environment (the sun slipping behind some clouds), or simply because the landscape changes dramatically as your flight path takes you over new terrain.

Still, manual exposure can come in handy in some situations. You might be wanting to achieve a silhouette effect and find that none of the exposure modes or EV correction features give you exactly the look you want, even with Spot metering. In Manual mode, you can set the exact ISO and shutter speed required, supplemented by neutral-density filters, if necessary. Manual exposure can be particularly useful when shooting night panoramas of such scenes as the full moon rising over a nearby lake, or a downtown cityscape in which lighting intensities and color temperatures can vary significantly.

Adjusting EV

Making EV adjustments is a way of applying exposure compensation to override the shutter speed and ISO settings calculated by the camera. You can add or subtract exposure in 1/3-stop increments, thereby making your image brighter or darker than if you'd allowed the Mini 3/Mini 3 Pro drone camera to choose its settings automatically.

F/STOPS VERSUS STOPS

Because of a lack of a current commonly used word for one exposure increment, the term *stop* is often used to mean *any* of the three exposure parameters. So a one-stop change can mean doubling or halving the shutter speed (from 1/250th to 1/500th or 1/125th second) or doing the same with ISO (from ISO 250 to ISO 500 or ISO 125). A one-stop adjustment can also be applied to opening or closing the aperture (which, of course, can't be done with your drone's fixed f/1.7 aperture). In this book, when I say "stop" by itself (no *f/*), I mean one whole unit of exposure, and am not necessarily referring to an actual f/stop or lens aperture. Similarly, 1/3-stop increments can mean either shutter speed or ISO changes, depending on the context.

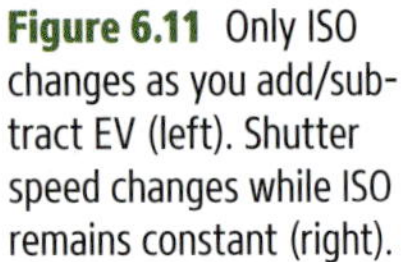

Figure 6.11 Only ISO changes as you add/subtract EV (left). Shutter speed changes while ISO remains constant (right).

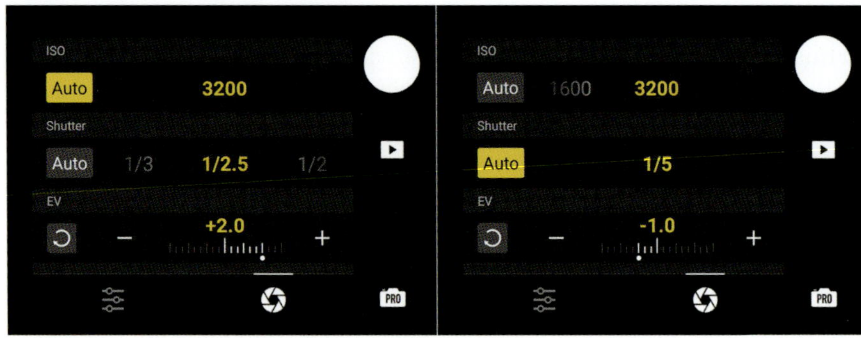

I showed you how to apply EV changes when Auto camera mode is active earlier in this chapter. In Pro mode, there are two ways to override the drone's exposure settings, using Touch Focus/Metering, as described above, and manually applying plus or minus values using the exposure controls shown in Figure 6.11.

As I mentioned earlier, when either Shutter Speed or ISO are set to Auto, or when both are in Auto mode, you can override their settings by applying exposure compensation, usually expressed in terms of EV (Exposure Value) changes. When you click the EV label, you're given the opportunity to add or subtract up to three stops of exposure, in one-third-stop increments. The EV effects of adjustments will be applied as described below:

- **Shutter Speed: Auto.** If Shutter Speed is set to Auto, then the shutter speed will increase or decrease while the ISO remains fixed as you add or subtract EV.
- **ISO: Auto.** If ISO is set to Auto, the ISO setting will change instead with the shutter speed remaining constant.
- **Shutter Speed/ISO: Auto.** If both are in Auto mode, then both will be adjusted.
- **Shutter Speed/ISO: Manual.** If you've disabled Auto adjustments for *both* shutter speed and ISO, then you are in Manual Metering mode, indicated by the M.M. label applied above to this EV setting, and EV changes are not possible.

Is Visual Noise a Problem?

With conventional cameras, the graininess we call "noise" can be an important concern. Visual image noise is that random grainy effect that some like to use as a special effect, but which, most of the time, is objectionable because it robs an image of detail even as it adds that "interesting" texture.

This noise is caused by three different phenomena:

- **Sensor area.** You'll often see assertions that larger sensors are subject to less visual noise because the individual photosites (pixels) are larger. That's not entirely correct. Some types of noise are actually a function of the total image area of the sensor; it makes no difference how the sensor is divided up into individual pixels. Larger sensors do allow more pixels and higher effective resolutions, but the actual *noise* levels of a given sensor size are the same whether it's a 12MP sensor or 48MP sensor. It's the increase in *total area* that lowers noise levels. Figure 6.12 shows the relative sensor sizes of a variety of digital camera digitizers, from a 36mm × 24mm full-frame sensor to the 9.8mm × 7.3mm sensor of the Mini 3/Mini 3 Pro.

  As you might guess, the Mini 3 and Mini 3 Pro have more visual noise resulting from sensor size than cameras with much larger sensors. In practice, you're more likely to see noise caused by sensor size than from length of exposure or high ISO.

- **Exposure time.** Longer exposures allow more photons to reach the sensor, increasing your ability to capture a picture under low-light conditions. However, the longer exposures also increase the likelihood that some pixels will register random phantom photons, often because the longer an imager is "hot," the warmer it gets, and that heat can be mistaken for photons. CMOS imagers, like the ones found in the Mini 3/Mini 3 Pro, contain millions of individual amplifiers and analog/digital converters, all working in unison. Because all these circuits don't necessarily process in precisely the same way all the time, they can introduce something called fixed-pattern noise into the image data.

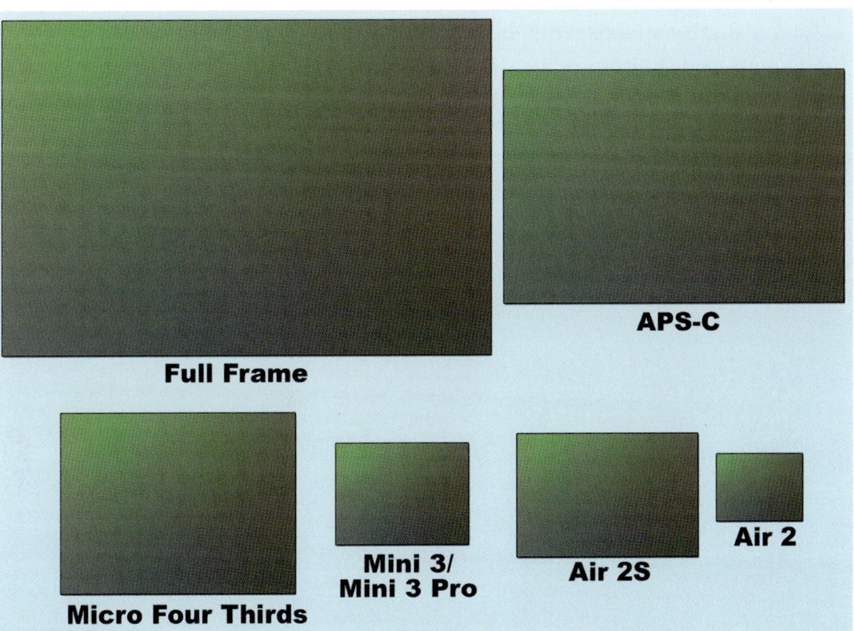

Figure 6.12 Comparing sensor sizes.

The good news is that it's unlikely you'll be capturing many images using long exposure times. Video shutter speeds are 1/30th second or shorter, and the vast majority of your still photos will be taken at even briefer shutter speed settings—frequently 1/250th or faster. In any case, the longest exposure time available with your Mini 3/Mini 3 Pro drone camera is 8 seconds, a duration that does not produce much long exposure noise.

- **High ISOs.** This kind of noise commonly first appears when you raise your camera's sensitivity setting above ISO 1600. This kind of noise appears as a result of the amplification needed to increase the sensitivity of the sensor. Because your sensor has twice as many green pixels as red and blue pixels, such noise is typically worse in areas that have red, blue, and magenta tones, because the green signals don't have to be amplified as much to produce detail. While higher ISOs do pull details out of dark areas, they also amplify non-signal information randomly, creating noise.

  Your drone is capable of using ISO settings that venture into the "noisy" zone. The Mini 3 can use up to ISO 6400 for video and 12MP still photos (ISO 3200 in 48MP mode), while the Mini 3 Pro can use up to ISO 6400 for video and ISO 12800 for still photos (both in Manual exposure mode). You'll rarely need those lofty settings, however, thanks to the fixed f/1.7 aperture. Under dim sunlight, you'd need an exposure of 1/8000th second at f/1.7 to push ISO to 3200 or an exposure of 1/4000th second at f/1.7 to require ISO 6400 at dusk.

If you do encounter objectionable noise in any of your still photos, most image-editing software includes noise-reduction features that will reduce the graininess, while masking a little detail. There's no reason to avoid high ISO settings, and keep in mind that the image stabilization built into your drone allows the use of longer shutter speeds while hovering aloft. Figure 6.13 shows Rick Murray's image of crescent moon (Venus and Jupiter are also visible in the original shot) rising over a town, captured at 1/8th of a second and ISO 1500, with subtle noise reduction applied in post-processing.

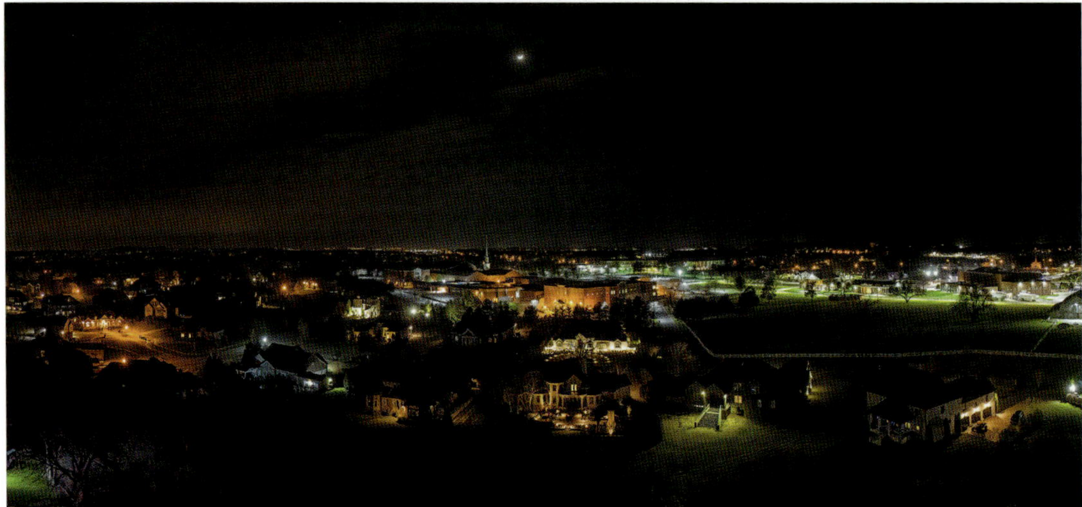

Figure 6.13 Long exposures and high ISO settings are useful for night shots.

Autoexposure Bracketing

Bracketing is a method for shooting several consecutive exposures using different settings, as a way of improving the odds that one will be exactly right. Before digital cameras took over the universe, it was common to bracket exposures, shooting, say, a series of three photos at 1/125th second, but varying the f/stop from f/8 to f/11 to f/16. In practice, smaller than whole-stop increments were used for greater precision. Plus, it was just as common to keep the same aperture and vary the shutter speed, although in the days before electronic shutters, film cameras often had only whole-increment shutter speeds available. Figure 6.14 shows a typical bracketed series.

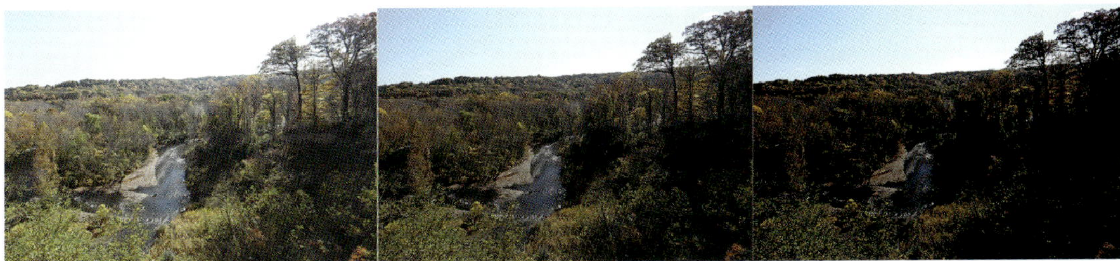

Figure 6.14 In this bracketed series, you can see underexposure (left), metered exposure (center), and overexposure (right).

Bracketing exposures automatically with your Mini 3/Mini 3 Pro couldn't be easier. AEB (Autoexposure bracketing) is one of the shooting choices available from Photo mode, as you can see in Figure 6.15. You can specify either 3 or 5 shots, and when you press the shutter icon/button, the drone automatically shoots a burst of the specified length, each at a different exposure value—one at the standard exposure, and the others with more or less exposure. For each, the shutter speed will change to provide the necessary exposure adjustment for the series.

- **3 shots.** The camera will capture one image at the *base* or standard exposure (usually the metered exposure). It then takes one additional shot that provides 2/3 stop *more* and one with 2/3 stop *less* exposure relative to that "base" image.

- **5 shots.** The camera captures one image at the base exposure, and then shots at 2/3 and 1 1/3 stops *less* and 2/3 and 1 1/3 stops *more* than the base exposure.

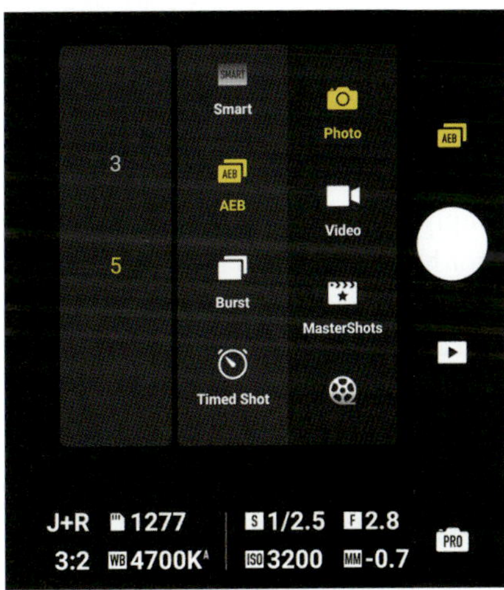

Figure 6.15 Choose 3 or 5 bracketed shots.

Note that I used the term *base* exposure rather than *metered* exposure. Most of the time, the initial shot will, indeed, be the one calculated by the drone based on your exposure settings, in exactly the way you might expect in both 3-shot and 5-shot modes:

- **Shutter Speed Auto/ISO Auto.** Both shutter speed and ISO will be adjusted to produce the over- and underexposures. You can safely use this mode if you have plenty of light, because there will be no danger of using a shutter speed that is too low to counter movement or an ISO sensitivity that will produce a noisy image.
- **Shutter Speed Auto/ISO Manual.** The ISO will remain at the setting you specify, and the shutter speed will be adjusted to produce less or more exposure around the base exposure. Use this mode when capturing bracketed images for manual HDR processing (described in the next section), because all your images will have similar noise characteristics.
- **Shutter Speed Manual/ISO Auto.** The shutter speed is constant at the setting you select, and ISO will be adjusted to produce the bracketed images. Use this mode when you want to freeze motion by locking in a fast shutter speed. Noise may vary between shots, particularly in 5-shot mode, but should not be objectionable if light levels are not low.

While your drone's bracketing feature is easy to use, it does have limitations, which you may notice if you have done a lot of bracketing with conventional cameras. Unlike its non-aerial counterparts, the Mini 3/Mini 3 Pro camera doesn't allow changing the increment between shots from the default 2/3-stop values. Some cameras let you choose increments of 2 to 6 whole stops, which gives you a more dramatic bracket spread, and up to nine separate shots rather than just 3 or 5. That flexibility can come in very handy with manual HDR photography.

One thing you *can* do, however, is bias your bracketing sequence toward over- or underexposure, simply by using exposure compensation. Say you've already captured a set of bracketed exposures and they all are too dark or too light. In Pro mode, simply tap plus or minus EV (up to three stops in either direction), and the drone will then adjust the metered setting upward or downward and use *that* as the base for the 3-shot or 5-shot bracketed sequence. This technique compensates, somewhat, for the inability to change the size of the increment; you're not getting more shots, but they are all biased in a more useful direction.

Working with HDR

High dynamic range (HDR) photography has been quite the rage for quite a while now, especially since vendors, including DJI, have been building HDR features into their devices. Entire books have been written on the subject. It's not really a new technique—film photographers have been combining multiple exposures for ages to produce a single image of, say, an interior room while maintaining detail in the scene visible through the windows.

Suppose you wanted to photograph an offshore lighthouse as sunset approached but found that if you exposed to represent the water accurately, the dramatic sky tones were overexposed, as shown at left in Figure 6.16. Reducing exposure to darken the sky also makes the water look murky and

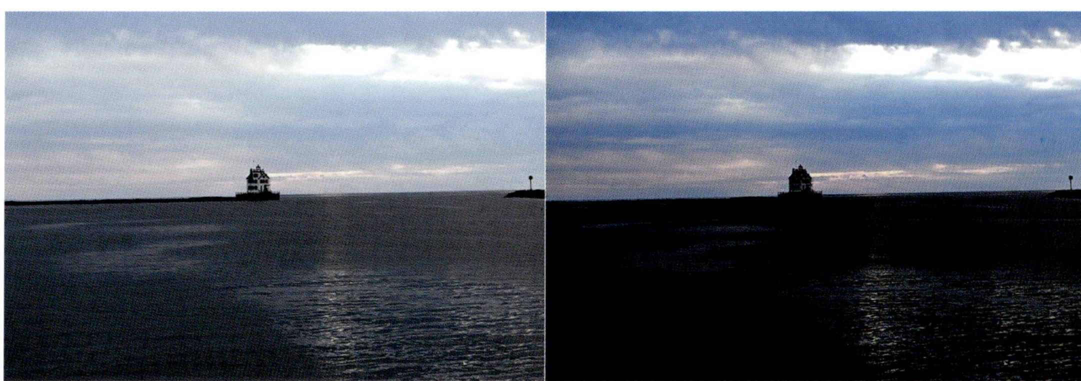

Figure 6.16 It's not possible to capture both the sky and water in the same image with one exposure.

lacking in detail, as seen at right in Figure 6.16. The solution is to capture multiple bracketed images, as described previously, and then combine them in an image editor or one of the stand-alone HDR processing utilities that are available.

That's what I did. I grabbed a five-shot bracketing sequence with shutter speed set on manual at about 1/320th second. The ISO is set to Auto to allow adjusting the ISO sensitivity during the bracketing. I used Photoshop's Merge to HDR Pro plug-in to combine four of the exposures, as shown in Figure 6.17. The resulting HDR image is Figure 6.18.

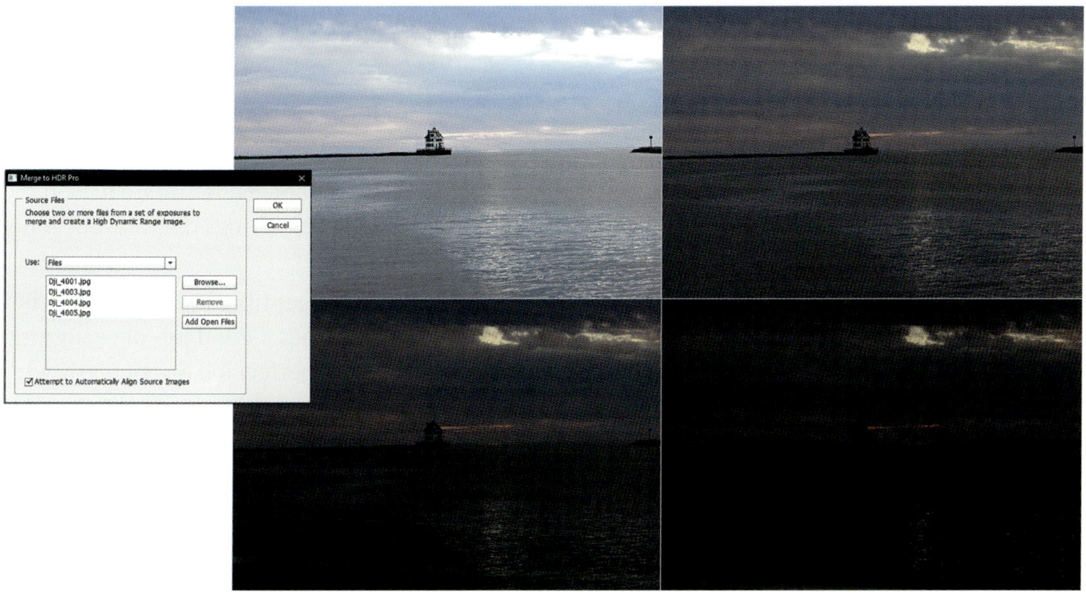

Figure 6.17 Multiple exposures using different values can be combined in an image editor like Photoshop.

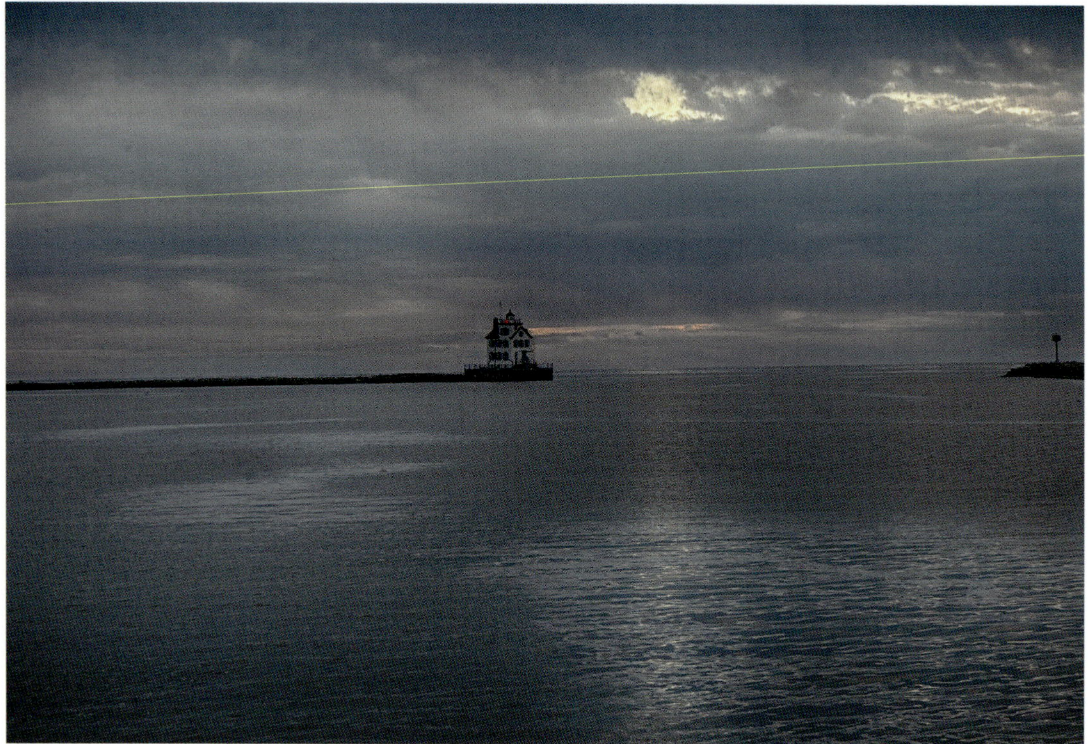

Figure 6.18 The combined image has more detail in bright and dark areas of the scene.

When working with HDR, there are a few things to keep in mind:

- **Moving objects may produce ghosts.** Even if the drone hovers steadily, there may be some *subject* motion between shots, producing "ghost" effects. For my example shot, a few birds, a flag on the lighthouse, and the relatively calm surface of Lake Erie were the only things that moved—only slightly—between exposures, so no ghosts are obvious.

- **Misalignment.** Your Mini 3/Mini 3 Pro may still shift almost imperceptibly between shots, but most HDR utilities feature an Auto Image Align function that does a good job of realigning your multiple images when they are merged. However, it can't do a perfect job, particularly with repetitive patterns that are difficult for the camera's "brains" to sort out. Some misalignment is possible.

- **Unwanted cropping.** Because the processor needs to be able to shift each individual image slightly in any (or all) of four directions in Auto Image Align mode, it needs to crop the image slightly to trim out any non-image areas that result. Your final image will be slightly smaller than one shot in other modes.

- **Weird colors.** Some types of outdoor lighting, including fluorescent and LED illumination, "cycle" many times a second, and colors can vary between shots. You may not even notice this when single shooting, but it becomes more obvious when using any continuous shooting mode, including HDR mode. The combined images may have strange color effects.

Fixing Exposures with Histograms

While you can often repair poorly exposed photos in your image editor, your best bet is to arrive at the correct exposure when your drone takes the original picture, minimizing the tweaks that you have to make in post-processing. However, you can't always judge exposure just by simply looking at the preview image on the screen of your controller, nor the review image when you tap the Playback icon to see an image you've already captured. Ambient light may make the screen difficult to see, and its rendition is not very accurate in any case.

Fortunately, you have two tools that allow you to evaluate exposure prior to capturing an image. One of these is the Overexposure Warning, which you can activate by accessing the System Settings menu (represented by three dots in the upper-right corner of the controller's display). Tap the Camera tab and scroll down to the Overexposure Warning switch (see Figure 6.19). Once activated, you'll view a "zebra stripe" pattern in any area of the frame that will be overexposed (see Figure 6.20).

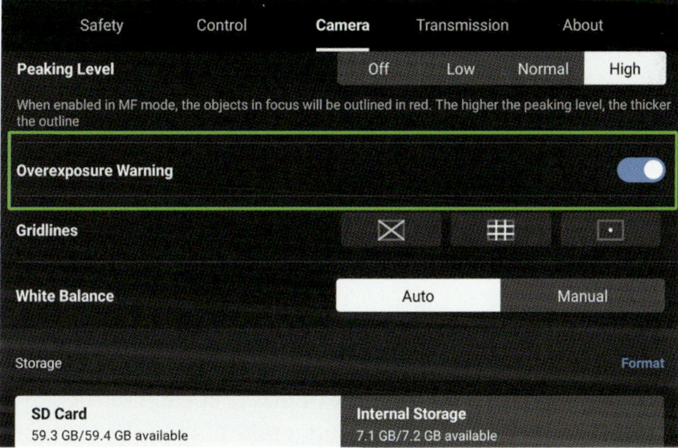

Figure 6.19 Turn on Overexposure Warning in the System Settings screen.

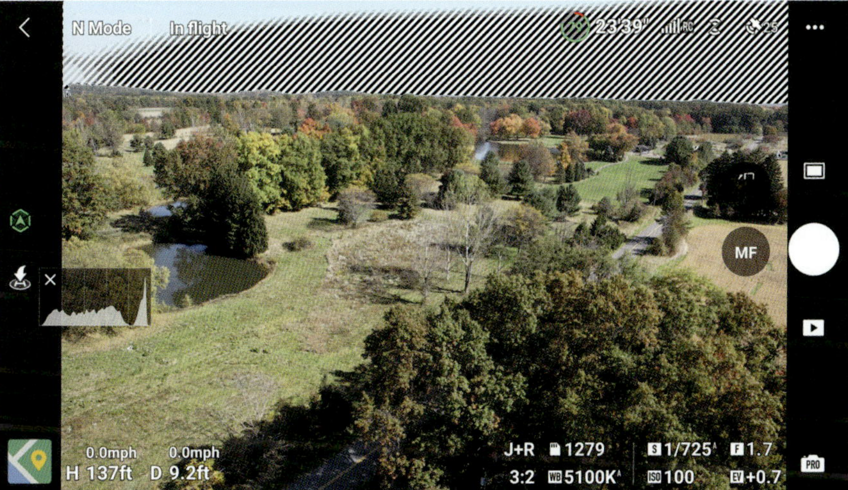

Figure 6.20 Overexposed areas will be highlighted with zebra stripes.

Depending on the importance of the "clipped" detail marked with the zebra stripes, you can adjust exposure or leave it alone. For example, if all the striped areas are in a background that you care little about, you can forget about them and not change the exposure, but if such areas appear in important details of your subject, you may want to make some adjustments.

Zebra stripes can be distracting, and don't provide any information other than warning that some areas are overexposed. A less intrusive tool for evaluating exposure is the histogram, a type of graph that represents the number of tones at a particular brightness level, so you can gauge the exposure in the shadows, midtones, and highlights. An example is shown in Figure 6.21.

Figure 6.21 A histogram is a graph representing the distribution of tonal values in shadows, midtones, and highlights.

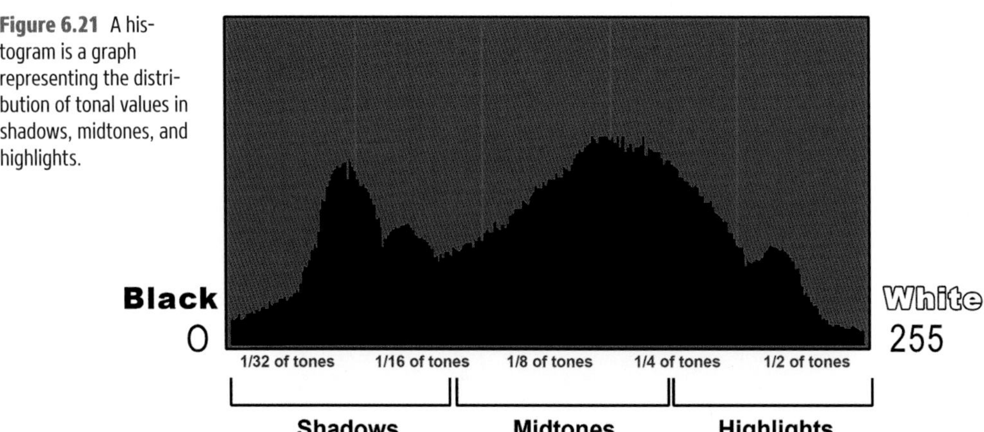

The horizontal axis represents each of 256 different tones, from the darkest blacks (zero) at the left end of the graph, to the brightest whites (255) at the right end. The curve of the graph is produced by vertical bars that represent the relative number of pixels at each of the 256 values. It's important to note that the 256 tones are not equally distributed. Only 1/32 of the available tones are contained in the left-most fifth of the graph, the second, third, fourth, and fifth sections are allocated 1/16, 1/8, 1/4, and 1/2 of the tones, respectively.

The bottom line is that the darkest shadow areas are represented by very few different tones, while highlights are allocated 16 times as many values. That's why it's much more difficult to recover detail in shadows than it is in highlights; there isn't much information in dark areas in the first place. I'll show you how to use that information shortly.

There are two ways to work with histograms. Your first line of defense should be to monitor the histogram shown on the screen of your controller. It is a "live" brightness (or luminance) histogram, which shows how the tones are arranged before and during capture, in real time. You can also view the distribution of your tones in your image editor, as all of them include a histogram feature you will find helpful in post-processing still images. However, it's better to get your exposure correct in the first place rather than try to fix it afterward.

Your first step is to activate the drone's histogram feature. Just follow these steps:

1. **Access System Settings.** Tap the System Settings trio of dots in the upper-right corner.

2. **Navigate to the Camera tab.** Tap the Camera tab and scroll down to activate the Histogram switch, seen in Figure 6.22.

3. **Exit.** Tap the Back icon or press the Back button (if present on your controller) to exit.

4. **Position histogram.** The histogram will appear on the screen, as in Figure 6.23. Touch your finger to the histogram and drag it anywhere you like on the screen.

5. **Hide histogram.** If you don't want to view the histogram, tap the X in its upper-left corner.

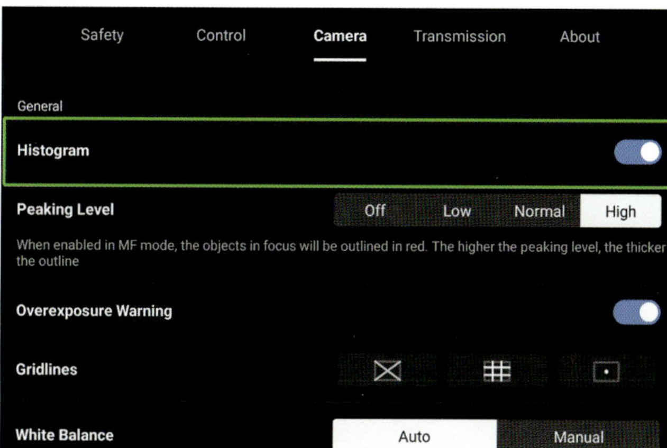

Figure 6.22 Activate the histogram from the Systems Settings menu.

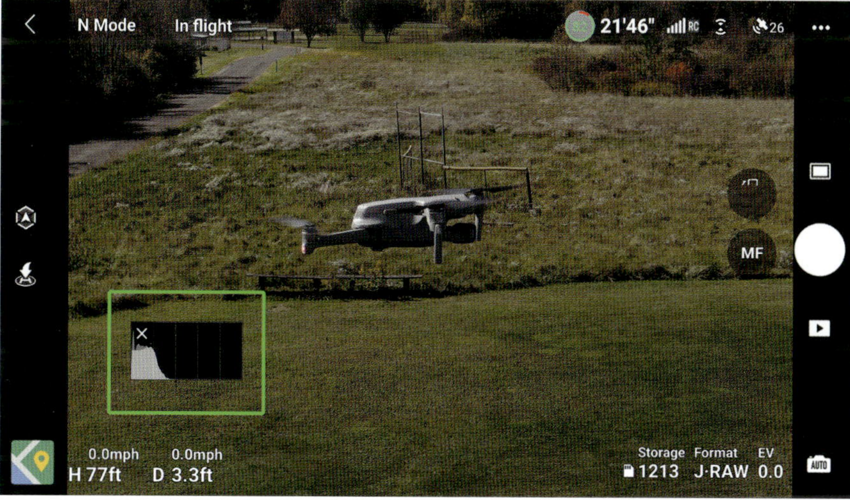

Figure 6.23 The live histogram will appear superimposed on the screen.

COLOR HISTOGRAMS

Your drone only offers the brightness/luminance histogram, and I'll show you how to interpret it in the next section. You'll find that image editors (as well as many digital cameras) offer a second type of histogram that shows the intensity of tones in each of the individual red, green, and blue color channels of an image. Obviously, a color image will have different proportions of each of the primary colors, depending on how much that color appears in the image.

As you become more adept in photography in general, and image editing in particular, you'll find color histograms increasingly useful. An example is shown in Figure 6.24. At left is an aerial image; at top right are the histograms for the red, green, and blue channels of that image. At bottom right, the three histograms are shown superimposed, which is a mode used by some image-editing software.

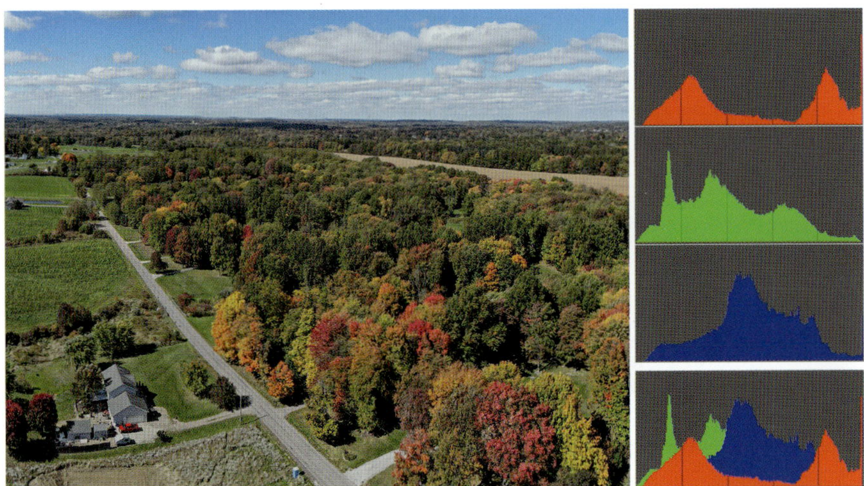

Figure 6.24 RGB histogram with separate channels (upper right); RGB channels superimposed (lower right).

Histograms and Contrast

Your camera's histograms are a simplified display of the numbers of pixels at each of 256 brightness levels, producing an interesting "mountain range" shape in the graph. As I mentioned earlier, each vertical line in the graph represents the number of pixels in the image for each brightness value, from 0 (black) on the left to 255 (white) on the right. The vertical axis represents the number of pixels at each level on a scale that is compressed or expanded to more or less fill the available vertical area of the graph.

Although histograms are most often used to fine-tune exposure, you can glean other information from them, such as the relative contrast of the image. Figure 6.25, top, shows a generic histogram of an aerial image having normal contrast. In such an image, most of the pixels are spread across the image, with a healthy distribution of tones throughout the midtone section of the graph. That large peak at the right side of the graph represents all those light tones in the sky. A normal-contrast image you shoot may have less sky area, and less of a peak at the right side, but notice that very few pixels hug the right edge of the histogram, indicating that the lightest tones are not being clipped because they are off the chart.

With a lower-contrast image, like the one shown in Figure 6.25, center, the basic shape of the previous histogram will remain recognizable, but gradually will be compressed together to cover a smaller area of the gray spectrum. The squished shape of the histogram is caused by all the grays in the original image being represented by a limited number of gray tones in a smaller range of the scale.

Instead of the darkest tones of the image reaching into the black end of the spectrum and the whitest tones extending to the lightest end, the blackest areas of the scene are now represented by a light gray, and the whites by a somewhat lighter gray. The overall contrast of the image is reduced. Because all the darker tones are actually a middle gray or lighter, the scene in this version of the photo appears lighter as well.

Going in the other direction, increasing the contrast of an image produces a histogram like the one shown in Figure 6.23, bottom. In this case, the tonal range is now spread over the entire width of the chart, but, except for the bright sky, there is not much variation in the middle tones; the mountain "peaks" in the midtones are not very high at all. When you stretch the grayscale in both directions like this, the darkest tones become darker (that may not be possible) and the lightest tones become lighter (ditto). In fact, shades that might have been gray before can change to black or white as they are moved toward either end of the scale.

The effect of increasing contrast may be to move some tones off either end of the scale altogether, while spreading the remaining grays over a smaller number of locations on the spectrum. That's exactly the case in the example shown. The number of possible tones is smaller, and the image appears harsher.

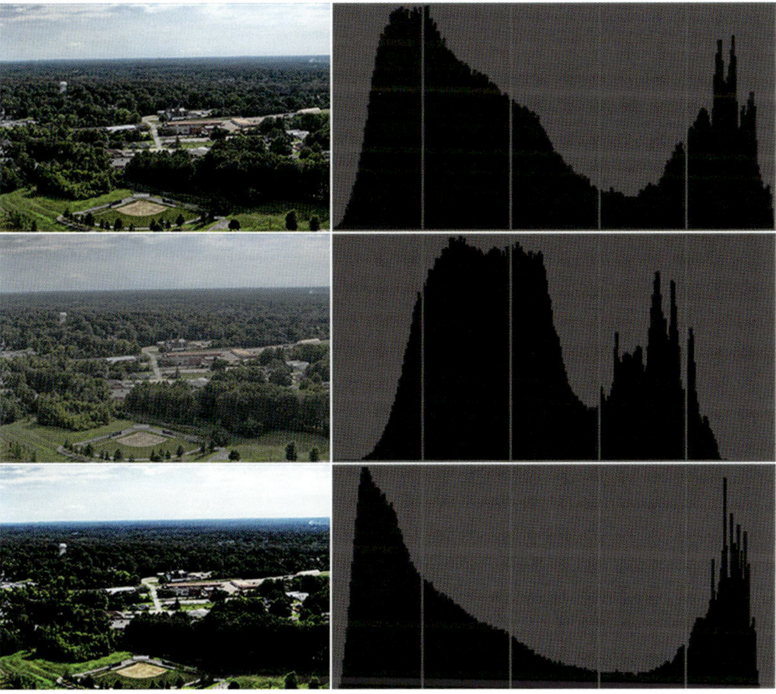

Figure 6.25 Top: This image has fairly normal contrast, even though there is a peak of light tones at the right side representing the sky. Center: This low-contrast image has all the tones squished into one section of the grayscale. Bottom: A high-contrast image produces a histogram in which the tones are spread out.

With drone photography there is very little you can do to adjust contrast. In daylight, the sunlight you have is the sunlight you have to use to capture your images. If lighting is too harsh, the best you can hope for are some clouds that will soften the illumination and fill in inky shadows. However, understanding contrast as displayed by the histogram can be useful when you need to match the shots you take today with those you capture on some other day. When I'm shooting construction progress images, I like to have light with good contrast to better show the details. I try to shoot at the same time of day for consistency, and perhaps wait, if necessary, for the same kind of light contrast when taking each set of images.

Histograms and Exposure

The important thing to remember when working with the histogram display in your camera is that changing the exposure does *not* change the contrast of an image. The curves illustrated in the previous three examples remain exactly the same *shape* when you increase or decrease exposure. *I repeat*: The proportional distribution of grays shown in the histogram doesn't change when exposure changes; it is neither stretched nor compressed. However, the tones as a whole are moved toward one end of the scale or the other, depending on whether you're increasing or decreasing exposure. You'll be able to see that in some illustrations that follow.

So, as you reduce exposure, tones gradually move to the black end (and off the scale), while the reverse is true when you increase exposure. The contrast within the image is changed only to the extent that some of the tones can no longer be represented when they are moved off the scale.

What you *can* do is adjust the exposure so that the tones *that are already present in the scene* are captured correctly. Figure 6.26, top, shows the histogram for an image that is badly underexposed. You can guess from the shape of the histogram that many of the dark tones to the left of the graph have been clipped off. There's plenty of room on the right side for additional pixels to reside without having them become overexposed. So, you can increase the exposure (by changing the shutter speed, ISO, or by adding an EV value) to produce the corrected histogram shown in Figure 6.26, center.

Conversely, if your histogram looks like the one shown in Figure 6.26, bottom, with bright tones pushed off the right edge of the chart, you have an overexposed image, and you can correct it by reducing exposure. In working with histograms, your goal should be to have all the tones in an image spread out between the edges, with none clipped off at the left and right sides. Underexposing (to preserve highlights) should be done only as a last resort, because retrieving the underexposed shadows in your image editor will frequently increase the noise, even if you're working with RAW files. A better course of action is to expose for the highlights, but, when the subject matter makes it practical, fill in the shadows with additional light, using reflectors, fill flash, or other techniques rather than allowing them to be seriously underexposed.

A traditional technique for optimizing exposure is called "expose to the right" (ETTR), which involves adding exposure to push the histogram's curve toward the right side *but not far enough to clip off highlights*. The rationale for this method is that extra shadow detail will be produced with a minimum increase in noise, especially in the shadow areas. As I noted earlier, half of a digital sensor's

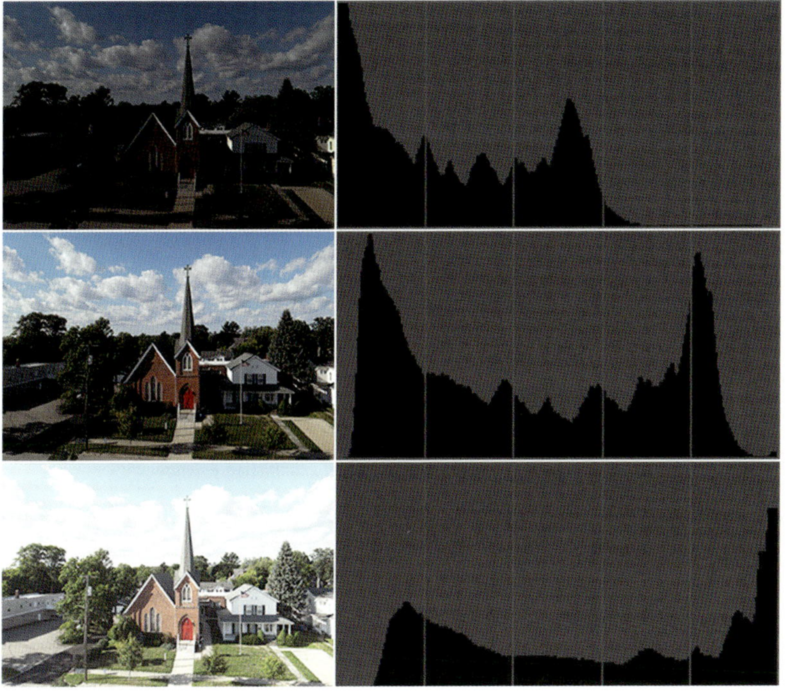

Figure 6.26 Top: A histogram of an under-exposed image may look like this. Center: Adding exposure will produce a histogram like this one. Bottom: A histogram of an overexposed image will show clipping at the right side.

response lies in the brightest areas of an image, and so require the least amount of amplification (which is one way to increase digital noise). ETTR can work, as long as you're able to capture a satisfactory amount of information in the shadows.

Exposing to the Right

Instead, you want to add exposure—as long as you don't push highlights off the right edge of the histogram—to brighten the shadows. Because there are roughly 8,000 tones available in the highlights, even if the RAW image *looks* overexposed, it's possible to use your RAW converter's Exposure slider (such as the one found in Adobe Camera Raw) to bring back detail captured in that surplus of tones in the highlights. This procedure is the exact opposite of what was recommended for film of the transparency variety—it was fairly easy to retrieve detail from shadows by pumping more light through them when processing the image, while even small amounts of extra exposure blew out highlights. (**Note:** I've rounded the numbers a bit for simplicity.) You'll often find that the range of tones in your image is so great that there is no way to keep your histogram from spilling over into the left and right edges, costing you both highlight and shadow detail. Exposing to the right may not work in such situations. A second school of thought recommends *reducing* exposure to bring back the highlights, or "exposing to the left." You would then attempt to recover shadow detail in an image editor, using tools like Adobe Camera Raw's Exposure slider. But remember, above all, that this procedure will also boost noise in the shadows, and so the technique should be used with caution. In most cases, exposing to the right is your best bet.

Focus Pocus

With conventional cameras, correct focus is both a major concern and a creative tool. Enthusiasts working with dSLRs or mirrorless interchangeable-lens cameras need to achieve sharp focus with a variety of subjects, and, in addition, use selective focus techniques as a creative tool to emphasize subjects or blur backgrounds. Drones, too, need to be able to focus accurately. This next section will tell you everything you need to know (or, perhaps, *more* than you need to know) about focus.

Simply put, focus is the process of adjusting the camera so that parts of our subject that we want to be sharp and clear are, in fact, sharp and clear. We can allow the drone to focus for us, automatically, or we can choose to focus manually. With conventional cameras, manual focusing is especially problematic because our eyes and brains have poor memory for correct focus. That's why your eye doctor conducting a refraction test must shift back and forth between pairs of lenses and ask, "Does that look sharper, or was it sharper before?" in determining your correct prescription. Too often, the slight differences are such that the lens pairs must be swapped multiple times.

Fortunately, sharp focus with the Mini 3/Mini 3 Pro does not generate the same trepidation you feel at the optometrist or with your traditional camera. Due to the physics of your drone's camera and the type of images you'll typically be capturing, excellent focus is usually very easy to achieve. DJI's own manual virtually ignores the subject of focus completely. I'm going to provide the missing information and a bit of background that will help you understand focus and how it works completely.

The reason that accurate focus is not generally an issue with drones like your Mini is that they typically have quite generous *depth-of-field* (DOF), which is the range of subject matter that is acceptably in focus. Technically, there is just one plane within your picture area, parallel to the back of the camera's sensor that is in sharp focus. That's the plane in which the points of the image are rendered as precise points. At every other plane in front of or behind the focus plane, the points show up as discs that range from slightly blurry to extremely blurry. In practice, the discs in many of these planes will still be so small that we see them as points, and that's where we get depth-of-field. Depth-of-field is just the range of planes that include discs that we perceive as points rather than blurred splotches. The size of this range increases as the aperture is reduced in size (which is not a factor with your drone's fixed f/1.7 aperture) and is allocated roughly one-third in front of the plane of sharpest focus, and two-thirds behind it. The range of sharp focus is always greater behind your subject than in front of it. (See Figure 6.27.)

Figure 6.27 The range of sharp focus is greater behind your subject than in front of it.

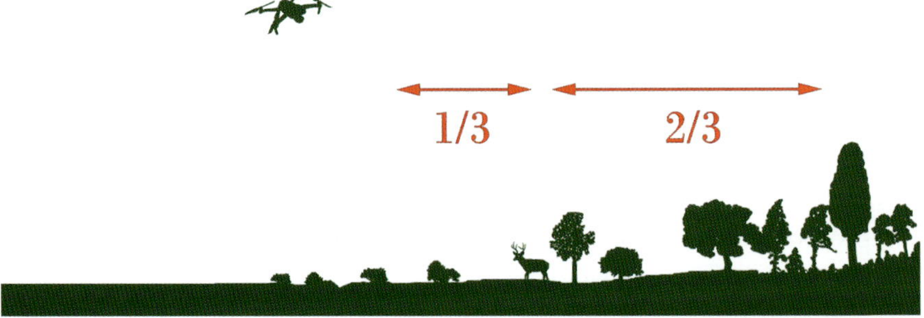

In addition to the aperture, the size of the sensor affects depth-of-field. Smaller sensors use shorter focal length lenses to achieve the same field of view. DJI describes the focal length of your drone's lens as an equivalent to the focal length of a lens providing the same field of view on a full-frame ("35mm") sensor measuring 36mm × 24mm.

Using that convention, the lens of the Mini 3 and Mini 3 Pro projects an image onto a sensor that has the equivalent field of view of a 24mm f/1.7 wide-angle lens, which provides an enormous depth-of-field range.

How enormous? Our perception of sharpness in an image depends on how close we are to that image, and how large it is. If you're looking at a print of one of your aerial images, its sharpness will be affected by the size of that print (say, it's a 16 × 20–inch print rather than an 8 × 10–inch print) and how close you are to it. (Of course!) That's because an image consists of a zillion tiny little points, which you can think of as pinpoints of light in a darkened room. When a given point is out of focus, its edges decrease in contrast and it changes from a perfect point to a tiny disc with blurry edges (remember, blur is the lack of contrast between boundaries in an image). (See Figure 6.28.)

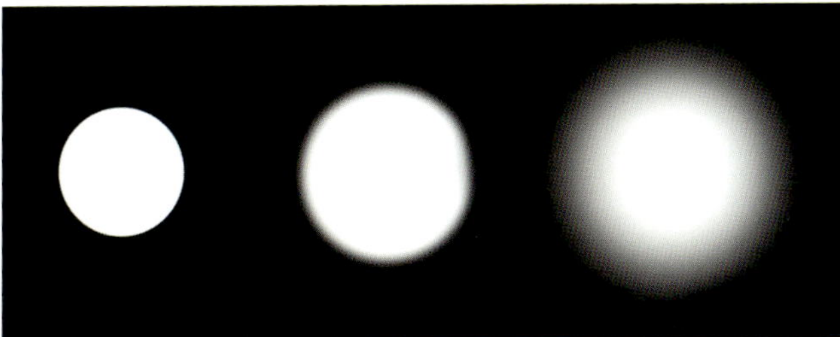

Figure 6.28 When a pinpoint of light (left) goes out of focus, its blurry edges form a circle of confusion (center and right).

When the disc grows large enough that we can see it as a blur rather than as a sharp point then a given point is viewed as being out of focus. You can see, then, that enlarging an image, either by displaying it larger on your computer monitor or by making a large print, also magnifies the size of each circle of confusion. Moving closer to the image does the same thing. So, parts of an image that may look perfectly sharp in a 5 × 7–inch print viewed at arm's length, might appear blurry when blown up to 11 × 14 inches and examined at the same distance. Take a few steps back, however, and the image may look sharp again. This is true for all viewing methods, for example, when you're viewing an image on a monitor. (Of course, the sharpness will be limited by the resolution of the display, too.)

To a lesser extent, the viewer also affects the apparent size of these circles of confusion. Some people see details better at a given distance and may perceive smaller circles of confusion than someone standing next to them. For the most part, however, such differences are small. Truly blurry images will look blurry to just about everyone under the same conditions.

The bottom line is that at normal aerial distances, the Mini 3 and Mini 3 Pro have prodigious amounts of depth-of-field, and at common altitudes everything farther away than 30 feet will be acceptably sharp. As a practical matter, you generally won't be shooting much closer than that—your drone's obstacle avoidance alarms will go nuts if you try to fly too close to a subject. However, some creative perspectives call for a more intimate approach to a subject. Commercial drone pilots may have a need to get close, say, to inspect a cell tower or inspect the roof of a dwelling.

Focus relies on *contrast detection,* which involves identifying the transitions between edges in an image. In Figure 6.29, left, the striations in the rocks are soft and blurred because of the low contrast between them. Whether the cracks in the stone are horizontal, vertical, or diagonal doesn't matter in the least; the focus system looks only for contrast between edges, and those edges can run in any direction at all.

At the right in Figure 6.29, the image has been brought into sharp focus, and the edges have much more contrast; the transitions are sharp and clear. Although this example is a bit exaggerated so you can see the results on the printed page, it's easy to understand that when maximum contrast in a subject is achieved, it can be deemed to be in sharp focus. Your eyes can visually evaluate contrast when you are focusing manually, just as the drone itself seeks the sharpest plane in autofocus mode.

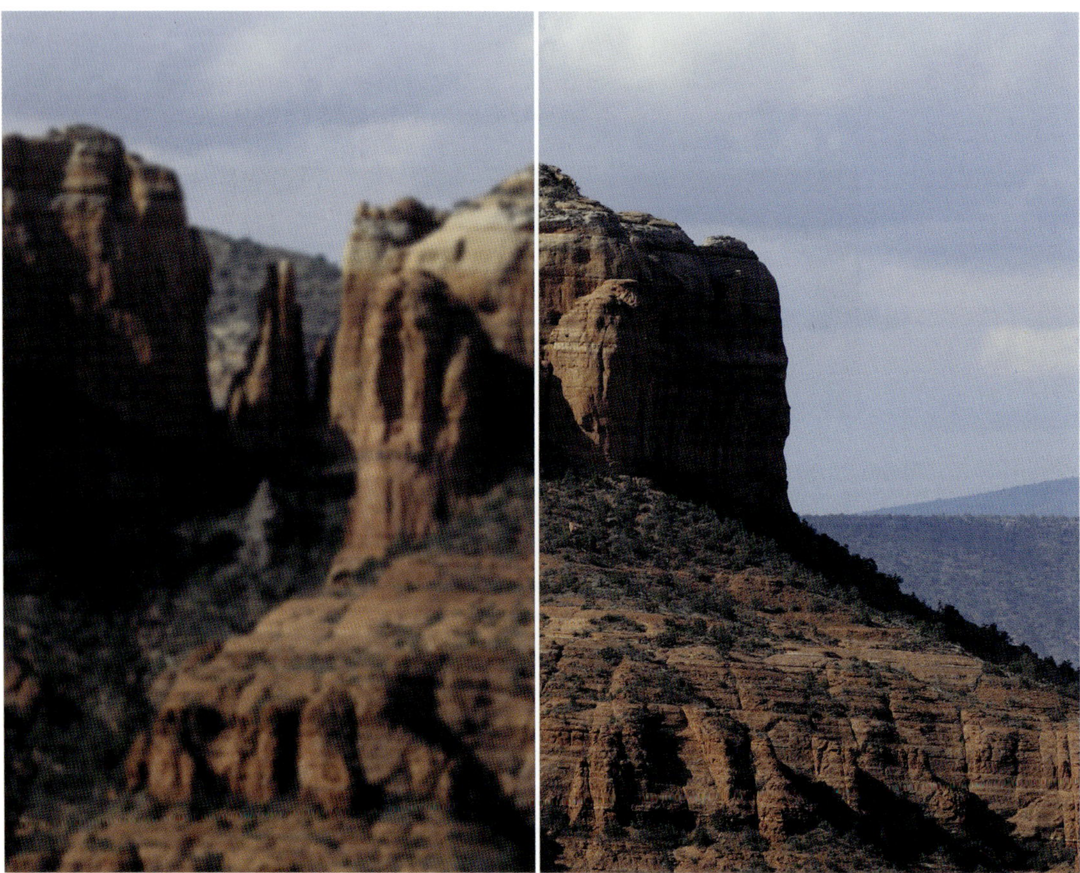

Figure 6.29 Edges are soft in an out-of-focus image (left). When edge contrast is highest, the image is in focus (right).

Autofocus and Manual Focus

Your drone will automatically focus when in AF mode. An icon located to the immediate left of the shutter-release icon on the controller screen will display either AF or an outline of a mountain range (which represents manual focus). Tap the icon to toggle between the two.

In AF mode, the drone will select a focus plane automatically. You can choose a particular subject to focus on by pressing a fingertip on that subject. The aircraft will focus on the subject within the yellow target shown in Figure 6.30, while calculating exposure at the same time. As I described earlier in this chapter, you can slide the "sun" icon upward or downward to add or subtract exposure compensation, and hold your finger down to lock exposure.

When you've toggled to MF, you can drag a yellow marker up and down a scale that has a mountain icon at its top (for distance subjects) and an icon of a person at the bottom (for close focusing). (See Figure 6.31.) You can visually evaluate manual focus on the screen of your controller or take advantage of the drone's Focus Peaking feature. You can activate Peaking Level in the System Settings menu's Camera tab (shown earlier in Figure 6.22). Choose Low, Normal, or High levels.

When activated, the drone will look for sharp edges for you, and outline them in red. The higher the peaking level, the thicker the outline will be, as shown in Figure 6.32. I use the highest level under bright, ambient-light conditions, because the red highlighting is much easier to view. However, the glowing red edges can make viewing your image difficult once focus has been achieved. DJI does not give you a choice of accent color (some platforms let you choose from blue, yellow, and red), so the contrast between edges can be difficult to discern if your subject has a great deal of red detail, which is the case in the Autumn example used for the figure.

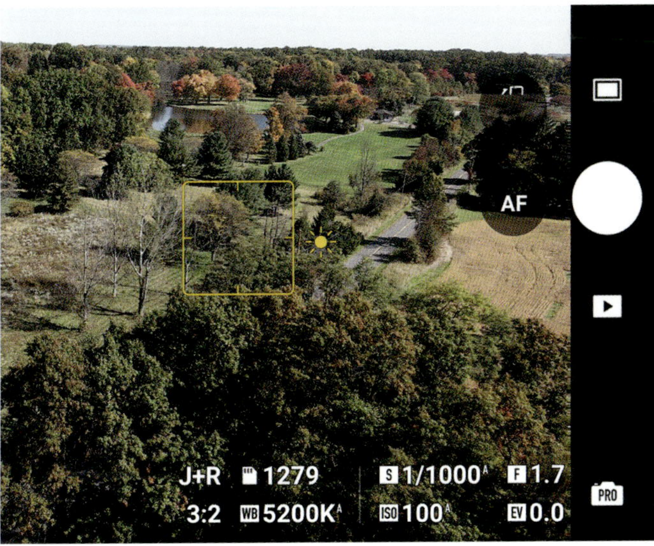

Figure 6.30 Focus on a desired point in the frame while measuring exposure.

Figure 6.31 Manual focusing.

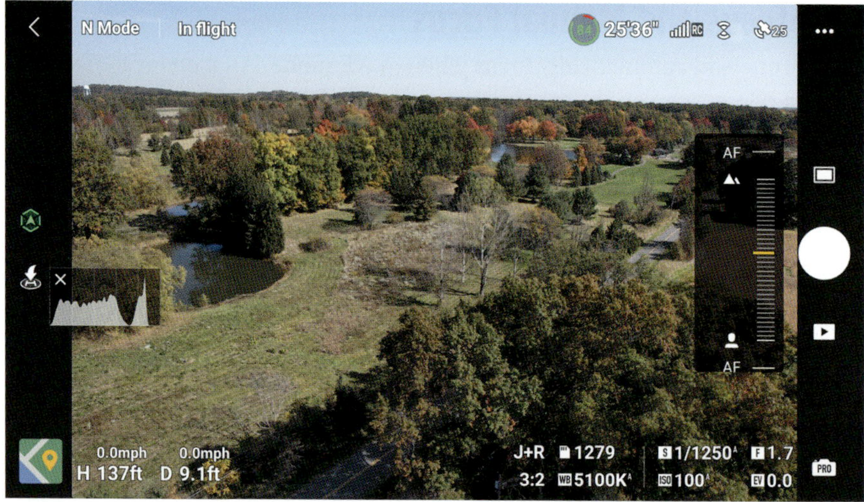

Figure 6.32 Focus peaking accentuates edges.

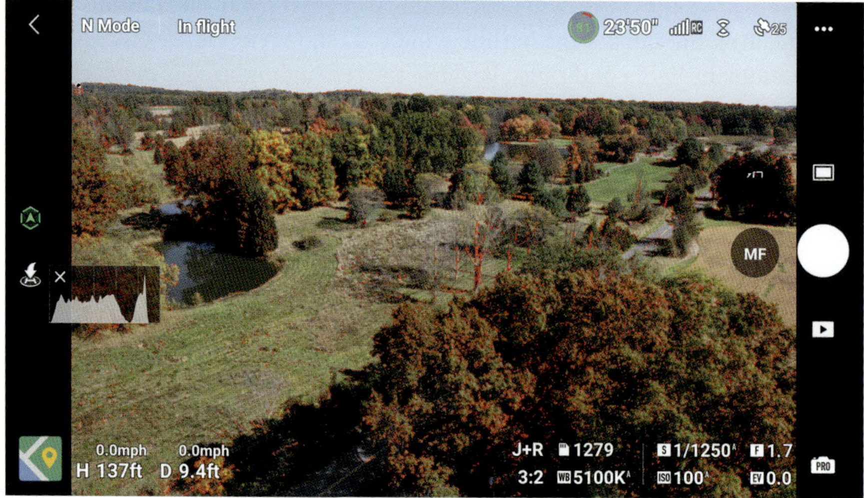

Working with Filters

Filters are an important tool for both still photography and video. They can be used to reduce the amount of light reaching the sensor so that longer shutter speeds can be used to add a blur effect to still photography, or to produce the desired cinematic "look" in video. Filters can take advantage of polarization to darken skies, enrich colors, and eliminate reflections. Special effects filters can produce unusual images not available with post-processing in image editors. And, at times, a filter can provide protection for your drone's camera lens. This section will take a closer look at the common application of filters for aerial photography.

The two most critical factors when choosing a particular type of filter for your drone are the quality and the weight of the filter itself. Cheap filters will degrade the image quality of your stills and affect the sharpness of your video clips. Don't go for the least-expensive filter you can find, particularly if it's a filter you will be using often.

Your filters should be designed to fasten onto the lens of your drone's camera using the same mounting system as DJI "official" filters, and the frame should be of lightweight aluminum or other material. You want a solid and reliable fit while not adding extra weight or balance issues to the drone's camera/gimbal component.

Neutral Density

There are times when you can have too much light. When reducing ISO isn't enough to get the desired shutter speed, you need a neutral-density filter to block additional light. *ND* filters, as they're known, come in a variety of "strengths," and vendors use somewhat confusing nomenclature to define how much of the light is blocked. You'll see neutral-density filters from one manufacturer labeled according to something called a *filter factor*, while others, from different vendors, are labeled according to their *optical density*. There are actually no less than *four* variations of naming schemes, all equally cryptic; and even if you understand the difference, you still probably won't know which is which, or why.

For example, one of the ND filters I own of a particular value is labeled, by different manufacturers, with the following names: ND8, 8X, ND0.9, and "Three Stop." All four monikers mean that the filter reduces the amount of illumination by three full f/stops. If the correct exposure were 1/500th second at f/8 without any filter at all, you'd need an exposure of 1/60th second at f/8 with the filter in place.

Because fast shutter speeds produce an undesirably hyper-realistic look in video, neutral-density filters are especially important when shooting movies. I'll cover their application in more detail in Chapter 6. Third-party vendors sell their own ND filters alone or in combinations. Several companies, such as Freewell and PGYTECH, offer variable neutral-density filters, which allow you to dial in 2- to 5- or 6- to 9-stop density by rotating a ring around the filter's circumference. Some ND filters are sold that also serve as polarizers (which I'll discuss shortly).

A special kind of neutral-density filter—the split ND or graduated ND filter—is a unique tool for landscape stills and video. In some scenes, the sky can be significantly brighter than the foreground and well beyond the ability of the camera's sensor to capture detail in both. An ND filter that is dark at the top and clear at the bottom can even out the exposure, restoring the puffy white clouds and clear blue sky to your images. These filters can be tricky to use. Here are some factors to keep in mind:

- **Don't tilt.** The transition in the filter should match the transition between foreground and background, so you'll want to avoid FPV (first-person view), in which the image rotates as the drone rolls during turns.
- **Watch the location of your horizons.** The ND effect is more sharply defined with a split ND filter than with a graduated version, but you need to watch your horizons in both cases if you want to avoid darkening some of the foreground. That may mean that you have to place the "boundary" in the middle of the image to properly separate the sky and foreground.
- **Watch the shape of your horizons.** A horizon that's not broken by trees, mountains, buildings, or other non-sky shapes will allow darkening the upper half of the image more smoothly. That makes seascapes a perfect application for this kind of neutral-density filter. However, you can use these filters with many other types of scenes as long as the darkening effect isn't too obvious. That makes a graduated ND filter a more versatile choice, because the neutral-density effect diminishes at the middle of the image.

Polarization

Polarizing filters are useful in many ways. Light becomes polarized (and therefore susceptible to the effects of a polarizing filter) when it is scattered by passing through a translucent medium. So, light from a clear-blue sky becomes polarized when it passes through the dust-laden atmosphere. Light striking, passing through, and reflecting off water also becomes polarized. The same is true of many other types of objects, including foliage, and the partially transparent paint on an automobile body (think about it: that's why cars need several coats of paint). Nontransparent or translucent objects, like the chrome *trim* on the automobile, aren't transparent, and don't polarize the light. *However,* if the light reflecting from the metal has already been partially polarized (that is, it is reflected skylight), you still might be able to see a reduced amount of glare reduction with a polarizing filter.

How does it work? A polarizer contains what you can think of as a tiny set of parallel louvers that filter out all the light waves except for those vibrating in a direction parallel to the louvers. The polarizer itself consists of two rings; one is attached to the lens, while the outer ring rotates the polarizing glass. This lets you change the angle of the louvers and selectively filter out different light waves.

A polarizing filter can be mounted on the camera to replace the empty frame that surrounds the lens. Rotate the frame to remove it, then attach the polarizer to the same mount. A ring around the outside of the filter allows adjusting the amount of polarization. (See Figure 6.33.)

You can rotate the ring until the effect you want is visible, but polarizers designed for use with drones will have a pair of marks on the rim of the filter that can be rotated to produce the best effect. Keep in mind that the amount of glare reduction depends heavily on the angle from which you take the photograph, and the amounts of scattered light in the reflections (which is determined by the composition of the subject). Polarizers work best when the sun is low in the sky and at a 90-degree angle from the camera and subject (that is, off to your left or right shoulder). Blue sky and water, which can contain high amounts of scattered light, can be made darker and more vibrant as glare is reduced. You can also reduce or eliminate reflections from windows and other nonmetallic surfaces.

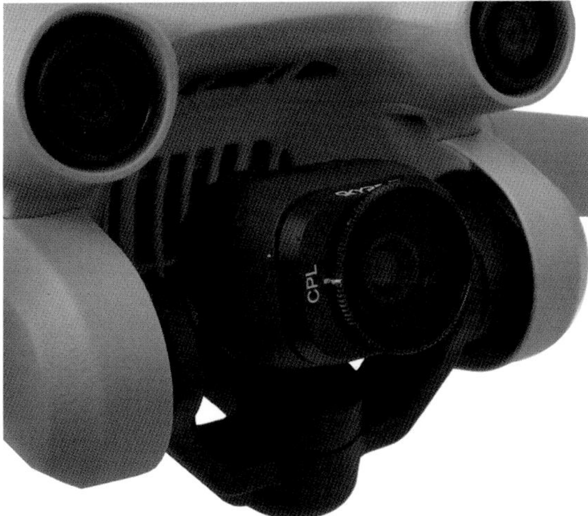

Figure 6.33 The filter replaces the empty frame on the camera.

As you might expect, polarizing filters solve problems and enhance images in several ways. Let's look at them:

- **Reduce or eliminate reflections.** Polarizing filters can reduce or eliminate reflections in glass, water, lacquer-coated objects, non-conducting surfaces, and plastic. They don't have any effect on reflections on metallic surfaces.
- **Increase contrast.** A polarizing filter is the only filter that can increase contrast in color imagery by eliminating those pesky reflections.
- **Darken pale skies.** Polarizing filters block a lot of light (as much as two f/stops), and because the effect is strongest when dealing with polarized light (such as light in the sky), this can help darken pale skies considerably. At the same time, it will also make clouds stand out more strongly. But take note of the potential undesirable effects I'll explain next.

As you gain experience, you'll learn what types of scenes benefit from polarization, and what types do not. Look at Figure 6.34, which shows two different shots taken with my Mini 3 Pro about 10 minutes apart from approximately the same location. (I had to land the drone after capturing the first image and install the filter to take the second shot.)

In the version at left, reflections in the ponds in the center provide a reverse image of the trees that surround them. The image at right, with the polarizer in place, has a darker sky and the colors of the Autumn leaves are richer. But the reflections of the trees are gone. That makes the ponds look duller and flat. I would have gotten a better picture by *not* using the polarizer and, perhaps, increasing saturation of the trees and sky in post-processing.

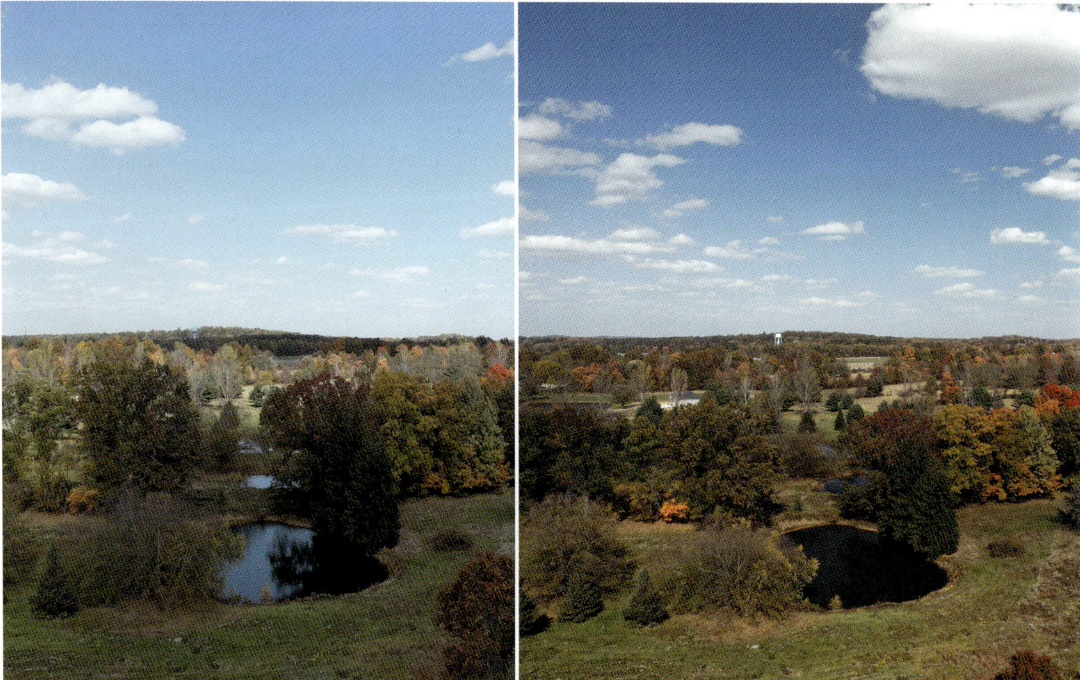

Figure 6.34 Unpolarized image (left); the same scene using a polarizer (right).

One thing to watch out for is the use of polarizers with wide-angle lenses, such as the 24mm optics installed on the Mini 3 Pro and Mini 3. Polarizers work best when the camera is pointed 90 degrees away from the light source and provide the least effect when the camera is directed 180 degrees from the light source, as when the light source is behind you. With longer lenses, the field of view is narrow enough that the difference in angle between the light source and your subject is roughly the same across the image field.

But the wide-angle lenses of your Mini 3 Pro and Mini 3 have a field of view of 82 degrees. It's possible for subjects at one side of the frame to be oriented exactly perpendicular to the light source, while subject matter at the opposite side of the frame will actually face the light source (at a 0-degree angle). The possibility is even more acute when shooting panoramas, which can extend the field of view to 180 degrees. With such broad perspectives, everything in between will have an intermediate angle. In this extreme case, you'll get maximum polarization at one location within your image, and a greatly reduced polarization effect at the extreme angles. Figure 6.35 shows how disruptive the effect can be; maximum polarization is applied at the center of the image, with much less visible in the left and right two-thirds of the photo. In this case, it would have been better to use no polarizing filter at all for this panoramic image. Use caution when using a polarizer.

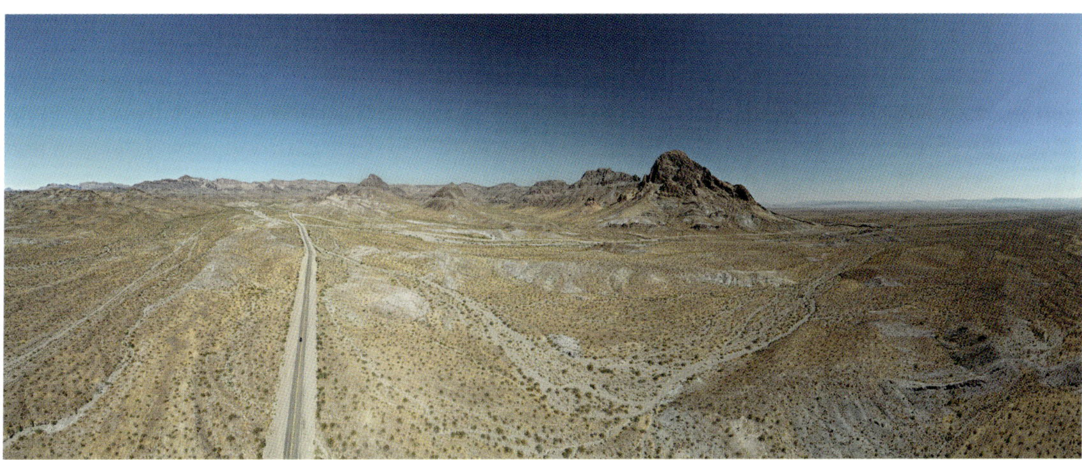

Figure 6.35 The polarization effect is strongest in the center of the image.

Filters for Protection

Several vendors offer UV filters for the Mini 3/Mini 3 Pro. Do you really need to use a filter to protect your camera's lens? I have a definitive answer: yes, no, and maybe.

Each of the three answers can be persuasive. No matter how careful you are, if you're not using a filter, some dust, mist, or other foreign substances can get on your lens during a flight, particularly if you are flying during bad weather or a dust storm kicks up unexpectedly. Your drone may suffer a "soft" crash. (I've collided with trees more than once, and my drone tumbled through the branches before hitting the ground without actually suffering any real damage.) In such cases, a filter can shield your lens from dust and debris, and absorb a few light scratches during minor collisions, assuming the gimbal itself is not harmed.

If you're clumsy, cleaning a filter may be safer than cleaning the lens itself. If you don't know how to clean a lens, or don't have the proper tools, the more often you have to clean your lenses, the greater the likelihood of leaving cleaning marks or clumsily rubbing off some of the vital multi-coating that helps prevent lens flare. Again, a filter may be appropriate for those who need to protect their camera from themselves.

As far as UV removal is concerned, it's known that general-purpose UV and skylight filters have little to no effect in the digital sensor world, so a UV filter offers nothing but a bit of protection, while adding weight to your gimbal. Lower-quality filters can degrade the image due to aberrations and flare. Why reduce the quality of every image you take to guard against an accident that may never happen?

My recommendation is to use a filter, such as an ND or polarizer, when you need to filter something. When conditions merit, the ND or polarizer you already have in place will serve as lens "protection." If unfavorable weather threatens, a UV filter can be useful.

Do It Yourself

If you like to experiment, you can make your own filters, using the empty frame around the lens as your filter holder. Carefully cut a piece of filter material to fit and mount it on the camera. Colored gelatin filters, pieces of fine window screen (for sunstar/starburst effects), and other experimental filters can be constructed and used to produce new and interesting special effects.

Next Up

This chapter covered a broad range of equipment-specific tips for improving your still photography. In Chapter 7, I'm going to describe some more general photographic concepts, including composition, cropping, and shooting at night. Budding photo enthusiasts may find the techniques eye-opening and especially helpful. I'm hoping that veteran photographers will use the chapter as a refresher, and discover some valuable nuggets they can apply to their current work.

Keys to Great Photos 7

Aerial snapshots are easy to create and fun to do. You may be an experienced shooter adding drone photography to your repertoire. Or, you may be a neophyte attempting to learn photography and drone operation at the same time. In either case, the ability to send an aircraft skyward as an aerial camera platform can be exhilarating. It's almost a given that your first hundred or so still photos will be views of your house from an altitude of 100 feet or so, followed by shots of your town's major (or minor) tourist attractions. Go ahead, enjoy random snapshooting. There's plenty of time to get serious about your drone-based photography.

Random snapshooting can sometimes yield lucky shots—happy accidents that look good and prompt you to say, "Actually, I meant to do that!" (even if it wasn't the case). Some Pulitzer Prize–winning photos have resulted from a photographer instinctively squeezing off a shot at what turned out to be a decisive moment in some fast-breaking news event. However, lacking a Pulitzer-winner's intuition, most photographers end up with a larger percentage of pleasing photos only when they stop to think about and plan their pictures before pressing or tapping the shutter release button or screen icon.

In this chapter, I'm going to help you take your aerial still photography to the next level, setting you on the road to taking great pictures. I'll introduce all the basic elements of good composition, such as selecting what to include in and what to leave out of a well-designed photograph. You'll find out some basic rules, such as the Rule of Thirds, and most importantly, when you should ignore these rules in order to get dramatic effect.

The very best photos are usually not accidents; they are carefully planned and composed. That is, such pictures display good composition, which is the careful selection and arrangement of the photo's subject matter within a frame. Planning can be challenging for drone photographers, who must pack a lot of activity into roughly 30 minutes of battery life. We can't wait for hours—à la Ansel Adams—in anticipation of the universe settling into exactly the right arrangement. Instead, simply understanding how good composition works and keeping that in mind on the fly when you shoot can make a world of difference. The following list gives you an overview of some elements in planning a great photo with your drone. I'll address the most important of these in more detail later in the chapter.

- **Selecting the picture orientation.** Some subjects look best when shown in a tall, vertically oriented frame. Some look best in a wide, horizontal format. A few need a square composition. To make the most of your camera's resolution, choose an orientation when you take the photo rather than cropping it later in an image editor.

- **Choosing your subject matter.** This isn't as easy as it appears to be. Your aerial vantage point and the wide-angle perspective of your drone's lens means the frame might be filled with interesting things to look at covering a broad range of the landscape below, but you need to decide which should be the subject of the picture.

- **Deciding on a center of interest.** One point in the picture should naturally draw the eye as a starting place for the viewer's exploration of the rest of the image. With a center of interest, the photo becomes focused and not simply a collection of objects.

- **What does your picture say?** A scenic photo can be composed in different ways, depending on what you want the image to say. For example, a photo taken in a park can capture the grandeur of nature showcasing a dramatic skyline with purple mountains' majesty and amber waves of grain. On the other hand, you might be tempted to make a statement about the environmental impact of humans by focusing on trash left behind by careless visitors or perhaps desiccated amber mountain majesties and chemically tainted waves of purple grain.

- **Directing the eye within the frame.** Use lines and curves to provide a guided tour of your image, directing the viewer from one portion to another to finally focus on the main center of interest. Balance the composition to keep the eye from wandering to "lopsided" parts of the image.

- **Planning for action.** If your subjects are moving, you need to anticipate where they will be and how they will be arranged when you take the picture.

- **Working with the foreground and background.** Objects and textures in the foreground and background can work for you or against you. The area surrounding your main subject is an important part of the composition.

Orientation

New photo enthusiasts using conventional cameras often fall into the trap of shooting all their photos at eye level and with the camera held in horizontal or "landscape" orientation. The first affliction isn't necessarily a problem for drone still images, which tend to be captured at various altitudes, and very seldom at what we would consider "eye" level. However, a dependence on horizontal compositions *does* plague aerial photographers, though, simply because the cameras built into the Mini 3 and Mini 3 Pro are, by default, oriented horizontally and limited to aspect ratios of 4:3 and 16:9. Fortunately, their cameras can be rotated 90 degrees by tapping the Rotate icon located just above the AF/MF control at the right of the DJI screen. Capturing vertical shots is remarkably easy.

In addition, while the most common panorama images, too, are generally taken in landscape format, you can opt to take a vertically oriented panorama, as well. (Panoramas can not be taken when the camera is rotated 90 degrees, or if you've attached the DJI wide-angle attachment, unfortunately.) But just because a wide perspective is urged upon you by the drone's camera, that doesn't mean all your images must use that format. You should keep in mind the option to rotate the camera and, also, that you can use *cropping* of an image captured in landscape format to carve a well-designed image out of the area encompassed by the entire frame.

Many times, the original image captured with your drone is just the raw material you work with in an image editor to create a compelling final image. Now, I'm not a fan of heavily processed images, and you won't find long chapters on using Photoshop or Lightroom in this book. (There are plenty of general-purpose image-editing books which do that more effectively.) But using an application to crop your drone images should be a regular part of your toolkit.

The orientation of a photo, in particular—whether it's a wide or tall picture—affects how you look at the image. When you see a landscape-oriented photo, you tend to think of panoramas and horizontal sprawl. A vertically oriented photo, on the other hand, provides expectations of height. Most subjects fit into one of these orientations; very few photos are actually composed within a perfectly square frame. Square photos are often static and uninteresting and are usually put to work only with subject matter that suits them, such as circular objects or images that have important horizontal and vertical components. If you fly the Mini 3 or Mini 3 Pro, you'll need to keep the limitations of square images in mind, because your drone's 4:3 aspect ratio is inherently more square, compared to the 3:2 layout of traditional digital cameras (other than Micro Four Thirds models).

Because of this built-in bias, many photographers unconsciously slip into the trap of viewing every potential photo in a horizontal mode. They consider a vertical orientation only when confronted by subject matter that simply can't be photographed in any other way, such as a tall structure or towering cliff. Figure 7.1, captured by Cleveland photographer Kolman Rosenberg, actually has a nice composition in default horizontal mode. The diagonal lines of the spit of land draw attention to the lighthouse at its tip. However, you can see that cropping the same picture to create a vertical image draws the eye from the foreground out to the lighthouse even more strongly. (See Figure 7.2.)

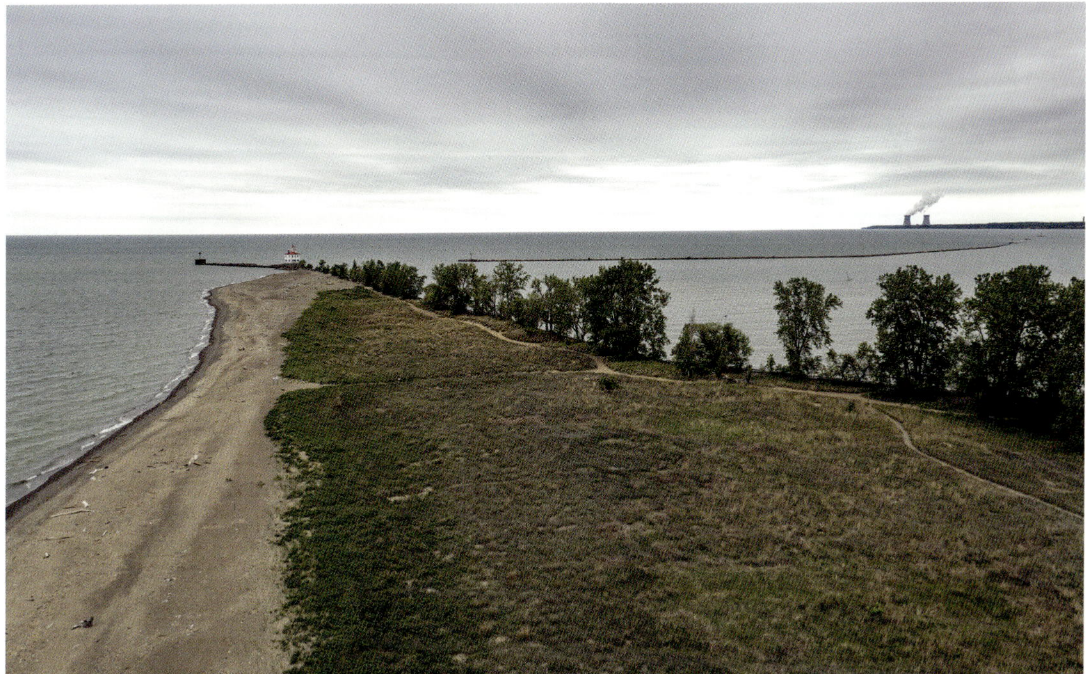

Figure 7.1 This horizontally oriented photo has strong compositional elements.

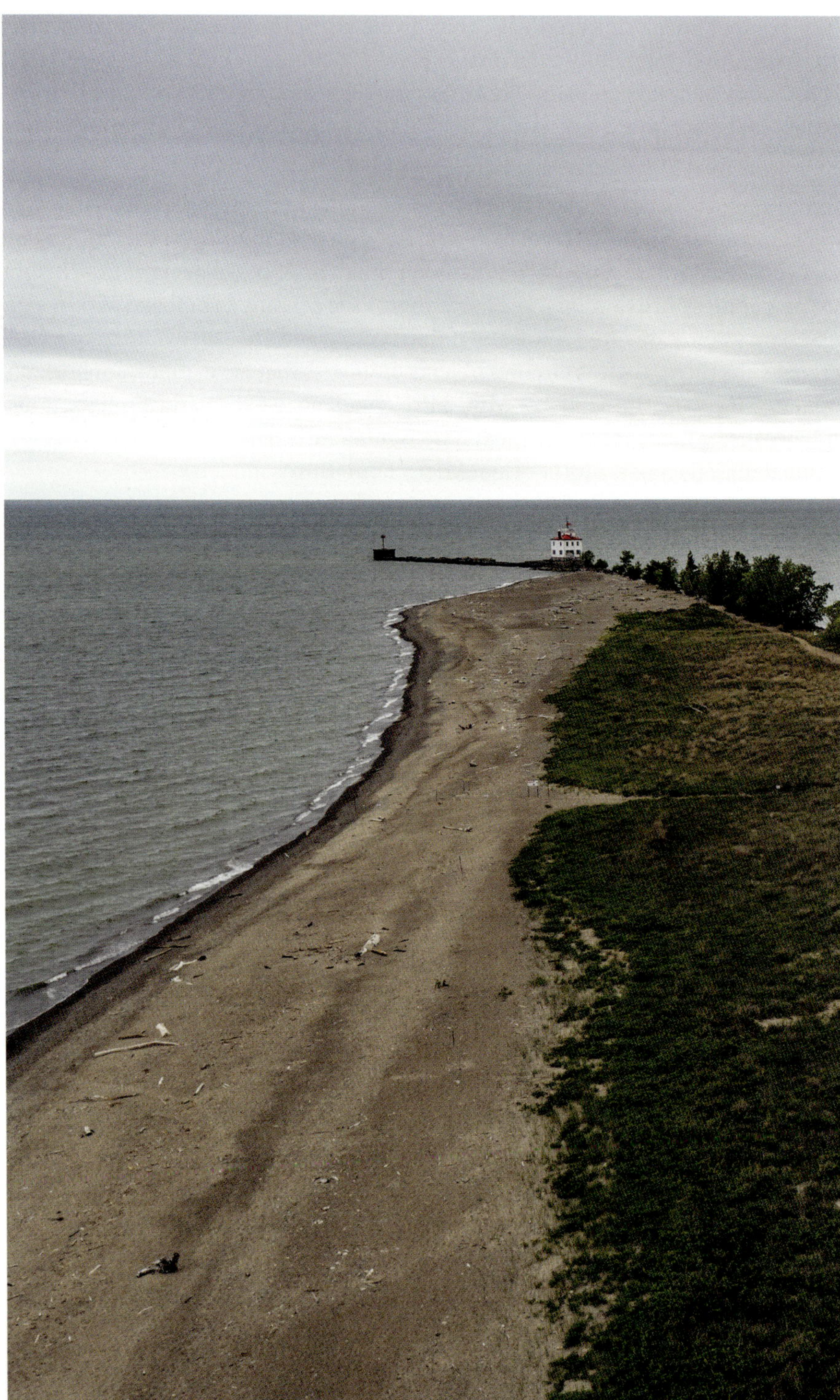

Figure 7.2 A vertical orientation adds depth.

Because your drone produces horizontally oriented images unless you think to rotate the camera, you'll need to think about the possibilities for vertical images *as you shoot*. Don't hesitate to make the decision to crop to a vertical image as you're reviewing your photos on your computer, too. Here are some tips that will help you decide when it's appropriate to use a vertical composition—and when you should think horizontal instead:

- If you're taking pictures specifically for a slide show or for a computer presentation, stick with horizontal pictures. Slide show images are seen sequentially and should all have the same basic frame that is often sized to fill up the horizontal screen as much as possible. Inserting a vertical picture might mean that the top and bottom of your photograph is cut off or appears odd on-screen.

- If your subject has dominant horizontal lines, use a horizontally composed image. Landscapes and seascapes that feature a prominent horizon, photos of sprawling buildings, or bridges spanning a waterway look their best in horizontal mode.

- If your subject has strong vertical lines, use a vertical composition. The tall buildings and towers, trees, and other lofty subjects all call for a vertical orientation.

- Consider cropping to a square composition if vertical and horizontal objects in your picture are equally important and you don't want to emphasize one over the other. A building that is wide but that has a tall tower at one end might look good in a square composition. The important vertical element at one end would keep the image from being too static. Circular objects lend themselves to square compositions because the round form fits comfortably inside a square "frame."

You may also find yourself boxed into a square format when you need to crop to eliminate distracting features outside the boundaries of your main subject. I captured a few aerial views of a Division III college football game from an adjacent vacant soccer field. My drone was never directly over any of the participants and spectators, and there were no temporary flight restrictions in the area.

But, as you might expect, the playing field was flanked at two ends with parking lots. By cropping the left and right sides of the image, I ended up with a square-ish picture. Cropping at top and bottom to produce a rectangular image would have eliminated the small-town flavor of this 1,300-student college. (Back in my day, I took a Sociology 101 course at a large university, with more freshmen than that packed into a single auditorium for its lectures.) (See Figure 7.3.)

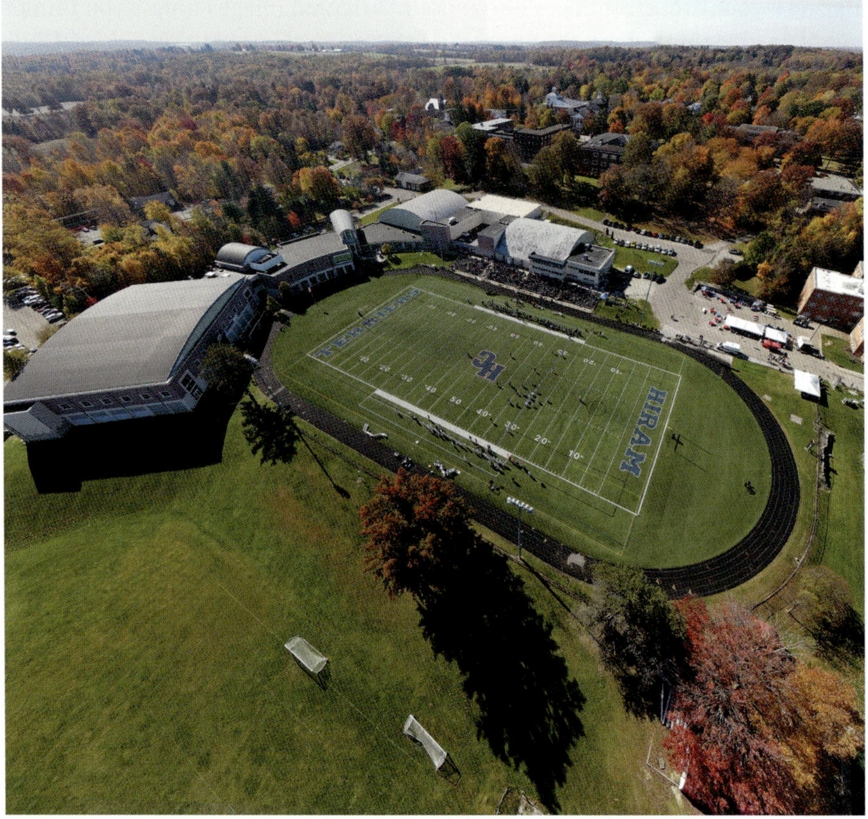

Figure 7.3 Go ahead and crop to a square to eliminate distracting image content.

Change Your Perspective

Earlier I mentioned the trap that enthusiasts of conventional cameras fall into: shooting everything at eye level. Stooping down or climbing a ladder can give you a whole new perspective for otherwise mundane snapshots. Drone photographers obviously seldom take photos from anywhere near eye level. However, there's no reason to shoot everything from an altitude of 400 feet, either.

One key to capturing more pictorial aerial photos is to stop thinking of them as aerial photos. Think like a ground-based photographer who happens to have the world's most versatile tripod platform at their disposal. I've been at several events where elevated work platforms (such as bucket trucks, "cherry pickers," or boom lifts) have been rented to allow taking photos of large groups of people from an angle that allows looking down on every smiling face. Today, you can take the same photo with a drone much more inexpensively and with less disruption.

Traditional aerial photos have their place, of course. The images of the high school shown in Figure 7.4 provide a decent overall perspective of the layout of the building. The version on top is a standard aerial view that really shows little of the building's character, although you get an excellent inspection of the structure's roofs. Taken from a lower elevation, the bottom image provides more detail about the high school's architectural style. Even so, it's still not something you'd want to put in the school yearbook.

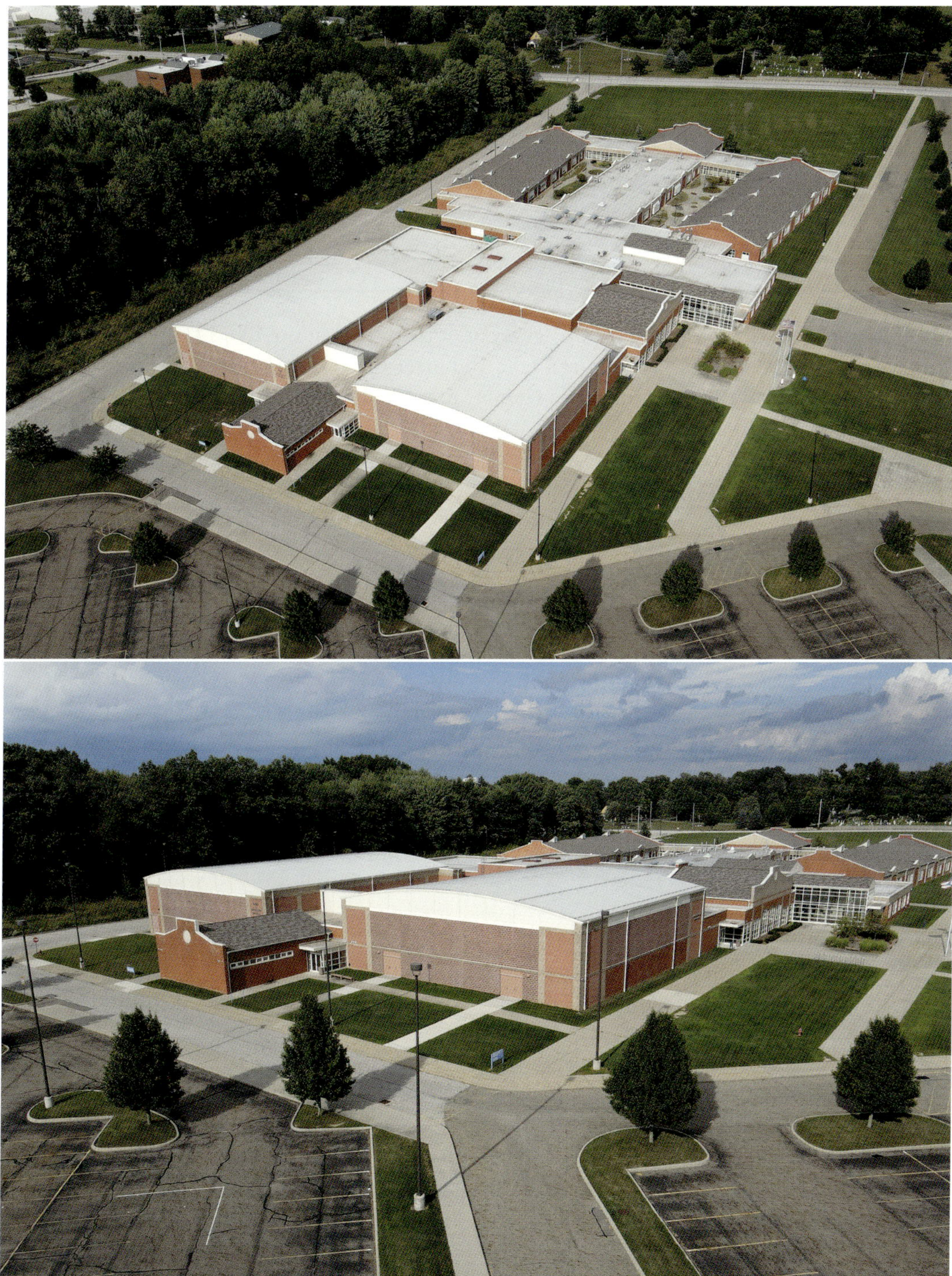

Figure 7.4 Aerial shots provide good overall views.

Figure 7.5, in contrast, was taken the same day using the same drone, but directly in front of the high school's main façade at an elevation of about 40 feet—much higher than any tripod I might have had available. The image doesn't scream "aerial photo."

SEE LEVEL

A large number of the photos I take, and which are included in this book, were taken at altitudes of less than 100 feet, with many of them captured at elevations of 50 feet or less. That's because my goal in each case was *not* to take an aerial photo. I just wanted to use my drone to take a particular picture that I couldn't get with my current digital mirrorless camera.

When I discovered this "versatile tripod" concept, it was a revelation. Even if an aerial view is not needed, your flying camera platform can take you places you couldn't easily venture to without superpowers. Like many beginners, when I got my first drone, I was initially leery about flying over water, because any sort of emergency incident or unplanned landing could easily result in a total loss of the aircraft. After a few months I realized that a dunk in the water wasn't any more likely than a crash in a forest or other inaccessible location and I became more daring.

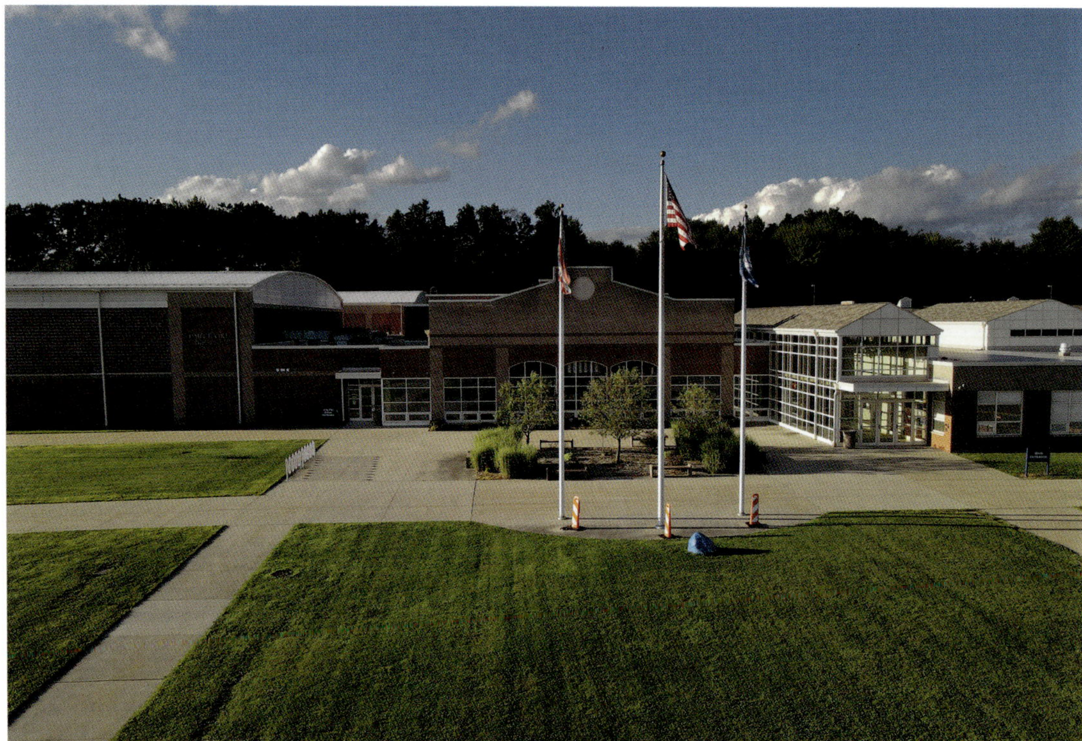

Figure 7.5 Shooting from a lower elevation provides a more conventional perspective.

I'm now fairly unconcerned sending my aircraft out over water, capturing aerial shots like the one shown at left in Figure 7.6. But I also don't hesitate to send my drone mounted on its virtual tripod up close for shots like the one seen at right in the figure. Some 30–40 feet in the air, I'm able to capture images from a vantage point I'd need a boat to obtain. Unless you happened to see this pair of images together, you might not guess that both were taken with a drone.

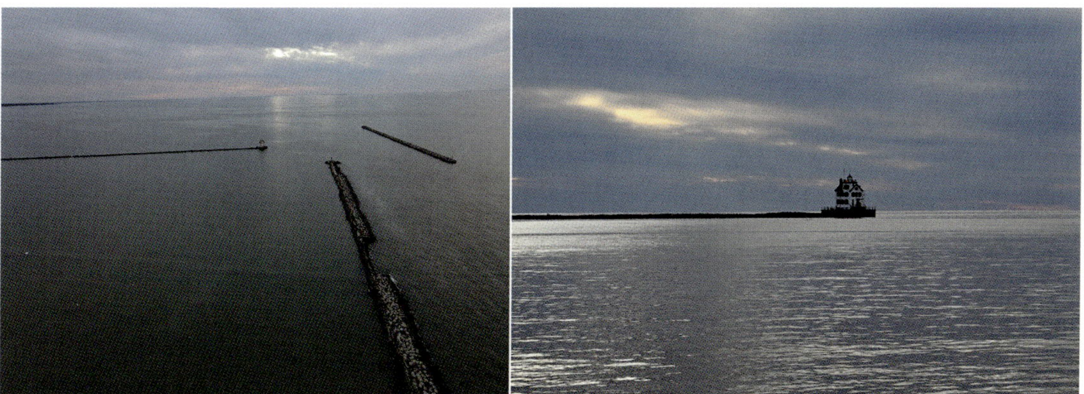

Figure 7.6 High vantage point (left); shooting from a lower altitude (right).

Center of Interest

Photographs shouldn't send the person looking at them on a hunting expedition. As interesting as your subject is to you, you don't want viewers puzzling over what's the most important part of the image or perhaps conducting a vote by secret ballot to see who has successfully guessed your intent. Every picture should have a single, strong center of interest. You want to narrow down your subject matter: rather than include everything of interest in a photo, choose one main subject. Then, if you can, find secondary objects in the picture that are also interesting (giving the photo depth and richness) but which are still clearly subordinate to the main subject.

On first glance, viewers might find it difficult to locate the center of interest in Figure 7.7, which shows an abandoned shack, photographed from a distance. The perspective of the 24mm (equivalent) lens emphasizes the isolation of the shack. A wide-angle lens will always convey a feeling of space and depth. The foreground area becomes more prominent, adding to the feeling of space. The lower angle takes in more of the sky and other surrounding area, giving additional depth. However, you may not want your subjects to appear too small; they should still be large enough to be interesting. Too much distance is the most common mistake amateur photographers make. If you're showing wide-open spaces in your picture, be certain that it's because you want to. But don't move so far back that the center of interest isn't obvious.

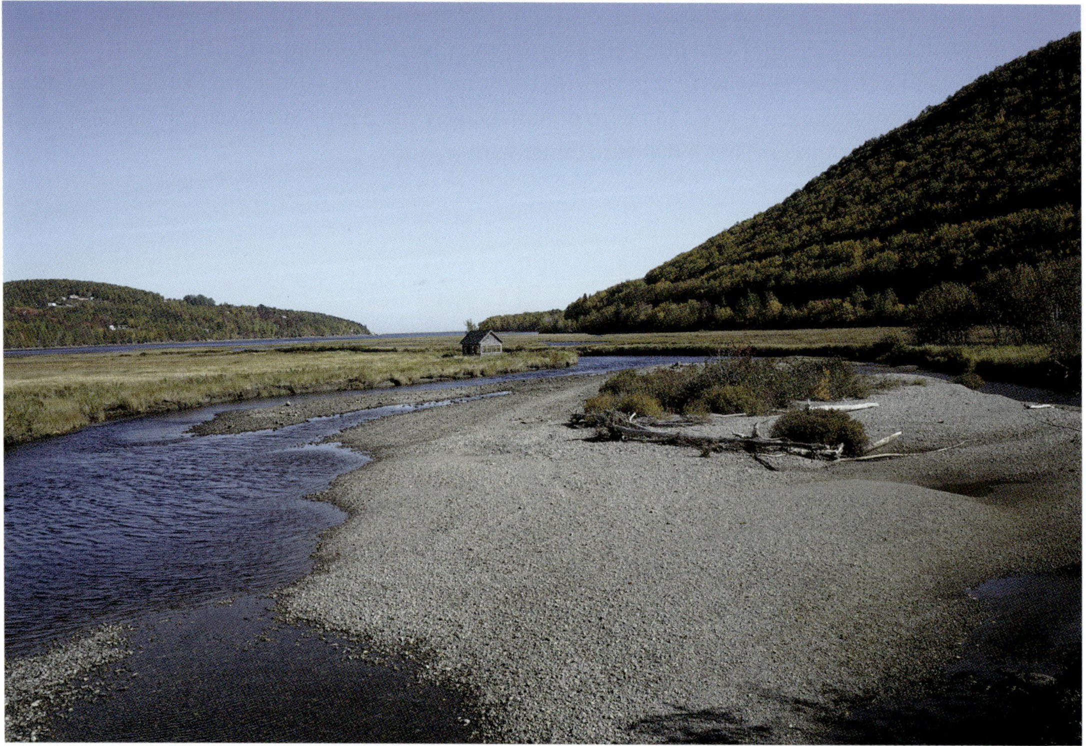

Figure 7.7 Too much distance may make your center of interest difficult to find.

A closer viewpoint, as seen in Figure 7.8, can make the center of interest easier to locate, and can add intimacy and show details and textures of a subject that can't be seen at greater distances. However, both examples highlight some other important considerations you should keep in mind:

- **Make sure that your composition has only one dominant center of interest.** Is the shack really the center of interest, or does the eye focus first on the driftwood at lower-center right and its surrounding foliage? Having more than one center of interest is confusing. Other things in a photo can be engaging, but they must clearly be subsidiary to the main center of interest. If you really have several things of importance in a single picture, consider taking several separate photos of each and using them to tell a story. Successful secondary subjects are clearly subordinate to your main center of interest.

- **Large, bright, colorful.** The center of interest is either the brightest or more vividly colored object in the photo or at least is one not overpowered by a brighter/more colorful object. Gaudy colors or bright shapes anywhere else in the image can distract viewers from your main subject. Some elements—such as a reflection of the sun on water—become part of the environment and aren't necessarily distracting. Other parts of a photo—such as a bright sail on a boat—can interfere with your carefully planned composition.

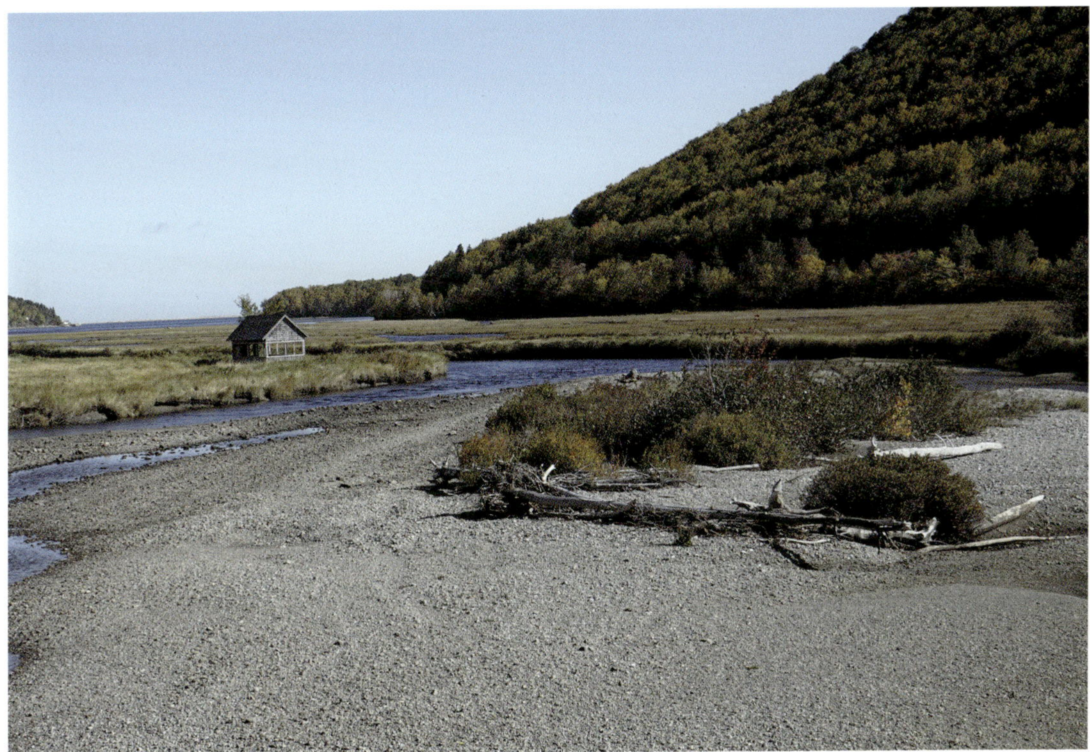

Figure 7.8 A closer shot helps reveal your main subject.

- **Avoid placing the center of interest in the exact center of the photograph.** There are many conventional occasions when it's okay to center your subject, such as for close-ups or portraits, but you won't be shooting many of those with your drone. But most of the time, you want to locate the important subject to either side and a little toward the top or bottom of the frame. Don't take "center" literally in all cases.

Tennessee photographer Rick Murray kept that in mind when he shot the image shown in Figure 7.9. He lifted off from the parking lot of the Tennessee Titans football stadium, across the Cumberland River from the Nashville skyline captured in the photo. The largest buildings were positioned in the upper left of the frame, with the diagonal of the river itself leading the eye from the left to right to take in the entire scene.

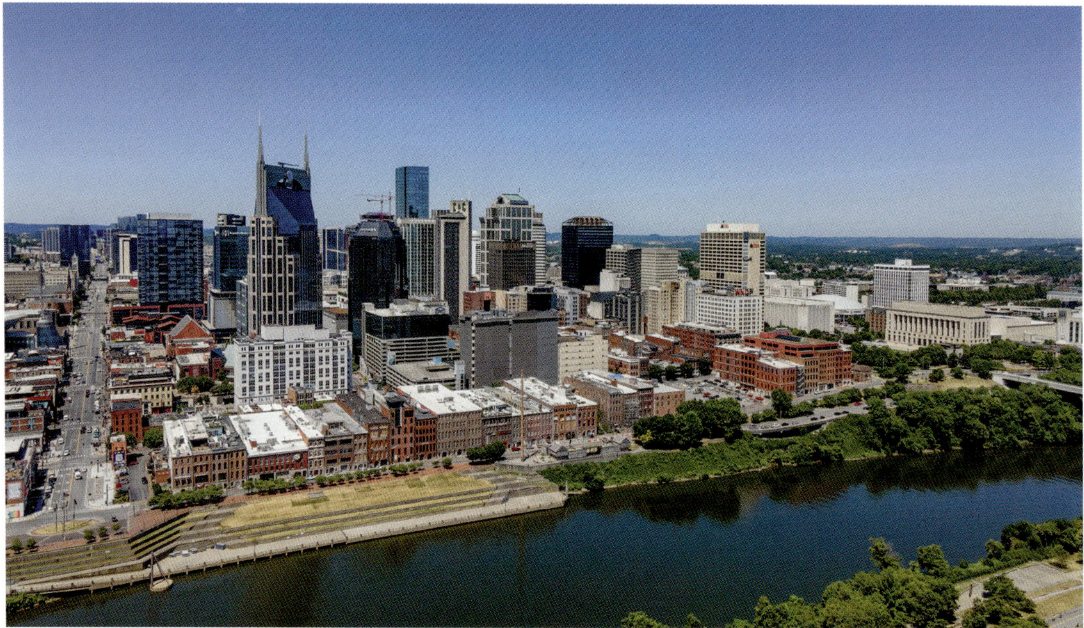

Figure 7.9 Position the center of interest outside the center of the photograph.

The Rule of Thirds and Composition

Photographers often consciously or unconsciously follow a guideline called the Rule of Thirds. It's simply a way of dividing your picture horizontally and vertically into thirds. An excellent place to position important subject matter is often at one of the points located one-third of the way from the top or bottom and sides of the frame. The Mini 3 and Mini 3 Pro each can overlay a Rule of Thirds grid over the frame using the Camera > Gridlines entry of the System Settings menu (see Figure 7.10), producing an overlay similar to the one shown in Figure 7.11. Note that you can combine any or all of the grid options, adding a crosshair and/or spot to your display.

Figure 7.10 Activate an on-screen grid in the Systems Settings menu.

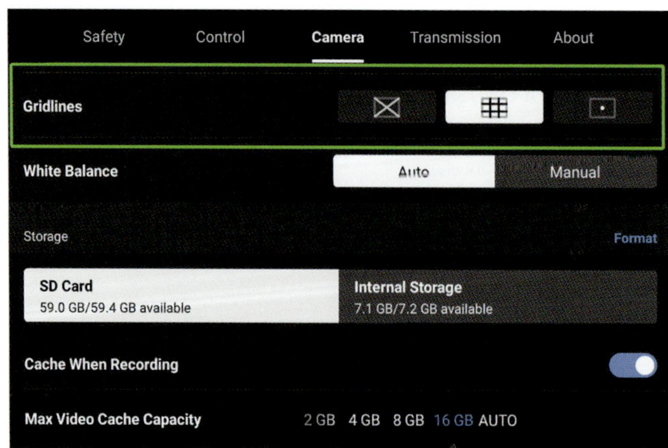

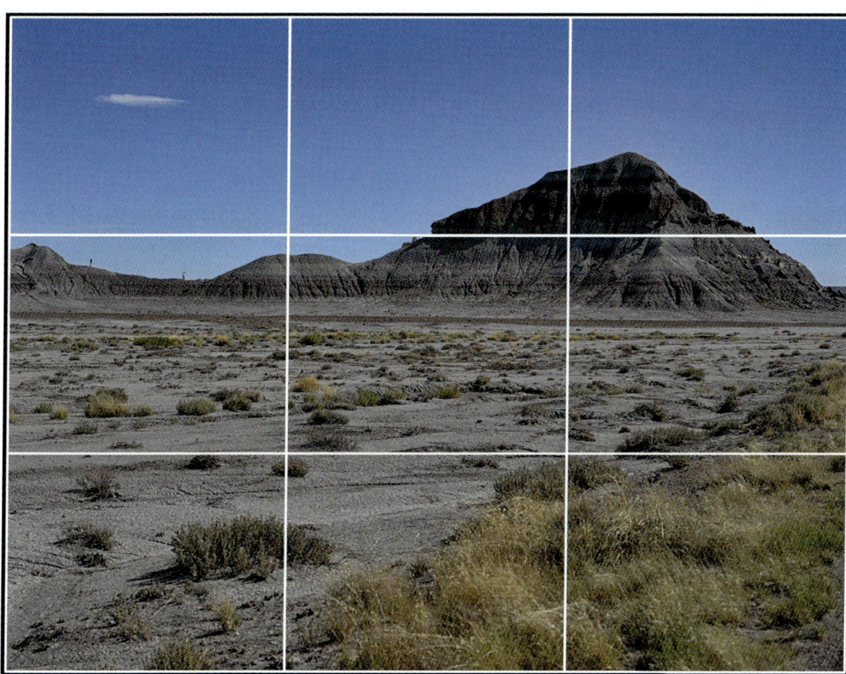

Use these guidelines to compose your pictures effectively using the Rule of Thirds:

- **Divide the frame into thirds horizontally and vertically.** Use the DJI Fly software's built-in grid as an aid. Above all, you want to avoid having your subject matter centered. By visualizing the frame in thirds, you automatically begin thinking of those ideal, off-center positions.

- **Use intersections.** Try to have important objects, particularly your center of interest, at one of the four intersections of the imaginary lines that divide the picture.

- **Be aware of edges.** Avoid having objects at the edge of a picture unless the part that isn't shown isn't important. Subjects with distinct "front" and "rear" components should be facing into the frame, rather than out it.

- **Portray motion.** Placing the subject at one of the intersection points implies motion or direction. A subject in the center is static and may appear motionless.

- **Use with other aspect ratios, too.** Don't get locked into the 4:3 (landscape) and 3:4 (portrait) default aspect ratios of the Mini 3 and Mini 3 Pro. You can use the Rule of Thirds with images shot using panorama or 16:9 proportions, too.

Often, you'll want to break the Rule of Thirds. There are almost as many exceptions to the rule as there are good reasons to apply it, which is why the rule should be considered only a guideline. Think of the Rule of Thirds as a lane marker on a highway. Sometimes you want to stay within the markers; other times, like when you see an obstruction in the road, you want to wander outside the lines. (If you happen to move from the United States to the United Kingdom, you'll find that it's wise to swap sides and use the lane markers on the opposite side of the road.)

You might want to ignore the handy Rule of Thirds when:

- **Subjects are large.** Your main subject matter is too large to fit comfortably at one of the imaginary intersection points. You might find that positioning an object at the "correct" location crops it at the top, bottom, or side. Move it a bit to another point in your composition if you need to see the whole thing.
- **Convey an idea.** Centering the image would help illustrate a concept. Perhaps you want to show your subject surrounded on all sides by adversity or by a threatening environment. Say you're photographing an area that has been devastated by a forest fire. A clump of trees that survived the fire, perhaps with a human dwelling in its midst, surrounded by scorched stumps can deliver a powerful message.
- **Isolate a subject.** As I noted, placing the subject at one of the intersecting lines intersection points can mean movement, as if the subject were about to flee the picture entirely. However, putting the center of interest in the middle of the picture gives the subject nowhere to go, nowhere to hide.
- **Show symmetry.** Centering a symmetrically oriented subject that's located in a symmetrically oriented background can produce a harmonious, geometric pattern that is pleasing, even if it is a bit static.

Incorporating Movement and Passage of Time

While video easily portrays movement and the passage of time, still photography must use other techniques to capture these changes. A still image can embody a feeling of motion through visual cues, while the passage of time can be represented by a series of shots taken at different moments that highlight the differences that have taken place between the first and last photos. The progression of the seasons throughout the year, or a collection of shots documenting a construction project are among the most common examples.

Motion and Direction

A photo composition creates an entire world for the viewer to explore. You don't want to destroy the illusion by calling attention to the rest of the universe outside the frame, or, even, something as mundane as the parking lot adjacent to the football field shown earlier. Here's how to orient your subjects in a picture:

- **Point of view.** If your subjects are people, animals, statues, or anything that you think of as having a point of view, make sure they are either facing the camera or facing into the frame rather than out of it. If the people in your image, whether individuals or a crowd, seem to be looking *out* of a picture, rather than somewhere *within* it, viewers will spend more time wondering what they are looking at than examining the actual scene. Your subjects don't actually have to be fixated on any object in particular, as long as they are looking somewhere within the picture.
- **Sense of direction.** A windmill, a palm tree bent over by a strong wind, stationary automobile, or anything with a sense of direction, such as the boat shown in Figure 7.12, should be facing *into* the frame for the same reason that a person should be looking into it. That's why the image at left in the figure looks "wrong." Even though the boat is at anchor, it looks more natural pointed into the frame, as in the version at right in the figure.

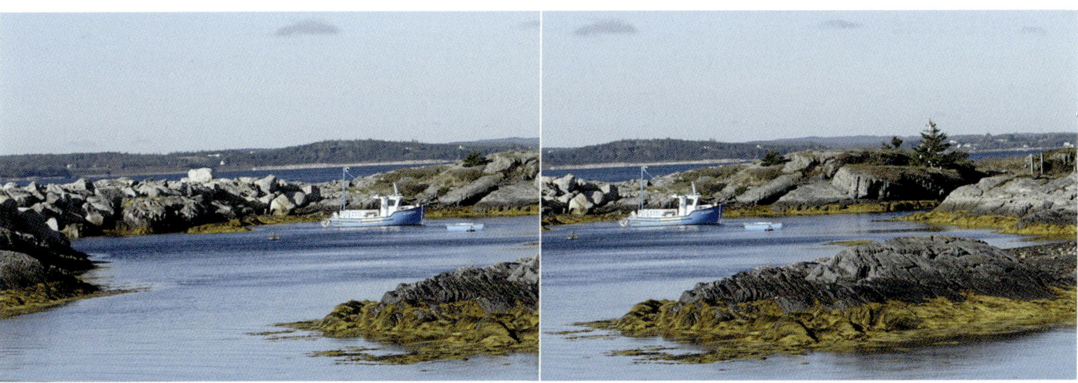

Figure 7.12 Objects should appear to be pointing into the frame.

- **Movement.** If objects in the frame are moving or pointed in a particular direction, make sure they are heading into the frame rather than out of it. Add extra space in front of any fast-moving object so that the object has somewhere to go while remaining in the frame, and it doesn't give the impression that it's on its way out of view.

Your cropping can actually create an artificial feeling of speed. Compare the top and bottom versions of the image shown in Figure 7.13. Both include enough space in front of the boat to form acceptable compositions. However, in the lower version the craft actually seems to be moving faster, because of the longer wake stretching out behind it.

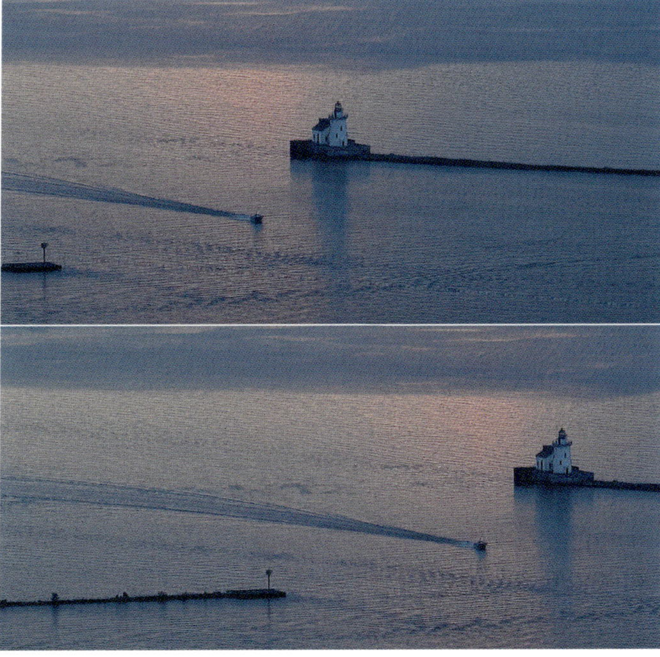

Figure 7.13 Cropping can add an artificial feeling of rapid motion.

Passage of Time

Still images can be used to illustrate the passage of time through the capture of multiple images. The Photo modes of the Mini 3 and Mini 3 Pro include Burst and Timed shot modes, which each provide you with a series of images you can use to illustrate different moments in time. Here's the difference:

- **Burst mode.** The drone will capture multiple images, one after another, as a series of stills. You can choose bursts of 3, 5, or 7 images. You'll find this facility useful when you want to grab a sequence of images of some action that is happening fairly rapidly, say, when shooting overhead coverage of motor sports. (I'm assuming you are following all the rules, such as not hovering over people or flying in any restricted air spaces.)

- **Timed shot mode.** This mode provides a type of interval photography, with the individual images captured automatically over a specified time at a desired interval. With both drones you can choose to take these sequences using intervals of 2, 3, 5, 7, 10, 15, 30, or 60 seconds.

In addition to these automatic modes, you can also shoot sequences at even longer intervals. In fact, if you have the patience and motivation, you can take individual photos from approximately the same location at intervals of days, weeks, or months. One project I've started is to take photos at different times of the year, creating a series of landscape images that show the same scene in spring, summer, fall, and winter. So far, I've captured summer and fall images, and will complete the sequence next year with winter and spring images.

Construction sites make interesting subjects for shots captured manually to document the work. They can move at a snail's pace for large structures, or quite quickly in the case of home construction. Figure 7.14 shows a series of images I shot of a house being built, illustrating the builder's progress from laying the foundation (at top, upper left) to completion of roofing (at top, center right), over the course of several months. At bottom, the home just needs a lawn and an extension of the driveway.

Here are some tips for getting an interesting set of construction progress images:

- **Consistent viewpoint.** It's likely you'll want a set of images taken from the same perspective so you can easily compare the progress of the construction. That can be tricky, and it requires some planning. It helps if you always take off from the exact same spot. Ascend straight up, and make a record of your altitude, heading, and degree of gimbal tilt so you can more or less repeat that perspective at a later date. (See Figure 7.15.)

- **Appropriate time of day.** Sunny weather at midday will provide the best contrast, with shadows helping to make the details of the construction clearly visible. Avoid early morning and late afternoon shots, as long shadows can be distracting. However, the weather may not cooperate, which was the case with my home construction series. At times, there were no sunny days at critical points in the construction, so some of my images have less contrast.

- **Shoot various angles.** Once you've captured your basic shot each time, go ahead and try different angles, using lower altitudes and/or positions to get a variety of views.

- **Add video.** Even if a series of still photos is your goal, as long as you're already aloft at the construction site, shoot some video using your drone's QuickShots feature, as described in Chapter 8. These clips will make a nice complement to the still images at some point.

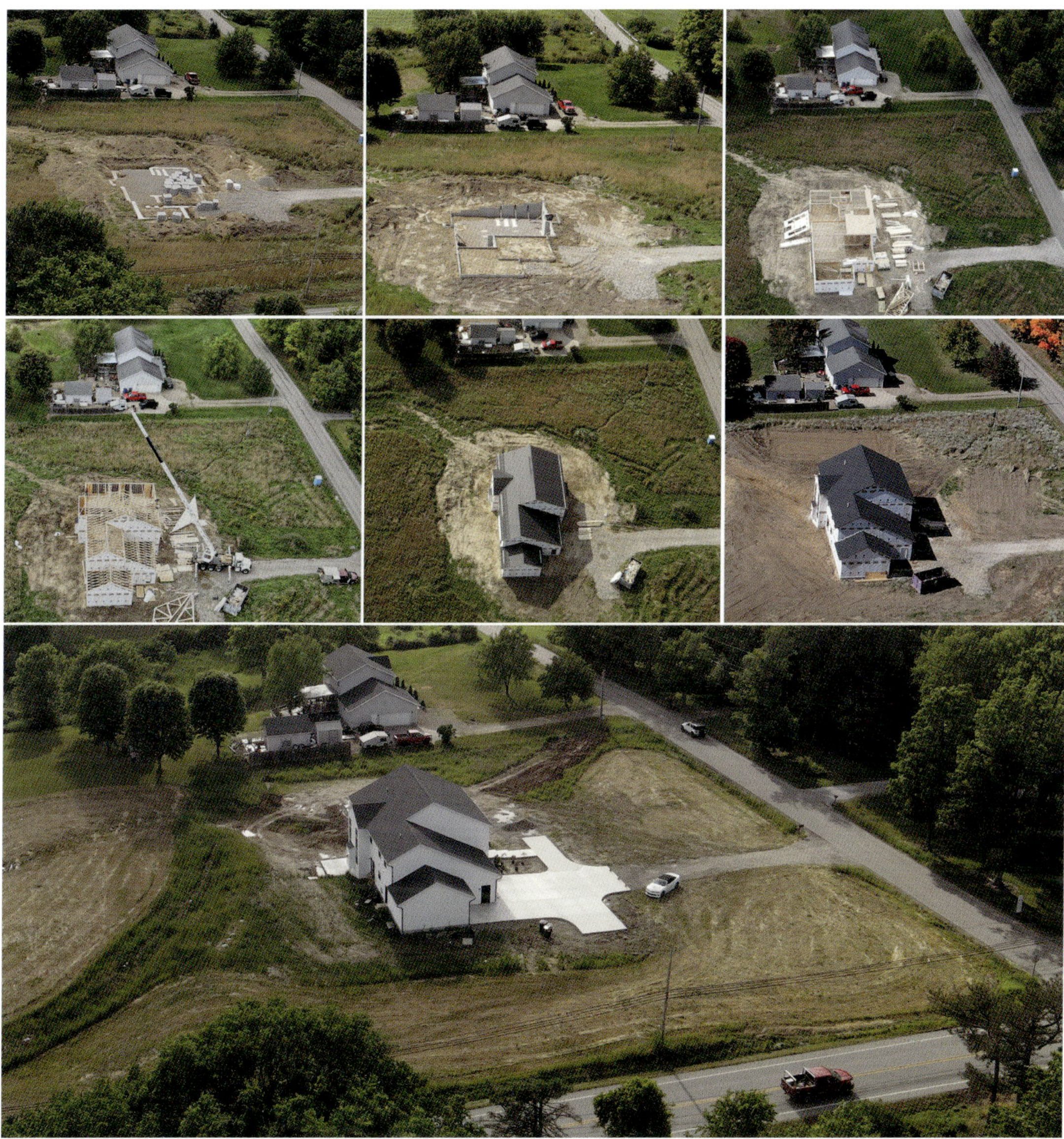

Figure 7.14 Construction progress shots.

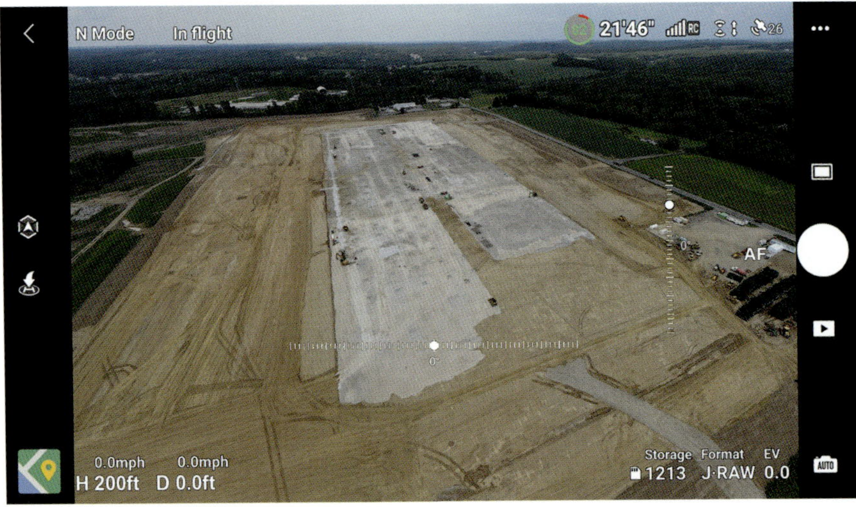

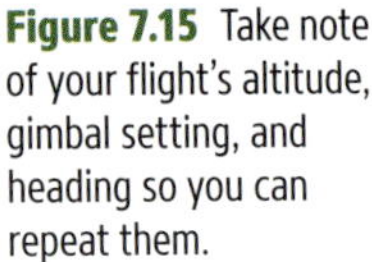

Figure 7.15 Take note of your flight's altitude, gimbal setting, and heading so you can repeat them.

Time-Lapse Movies

Humans have been capturing still photos as documentation for ages. Combining all those stills into time-lapse movies is relatively new. They are nothing more than a series of still photo images taken at specific intervals and then displayed continuously as a motion picture that shows in a few seconds or minutes of action that actually takes place over the course of hours, days, or months. Invented in the early 1950s by John Ott, the technique caught the public eye when he used it for a sequence in an Academy Award–winning nature film by Walt Disney. A film documenting the building of Disneyland in California was probably the first use of time-lapse to picture construction progress. Your drone can automatically apply a version of this concept during a single flight with its Hyperlapse feature, which I'll describe in Chapter 8.

Using Straight Lines and Curves

After you have the basics out of the way, progressing to the next level and creating even better compositions is easy. All you need to know is when to apply or break some simple rules. Just remember that one of the key elements of good composition is a bit of surprise. Viewers like to see subjects arranged in interesting ways rather than lined up in a row.

Lines within your image can help your compositions by directing the eye toward the center of interest. The lines don't have to be explicit; subtle shapes can work just as well. Try these techniques:

- **Use repetitive lines or shapes to create an interesting pattern.** Repetitive lines or shapes could be multiple lines within a single object, such as the grout lines in a brick wall. Repetitive lines could also be several different parallel or converging objects, such as a road's edges, the centerline of the road, and the fence that runs along the road.

Figure 7.16 is Cleveland photographer Kolman Rosenberg's shot of the aftermath of a sandcastle-building competition. A week after the contest, only sad lumps of flattened sand remain at lower right in the photo, with a few of the larger sculptures retaining their shape. The lines of the canvas walking path and sole human walking past add interest. The patterns formed by strong repetitive lines and shapes can become a pleasing composition in themselves.

- **Diagonals.** Find diagonal lines to direct the attention to the center of interest. Diagonal lines are better than horizontal or vertical straight lines, which are static and not particularly interesting. Figure 7.17 features the diagonal line of the Smolen-Gulf Bridge over the Ashtabula River in Ohio, at 613 feet, the longest covered bridge in the United States and the fourth-longest covered bridge in the world.

I needed to fly at an altitude of 100 feet to capture the full length of the bridge, so I ended up with a typical aerial shot. The strong diagonal line did add some interest.

REMINDER

If you need to know the exact altitude used for a particular shot (or the latitude, longitude, or exposure settings), you'll find it in the EXIF information embedded in the image file, accessible from many image editors and utilities.

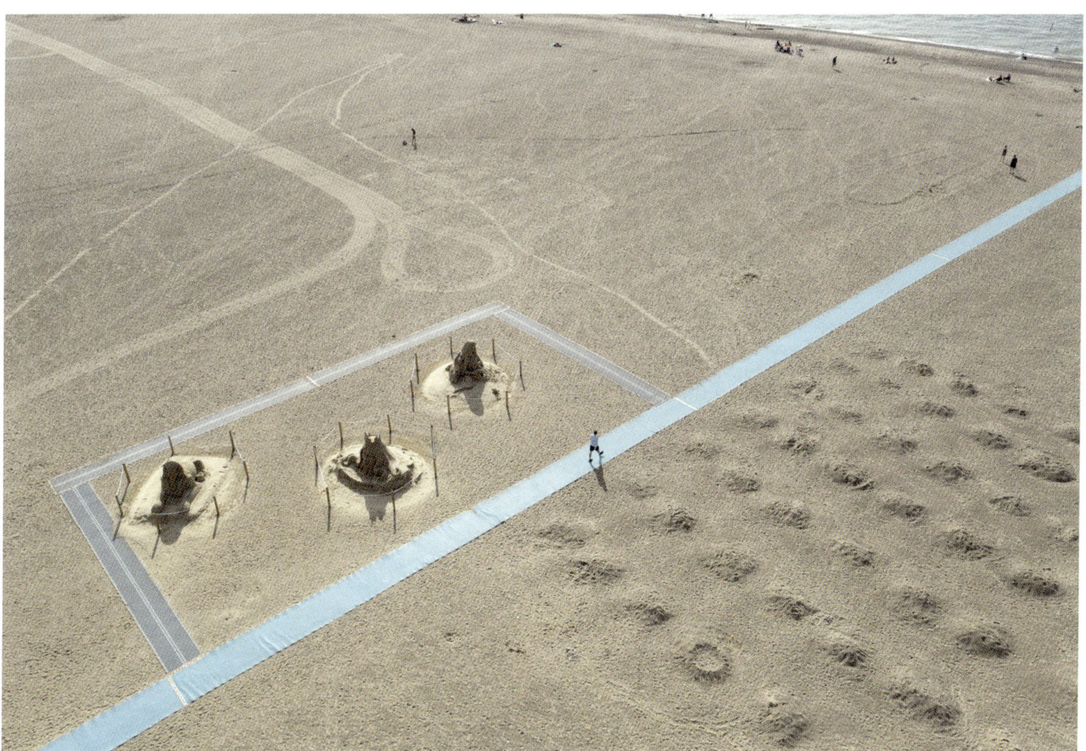

Figure 7.16 Using repetitive shapes.

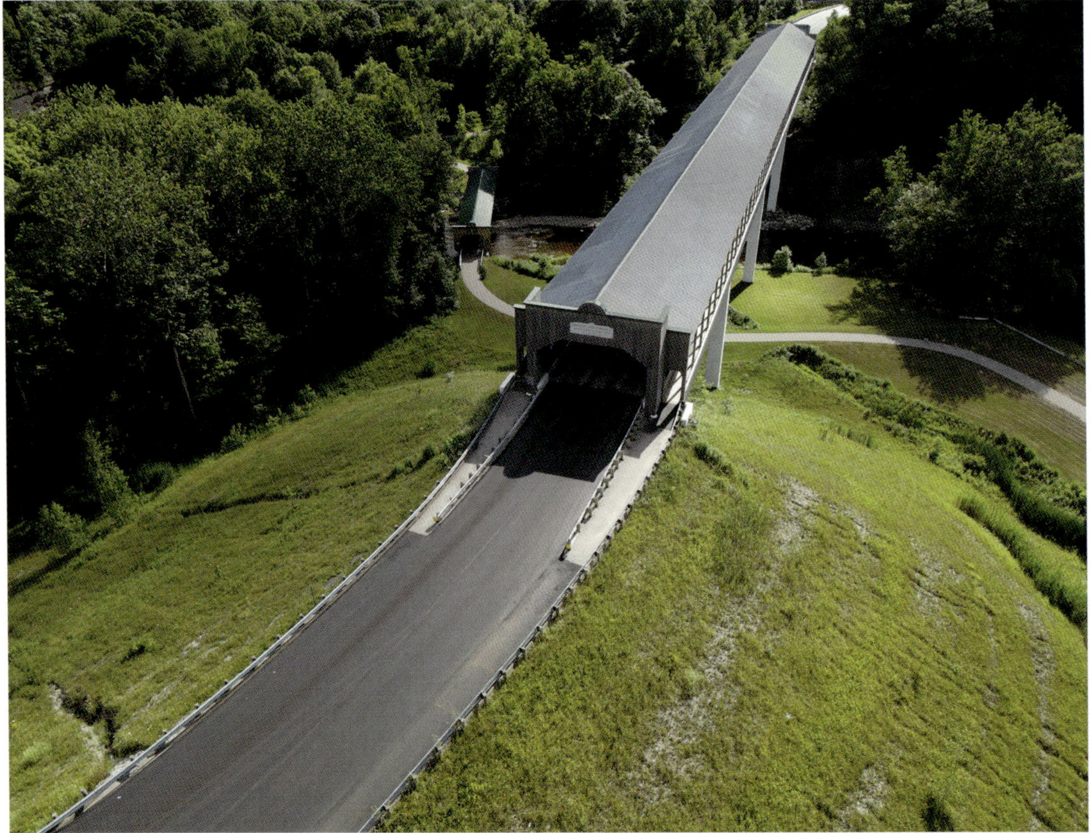

Figure 7.17 Diagonal lines can be more interesting than horizontal or vertical lines.

- **Curves.** Curved lines, which are more graceful than straight lines, can lead the viewer gently from one portion of the composition to another. Curving roads are a good example of arcs and bends that can contribute to a composition. Figure 7.18 shows the same Smolen-Gulf bridge a few hours later from an altitude of just 25 feet. The reduced elevation and curve of the road provides a much-improved composition.

- **Leading lines.** Look for lines in your image and try to use them to lead the eye to the main subject area. Some lines are obvious, such as roads, fences, or a seashore leading off into the distance. These kinds of lines are good when you want a dramatic composition.

Figure 7.19 shows the historic Jasper County Courthouse in Carthage, Missouri, a popular Route 66 attraction. The town itself is interesting, so I decided to include as many of the surrounding buildings in the image as possible. The triangular shape of the leading lines draw your eye into and through the picture. I was lucky enough to visit the town on a Sunday evening, when the streets were completely deserted and free of distracting vehicles and residents.

Experimenting with panorama mode, I also captured the version shown in Figure 7.20, which distorted the image a bit, producing what I think is an even stronger example of how leading lines can lure you into exploring all the details in an aerial image.

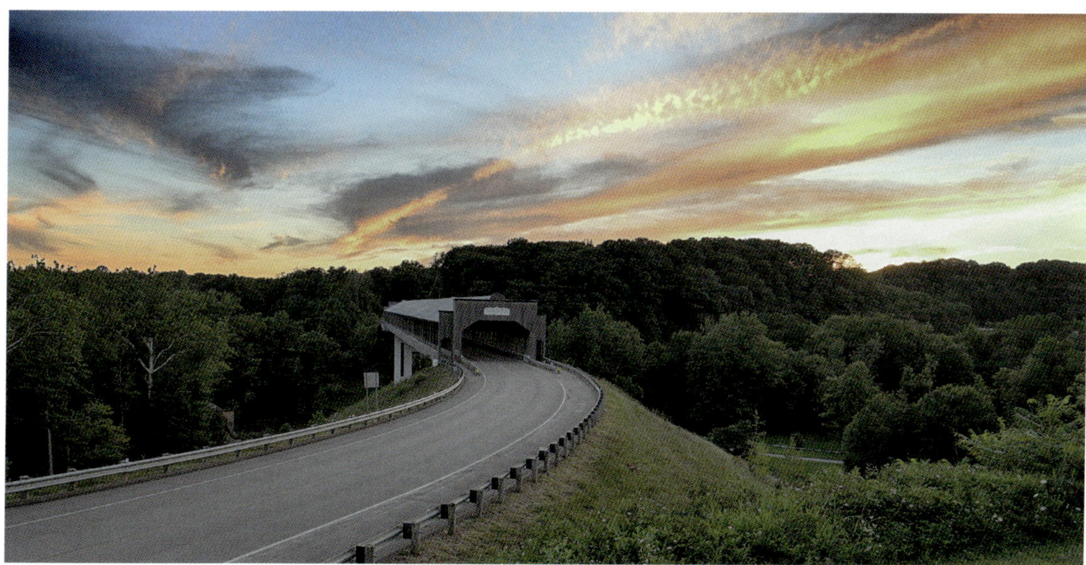

Figure 7.18 Curved lines are more graceful.

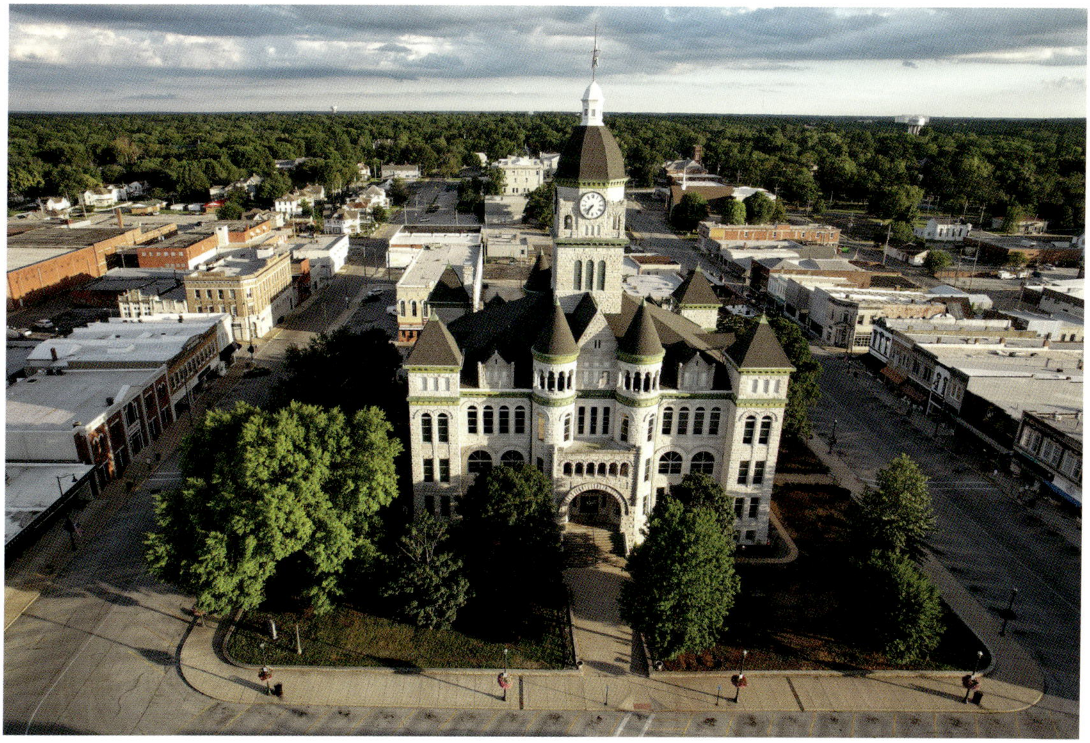

Figure 7.19 Leading lines draw the eye into a composition.

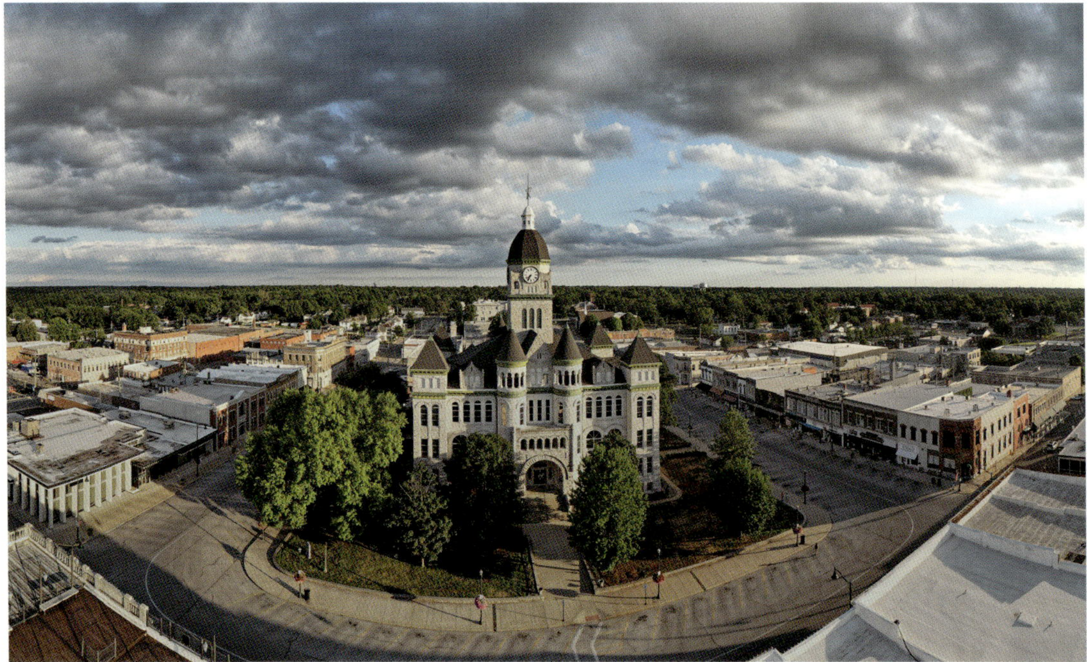

Figure 7.20 Straight and curved lines can combine to focus the viewer's attention.

Working with Shapes

Interesting shapes can attract the eye, too, as long as the shapes are dynamic. For example, three objects arranged in a triangle make a picture inherently more interesting than if the objects form a square shape. Your eye naturally follows the lines of the triangle toward each of the three points, or apexes, whereas squares or rectangles don't point anywhere. Figures 7.19 and 7.20 provide a good example of how triangular compositions work.

Keep in mind that wide images, especially panoramas like the one shown in Figure 7.21, express a feeling of spaciousness, while tall compositions invoke height, loftiness, and stature. The next three figures show how you can use these concepts to approach a subject from different angles, so to speak. Figure 7.22 is an aerial panorama, using the Mini 3's/Mini 3 Pro's 3328 × 8000–pixel vertical panorama mode, taken from an altitude of 70 feet. The vertical orientations provide an image slice that includes a healthy chunk of sky, a Great Lake, some breakwalls, and a spit of sand that's punctuated by tire tracks that have carved out repetitive lines. The shapes combine to form an interesting composition.

I used "tall tripod" mode to shoot the image shown in Figure 7.23, taken at a height of just 11 feet. The curve of the beach and white-on-brown pattern of the gulls and sand was interesting. This particular flock had grown accustomed to ignoring my drone, which I kept at a safe distance. I do *not* recommend trying this at home. You don't want to annoy them and set off an erratic retreat that could damage your drone or, much worse, injure a bird. For Figure 7.24, I moved the drone up to 25 feet, oriented so I could capture the triangular shape of the beach, the horizon, and the flock of gulls. I like this shot the best.

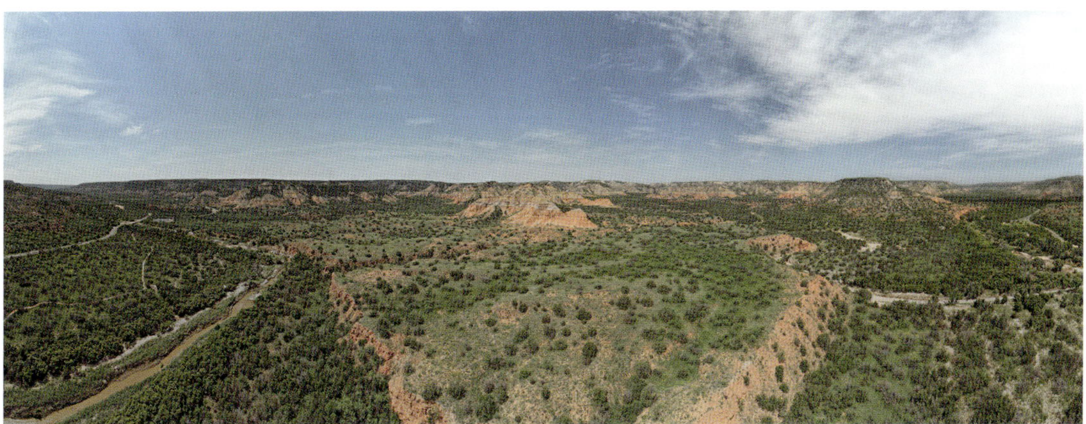

Figure 7.21 Broad landscape-oriented images convey a feeling of wide-open spaces.

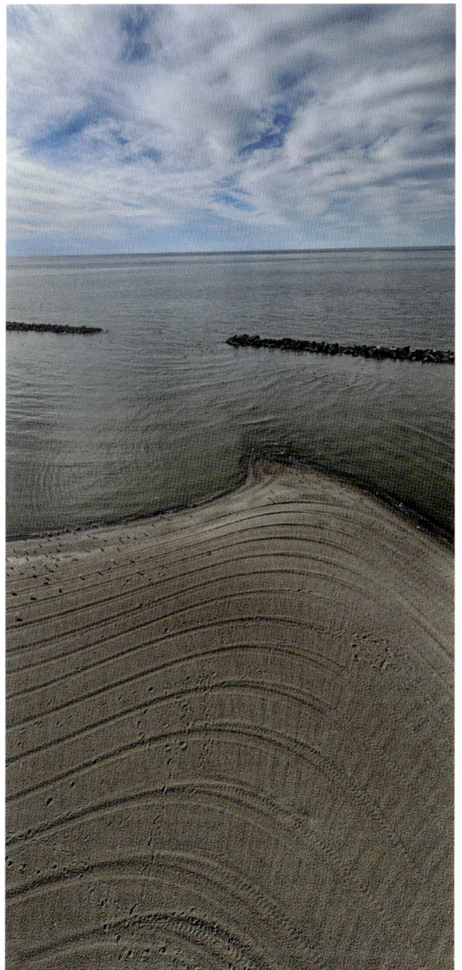

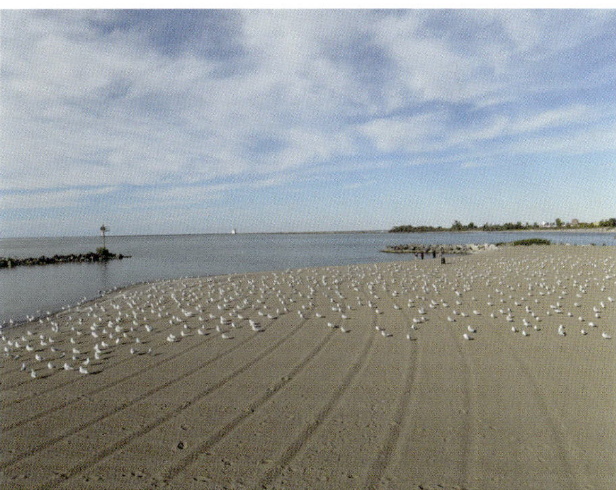

Figure 7.23 Shooting in "tall tripod" mode.

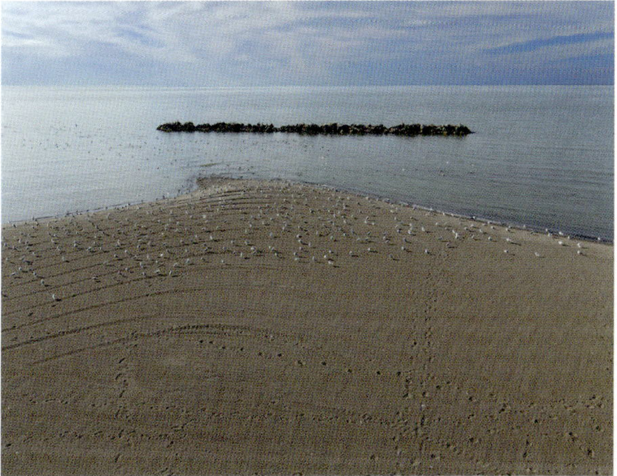

Figure 7.22 A vertical panorama.

Figure 7.24 Combining shapes and lines.

Vivid colors are another way of using shapes to create an appealing image. You can always make an image come alive by using an image editor to boost the saturation or vibrance of a photo. Saturation increases the richness of all the colors in an image, often unnaturally, while vibrance affects only the muted colors while leaving already-saturated hues alone. However, I tend to prefer getting the shot in the camera rather than in post-processing and recommend looking for colors that pop naturally. You may find them in sunsets and sunrises or richly colored skies (perhaps by using a polarizer to deepen the colors). Or you may discover subject matter that itself jumps to life because of its vibrant colors. That was the case when I visited one of the many umbrella-based art installations that have popped up in many locales. This particular "umbrella alley," which featured nearly 200 colorful parasols, hung over a narrow street between two buildings. I captured the image shown in Figure 7.25, some 60 feet above the installation.

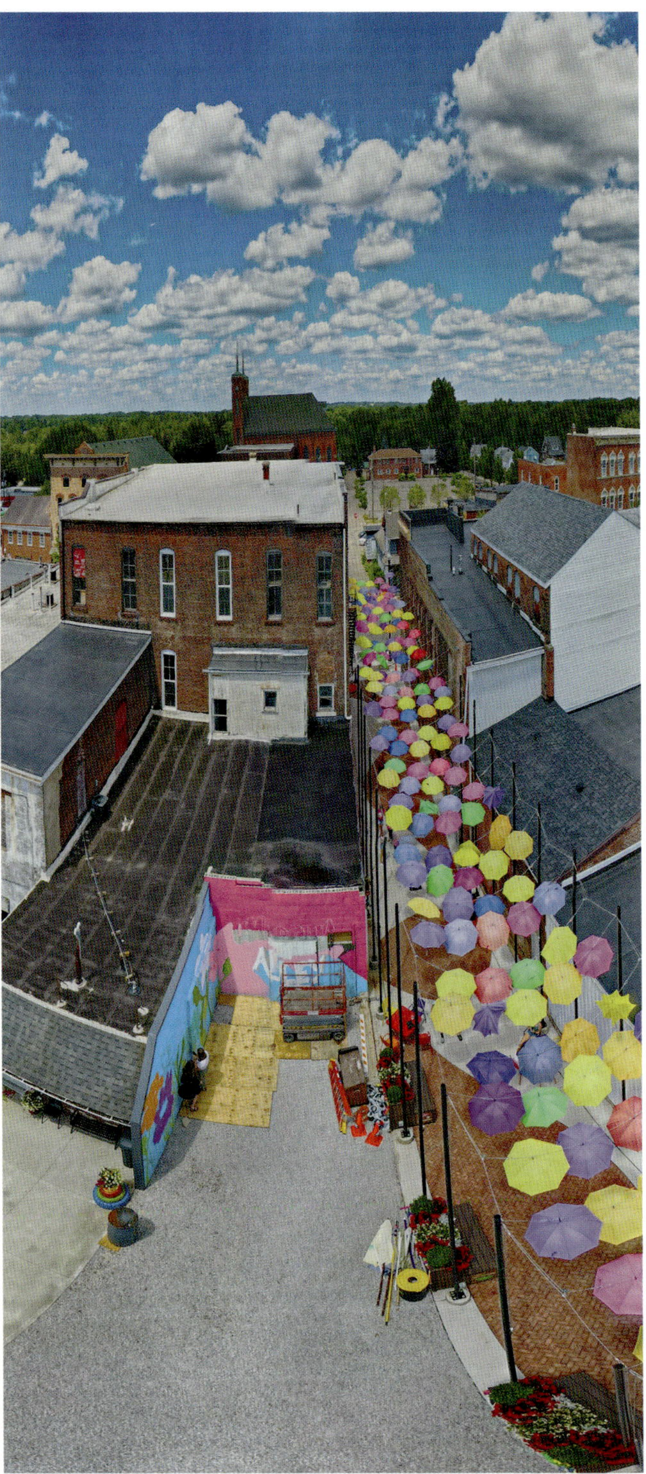

Figure 7.25 This "umbrella alley" is festooned with brightly colored shapes.

Framing an Image

Framing is a technique that is frequently used in conventional photography, most often using some foreground objects to wrap around a more distant subject to create a border. The edging around an image defines the picture's shape and concentrates attention on the image within the frame.

Foreground frames, which are typically trees or architectural features, are problematic for drone photos, although you can sometimes use your surroundings as attractive borders around your own pictures. But even if you are unable to provide a frame in the foreground, you can still compose your images such that your subject is, indeed, "framed" by its surroundings.

Look for obvious framing shapes in which you can place your composition. With shots taken in "high tripod" mode, you can readily find frames in the form of canopies of trees, arches (when shooting below towering bridges), and space between buildings. These have the advantage of being a natural part of the scene, and not something you contrived in order to create a frame.

You can make your own frames by changing position until objects create a border around your image. Find a curving tree branch and back up your drone until the scenic view you want to capture is wrapped in its leafy embrace. One advantage of a foreground frame is that it creates a feeling of depth. A flat-looking image can jump to 3D life when it's placed in a frame.

For Figure 7.26, I originally wanted to crop the image to create a vertical composition of the stream emptying into the pond. Then, I decided to instead crop to a panoramic shot with the natural cliffs on the left side and the structure on the right forming a foreground frame for the waterway that extended off into the distance.

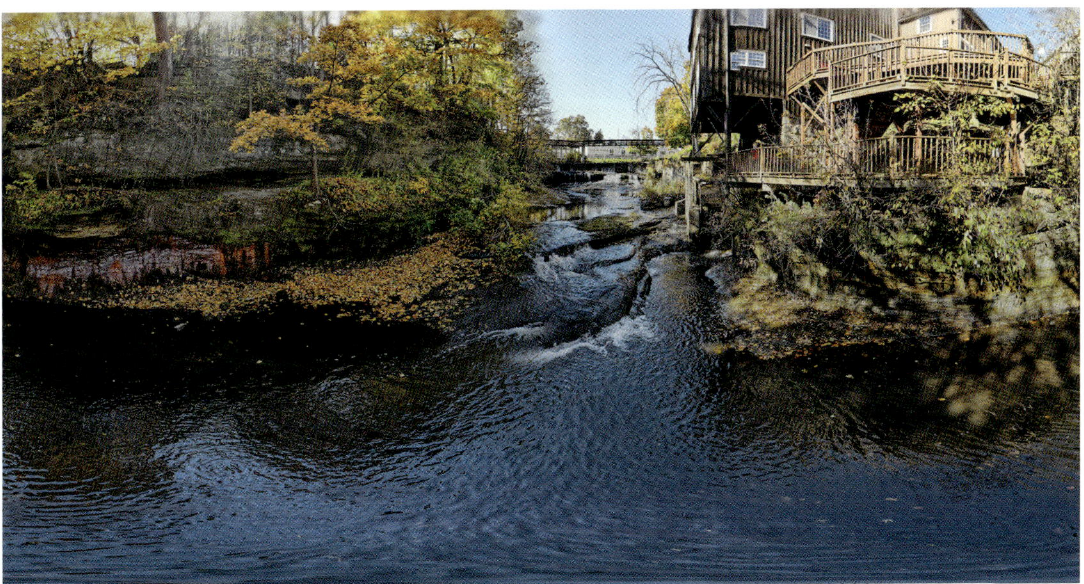

Figure 7.26 Foreground shapes can create a frame.

Because of the unusual perspective provided by aerial photography, I often like to create somewhat abstract images that are abstract simply because of their unusual viewpoint. When I posted Figure 7.27 on a website without a detailed description, one of the first comments I received was "I had to look at this photo for several minutes before I realized it was an overhead shot of a covered bridge." That was exactly my point. The four clumps of trees dressed in their Autumn colors formed a four-point "frame" around the country river road and its bridge.

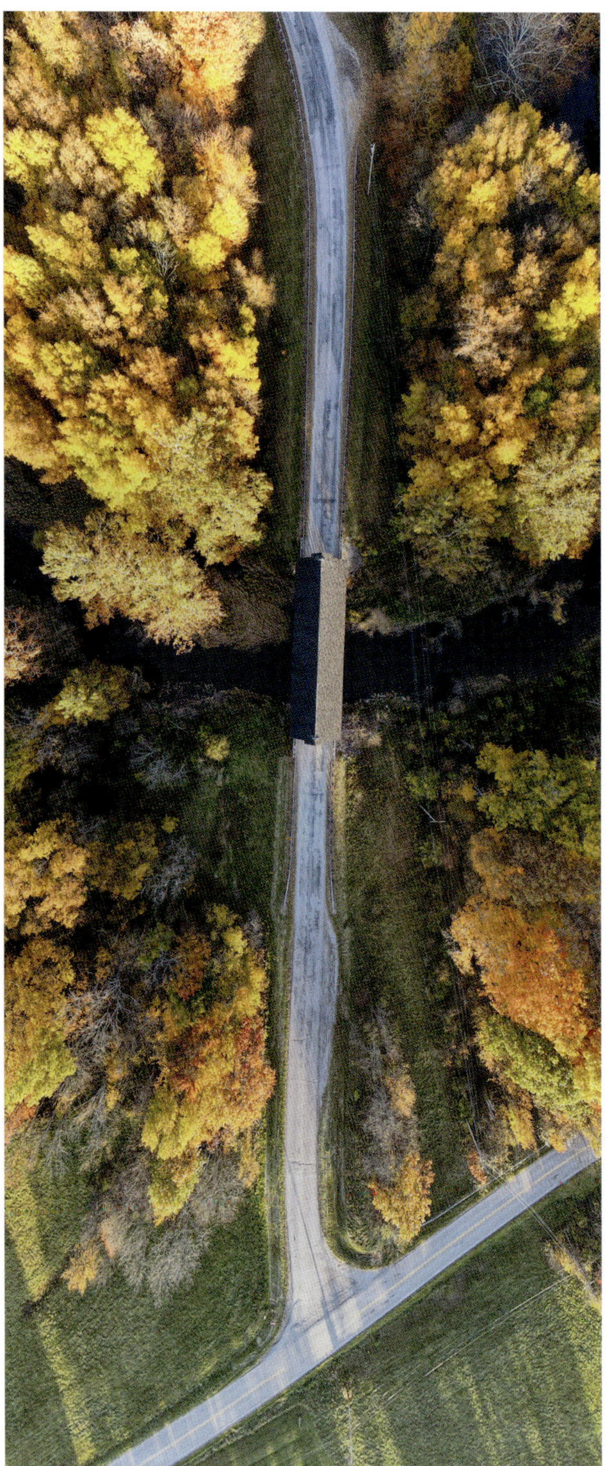

Figure 7.27 Abstract images engage the viewer as they explore their content.

Creative Cropping

Both the Mini 3 and Mini 3 Pro produce images with enough resolution to withstand a reasonable amount of cropping. You can crop your images to improve the composition and to transform one type of image, say, a horizontally composed photo, into a panorama or vertically oriented shot. You can even "find" a new image hidden within a photo you've already taken.

Creating Balance

When working with shapes, you should consider the balance of the objects in your image. If you place every element of interest in a photograph on one side or the other, leaving little or nothing to look at on the opposite side, the picture is unbalanced, like a seesaw with a child at one end and no one on the other. The best pictures have an inherent balance that makes them look graceful.

If the photo you took doesn't already have inherent visual equilibrium, you can create balance with cropping. To balance your image, try to arrange objects so that anything large on one side is balanced by something of importance on the other side. This is not the same as having multiple centers of interest. You can balance objects in two ways:

- **Symmetrical balance.** Have the objects on either side of the frame be of roughly similar size or weight.
- **Asymmetrical balance.** Have the objects on opposing sides be of different size or weight.

Refining the Composition

Many images can be improved by cropping out extraneous objects and reorienting the frame. For the last five years, I've spent a month each winter in Cedar Key, Florida, writing and taking photos using a Fifties-era motel as my base of operations. Most nights, I go out and shoot the spectacular sunsets, either from ground level or from the vantage point of my drone.

One evening, I captured the image seen in Figure 7.28, but decided I wanted one that pictured the motel and its environs. I adjusted the gimbal so that the sun itself was not within the frame, so that the exposure would allow representing the foreground. Unfortunately, the full frame, seen at left in Figure 7.29, is cluttered with parked cars and trucks, buildings, and the roadway. Cropping the image as shown at right in the figure yielded the image I wanted.

Twilight, Night, and Winter Shooting

Don't be trapped into confining your aerial photography to traditional times of the day or limit your flights to only certain times of year. Sunsets do tend to be a favorite subject for drone photographers because of the dramatic lighting and colors. But few actually explore the full range of exciting pictures you can capture at twilight, with even fewer experimenting with night photography, which yield some exciting pictures. In areas that experience frigid weather, many drone pilots shut down entirely for the Winter months. You're missing some great opportunities.

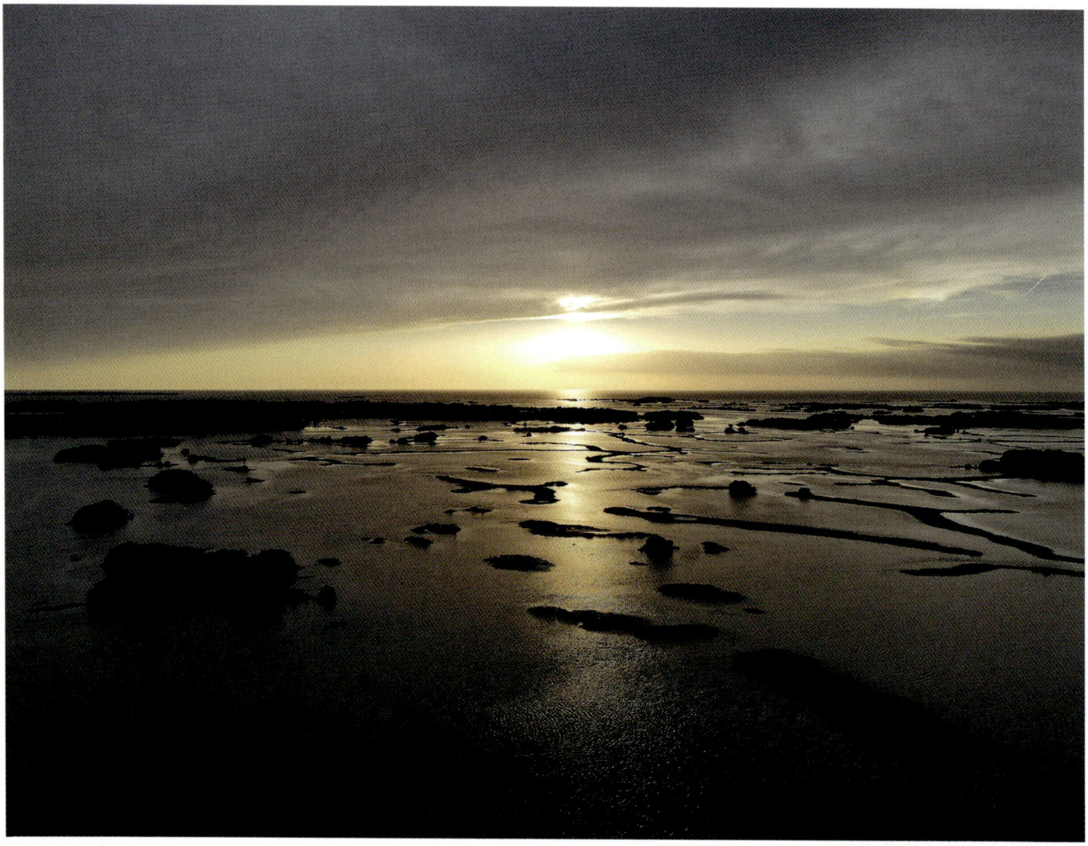

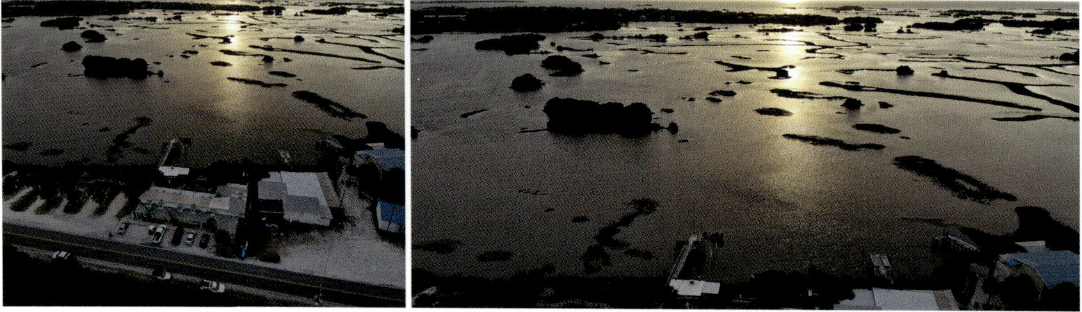

Figure 7.28 Initial shot of the sunset only.

Figure 7.29 Final shot full frame (left) and cropped (right).

Golden Hours and More

Earth-bound photographers have long coveted the times of day called "golden hours" or "blue hours." The most common subjects captured during these times involve sunsets, or landscapes filled with the twinkling lights of buildings, parking areas, or other sights. I photographed the scene shown in Figure 7.30 just as the sun was setting and the lights of a nearby marina and community were already illuminated.

Golden hours are the periods just before sunset or just after sunrise, and can last anywhere from 20 minutes (at the equator) to several hours, depending on your latitude. (I first noticed this on one of my annual visits to Florida, where the sunsets always seemed to happen *a lot* faster.) While the orange glows and dramatic shadows can be gorgeous, it's important to note that the dynamic range of golden hour scenes is reduced; there is less difference between the lightest and darkest parts of a scene. Artificial light—from homes, streetlights, or boats floating on water—will more closely match the natural lighting. You generally often won't need to use HDR.

Once the sun has dipped completely below the horizon, you'll experience blue hours for a period of time. The orange glow will be gone, the sky will not have a direct light source, and your scene will be illuminated by extremely soft blue lighting. Shadows will be gone and your images will take on a calm appearance.

Both Part 107–certified and recreational drone pilots are allowed to fly their drones at night without needing to undergo the previously lengthy process of obtaining a waiver, which was required of professional drone pilots until mid-2021. However, you are required to have attached to your drone anti-collision lighting visible for at least three statute miles with a flash rate sufficient to avoid a collision. Your Mini is not equipped with such lighting, so you will need to add a strobe in order to comply. You must also abide by all the appropriate safety rules, including not flying over people. Professional Part 107 pilots may need to take a new online course available at the FAA Safety website.

Note that the rules also apply to dawn and dusk, which the FAA defines as the period 30 minutes before official sunrise and 30 minutes after official sunset. These periods are known as *civil twilight*.

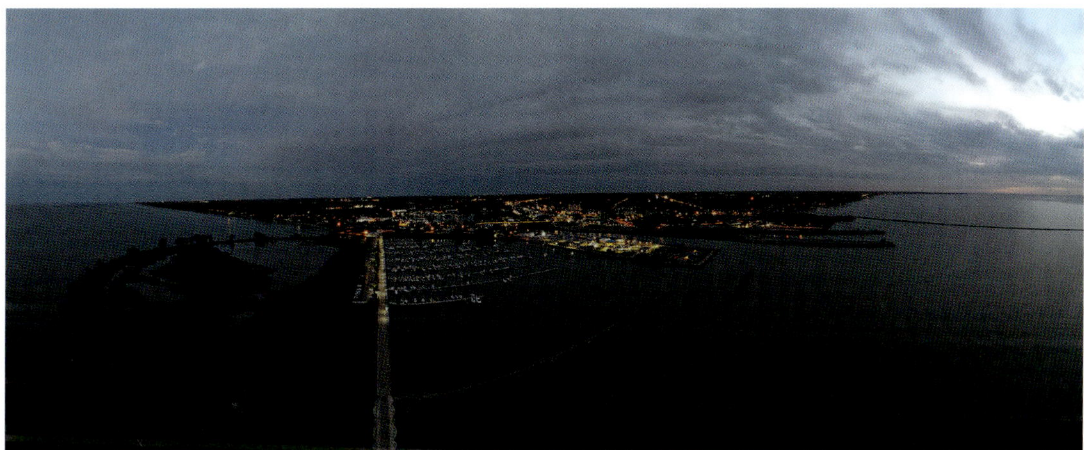

Figure 7.30 A shoreline photographed at twilight.

An exception is made for Alaska. Why does Seward's Icebox get special treatment? The 48th state is the only part of the U.S. that *doesn't* have conventional twilight for part of the year, during its "midnight sun" in summers, and what are termed *polar nights* during winter. Civil twilight for Alaska is specified in the Air Almanac.

> **TWILIGHT TIME**
>
> Civil twilight is defined as the period when the sun is less than 6 degrees below the horizon. There is also nautical twilight when the sun is between 6 and 12 degrees below the horizon, and astronomical twilight that kicks in when the sun is between 12 and 18 degrees below the horizon. Night officially begins when the sun is 18 or more degrees below the horizon.

I don't recommend twilight or night shooting for beginning recreational pilots, as there are multiple complications and risks involved. It's easier to lose your required visual line of sight, even with the LED auxiliary light in the drone's belly activated using the defined button. Moreover, you will be unable to reliably detect obstacles, and your drone's vision systems will be ineffective.

In effect, the operational range of your drone is reduced because it is difficult to discern location, attitude, altitude, and direction of flight. In its training materials, the FAA points out the phenomena involved with *night physiology* and *night illusions*. You probably learned about the eye's rods and cones in high school science classes. The cones near the center of the eye perceive fine detail and color, while the rods are used for peripheral vision. We all have a night-blind spot in the center of the field of vision, causing us to lose perception of sharpness, color, depth, and size. The FAA recommends looking 5 to 10 degrees off-center of the direction where your drone is flying to help compensate for the blind spot.

We also suffer from illusions and distractions at night, which include:

- **Motion parallax.** At night, stationary objects may appear to move, which can cause confusion.
- **Geometric perspective.** Objects may appear to have different shapes when viewed at different distances and angles.
- **False horizon.** Because it's dark, lights on the horizon may cause the drone to appear to be higher than it really is, so its visual appearance may differ from what you see on the controller's telemetry.
- **Reversible perspective illusion.** Apparently, when two aircraft are flying at night roughly in parallel, they may actually appear to be moving away from each other when they are actually converging.
- **Fascination.** When humans are fixated on one task, they may not notice other things going on around them. There was a famous experiment in which half of the observers assigned to monitor the play in a basketball game didn't notice a woman dressed in a gorilla suit cavorting at the sidelines.

You should also avoid looking at bright lights and, if at all possible, use a companion as a visual observer to scan for other aircraft. You'll also need a landing area that's illuminated, although the lights can be dimmed until needed. And, of course, all the rules about operating within controlled and uncontrolled airspaces must be followed, and you must get authorization through FAA Drone Zone or LAANC when appropriate.

Once you're comfortable shooting at twilight, you'll want to explore shooting the same scene in both daylight and twilight hours to provide an interesting comparison. Our Volunteer State friend Rick Murray had that in mind when he covered Sumner Fest, the annual hot air balloon festival in Hendersonville, Tennessee. Although the weather was a bit gloomy with heavy dark clouds and periodic light rain, he took advantages in breaks from the precipitation to capture the images shown in Figure 7.31, both in daylight (top) and twilight (bottom). Both photos were 180-degree panoramas, with a bit of noise reduction applied using the Topaz Denoise utility.

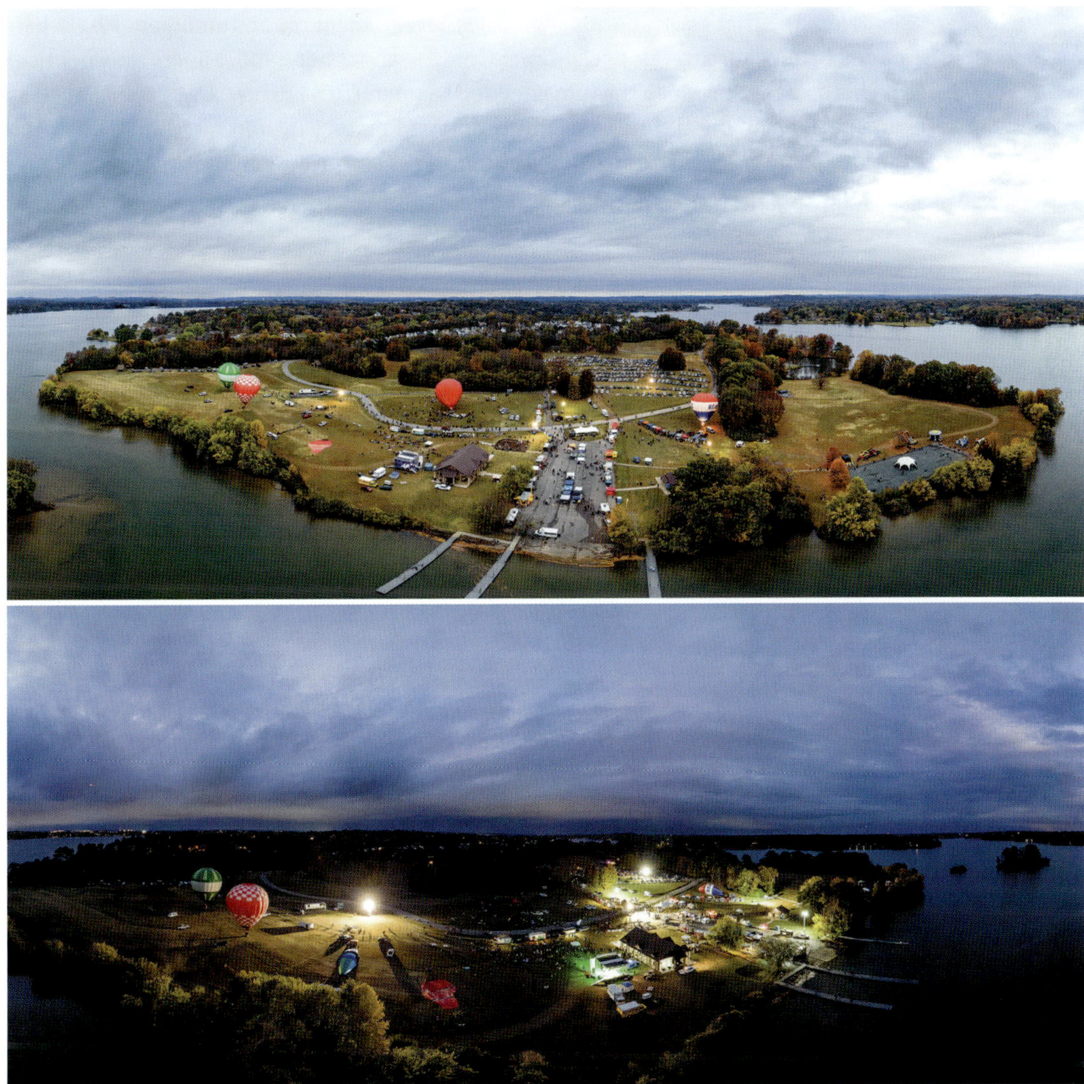

Figure 7.31 Daylight and twilight versions of the same scene.

Winter Shooting

In many ways, drone photography in the winter is much like aerial shooting at other times of year. You have to contend with the weather, looking out for sleet or snow instead of rain. High gusts of wind can prevent you from flying at all. The chief difference is that, in many climes, winter is *cold*, sometimes extremely so. Frigid weather imposes several different restrictions:

- **Reduced battery power.** Heat and cold both have an effect on your drone's batteries. Under some conditions, especially those found in summer, batteries can heat up and may even swell, as a flight increases in length. That's why it's not advisable to try to recharge an Intelligent Flight battery right after you bring your aircraft back home. Cold, on the other hand, affects the chemical reactions in the battery that produce the juice needed to operate the drone. I've experienced as much as 40 percent reduced flight time with a fully charged battery in cold weather. Winter is a good time to have the more powerful Intelligent Flight Plus batteries on hand.

- **Reduced human enthusiasm.** Before I got into aerial photography, I spent many a winter shooting lovely snow scenes. I traveled to Sainte-Anne-de-Beaupré in Quebec, Canada this past February, in fact, and nearly froze my feet off taking conventional still photos of some folks at a ski resort there who were enjoying the weather more than I was. I have to confess that most years I head to Florida when the weather gets cold, and that's where I do most of my winter aerial photography.

  Don't be like me. Be like Rick Murray, who captured the great image seen in Figure 7.32. He took his Mini Pro 3 out to capture some freezing fog moving across Old Hickory Lake, northeast of Nashville in sub-zero temperatures.

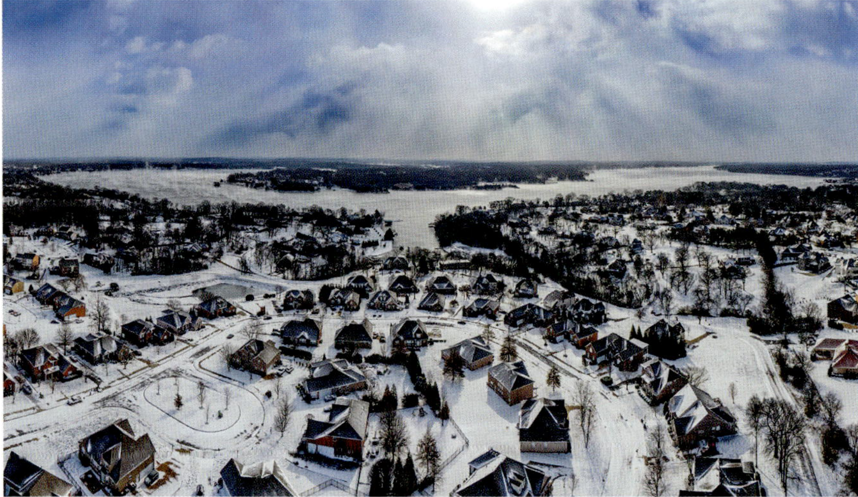

Figure 7.32 Bundle up, and you can capture impressive images in frigid winter weather, too.

Next Up

Now it's time to learn everything you need to know to get started shooting great videos from your aerial perch in Chapter 8.

Shooting Video 8

The still photography capabilities of your Mini 3 or Mini 3 Pro may be amazing, but the video features are even more remarkable. In video mode, your "Tripod in the Air" becomes a "SteadyCam in the Sky," capable of capturing a variety of cool cinematic moves automatically, and dozens of other impressive video shots manually. It can shoot Full HD (high-definition) and 4K (ultra-high-definition) clips, plus 2.7K resolution at your choice of frame rates. Slow-motion and fast-motion video are also available. Advanced users will love the drone's ability to use the D-Cinelike color profile option to enable advanced editing of color, saturation, sharpness, and some video-centric attributes using the color-grading tools of a video editor.

This chapter provides an introduction to video shooting, with the recreational drone pilot in mind. I'm going to show you how to practice a full range of useful manual maneuvers and describe the automated QuickShot features and MasterShots (a Mini 3 Pro–only option). You'll easily be able to capture compelling clips you can show as-is, or edit them into complete mini-productions.

If you're a serious videographer interested in incorporating drone video into your movies, you'll want to check out the entire books dedicated to the techniques of video, and sample some of the YouTube tutorials. It's not really possible to cover all the video capabilities of your drone, so my goal is to help video neophytes engage with what is one of the most interesting capabilities of the Mini 3 and Mini 3 Pro aircraft.

Preparing to Shoot Video

Whether you're looking to record informal clips of the family on vacation, the latest viral video for YouTube, or a set of scenes that will be painstakingly crafted into a cinematic masterpiece using editing software, your drone will perform admirably.

The first step is to switch the drone to video shooting mode within the DJI Fly app. Just follow these steps:

1. **Access shooting mode.** When connected to the aircraft using the DJI Fly app, tap the Shooting mode icon located at the right edge of the screen, just above the Shutter/Recording icon, as seen in Figure 8.1. The Mini 3 Pro version is shown in Figure 8.1; the Mini 3 screen is very similar but lacks a MasterShots option.

2. **Choose Video.** Tap the video icon in the middle column and the available video mode icons will appear in the left-most column.

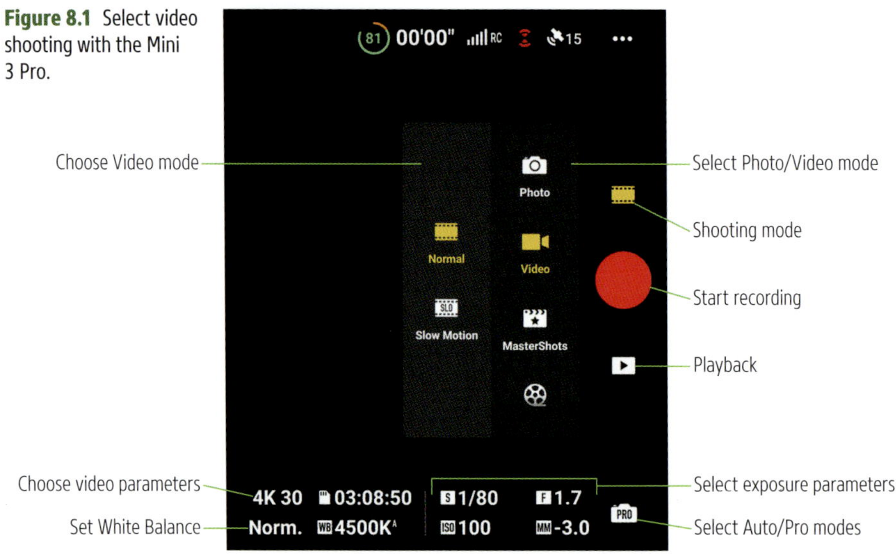

Figure 8.1 Select video shooting with the Mini 3 Pro.

Choose Video mode
Select Photo/Video mode
Shooting mode
Start recording
Playback
Choose video parameters
Select exposure parameters
Set White Balance
Select Auto/Pro modes

3. **Select Auto or Pro mode.** Both Auto and Pro adjustment modes are available for video shooting. As I'll explain shortly, you'll have more options in Pro mode.

4. **Choose video parameters.** In Auto mode, you can choose video resolution, frame rate, and add or subtract exposure compensation. In Pro mode, you can also select shutter speed, aperture, and ISO. I'll describe these options in the following sections.

Resolution and Frames Per Second

Two of the parameters you'll need to specify before shooting video are *resolution* and *frames per second*. Tap the area labeled Choose Video Parameters in Figure 8.1, and, with the Mini 3 Pro, a screen like the one shown in Figure 8.2 appears. (The Mini 3 will display only Resolution and Frames Per Second choices, as these are the only video parameters it makes available.)

Resolution is the dimension, in pixels, of each individual video frame, while the frames-per-second setting determines how many individual images (frames) are captured per elapsed second. I'm going to explain them and tell you why each individual value is important.

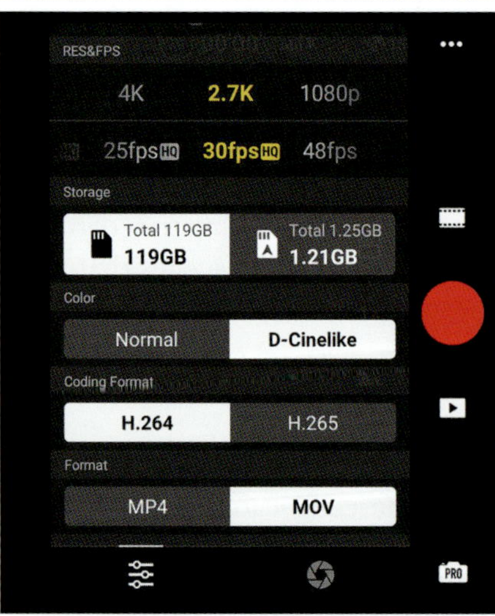

Figure 8.2 Select video resolution and frame rate.

Resolution

The kind of high-definition video drone pilots shoot always uses a consistent aspect ratio of 16:9. (Wide-screen motion pictures intended for theaters may use other proportions, such as 1.85:1.) Resolution is expressed in terms of the width times the height of the frame. Because the proportions are fixed, video resolution is sometimes expressed using only the height: 720p, 1080p, 3840p, and so forth. The "p" means that progressive scan was used (each line of pixels, top to bottom, is captured one after another), rather than using *interlaced* scan (odd-numbered lines captured first, then even-numbered lines). Common resolutions include:

- **1280 × 720.** *Standard HD.* This lowest-resolution HD format is on the way out, and neither the Mini 3 nor Mini 3 Pro can *capture* video at this resolution, although transmission of 720p video for display on a controller like the RC-N1 remote is available.

- **1920 × 1080.** *Full HD.* This is the minimum resolution used by most television screens and computer monitors, although a few 720p devices are still sold. It was the standard video resolution for a long time, but it is rapidly being replaced by higher-definition devices.

- **2688 × 1512.** *2.7K.* This resolution is useful for advanced users working with video-editing software. It enables you to crop a 1920 × 1080 region to improve the composition of a scene. Videographers sometimes like to "overshoot" and then decide in post-processing how to frame the image. Some believe that video captured at a higher resolution and then downsized looks better. Improvements from using 2.7K clips are likely to be minimal.

- **3840 × 2160.** *4K.* This resolution used by the drones is on the way to becoming the new "minimum" standard, with more devices and streaming services supporting it. It's sometimes called Ultra High Definition (UHD), although 8K video currently shares the UHD designation. Note that digital cinema defines 4K as 4096 × 2160—256 pixels wider than your drone's 4K mode.

- **5472 × 3078.** *5.4K.* This higher resolution is available on some upscale DJI drones, but not the Mini 3 or Mini 3 Pro. Its availability exists for the same logic as 2.7K resolution. You can crop 5.4K video down to 4K resolution, or, theoretically, end up with slightly better quality 4K using downsizing. The editor must know what they are doing and choose the appropriate encoder settings.

- **7680 × 4320.** *8K.* Your drone cannot capture conventional video at this high-end resolution, either. While it's making inroads in terms of devices able to handle it, right now 4K remains the mainstream video resolution of choice.

Frame Rates

Frame rates are the number of individual images captured per second. As I mentioned earlier, your drones do not use *interlaced scanning*, in which odd-numbered lines (lines 1, 3, 5, 7, and so forth) are captured with one pass, and then the even-numbered lines (2, 4, 6, 8, and so forth) are grabbed. Instead, video is captured using *progressive* or *sequential scanning*. This happens at a rate of 30, 60, or 120 frames per second, corresponding to the number of video fields captured. Two additional frame rates—24 fps and 48 fps—are available for shooting the so-called "cinematic" look, which I'll explain shortly.

All these numbers apply to the NTSC television system used in North America, Central America, parts of South America, and in Japan, South Korea, and some other countries. Other places, including Europe, most of Asia, Oceania, and Africa, and parts of South America use PAL, where the nominal scanning figures are 25/50/100 rather than 30/60/120. I used the term *nominal* because the actual frame rates may technically be slightly different. You'll sometimes see 23.976, 29.970, or 59.940 progressive scan frame rates. In practice, the nominal figures are good enough.

Your choice between 30/60/120 fps (NTSC) or 25/50/100 fps (PAL) and 24 or 48 fps is determined by what you plan to do with your video. The short explanation is that, for technical reasons I won't go into here, shooting at 24 fps gives your movie more of the "cinematic" look that film would produce, excellent for showing fine detail. However, if your clip has moving subjects, or you pan the camera, 24 or 48 fps can produce a jerky effect called "judder." The 30 and 60 fps (or 25 and 50 fps) options produce a home-video look that some feel is less desirable, but which is smoother and less jittery when displayed on an electronic monitor. I suggest you try each type and use the frame rate that best suits your tastes and video-editing software. **Note:** As I'll explain later, the shutter speed you use can also contribute to a jerky look when the speed is too fast for a particular frame rate.

When video is played back at the same frame rate at which it was captured, the motion appears at normal speed. If the clip was captured at a higher speed (such as 120/100 fps), action seems to be moving in *slow motion*. Image-editing software can be used to seamlessly meld slo-mo video with normal video as a special effect. Interestingly, when you play back video at a speed that is faster than the speed at which it was captured, you get speeded up motion with a time-lapse look. That's what your drone's Hyperlapse setting does. Individual frames are captured at intervals greater than the 24/30 fps norm so that, when played back, the motion is speeded up and somewhat frantic in appearance.

Video Settings (Mini 3 Pro Only)

The Mini 3 Pro has three additional video settings available. I'll explain each of them in the following sections. The basic settings include:

- **Format: MP4, MOV.** These are the container files that hold the video data, as I'll describe shortly.
- **Color: Normal, D-Cinelike.** These are your color profiles, also described shortly.
- **Coding Format: H.264, H.265.** These are the codecs (coder/decoder) used.

Format (Mini 3 Pro Only)

Both MP4 and MOV are multimedia file storage formats which serve as digital container files that hold compressed video data, audio tracks, still images, subtitles, and metadata needed to play back the video. You can select which format to use in the Systems Setting menu, or from the main screen, as shown in Figure 8.2. Both encode their contents using the MPEG-4 codec (coder/decoder). You can think of container files as a library shelf that may contain DVDs, audio CDs, photo albums, and a card catalog telling you where to find each and how to access them. The container is not the video itself, but, rather a place where the video and its components can be stored.

MP4 is an international standard and the most widely used video format and is compatible with a vast range of devices, software, and streaming platforms. It uses lossy compression to save space and can be smoothly translated to MOV as long as the same codec (such as H.264, described shortly) was used for both.

MOV is a proprietary format developed by Apple for use with its QuickTime multimedia framework back in 1991. Although Apple ceased support for QuickTime more than five years ago, MOV lives on, because MOV files are less compressed than MP4 and sometimes higher in quality. They may be better for editing on Mac platforms, but most software can handle both MOV and MP4 and convert between them. YouTube and Vimeo video-hosting services accept both.

Color (Profiles)

By Color, in this case, DJI actually means something you can think of as video color profiles. Profiles are a way of adjusting the tonal values of a video as it is captured to produce a desired range of values and dynamic range. When processing the resulting footage in an image editor, a technique called *color grading* can be applied to produce the widest possible range of detail in shadows, highlights, and midtones. Color grading is a skill to be mastered in itself, but when used well, results in stunning video. DJI offers two different profiles with the Mini 3 Pro—Normal and D-Cinelike.

If you've been taking photos for a while, you're probably familiar with all the fixes and tweaks you can do with your still images within image editors like Photoshop. It's relatively easy to adjust color tones, contrast, sharpness, and other parameters prior to displaying or printing your photo. Movies are a little trickier, because any given video typically consists of *thousands* of individual photos, captured at 24 frames per second (or faster), with the possibility that each and every frame within a particular sequence might need fixes or creative adjustments.

Fortunately, shooting video does not preclude doing post-processing during editing. Indeed, many videographers deliberately shoot relatively low-contrast video in order to capture the largest dynamic range possible, and then fine-tune the rendition later using their editing software. The profiles offered by the Mini 3 and Mini 3 Pro allow you to adjust your camera so that the video you capture is somewhat *pre-fine-tuned* in order to reduce or eliminate the amount of post-processing you do later.

Needless to say, creating and using profiles is a highly technical aspect of video making, at least in terms of the amount of knowledge you need to have to correctly judge what changing one of the parameters will do to your video. I hope to get you started with a quick description of what those parameters do, so you'll have a starting point when you start to explore them.

Thanks to our evolutionary heritage, humans don't see differences in tones in a linear manner. An absolutely smooth progression of pixels from absolute black to pure white (with 0 representing black and 256 representing white) would not look like a continuous gradient to our eyes. We'd be unable to detect differences in shadows and highlights that have the same change in tonal values as midtones. So, everything from computer monitors to printers use a correction factor (gamma) to cancel out the differences in the way we see tones.

This correction takes the form of a curve, called a *gamma curve*. If you remember your geometry, the x and y axes on a graph are used to define the shape of a curve, and in the case of gamma curves, the values use logarithmic units (ack!) to define the slope. The whole shebang is needed to reconcile the ability of sensors to capture, video systems to display, and printers to output a range of tones in a linear way with the actual tones we perceive non-linearly. Gamma correction and gamma compression are used to help make sure that what we get is what we see. While gamma correction between computer platforms (that is, between Macs and PCs) may be different, the actual gamma values defined by video standards like NTSC and PAL are fixed and well-known. Profiles allow you to configure your camera to capture video using a desired amount of gamma and color tone correction, and then make adjustments during color grading.

Video signals normally encompass brightness levels from 0 percent to 109 percent (you read that right: modern video cameras can record detail in highlights that are actually brighter than was possible when the video age began; the old scale was retained, reminiscent of Nigel Tufnel's 11 setting on his amp). However, even the 109 percent provides too much of a limitation; cameras can capture detail in highlights that are even brighter than *that*. So, a log gamma curve like D-Cinelike is used to *compress* all that image detail to fit into the space allowed for conventional video signals. Post-processing in a video editor allows working with all that information and produces a finished video that contains the filmmaker's selection of tonal values in a form that can be displayed comfortably. The full dynamic range can be used to produce the finished movie. You might find that useful when exposing for highlights while avoiding blowing out the sky, or for capturing detail in shadows without losing midtones and highlights. The next sections will help you understand your profile choices with the Mini 3 Pro.

Normal

As you might expect, Normal is the default, unaltered video profile, which produces great results with a generous range of tones, even when shooting video that encompasses a fairly bright sky and darker subject matter on the ground. It provides bright, saturated colors and excellent contrast under most conditions. It looks good and is ready to use or edit with no additional processing, unlike the optional color profiles, which produce very, very flat footage prior to grading.

The Normal color profile is frequently the best option for amateur drone pilots who want ready-to-use aerial footage. However, Normal videos may lack some of the fine detail contrast and dynamic range improvements found in professional video.

D-Cinelike

D-Cinelike offers a flatter, more muted color profile for Mini 3 Pro users than Normal. However, it is able to capture a longer dynamic range than Normal, with improved contrast and detail. It prevents highlights from being too bright or washed out, and avoids inky shadows, which can be a particular problem late in the day when the sun is low in the sky. You'll end up with fewer image areas that are completely white or black, with the brightest highlights becoming slightly darker and darkest shadow brightened a bit.

Straight out of the camera, your D-Cinelike video will have lower contrast and appear duller. However, the color grading process for D-Cinelike footage can be considered fairly simple, often requiring just a few changes to exposure and saturation to produce crisp footage.

Coding Format

Here you'll select one of two widely used video compression standards, or codecs (coder/decoder), shown earlier in Figure 8.2. Your choices include:

- **H.264.** Also known as MPEG-4 Part 10 or Advanced Video Coding (MPEG-4 AVC), it compresses video so it requires only half the storage space or transmission bandwidth of MPEG-2, with the same video quality. Used with the Normal profile, it can be used to produce video quickly when you need fast turnaround. It is your best choice if you have a slow computer, don't want to use color grading, and will be working with MP4 to get the highest degree of compatibility. However, if you're shooting 4K, the file sizes will be larger and more demanding of your computer's power.

- **H.265.** For the best quality, you'll want to use H.265, also known as H.265/HEVC (High-Efficiency Video Coding), even when using the Normal profile. It uses less compression but can produce 10-bit files with a maximum amount of information, which comes in handy when doing color grading. However, you'll need a fairly powerful computer to edit any footage you capture using this codec.

Exposure Considerations

I covered the elements of exposure in Chapter 5, and pretty much everything written there applies equally to shooting video. In general, you can apply the same exposure compensation/EV adjustments, white balance settings, histogram interpretation, and other parameters you use for still photography to capturing videos. In Auto mode, the drone will select shutter speed and ISO setting for you, but you can still compensate with EV adjustments. In Pro mode, you can select shutter speed, ISO, and EV adjustments yourself. I won't repeat the other discussion of exposure in Chapter 5 here.

However, two particular aspects of exposure control have special significance for videography. One of them is the need for consistent exposure while shooting. The other is the use of shutter speeds, and returning to that topic also calls for revisiting my earlier discussions on working with neutral-density filters.

Consistent Exposure

If most of your previous experience has been in shooting stills, you may not have given a lot of thought about why exposure consistency may have much more importance when capturing video. Every photographer wants to achieve well-exposed stills and video, and knows that exposure itself is an important tool in creating the look and mood of a finished image or video sequence. You may want a dark and gloomy look, or a bright high-key atmosphere. If your exposure is a bit off, it can often be corrected using an image editor, video editor, or during color grading of movie footage.

Where video shooting differs from stills is the need for exposure consistency and continuity during and between shots. If a scene or an intercut sequence is suddenly darker, lighter, or has different lighting, the difference can be as jolting as the appearance of a Starbuck cup on a dinner table in Westeros.

You'll have lots of opportunities to put your experience to work. For example, you can also lock exposure to keep the same exposure settings as lighting changes or you reframe your scene from the air. Occasionally, you may find that you start having an exposure problem during recording; this might happen when pointing the lens toward a light-tone area that causes the camera to begin underexposing. Don't let that happen. Before pointing the camera toward a backlit area, lock the exposure. This will prevent the exposure from changing as you point the lens toward the backlit part of the scene. This is preferable to waiting until an underexposure problem starts and then setting plus exposure compensation that suddenly makes the video brighter.

If you're producing any sort of ambitious amateur or professional video, you'll want lighting and exposure to remain consistent, when need be, from shot to shot. It's up to you to decide whether to use your drone's autoexposure and auto ISO modes, or to make the necessary adjustments manually.

Once you realize that your video is not a still photograph, or even a series of still photographs, but, instead is the capture of a series of moments in time, you'll put exposure consistency and continuity at the top of your list of priorities.

Appropriate Shutter Speed

Your drone has a fixed f/1.7 aperture, so, as I described in Chapter 5, you must control exposure using only shutter speed and ISO, supplemented by neutral-density filters when even the lowest ISO setting won't let you choose the desired shutter speed. You have several options, which I introduced in Chapter 5:

- **Auto ISO/Manual shutter speed.** You select a shutter speed and the drone will choose an ISO sensitivity that will provide the correct exposure.
- **Manual ISO/Auto shutter speed.** You choose a fixed ISO sensitivity and allow the camera to adjust the shutter speed to arrive at an appropriate exposure.
- **Exposure compensation.** In either of the modes listed above, you can override the automatic setting by applying a plus/minus EV adjustment, as seen in Figure 8.3.
- **Manual ISO/Manual shutter speed.** You select both yourself.

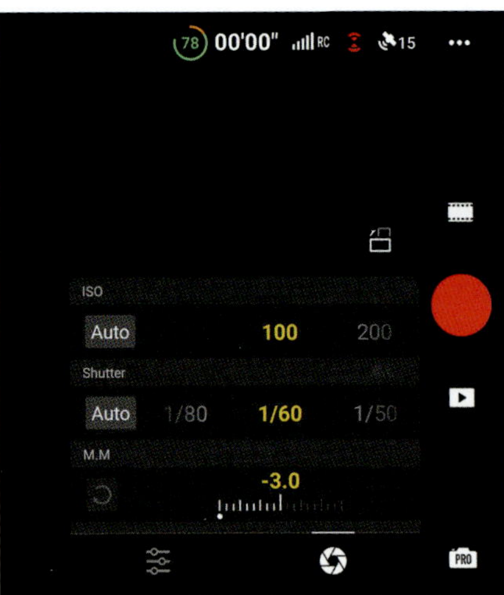

Figure 8.3 You can use EV settings to adjust video exposure, too.

The choice of a shutter speed for video is not as simple as you assume. You might think that setting your camera to a faster shutter speed will help give you sharper video frames. Actually, it *will,* but that's frequently not a good thing. In most cases it's best to leave the shutter speed at no more than *double* the frame rate (in other words no higher than 1/50th to 1/250th second) and allow the overall exposure to be adjusted by varying the ISO sensitivity or by using a neutral-density filter.

A "slow" 1/30th- or 1/60th-second shutter speed doesn't mean your movies will have the same amount of blur that a typical still photograph will have using those shutter speeds. We don't normally stare at a video frame for longer than 1/30th or 1/24th second, so while the shakiness of the *camera* can be disruptive (and usually corrected by the image-stabilization feature), if there is a bit of blur in our *subjects* from movement, we tend not to notice. Each frame flashes by in the blink of an eye, so to speak, so a shutter speed of 1/30th or 1/60th second works a lot better in video than it does when shooting stills.

Indeed, higher shutter speeds actually introduce problems of their own. If you shoot a video frame at 30 fps using a shutter speed of 1/250th second, the actual moment in time that's captured represents only about 12 percent of the 1/30th second of elapsed time in that frame. Yet, when played back, that frame occupies the full 1/30th of a second, with 88 percent of that time filled by stretching the original image to fill it. The result is often a choppy/jumpy image, and one that may appear to be *too* sharp.

In addition, because we are accustomed to viewing Hollywood productions that use slower shutter speeds, we *expect* to see a bit of blur to smooth out the transitions as an object moves within the video frame. It's thought that this effect is more social imprinting than scientific: we've all grown up accustomed to seeing the look of movies that, by convention, were shot using a shutter speed that's half the reciprocal of the frame rate (that is, 1/48th second for a 24 fps movie). Movie cameras use a rotary shutter (achieving that 1/48th-second exposure by using a 180-degree shutter "angle"), but the effect on our visual expectations is the same. For the most "film-like" appearance, use 24 fps and 1/60th-second shutter speed.

Faster shutter speeds do have some specialized uses for motion analysis, especially where individual frames are studied. The rest of the time, 1/30th or 1/60th of a second will suffice. If the reason you needed a higher shutter speed was to obtain the correct exposure, use a slower ISO setting, or a neutral-density filter to cut down on the amount of light passing through the lens. A good rule of thumb is to use 1/60th second or slower when shooting at 24 fps; 1/60th second or slower at 30 fps; and 1/125th second or slower at 60 fps.

Working with ND Filters

I covered neutral-density filters in considerable detail in Chapter 5, so you should just need a reminder of how important they are when shooting video. The lowest ISO sensitivity setting available for your drone is ISO 100. With a typical daylight scene, shutter speeds will rarely be slower than 1/750th second at ISO 100. So, if you want the best cinematic effect, you'll need at least a 4-stop ND filter to reduce a 1/750th-second shutter speed to the 1/50th-second range suitable for a 24 fps frame rate. The ND filter sets packaged with the Mini 3 and Mini 3 Pro both include 4-stop filters, labeled ND16. (Remember that the density of these filters doubles for each stop reduction; four stops: $2 \times 2 \times 2 \times 2 = 16$.)

To give yourself a little wiggle room under bright conditions, you might want to use an ND filter with more density, such as an ND64 or ND128 (6 and 7 stops). Such filters can help retain a desired shutter speed even under brighter conditions at ISO 100; in *dimmer* light, they'll continue to do the job. You'll just need to boost the ISO sensitivity, say, to ISO 200 to 400 to produce the appropriate exposure with little quality loss due to the higher sensitivity setting.

In practice, you can probably skip using an ND filter entirely for fairly static video clips with limited movement of the drone and your subject matter. Lacking motion, any jerkiness caused by a fast shutter speed may not be noticeable. But once you start doing fly-bys or fly-overs of any type, you'll want to have an ND filter in place to preserve the smooth cinematic look. Some ND filters are sold that double as polarizers. Specialized split ND and graduated ND filters can help balance a bright sky with a darker foreground.

Using Digital Zoom

Neither the Mini 3 nor Mini 3 Pro have an optical zoom lens to provide adjustments to the field of view. Their cameras have fixed focal length lenses with a wide-angle perspective equivalent to a full-frame camera's 24mm with a fixed f/1.7 aperture.

Depth-of-field (the range of sharp focus) extends from 39 in./1m to infinity. You generally won't be capturing images at a distance of one meter or less, so effectively, every still photo or video you capture should have an acceptable range of sharp focus.

However, in Single Photo and Video modes, both the Mini 3 and Mini 3 Pro can *simulate* an optical zoom by enlarging a cropped area of the sensor to fill the frame. While this cropping reduces the resolution and image quality of the area captured, it does allow zooming in to produce an enlarged image from the same aerial position.

When a circle with a zoom ratio (1X, 4X, etc.) appears to the upper left of the Record icon on the controller screen, as shown in Figure 8.4, left, you'll know zooming is available. If it does not appear, then you've chosen a conflicting mode and must adjust the errant parameter. Typical maximum zoom ratios are shown in Figure 8.5.

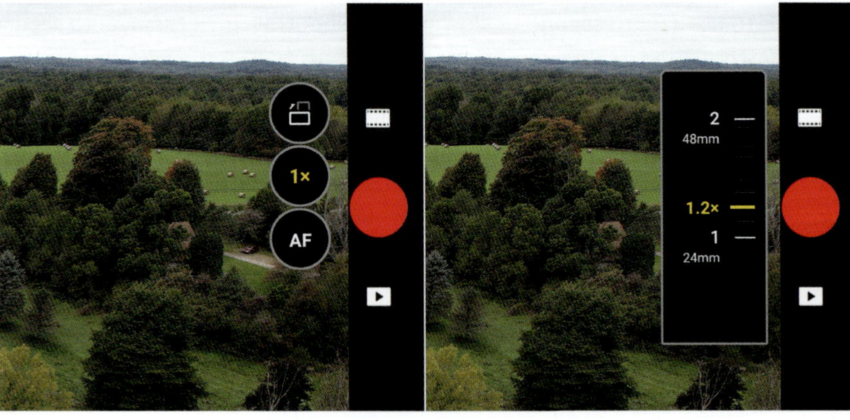

Figure 8.4 Tap the Zoom ratio icon to zoom in whole increments (left), or use a sliding scale (right).

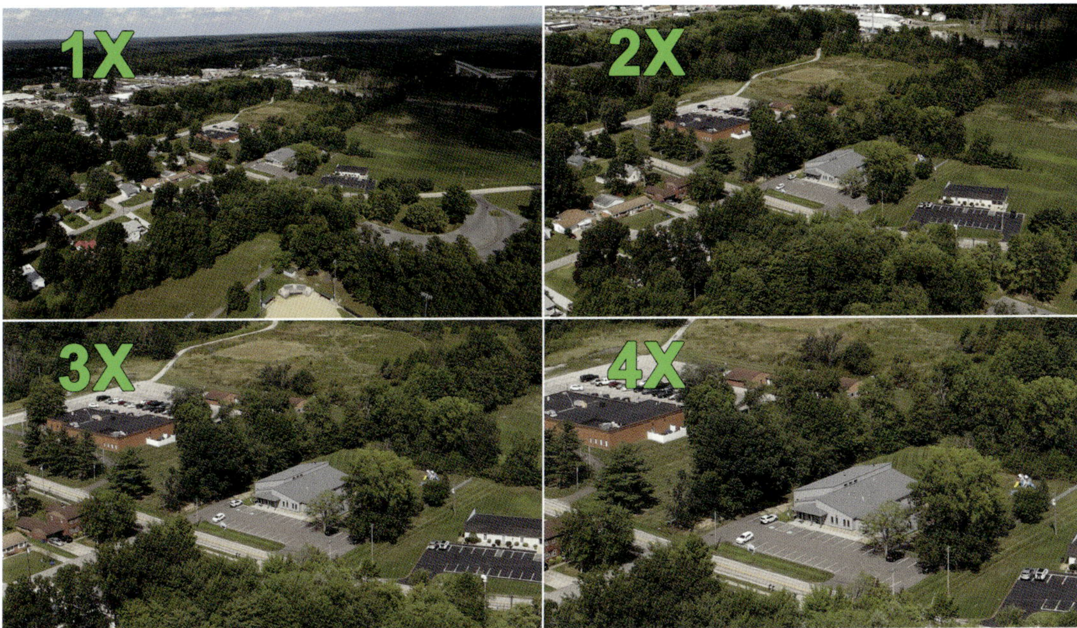

Figure 8.5 Typical zoom factors.

There are three ways to zoom:

- **Tap Zoom ratio icon.** Tapping the icon repeatedly will cycle among the available zoom settings. The live display on your controller's screen will zoom to reflect the new zoom setting. (Check out Figure 8.4, left, again.) Only whole increments (e.g., 2X, 4X, etc.) are available in this mode.

- **Press and hold the Zoom ratio icon.** As you press a finger on the icon, a zoom scale will appear, as seen in Figure 8.4, right. You can slide up and down to change the zoom setting. The equivalent focal length appears next to the scale. You can choose any intermediate equivalent focal length between the whole increments as you slide.

- **Use your controller's "zoom" dial.** With the DJI RC-N1, hold down the Fn button on the *left* side of the controller while rotating the gimbal dial. (The dial will tilt the gimbal if the Fn button is not held down.) If you're using the DJI RC or DJI RC Pro, just rotate the Camera Control (Zoom) dial on the right top of the controller; no button press is necessary. The location of these controls was shown in Chapter 3. You can select any of the intermediate focal lengths when using this method.

Zoom Effects

Now that you know how to "zoom" with your drone, what do you do with it? In general, it's a good idea to limit the zoom sequences you capture, especially *while recording*. It can be useful to be able to adjust the field of view and zoom in between shots to provide different perspectives, although having a scene suddenly appear larger can be disconcerting. You'll probably want to reposition your aircraft between takes at different zoom settings.

But zooming during a sequence can be even more jarring and may be reminiscent of techniques used in '70s-era kung-fu movies. You'll want to plan any zoom carefully, and use your drone's zoom dial to get the smoothest zoom possible.

Of course, there are exceptions to every rule, and sometimes it takes a genius—or two of them—to find the exception. Cinematographer Irmin Roberts came up with something called a *dolly zoom* that was most dramatically used by Alfred Hitchcock in his 1958 film *Vertigo*. (It's sometimes called the Vertigo Effect for that reason.) To achieve this effect conventionally, the camera and its mount are attached to a smooth track. In its most common implementation the camera is moved *forward* or *backward* on its track, *closer to* or *further away* from the main subject. The field of view is changed simultaneously using zoom, so that the subject remains the same size.

If the camera moves closer while zooming out, the background seems to grow and become more dominant. If the camera moves *away* while zooming *in*, the foreground subject is emphasized as the background grows relatively smaller. The effect can be striking and is often used to convey reactions to dramatic events.

Although the dolly zoom is most effective when combined with selective focus to isolate the foreground subject, you can apply it to your drone videography in many ways. It does take some practice, but so does maneuvering your aircraft with agility. Just follow these steps:

1. **Select a dramatic foreground subject.** A large, impressive building or statue against an interesting background would be ideal. Personally, I'd try this using the *Cristo Redentor*, atop Corcovado Mountain in Rio de Janeiro, if it were legal, I could afford it, and had the necessary skills.

2. **Choose N (Normal) mode.** Although this is a cinematic effect, oddly enough, Cine/Tripod mode won't work too well, because the drone's movement is too slow for a dramatic change. Conversely, Sport mode is too fast.

3. **Hover at an appropriate distance.** You'll want to fill as much of the frame as you can with your subject.

4. **Begin recording.** Tap the Record button and begin capturing video. You can trim any excess footage at the beginning using your video-editing software.

5. **Prepare to zoom.** Hold down the Fn button if using the RC-N1 controller and position your left index finger on the gimbal dial. If you're using the DJI RC or DJI RC Pro controller, position the index finger of your right hand on the camera control dial.

6. **Zoom smoothly while flying backward.** This is the tricky part. You'll want to zoom in while pressing the right stick backward to move the drone in that direction. You'll want to try and match the drone's backward movement with the zoom-in effect, so the main subject remains the same size. It's not easy to rotate the zoom dial while coordinating backward flight. Be prepared to practice and also capture several takes until you get it right.

Other Useful Maneuvers

I explained basic maneuvers in Chapter 5. The manually implemented maneuvers I described earlier are just the beginning of the aerial movements and techniques you can use to transform your videos into engaging and compelling clips and motion pictures. As I noted earlier, my goal is to introduce you to the basics, so you'll be interested in exploring the full range of videographic techniques that drones are capable of. This next section provides you with a checklist of cool techniques you can explore as your skill grows.

- **Flyover.** The use of flyovers taken from a birds-eye view have become a key movie establishing shot, supplementing the familiar skyline shots of cities like San Francisco, New York, Paris, and London. Given a familiar enough landmark—say the Pyramids of Egypt—a well-done flyover can replace the skyline (or monument-line) shot entirely. Recreational flyers may not be able to do flyovers of major metropolitan areas, but a birds-eye perspective can still be used to provide an interesting view in your video.

- **Dolly.** I described the dolly zoom earlier in this chapter, but other dolly shots can be a staple used in other ways. In Hollywood, the camera mount often resides on a special set of rails, such that the camera either slides in seamlessly toward or away from the subject or maintains pace alongside it. You can imitate the in/out dolly move by maintaining a particular altitude with the drone on the same level as your subject and flying toward or away from your subject at a constant speed. Moving the drone facing your subject in parallel with it provides a side-slide shot. You can achieve the same look with the drone's automatic ActiveTrack (Parallel) Intelligent Flight mode, but you can learn to duplicate the move manually, too.

- **Flythrough.** With a flythrough, you're moving the drone right through a scene, with objects passing by (such as trees, buildings, or, say, the interior of a covered bridge) during the maneuver. You can fly through as a forward motion with the camera facing ahead, or looking backward as the aircraft flies in reverse. Since you're actually flying through an area, you'll need to take extra precautions to avoid collisions.

- **Flyby.** You can execute this maneuver by flying past a subject in a straight line, while pressing the left stick left or right so the drone rotates in sync with your subject. It's as if you were moving past a subject while turning your head to keep the subject in the center of your view. It will take some practice to synchronize the rotation smoothly.

- **Elevator.** All you need to do is point the drone at the lower edge of a vertical subject (such as a tower), and then push the left stick forward smoothly to cause the aircraft to rise, revealing more and more of the subject's upper structure. The reverse maneuver can also be executed, by reducing the drone's altitude.

- **Pan/Tilt.** To capture a pan shot, all you have to do is press the left stick to the left or right, so the drone rotates horizontally. You can use this to follow action as a subject moves from one edge of the movie frame to the opposite edge, or simply to show an impressive vista. The technique is similar to still photo panoramas, but you're revealing the scene gradually as the camera rotates.

A tilt is similar to a pan, but the change in perspective is caused by the tilting of the drone's camera on its gimbal up and down. The range is more limited, as the gimbal can't start its tilt upward (unless you enable that feature in the Control tab of the System Settings menu). You can use a tilt to gradually show the whole of a vertical structure, overcoming the tilt limitation by combining the movement of the gimbal dial with an elevator shot.

- **Chase.** You've watched commercials where the tough off-road vehicle climbs up a mountain, with the camera following it all the way to the top. Perhaps the commercial cuts to shots from the front of the vehicle, as it "chases" the camera. You can duplicate this type of shot manually, but I recommend learning how to use the FocusTrack mode's ActiveTrack option in Trace mode (discussed soon) instead.

- **Bank.** This kind of shot abandons the gimbal's horizontal stabilizing capabilities and lets the view tilt as the drone banks while making turns. This resembles the looks you get with racing drones that use first-person view. In fact, all you need to do to enable it is to go to the Control tab of the System Settings menu and change the gimbal's behavior from the default Follow setting to FPV.

FocusTrack (Mini 3 Pro Only)

FocusTrack is a versatile Intelligent Flight mode that allows you to keep your subject in the center of your shot while your drone flies autonomously or manually. It includes three variations, Spotlight 2.0, ActiveTrack 4.0, and Point of Interest 3.0. When using any of these, you or an observer will need to remain alert to spot safety hazards or obstacles.

You'll need to use some caution when using FocusTrack to "chase" your subjects while shooting, especially in areas with obstacles that may be difficult for the drone to detect, such as tree branches, power lines, transparent objects such as glass or water, and blank walls, or subjects moving on snow. The drone may lose a subject if it changes direction or shape drastically, moves out of sight for more than a short time, or has a similar color, texture, or pattern as its surroundings. FocusTrack can also be thrown off by dim illumination, intervening subjects that "catch" its attention, or when the aircraft is near its flight height/distance limits or a GEO Zone.

SUBJECT SCANNING

Although you will generally select your subject by drawing a box around it on the screen, the DJI Fly app has a Subject Scanning option in the Control tab of the System Settings menu. When activated, the app will examine your scene and place plus icons on possible targets. (See Figure 8.6.)

You can enable any of the three tracking modes by taking off and hovering about six feet off the ground. Then, select a subject by drawing a box around it on the screen with your finger. If your subject is a human being, they can raise one hand above shoulder level and the drone will interpret this as a signal to lock on. The default FocusTrack mode is Spotlight, but you can switch to any of the other modes by tapping their icons that appear at the bottom of the screen. (See Figure 8.7.) Exit FocusTrack by pressing the Pause button on your controller.

- **Spotlight 2.0.** This mode is an excellent choice for subjects that don't move, including people. You can fly the drone all around the subject at different angles and altitudes, and the subject will remain in the center of the frame. The water tower shown in Figure 8.7 is an example of the kind of subject you might choose.

This mode is a mix of autonomous and manual flight. The drone will adjust the gimbal to keep the subject centered automatically, but you have control over the flight path. As with any manual flight, you can push the right stick forward or back to adjust the distance from the locked-in subject or left/right to circle around it. Adjusting the left stick forward or back changes the altitude and pressing the left stick left/right rotates the drone to adjust the frame. As you're recording, if the drone loses the subject, it will exit Spotlight mode and hover, awaiting new instructions.

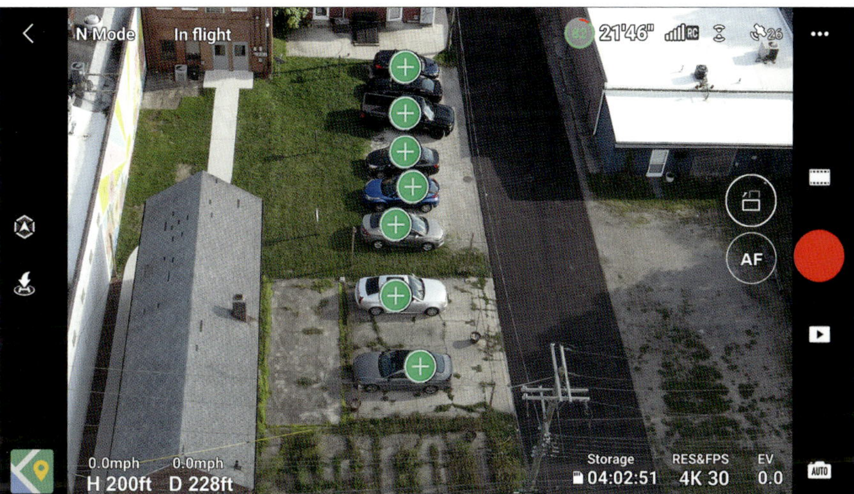

Figure 8.6 Subject Scanning can find target subjects for you.

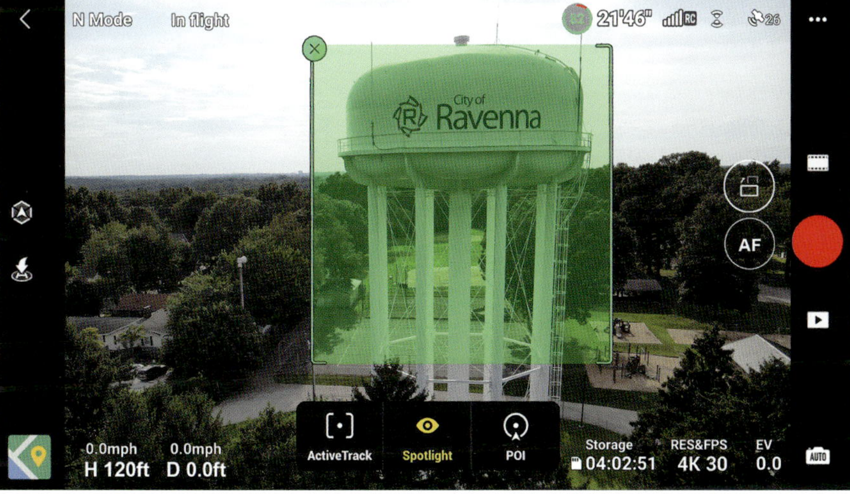

Figure 8.7 Spotlight mode.

- **ActiveTrack 4.0.** This mode allows you to follow a moving subject around from two different angles, either behind or alongside. When you've drawn a box around your subject, a pair of options, Trace and Parallel, pop up. Tap the one you want, and then tap Go to begin tracking.

  The screen will look like the one shown in Figure 8.8. The drone can differentiate between people and vehicles, and an appropriate icon for each will appear below the box.

  In Trace mode: The aircraft follows the subject from a constant distance, as if it were chasing it. It will sense and avoid obstacles in front of it as it follows the subject. However, the maximum speed in Normal mode is 22 mph; in Cine/Tripod mode, 13.4 mph upped to 36 mph in Sport mode, so you'll be unable to follow any subject faster than that.

  In Parallel mode: Move the drone to the side of your subject, and the drone will automatically track it from a constant angle and distance, while maintaining the same altitude—even if the subject moves upward or downward on its path. The aircraft *will* change altitude to avoid collisions with obstacles.

- **Point of Interest 3.0.** In this mode, you draw a box around the subject, then choose the speed and direction of the drone's travels as it orbits your subject by dragging the circle icon of the arrow that appears on the screen. As you drag it from right to left, the travel speed in a clockwise direction increases, until you reach the left end of the arc, where the direction reverses to counter-clockwise. The altitude of the aircraft does not change from its initial height. (See Figure 8.9.)

  Once you've started recording, the drone moves slowly at first as it calculates the diameter of the circle that will be flown. It then speeds up to the velocity you specified. You can move the drone closer or further from the subject, and it will make any corrections needed to continue circling around your subject.

Figure 8.8 ActiveTrack.

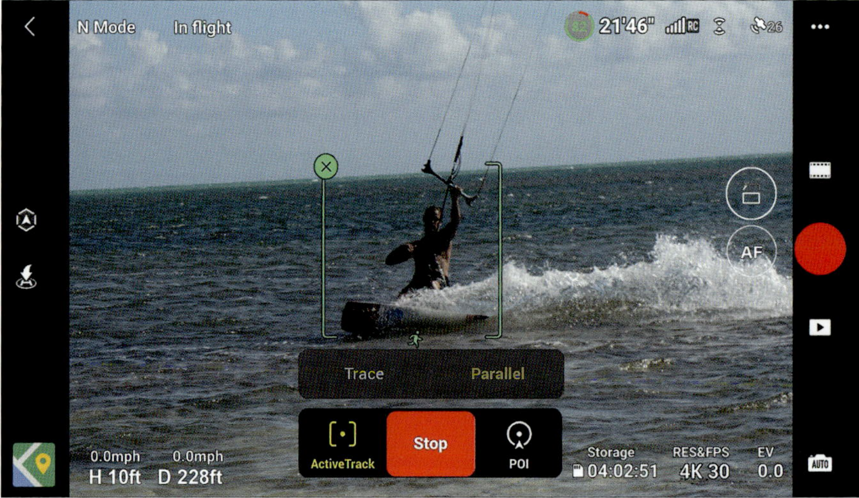

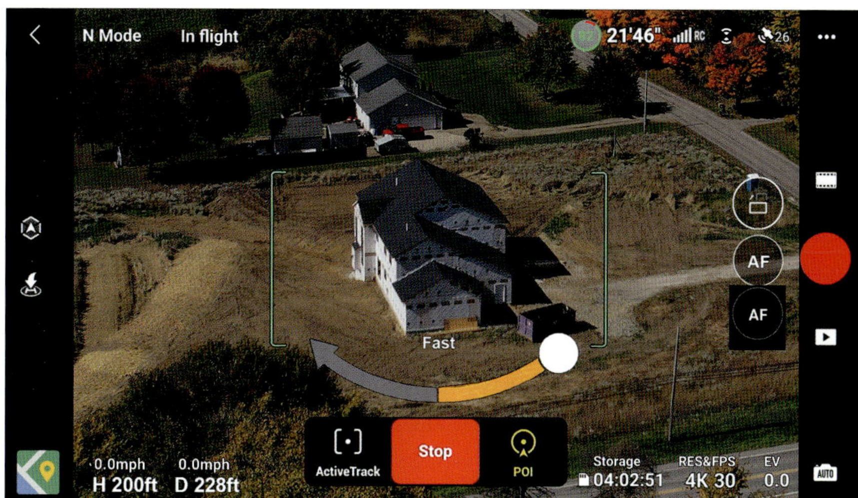

Figure 8.9 Point of Interest mode.

QuickShots

Many still photography instructors have their students learn how to shoot using manual exposure controls first, before branching out to learn semi-automatic exposure options like shutter-priority or aperture-priority. In a similar vein, I had you practice doing basic maneuvers manually before introducing your drone's more automatic options like FocusTrack. Now that you're capable of using a full range of video techniques with your controller specifying every move, you're in a better position to appreciate the autonomous and semi-autonomous video modes available with the Mini 3 and Mini 3 Pro.

QuickShots are shooting modes that guide the drone through various useful shots using its sensors and intelligence to handle nearly all the details required to capture a specific kind of clip. Your input may be limited to choosing the subject, specifying the starting point of the aircraft, its distance, or perhaps direction. Your options include Dronie, Rocket, Circle, Helix, Boomerang, and Asteroid. (The Mini 3 does not have the Asteroid mode.) The drone captures a clip using the parameters for that type of shot and automatically creates a short video, which can be viewed, edited, provided with a soundtrack, and, if you like, shared to Facebook or other social media.

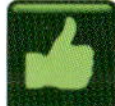

NOTE It's especially important to be aware of potential obstacles, such as powerlines, buildings, or tall trees, as well as the presence of any people you might fly over, when using Quick-Shots. Neither the Mini 3 nor Mini 3 Pro have side sensors and can easily collide with obstacles when flying in the large circle maneuvers some QuickShot modes use. Make sure your flight distance and altitude are appropriate before flying. If you misjudge, you can exit a QuickShot mode or pause and hover the aircraft (use the Pause/Return to Home button). You should not use QuickShots when the GNSS signal is weak, or when close to buildings (which can interfere with GNSS).

QuickShot Quick Start

As I described above, capturing a QuickShot is as easy as selecting a subject, a few parameters, and tapping Start. The full set of steps looks like this:

1. **Launch.** Take off and hover at least six feet above ground level.

2. **Choose QuickShot mode.** Scroll through the shooting modes, select QuickShots, and tap on the QuickShot mode you want to use.

3. **Set parameters.** Some modes will let you choose a distance, flight time, or flight direction.

4. **Specify subject.** You can draw a box around your subject, or, a human subject can wave or raise their arm so their elbow is above shoulder level. If the drone detects a likely subject on its own, you can tap the green circle with the plus symbol (as shown earlier in Figure 8.6) to accept it.

5. **Move to start.** After specifying your subject, you can manually move the drone to your selected starting point.

6. **Begin.** Tap the red Start/Record icon at the right side of the screen and the drone will begin shooting after a short countdown. A progress indicator circle will advance around the red icon, which now contains an X you can tap to cancel. (See Figure 8.10.)

7. **Monitor progress.** Watch carefully for obstacles as the drone captures your clip. If the aircraft detects an obstacle, it will halt and hover in place.

8. **Cancel (optional).** You can exit at any time by tapping the red circle X, or by pressing the controller's Pause/RTH button.

9. **Drone returns.** After capturing the QuickShot, the drone will return to its initial position.

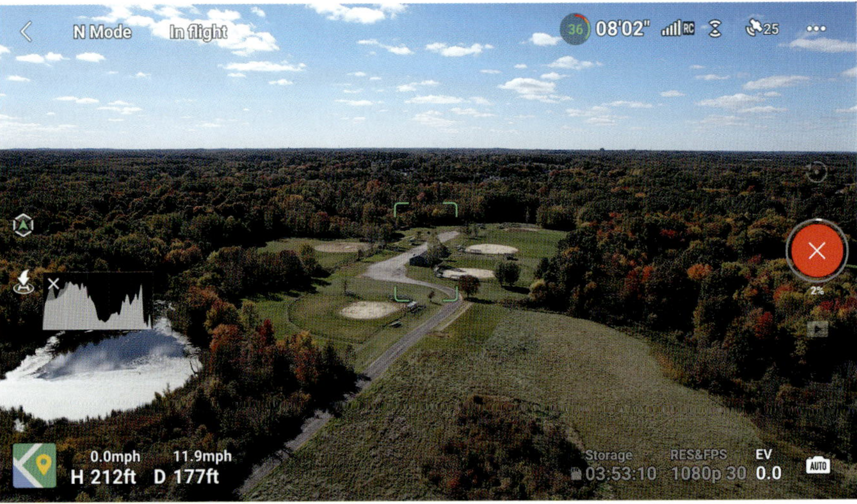

Figure 8.10 You can monitor the progress of the QuickShot on-screen.

You have a wide selection of useful QuickShot modes to choose from, detailed in the sections that follow. While all of these are helpful, you should keep in mind that they're intended to be a shortcut, and not really the primary source of clips for a professional-quality video. One mistake beginners make is to use them exclusively, which can make all their videos look the same.

Dronie

This maneuver is often used to create a video selfie (or if more than one person is involved, an *ussie*). When you select Dronie, an animated reminder screen, like the one shown in Figure 8.11, appears. When you minimize the reminder, you can select your subject and a maximum distance from the subject the drone should maintain, as seen in Figure 8.12. When Dronie is activated, the aircraft ascends slowly with the gimbal pitching slightly downward to follow the selected subject, which can remain motionless or move. The drop-down menu shown can be tapped to specify the maximum height for the sequence. Once recording of the dronie is finished, the aircraft will fly back to its original position, slowly at first, then accelerating.

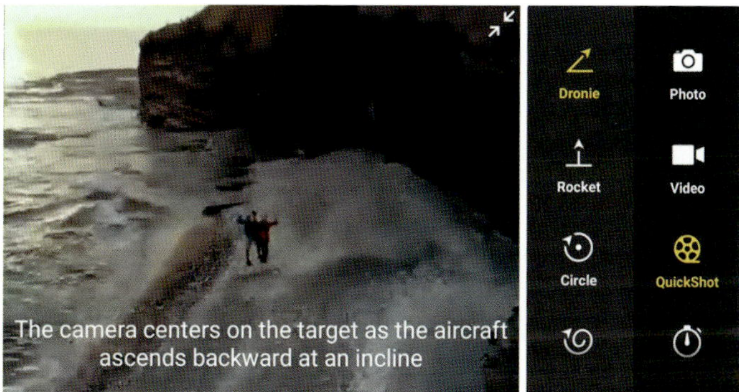

Figure 8.11 The app shows a preview of the dronie effect.

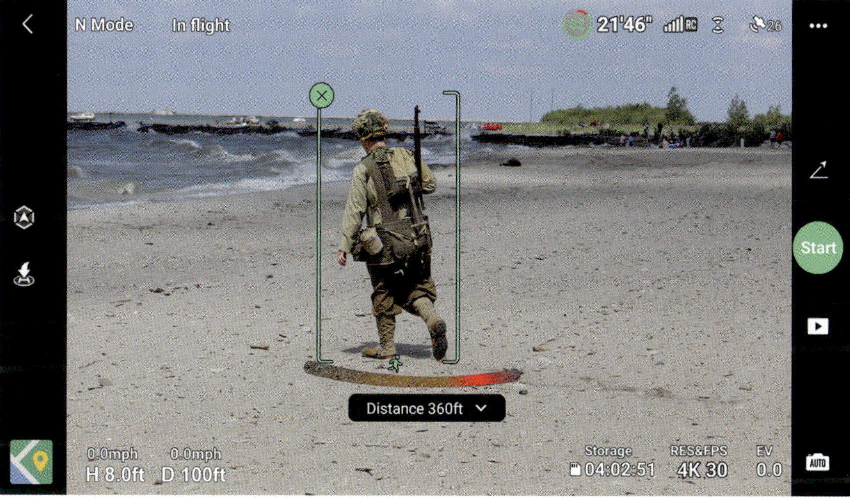

Figure 8.12 You can lock in a subject and specify a maximum height.

Rocket

The Rocket maneuver is another quick shot that can be used for reveals. (See Figure 8.13 for the reminder screen.) You can position the drone in front of your subject, at a distance you select, and choose a maximum altitude for the sequence, as shown in Figure 8.14. The clip ends up as a shot directly over your subject, and, as such, should be used with human subjects only with permission and when allowed. The maneuver begins in front of the subject and the drone increases altitude, slowly at first, and then accelerating while moving forward and tilting the gimbal downward to end above your subject. As with the other QuickShots, once recording is completed, the drone will fly back to its original position.

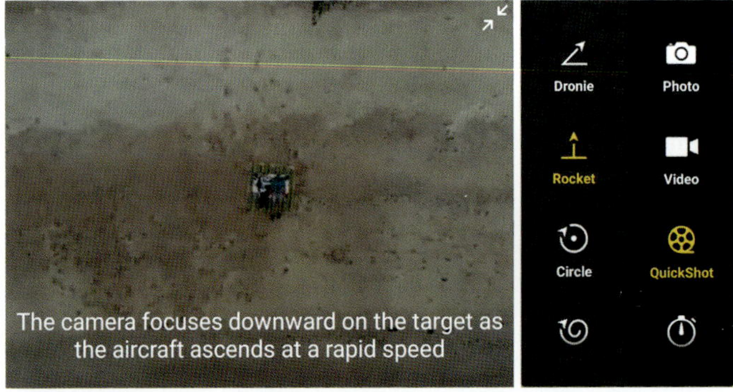

Figure 8.13 Select Rocket as your QuickShot.

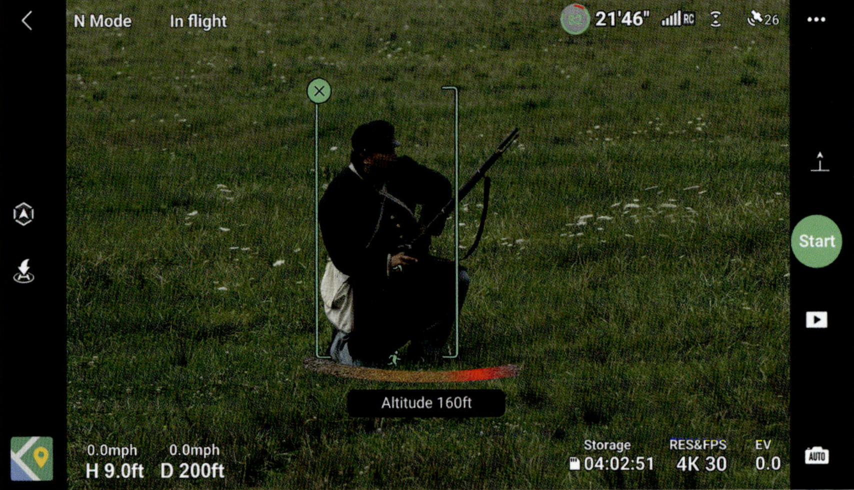

Figure 8.14 Manually choose the starting position and specify the maximum altitude.

Circle

The Circle maneuver (see Figure 8.15) is an automated version of the Orbit, with the drone circling around the subject you select. Move the drone to the height and distance you want and then choose the person, object, or structure to highlight using the same options available for the other QuickShots. Note that if your starting point is too far away for the drone to find a suitable subject automatically, you'll definitely need to draw a box around it. Finally, select the direction of rotation (clockwise or counterclockwise) and tap Start to begin. (See Figure 8.16.)

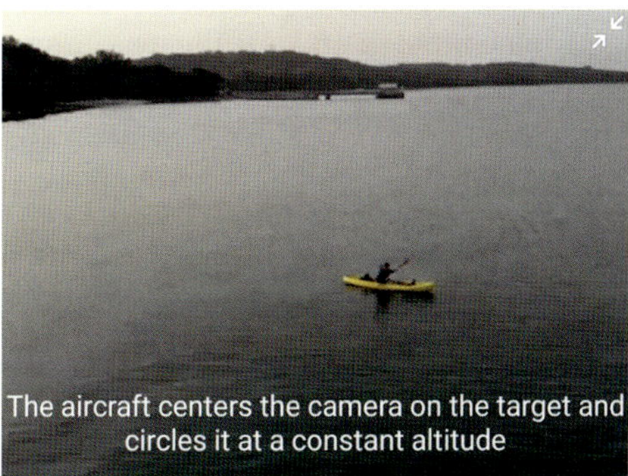

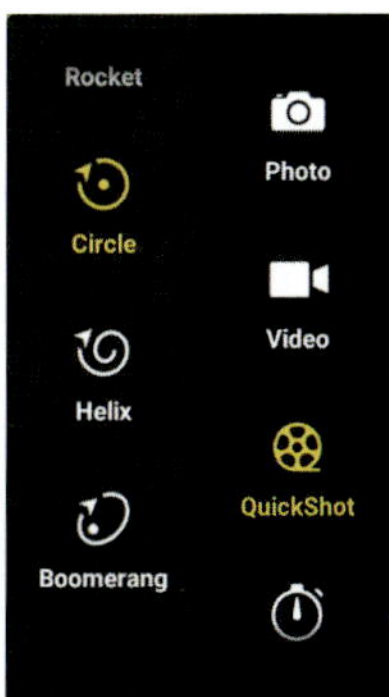

Figure 8.15 You can monitor the progress of the QuickShot on-screen.

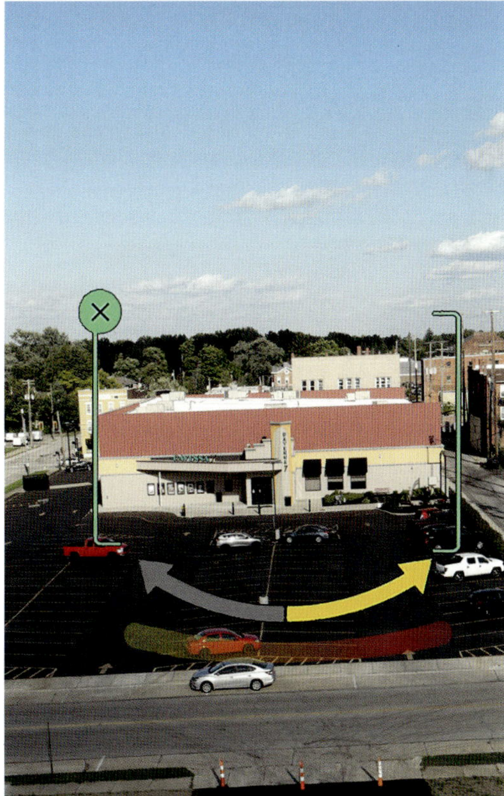

Figure 8.16 Choose clockwise or counter-clockwise directions.

The drone will circle around your subject at a constant altitude and distance from your starting point, and, as the circle is completed, return to that position to finish. The greater initial distance you choose, the larger the circle will be, and the faster the drone will move in flying its circular route. That keeps the elapsed time reasonable, and also appropriate visually.

Helix

With the Helix maneuver (see Figure 8.17), the drone flies upward and backs away from your subject gradually, with the gimbal moving downward and rotating to keep the subject centered in the frame as the aircraft works its way through a spiraling course to finish at the maximum radius you specify. You can choose clockwise or counterclockwise directions. The drop-down radius slider operates like the distance and altitude controls of the previous QuickShot modes, so I won't provide a screenshot of it. Because the Helix rises and curves dramatically, you should carefully assess the area for hazards before attempting this shot. (See Figure 8.18.)

Figure 8.17 Helix provides a spiraling path for the drone.

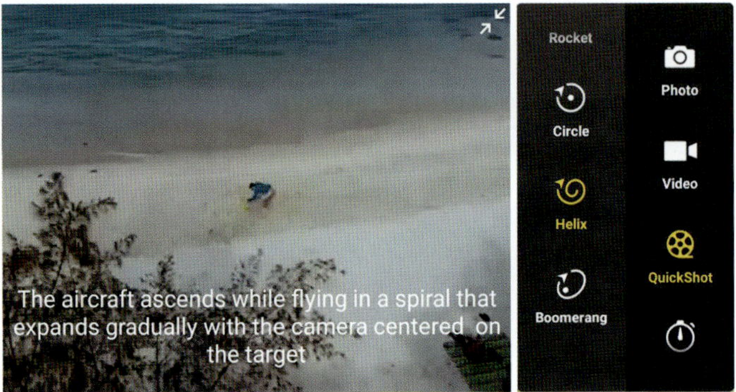

Figure 8.18 Make sure the surrounding area is clear before initiating the Helix maneuver.

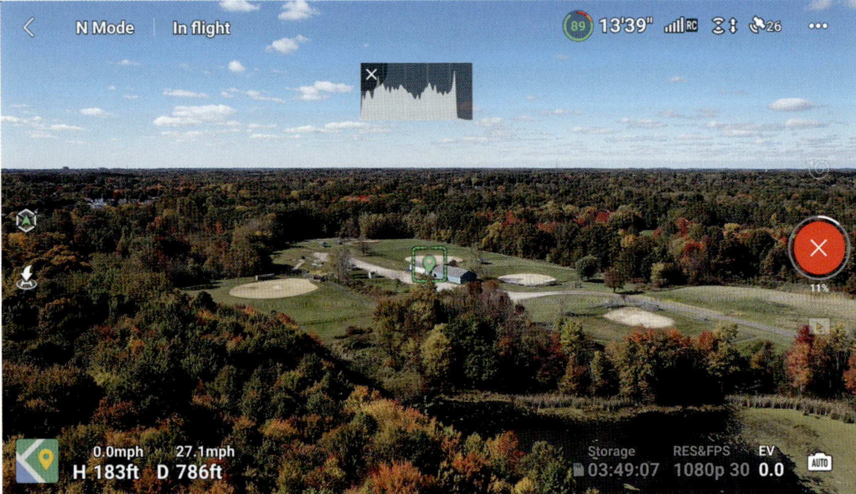

Boomerang

Many drone users say this maneuver is their favorite. (See Figure 8.19.) The drone flies an oval path, ascending as it leaves its starting point. When it reaches a point behind the subject, the aircraft slows almost to a stop, then increases altitude while tilting the gimbal downward as it starts its return. Descending boomerang-like, the drone ends up in front of the subject at its starting altitude.

You choose the starting altitude and position. It's a good idea to make sure a space of at least 100 feet around the aircraft is clear of obstacles, and that there is room to ascend safely within that area. As with Circle and Helix, you can select either clockwise or counterclockwise movement.

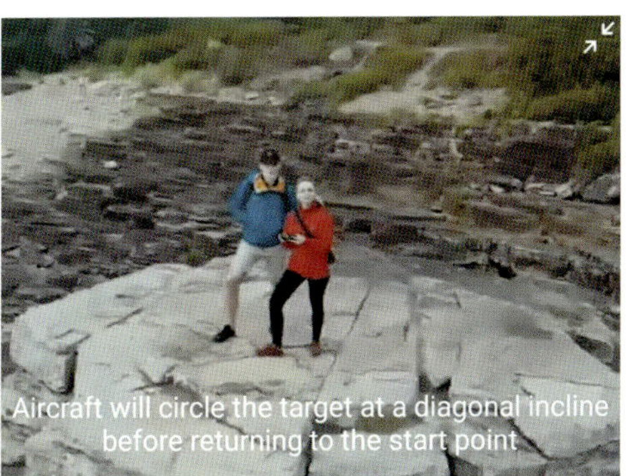

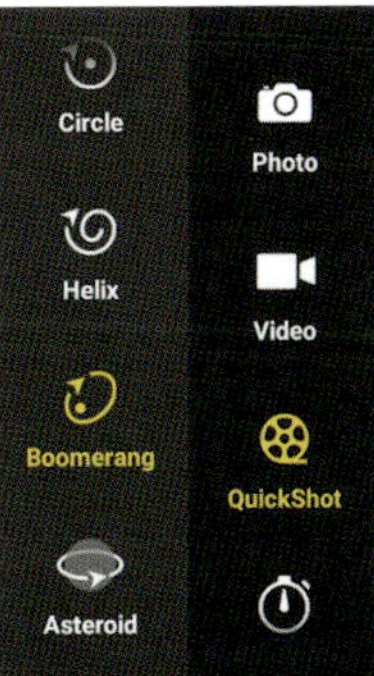

Figure 8.19 Boomerang causes the drone to fly out and behind you, then return to its starting position.

Asteroid (Mini 3 Pro Only)

Asteroid is an odd duck. The drone flies backward and upward and takes enough still photos to create a 360-degree panorama, then flies back to the starting point you specify. A video is generated that starts with the panorama captured at the highest position, then displays the descent back to the initial location. This is another QuickShot that requires a lot of space. You should make sure there is at least 120 feet behind the start point with no obstacles, and 150 feet or more above it. (See Figure 8.20.)

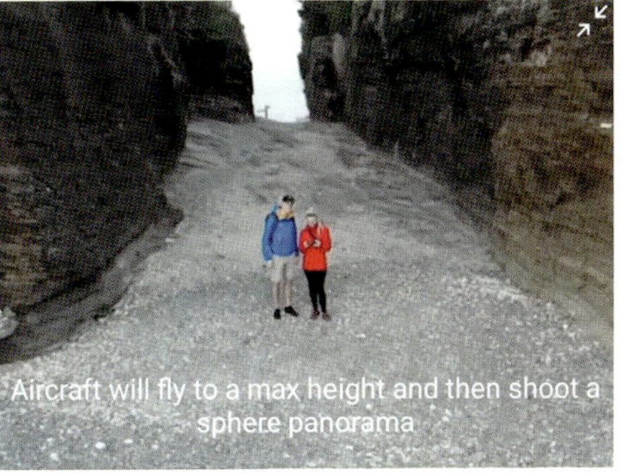

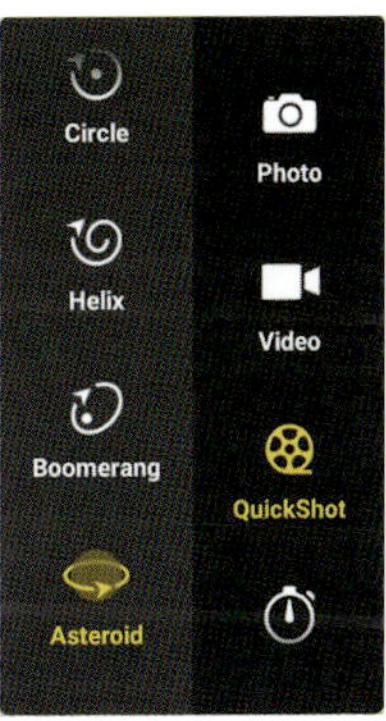

Figure 8.20 You can monitor the progress of the QuickShot on-screen.

Hyperlapse

Your drone's Hyperlapse feature is an automated time-lapse video mode that allows the drone to take a series of still images at a 16:9 aspect ratio and then combine them to produce a video that shows the motion over the elapsed time speeded up tremendously. Where time-lapse photography consists of a series of images captured with the camera remaining in one place, hyperlapse involves capturing that series from a moving camera. In both cases, many individual images are stitched together to produce a video that can be played back at a normal rate, but with the subject matter changing significantly between frames. Here are some considerations to take into account when creating hyperlapse movies:

- **Shutter speed.** Some blurring is desirable between frames to emphasize the feeling of motion, so you'll want to use the lowest ISO setting and the densest neutral-density filter you have. In daylight, exposure times of 2 to 6 seconds are used most often, with the longer intervals advisable only if there is little or no wind. The drone needs to achieve a precise position for each shot and gusts only make that more difficult.

- **Interval.** The drone needs to be able to fly to its next position between shots, which may require longer intervals when greater distances are involved. A 2-second interval may not allow enough time for the drone to navigate to its next position.

- **Weather.** Daytime hyperlapse clips are most dramatic when there are moving clouds in the sky. Without clouds, the footage can appear a little bland. Just keep in mind that fast-moving clouds, while desirable from a visual point of view, may mean stronger winds at the altitude at which you are flying.

- **Speed.** Your speed needs to match the length of your drone's route so it can cover that distance during the flight.

- **Duration.** When you see the duration of your flight (it will be shown on the screen), you should check to make sure you have sufficient battery power to complete the mission. Hyperlapse videos lasting about five seconds when played back are often the most dramatic. You can edit several of these together to create a compelling video. But, with a 2-second interval between shots, a clip that plays back over 5 seconds will require 125 frames that will take 4 minutes, 10 seconds to capture at 30 fps. It will take you time to set up and get into position. You wouldn't want to commence such a sequence with, say, only 8 minutes of battery power left. Remember, you'll need to have sufficient power to Return to Home when finished. If you miscalculate, the Low Battery Return to Home feature will kick in and abort your recording.

Your drone has four different Hyperlapse modes: Free, Circle, Course Lock, and Waypoints. You can select the mode using the screen shown in Figure 8.21.

- **Free.** You have full control over the aircraft's movement and gimbal position. It's the only Hyperlapse mode you can fiddle with before the drone takes off. That gives you plenty of time to make your settings DJI without the motors running and seriously impacting your battery power/flight time. This is the only mode that lets you use Cruise Control, described in the next section, which is useful for stabilizing the aircraft and maintaining the same speed as you direct it manually.

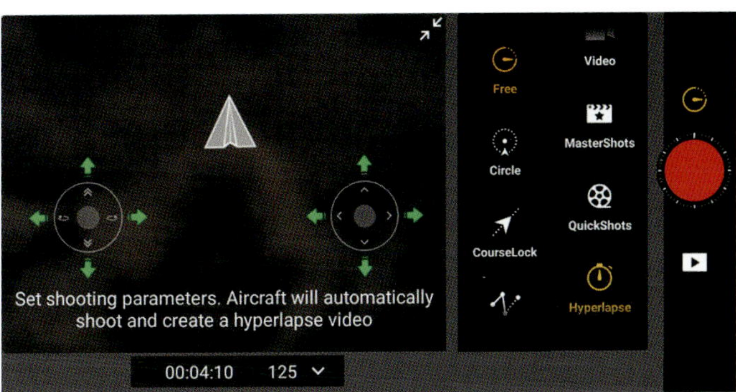

Figure 8.21 Selecting a Hyperlapse mode.

You can select the interval, duration of the video, and maximum speed, as shown in Figure 8.22. The number of frames that need to be captured using your parameters and the length of time needed to shoot the video is displayed (so you can make sure you have sufficient battery power). As with all the Hyperlapse modes, you commence shooting by pressing the shutter/record button to begin.

- **Circle.** In this mode, the aircraft flies a circular route automatically. You select a subject by drawing a box around it, and, as with Free mode, you select the interval, duration of the video, and maximum speed. Specify a clockwise or counterclockwise flight path, as shown in Figure 8.23. You're shown the number of photos that will be taken and how long the shooting time will be. Once recording begins, adjust the gimbal, speed, and position of the drone with the controls.

- **Course Lock.** With Course Lock, the aircraft will fly only in the direction the camera is pointed with a fixed orientation achieved by framing using the gimbal dial and rotation control (moving the left stick left or right). It will fly in that straight line once you lock the direction, regardless of which way the drone is facing. (See Figure 8.24.) It's useful when flying in narrow spaces, as the aircraft will not move from the path you've locked in. You can select a subject after drawing a box; if not, the drone will just fly in the direction of the camera.

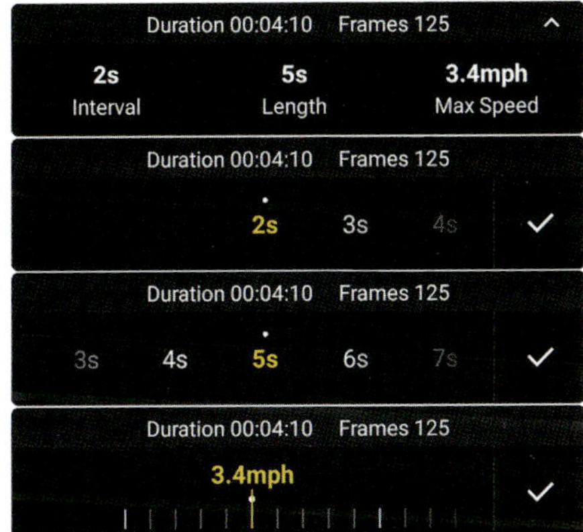

Figure 8.22 Choose parameters in Hyperlapse Free mode.

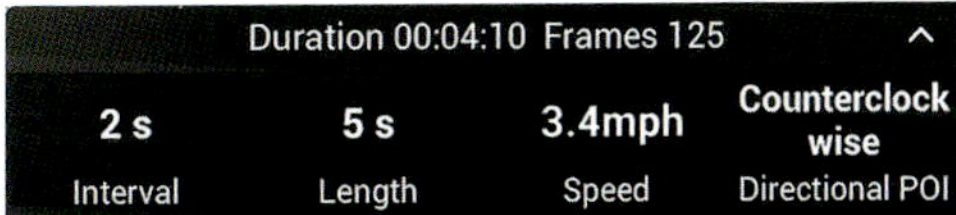

Figure 8.23 You can choose clockwise or counterclockwise direction in Circle mode.

Figure 8.24 Lock the drone to a straight-line path with Course Lock.

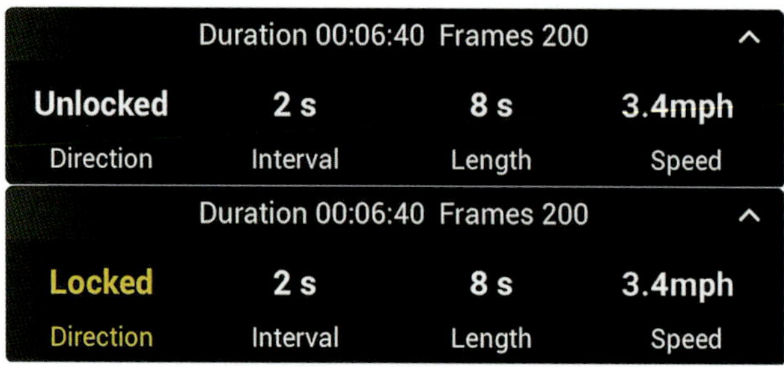

Figure 8.25 Choose up to five waypoints.

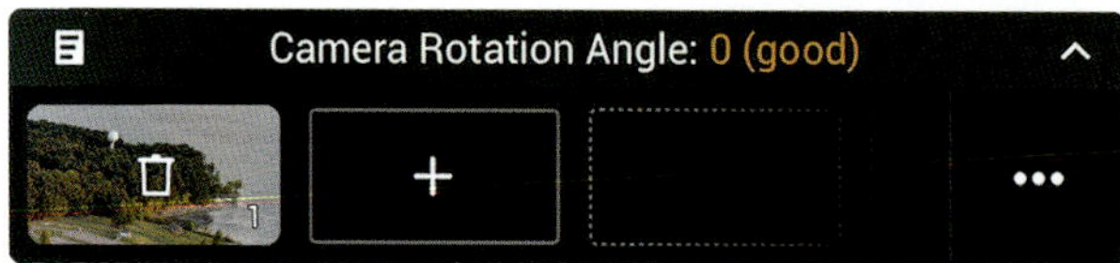

As with the other modes, you set the interval time, video duration, and max flight speed, and the screen shows the number of photos taken and length of shooting time. You can push the right control stick forward and back to control the horizontal flight speed, or side-to-side to move the drone to a different parallel forward path. (Rotating with the left stick is disabled once the maneuver has begun.)

- **Waypoints.** The aircraft automatically captures the images using a flight path you designate comprised of two to five different waypoints. (See Figure 8.25.) You can specify the points individually and, if you like, reverse them so the drone flies the same route in the opposite direction. This mode is especially useful when you want to capture a series of hyperlapse videos over an extended period of time. It's easy to capture a daylight hyperlapse of a scene, then return and generate one at twilight using the same route. You specify the waypoints and lens direction, interval time, video duration, and maximum speed.

More On Cruise Control (Mini 3 Pro Only)

Cruise Control, available with Hyperlapse Free mode, is a useful cinematic feature that allows you to set your drone on a desired course, and then lock that behavior so the aircraft continues smoothly at the same pace. You can still adjust the drone's direction, altitude, and gimbal position, if you like. Cruise Control works best in conditions that are not too windy; it won't produce the desired results if gusts are strong enough to exceed the drone's ability to compensate.

Cruise Control has previously been available only when using the Hyperlapse Free mode. More recently, however, DJI has been making it available in normal video modes, too, with some of its other drones, and may eventually be added to the Mini 3 Pro, as well, through a firmware update.

The feature is simple enough to use. You need to assign Cruise Control to a custom button, as I'll show you shortly. Then, when your drone is aloft, after you've made your desired flight adjustments, you can activate your drone's autopilot feature by pressing that button. A "Cruise Control In Use" message appears at left on the controller screen, next to an X you can tap to disable Cruise Control. (See Figure 8.26.) When the feature is enabled, you can concentrate on other aspects of the flight.

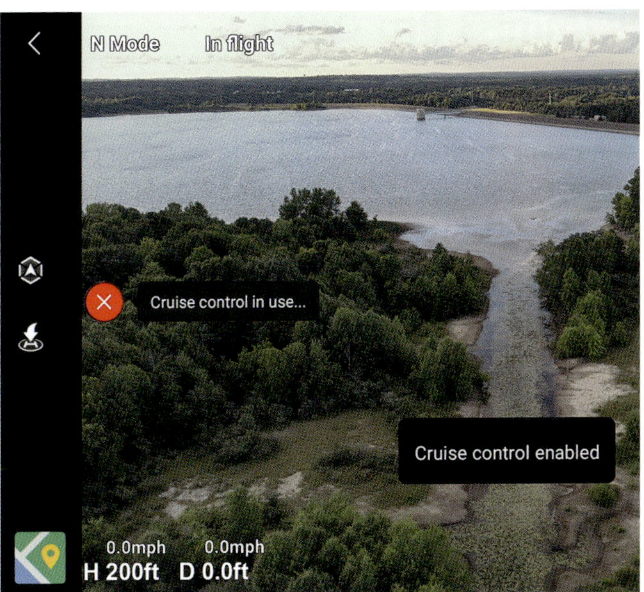

Figure 8.26 Activate Cruise Control by pressing the defined custom button.

To set up Cruise Control on your drone, just follow these steps:

1. **Access System Settings.** Tap the three dots in the upper-left corner of the main controller screen to open the Systems Settings menu. Navigate to the Control menu, as seen in Figure 8.27.

2. **Customize button.** Tap the Button Customization option in the Control menu.

3. **Select button.** Choose the button you want to use to invoke Cruise Control. Although I've highlighted the C3 button (available on the DJI RC Pro controller) in the figure, you can choose any other programmable button. You might actually want to use one of the buttons on the back of the controller and avoid a front button that you could press by accident while using the control sticks.

4. **Choose function.** In the figure, I've specified Hyperlapse Cruise Control. When the expected firmware update adds the full Cruise Control feature, that choice will appear as well.

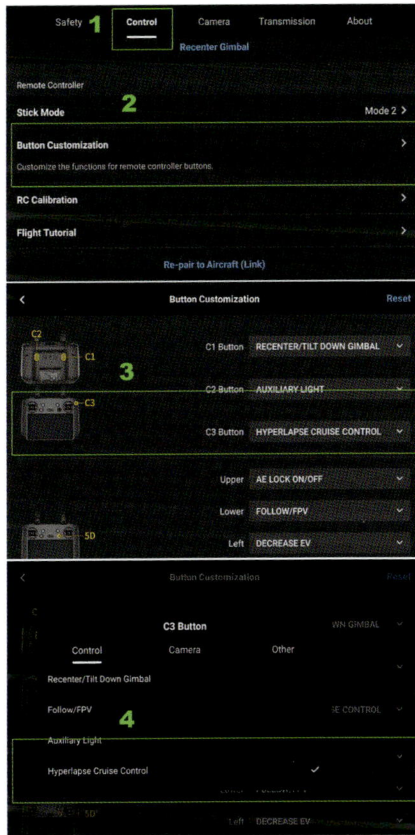

Figure 8.27 Adding Cruise Control to a custom button.

MasterShots (Mini 3 Pro Only)

MasterShots is a cool feature that lets you create a mini movie with a variety of shots while letting your drone do all the work. All you need to do is select a subject and enter some parameters affecting the width, height, and duration of the video, and let your aircraft boogie through its routine. You'll end up with a 2- to 3-minute cinematic video that you can edit yourself or convert into a finished video with a soundtrack using one of DJI Fly's built-in templates. Here are some things to consider:

- **Static subjects.** MasterShots works best with subjects that do not move. When the drone switches from one shot mode to the next it can often "lose" its original target if it is moving. You can experiment with moving targets if you like, but don't expect consistent results.
- **Full HD.** MasterShots is able to use the zoom capabilities available in 1080p mode, so full-featured 4K MasterShots will have to come with some updates from DJI.
- **Edit yourself.** The basic MasterShot clip can be saved as-is without applying a template, and then you can extract that footage and edit or use it as you like. Even the most skilled videographer can't capture five different professional-looking shots in a couple of minutes.

Using MasterShots

In capturing a MasterShot, the Mini 3 Pro will attempt to keep a subject you select centered in the frame while executing a series of cinematic maneuvers that will be combined to produce a short, professional-looking video. You should choose a location that is free of intervening obstacles, such as buildings, and living things, including trees, people, and wildlife. The drone will look for obstacles on its own and brake and hover in place if an object is detected in front of or behind it. (Remember, the Mini 3 Pro does not have side sensors.) You can adjust the drone's flight path during capture, if necessary.

Because you don't want the Mini 3 Pro to "lose" its subject, you should not use MasterShots when the subject is similar in color or texture to its surroundings, moving fast (especially if the subject is airborne, as well), or lighting is dark. Avoid situations where the subject is blocked from the drone's view by intervening objects or outside the aircraft's line of sight. If there are buildings nearby, these structures may block GNSS signals. When GPS signals are weak, the Mini 3 Pro's flight path may become unstable.

Once aloft to a height of at least 6.6 feet, you can activate MasterShots and select your subject by dragging a box around it on the screen. A panel appears with choices for setting the width, length, and height of the flight path. Once you've entered those parameters, you'll be shown the estimated flight time for your MasterShot-to-be. (See Figure 8.28.) Tap Start to begin recording.

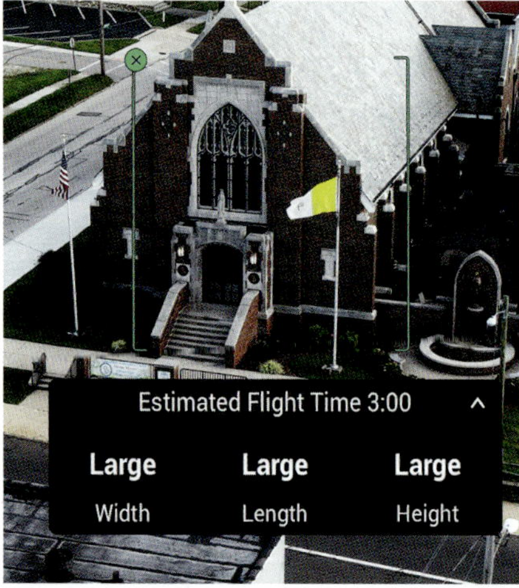

Figure 8.28 Define the width, length, and height of your MasterShot.

Once the automated flight has begun, you'll see a series of progress messages on the controller screen, like those I've collected in Figure 8.29. (They appear one at a time in the same location, and not arrayed as in the figure.) You can exit MasterShots by pressing the Flight Pause button or tapping the X that appears on the DJI Fly screen. After the Master-Shot is done, the drone will return to its original location.

When finished, I recommend downloading your original footage, as indicated by the green box I placed in Figure 8.30. Then, if you like, you can scroll through the list of available templates and let the DJI Fly app do its thing with the MasterShot you've just captured. If you like the results, that's fine, but since you have the original available, you can re-edit it or tweak it any way you like.

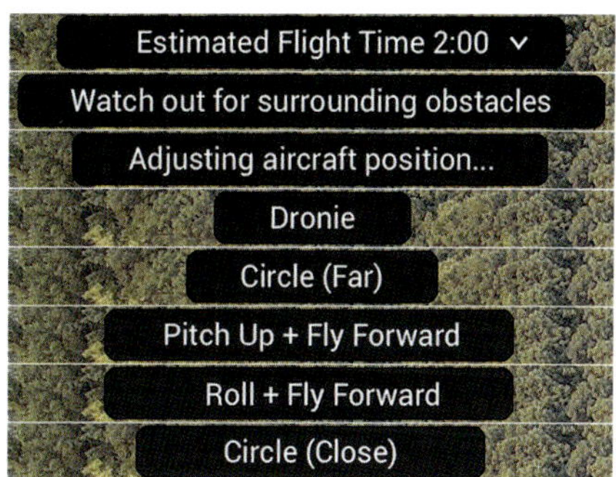

Figure 8.29 You'll see progress messages as the flight is underway.

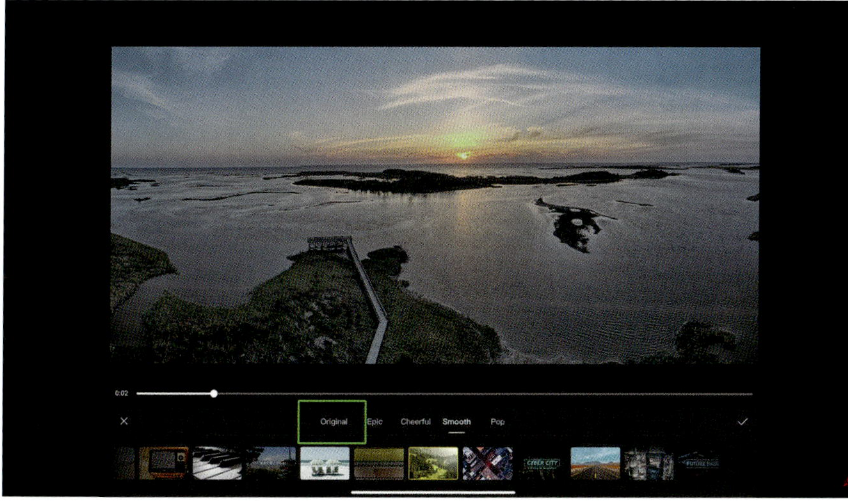

Figure 8.30 Save your MasterShot or use a template to compile a finished video.

DON'T GIVE YOURSELF PROPS

One problem with MasterShots is that the drone's propellers sometimes appear in the sequences. That's because obstacle sensing capabilities are enhanced to avoid collisions as the drone performs its MasterShot maneuvers. The gimbal may tilt at angles that allow the props to be captured.

To reduce or eliminate this effect, just follow these steps:

1. **Take off and enable MasterShots.** The menu entry you need to adjust is only available when the Mini 3 Pro is in flight.

2. **Access System Settings.** Tap the three dots in the upper-left corner of the screen to open the Systems Settings menu and tap the Camera tab.

3. **Disable obstacle avoidance.** A new Shooting Priority entry will appear. Select Composition, as shown in Figure 8.31. The gimbal will not adjust to include the props in your video, but you'll need to pay special attention to surrounding obstacles.

Figure 8.31 Choose Composition to keep propellers from appearing in your MasterShots.

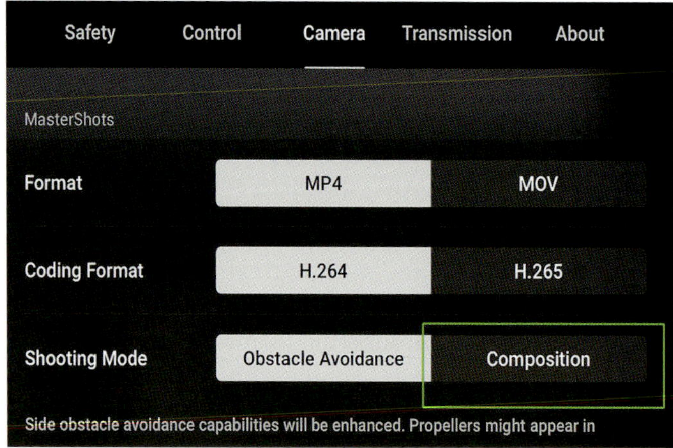

Editing QuickShots and Other Videos

Beginners will like the fact that DJI gives you a basic editor for videos right within the DJI Fly app. You can choose to generate videos from a series of clips automatically, using a Template option. Or, as your skills improve, you can perform more advanced editing adjustments to produce a polished movie ready for sharing on social media without resorting to Final Cut Pro or DaVinci Resolve. This section will introduce you to your options available within the versatile DJI Fly app.

The DJI editor is hidden on the startup screen, accessible by tapping on the Album icon at lower left. The content available on your drone (if connected) or your smart device will be displayed, as seen in Figure 8.32, with an option at the top of the screen of viewing All, Photos, Videos, or Favorites. You'll see thumbnails of each video, along with its duration. Only a low-resolution version of each clip is stored on your device; you'll need to transfer or download the video to the device to work with the full-resolution clip.

Figure 8.32 Download clips from your drone to your controller or device.

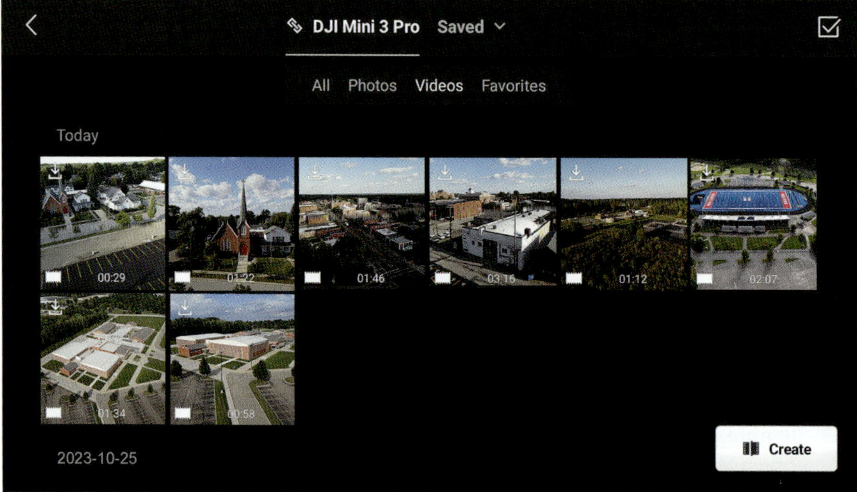

A downward-pointing arrow icon in the upper-left corner of each thumbnail will be shown if you need to download that clip to your controller or smart device. Once all the sequences you want to use are available, click on Create in the Album screen. It's located in the lower-right corner in Figure 8.32. You'll then progress to the screen shown in Figure 8.33, where you can choose to work with Templates, or create your own video in Pro mode. The available templates are stacked in the right-hand column, with the template's theme, number of shots required, and duration in seconds shown. Highlighting a template displays a sample of its theme. If you haven't used a template before, you'll be advised to download it. You can then tap Apply to proceed to the next step.

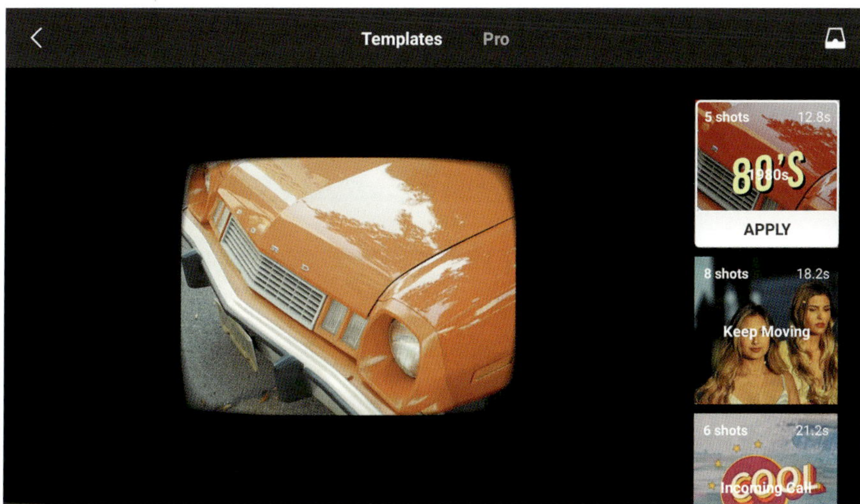

Figure 8.33 In Template mode, choose which canned video format to use.

You'll need to select the number of shots specified for your selected template. (See Figure 8.34.) Click the Add panel in the upper-right corner to add the selected clips to the template. You'll be whisked to the editing screen shown at left in Figure 8.35, and the app will provide a preview of the video in progress. Five thumbnails are displayed, showing the duration, in seconds, of each of the clips (in this example, 2.5, 2.4, 1.8, 2, and 3.8 seconds).

Underneath the thumbnail array you'll find icons representing seven different tools you can use to edit the video. Tap one of the thumbnails to use the tools on that portion of the video. Each thumbnail sequence can be edited separately. The tools include:

- **Extract.** The template has chosen a portion of each of the individual clips to use in the video. This utility lets you choose from different sections of that clip, presented as thumbnails you can sample and preview. A Speed slider lets you adjust how fast the extracted excerpt plays.
- **Clip.** Allows you to zoom in and out of the current clip, rotate it, or resize it to fit by using two fingers to pinch the screen. (See Figure 8.35, center.)
- **Replace.** Here you can swap out any of the clips for another one in your album.
- **Sort.** You can change the order of the clips.
- **Filter.** Add special effects, such as the ones shown in Figure 8.35, right.

Figure 8.34 You'll need to select the specified number of clips required for the template.

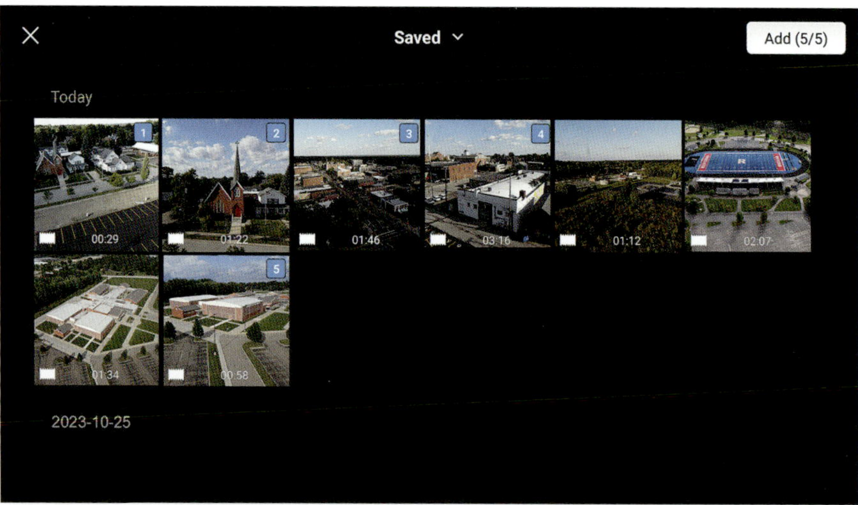

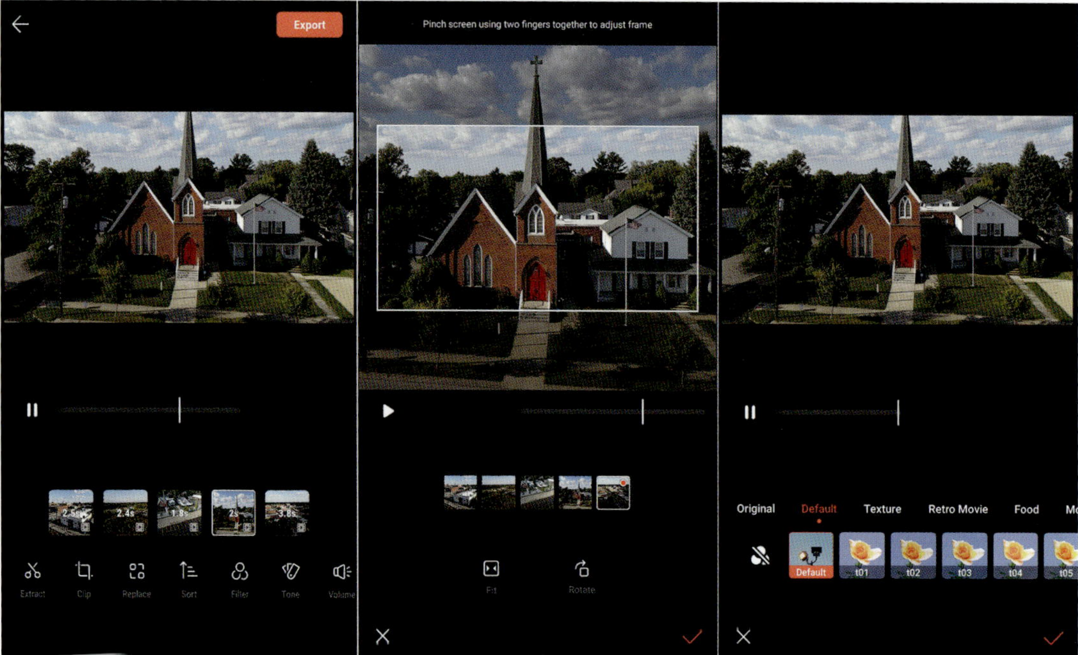

Figure 8.35 The Template editing screen (left) offers tools like Clip (center) and Filter (right).

- **Tone.** Change brightness, contrast, saturation, temperature (white balance), add a vignette effect, or sharpen. You can apply these changes to an individual clip or all the clips in the video.
- **Volume.** A slider appears letting you adjust the volume of the soundtrack for one clip, or all of them.

When you've finished your edits, tap the red Export label in the upper right of the screen (shown at left in Figure 8.35). The app will show you the progress as it generates your video (see Figure 8.36) and, when finished, presents you with the option to view the video or, selecting from an array at the bottom of the screen, post the video to Facebook, Instagram, WhatsApp, TikTok, or SnapChat. (You must have the appropriate social media app installed on your device to share the video.) (See Figure 8.37.) Click Done when finished.

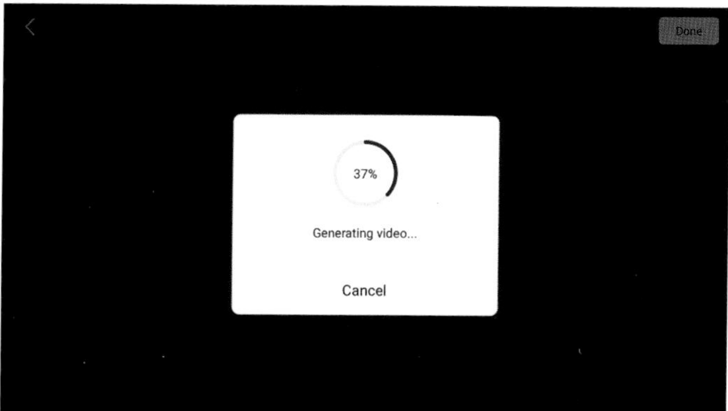

Figure 8.36 Generating the video.

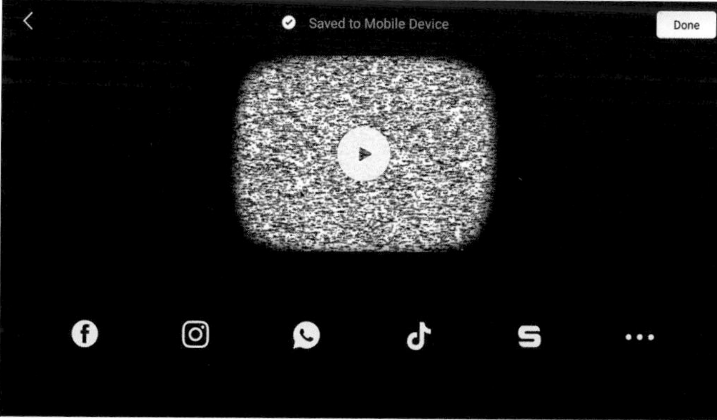

Figure 8.37 Your video can be shared to Facebook, Instagram, WhatsApp, TikTok, or SnapChat.

Pro mode starts out similarly to Template mode, with you selecting which clips to include. Note that all your video clips do not need to be aerial footage from your drone. You can add other video with the same resolution captured from other sources. The editing screen in Pro mode has many more options than are available in Template mode, as shown in Figure 8.38. At the bottom resides a row with icons representing volume and playback speed controls and options to delete, copy, or reverse playback direction. Underneath are icons for editing and cutting frames from the clip, adding music tracks, filter effects, text subtitles, and stickers.

Some of your editing options are shown in Figures 8.39 and 8.40. Advanced video-editing procedures are beyond the scope of this book, but you can see that even a basic editor like the one supplied with the DJI Fly app has many options.

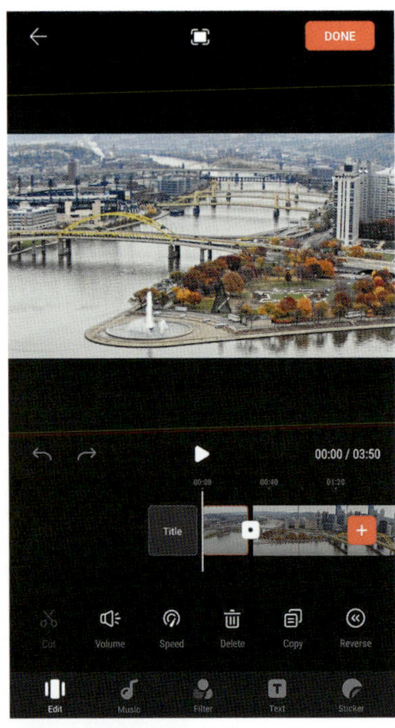

Figure 8.38 The Pro editing mode has more options.

Figure 8.39 Editing (upper left), volume control (upper right), speed control (lower left), and three varieties of filters (lower right).

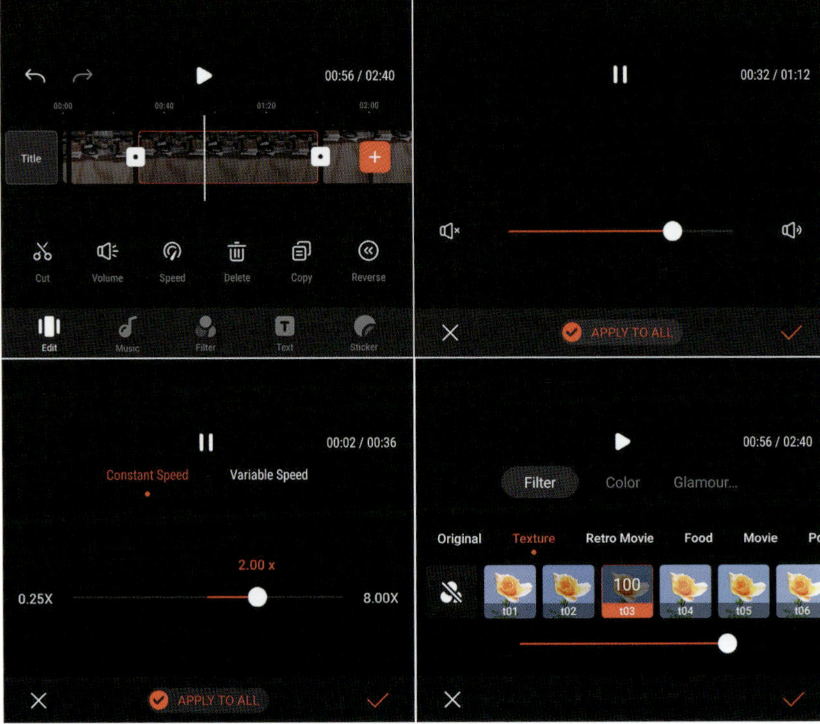

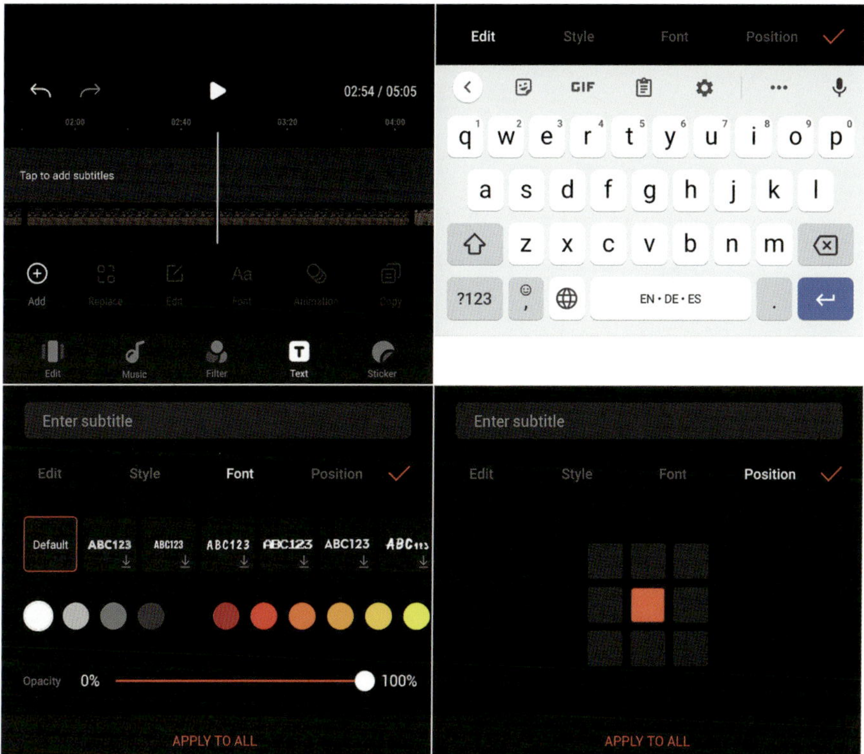

Figure 8.40 You can add text and subtitles to your videos using the DJI Fly app's tools (upper left). A virtual keyboard is available with multiple options for inserting items into your video (upper right). You can select font, style, color, and text transparency (lower left). Subtitles can be placed in several different positions within the frame (lower right).

Stills from Video

Guess what? Video from your Mini 3 and Mini 3 Pro can be used to create still images that are difficult to capture with a conventional camera, and even more tricky to shoot with drones in Photo mode. I'm talking about exciting shots of transient subjects, such as fireworks or lightning. Of the two, fireworks are easier to shoot, simply by using a long exposure that captures the explosion and blossoming arc of lights. Lightning typically requires some sort of light-detecting trigger to take a picture at the correct—and unpredictable—instant.

Simply by shooting video at 4K 60p, you can capture action at a continuous shooting speed of 60 frames per second. Then, using the video editor of your choice, extract an 8 megapixel still image. You'll often find that an 8MP still is sharp enough for most purposes, even though as a still photographer you are probably accustomed to capturing images at 24MP or more. Just choose an appropriate ISO setting and shutter speed and shoot: the need for sticking to shutter speeds between 1/30th and 1/125th second goes out the window if your final product isn't video. Tennessee drone veteran Rick Murray extracted the dramatic image shown in Figure 8.41 using Apple's iMovie application, and post-processed in Adobe Lightroom and Photoshop.

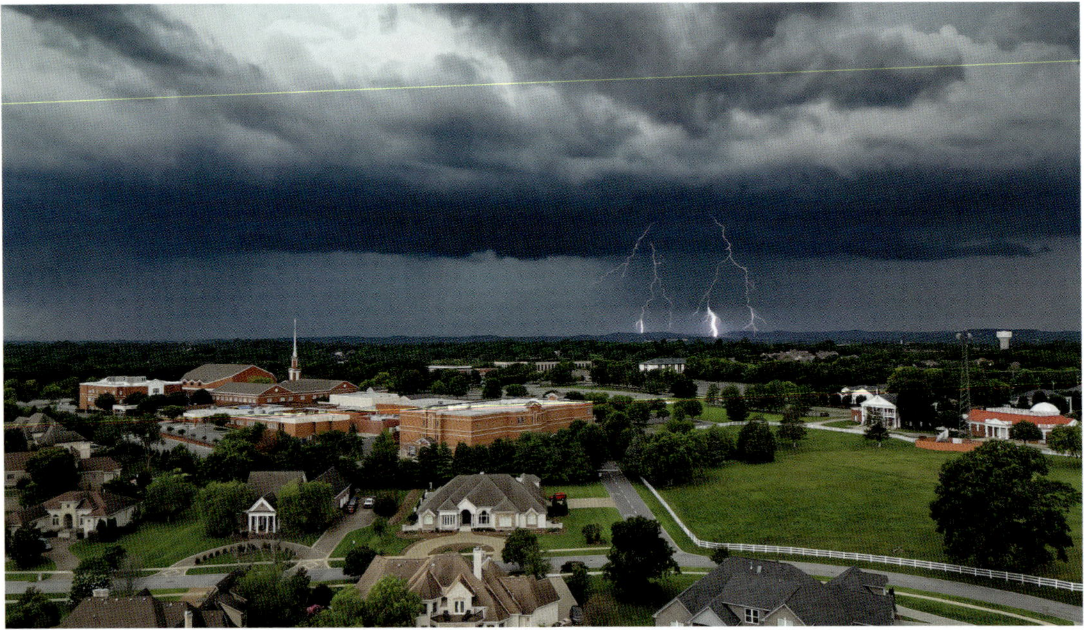

Figure 8.41 A frame extracted from a 4K video produced this dramatic shot of lightning.

Tips for Movie Making

I'm going to close out this introductory video chapter with just a couple of tips you can use to improve your moviemaking as you move toward more polished video production. Each of these concepts will be familiar to experienced videographers, but photographers who have concentrated on still images may need to learn about these essential considerations.

Shooting Script

A shooting script is nothing more than a coordinated plan that covers both audio and video and provides order and structure for your video when you're in planned, storytelling mode. A detailed script will cover what types of shots you're going after, the audio soundtrack you'll be laying over your footage, and any special effects you plan to use in post-production, transitions, and graphics. A good script needn't constrain you: as the director you are free to make changes on the spot during actual capture of your aerial footage. But, before you change the route to your final destination, it's good to know where you were headed, and how you originally planned to get there.

When putting together your shooting script, plan for lots and lots of different shots, even if you don't think you'll need them. Only amateurish videos consist of a bunch of long, tedious shots. You'll want to vary the pace of your production by cutting among lots of different views, angles, and perspectives, so jot down your ideas for these variations when you put together your script.

If you're shooting a documentary rather than telling a story that's already been completely mapped out, the idea of using a shooting script needs to be applied more flexibly. Documentary filmmakers often have no shooting script at all. They go out, do their interviews, capture video of people, places, and events as they find them, and allow the structure of the story to take shape as they learn more about the subject of their documentary. In such cases, the movie is typically "created" during editing, as bits and pieces are assembled into the finished piece.

Storyboards

A storyboard is a series of panels providing visuals of what each scene should look like. While the ones produced by Hollywood are generally of very high quality, there's nothing that says drawing skills are important for this step. Rudimentary drawings work just fine if that's the best you can do. The storyboard just helps you visualize locations, placement of subject matter, and helps show how you want to frame or compose a shot.

Today's audience is used to fast-paced, short-scene storytelling. In order to produce interesting video for such viewers, it's important to view video storytelling as a kind of shorthand code for the more leisurely efforts print media offers. Audio and video should always be advancing the story. While it's okay to let the camera linger from time to time, it should only be for a compelling reason and only briefly. It only takes a second or two for an establishing shot to impart the necessary information.

Provide variety too. If you put your shooting script together correctly, you'll be changing camera angles and perspectives often and never leave a static scene on the screen for a long period of time. (You can record a static scene for a reasonably long period and then edit in other shots that cut away and back to the longer scene with other views.)

When editing, keep transitions basic! I can't stress this one enough. Watch a television program or movie. The action "jumps" from one scene to the next. Fancy transitions that involve exotic "wipes," dissolves, or cross fades take too long for the average viewer and make your video ponderous. An exception can be made when the time gaps or subject changes between scenes are too abrupt; in such cases, a cross fade can be effective in creating the necessary separation between those scenes.

Composition

In movie shooting, several factors restrict your composition, and impose requirements you just don't always have in still photography (although other rules of good composition do apply). Here are some of the key differences to keep in mind when composing movie frames:

- **Horizontal compositions only.** TikTok and cellphone videos aside, conventional movies are generally shot and shown in horizontal format only.
- **Wasted space at the sides.** For some shots, you may want to get close enough to your subject to fill up as much of the frame as possible. (Of course, you can fill that space with other interesting stuff, but that defeats your intent of concentrating on your main subject.)

- **Seamless (or seamed) transitions.** Unless you're telling a picture story with a photo essay, still pictures often stand alone. But with movies, each of your compositions must relate to the shot that preceded it, and the one that follows. It can be jarring to jump from a long shot to a tight close-up unless the director—you—are very creative. Another common error is the "jump cut" in which successive shots vary only slightly in camera angle, making it appear that the main subject has "jumped" from one place to another. One rule of thumb is to vary the camera angle by at least 30 degrees between shots to make it appear to be seamless. Unless you prefer that your images flaunt convention and appear to be "seamy."

- **The time dimension.** Unlike still photography, with motion pictures there's a lot more emphasis on using a series of images to build on each other to tell a story. Static shots where the camera is mounted on a tripod, and everything is shot from the same distance are a recipe for dull videos. Watch a television program sometime and notice how often camera shots change distances and directions. Viewers are used to this variety and have come to expect it. Professional video productions are often done with multiple cameras shooting from different angles and positions. But many professional productions are shot with just one camera, and with careful planning you can do just fine with your drone.

Next Up

The final chapter of this book is a ready reference to the five menu tabs of the DJI Fly's System Settings screen, which provides a full set of adjustments for the most important settings that apply to your Mini 3 or Mini 3 Pro's safety features, controls, flight modes, camera operation, and transmission parameters. It also includes a description of the features in the DJI Fly app's main screen.

Menu Reference

9

The Systems Settings screen in the DJI Fly app has five individual menu tabs that let you specify adjustments for the most important settings that apply to your Mini 3 or Mini 3 Pro's flight modes. You can access the screen any time your controller is connected to your aircraft by tapping the three dots in the upper-right corner of the Camera View screen, or, if you have the DJI RC Pro controller, by pressing the 5D button.

The Systems Settings screen can still be viewed when not connected to your drone by tapping the Connection Guide label on the DJI Fly introductory screen, and then tapping on Camera View within the guide. That will take you to the camera view, even if no drone is connected, and you can then tap the three dots in the upper-right corner to view the Systems Settings screen. However, the menus and options available will be slightly different because the app needs to "know" which aircraft the settings will be applied to display them properly.

This chapter provides a reference to the key settings available with the System Settings screen. You've been using many of them already as you learned to fly your drone, but you'll encounter some new ones here for functions like gimbal calibration. I'll provide a brief overview of commands discussed elsewhere in this book and not duplicate the explanations from earlier chapters. I'm providing longer descriptions of the others.

DIFFERENT STROKES

As you've learned, the Mini 3 Pro and Mini 3 differ slightly in features and their implementations, and I've pointed out the distinctions as we've proceeded. In this chapter, I'm going to provide illustrations of the menus for each aircraft side-by-side, with the (generally more complex) Mini 3 Pro screens on the left and those of the Mini 3 on the right. Where functions and operations differ, I'll point out those, as well. Sometimes the order in which specific menu entries appears differs between the Mini 3 Pro and Mini 3; the following sections follow the Pro aircraft's listing order.

Safety Menu

Tap the leftmost tab in the Systems Settings screen to produce the Safety menu, shown in Figure 9.1. It's a scrollable menu and you won't see all the entries at once, as in the figure. The Safety menu has entries for making obstacle avoidance settings, flight protection, calibrating sensors, battery information, and other functions. Some settings can be made by tapping a label, toggling a switch, or moving your finger along a slider. If an entry has a > symbol at its right edge, you can tap that symbol to view a sub-entry with additional settings.

Figure 9.1 Safety menu.

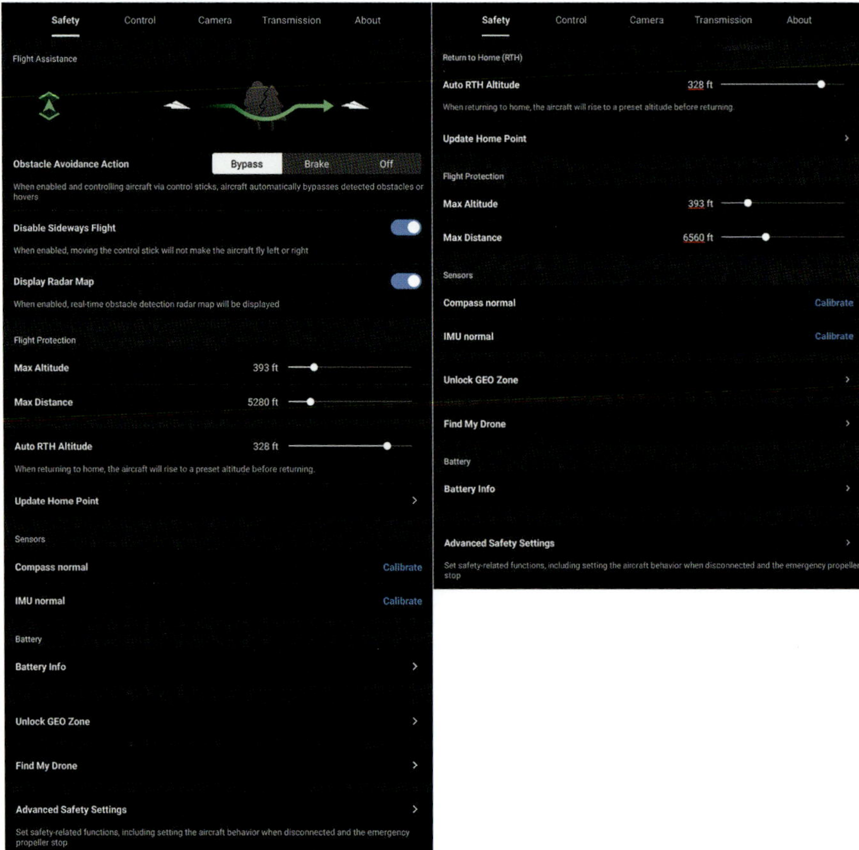

Obstacle Avoidance Action (Mini 3 Pro Only)

This is where you tell your drone what to do when it encounters an obstacle. Your choices are Bypass, Brake, or Off. So, you can tell the Mini 3 Pro to use its sensors and GNSS data to calculate a safe route around the obstacle, or stop, hover in place, and await further instructions from you. You can also disable obstacle avoidance completely (it is disabled automatically in Sport mode). You might want to turn it off under some circumstances, as it may be too sensitive when, say, flying through a group of trees, or disable sideways movement (as described next). If you're certain you can avoid the obstacles manually, working without the drone's safety net is an option.

Disable Sideways Flight (Mini 3 Pro Only)

This option appears only when Obstacle Avoidance Action is set to Bypass in the System > Safety menu. When enabled, as the drone responds to your navigational commands and uses APAS to detect and avoid obstacles in its path, the Mini 3 Pro will *ignore* left/right joystick movement and will fly only in forward/backward directions. This capability is especially useful when flying through hazardous areas to avoid accidentally hitting trees or structures located to either side of the drone, or when you deliberately want the aircraft to proceed smoothly forward or backward without accidental deviation.

Display Radar Map (Mini 3 Pro Only)

When enabled, this map can appear in the lower-left corner of the screen. Once you've taken off and the Home Point has been updated, you'll be able to view the location of key components, shown in Figure 9.2.

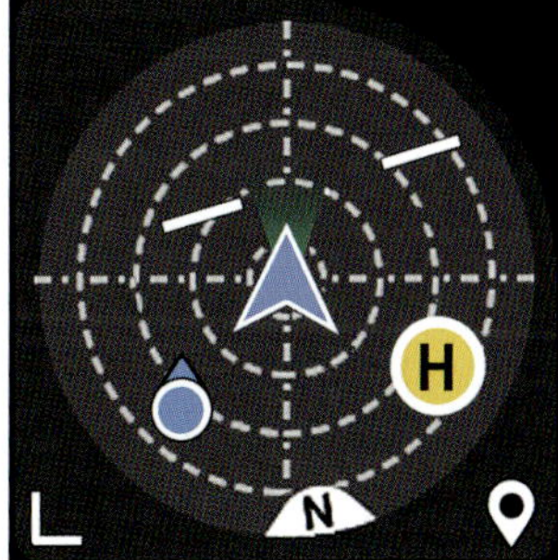

Figure 9.2 Displaying the radar map.

- **Drone.** The blue and white arrowhead icon shows the location of the drone.
- **Attitude.** The horizontal or slanted lines indicate the tilt of the drone when it is banking into a turn or trying to maintain position against winds. If you see the lines tilting when the drone should be hovering or moving straight forward or backward, it may mean that the aircraft is fighting strong winds. The lines will be in the upper half when the drone is moving forward (the nose is tilted down) and in the lower half (the nose is tilted up) when moving backward.
- **Remote control.** The blue and white dot shows the position of the remote control in relation to the Home Point. In practice, it may remain very close to and overlap the Home Point on the map and only diverge when you move away from it. The arrow on the dot indicates the direction in which the controller is pointed.
- **Compass direction.** In Figure 9.2, North, as it relates to the drone's orientation, is shown at the lower-right edge of the map.
- **Enlarge/Reduce radar map.** Tap the L shape at lower left to reduce the map to an icon.

Max Altitude/Max Distance

The order in which this pair of options appears in the Safety menu differs between the two drones. It's displayed immediately *after* the Display Radar Map entry with the Mavic 3 Pro, and *following* the Update Home Point entry of the Mini 3, as shown earlier in Figure 9.1. These two entries allow you to drag the sliders to specify the maximum altitude the drone can rise to, and the maximum distance it can travel away from you. The altitude should be set to no higher than 400 feet *above ground level*. You can set a lower limit if you like. Keep in mind that you must keep your drone within your line of sight when setting the distance level. Under dim lighting conditions, especially twilight, your drone's required add-on strobe (*required* for night flying) can help you maintain line of sight at greater distances.

Auto RTH Altitude

As explained in Chapter 4, the automatic RTH features enable the drone to return it its last registered Home Point, by default registered as the first location where the drone received an acceptable GNSS signal. When you invoke automatic RTH, the best procedure is to have the aircraft first ascend to an altitude that is high enough to allow it to move horizontally without encountering any obstacles.

You can use this slider to define how high the drone will rise before starting to return. The higher the altitude, the longer the return will take and the greater amount of battery power that will be consumed. You can decide for yourself what a general-purpose safe altitude is, or change it to suit your specific circumstances. It's usually a good idea to compromise using an altitude that is higher than trees or nearby structures.

Update Home Point

You can update the Home Point at any time during an actual flight by tapping on the Camera View map or by using this entry, which allows you to switch the Home Point to the current location of the drone, to the current location of the remote control, or to a position you specify by dragging the H icon on the map.

Compass Calibration

The Mini 3 Pro (but not the Mini 3) includes a compass automatic calibration feature which will detect and correct errors, then display a prompt on the DJI Fly screen. Both drones can be calibrated manually, however, and this may be required from time to time. If manual calibration is needed, a warning message will notify you. Visit the Safety menu, and tap the Compass Calibrate option to proceed. As I've mentioned before, the presence of metallic objects can interfere with the compass's operation and calibration. Large metal objects or even the rebar in concrete slabs can affect it, so you should move as far away from such interference when recalibrating. I usually visit a nearby open field with nothing around the drone except vegetation.

The drone needs to be at least five or six feet above ground level when you begin the process. You'll see screens like the ones shown in Figure 9.3. Follow the prompts and rotate the drone until calibration is complete. Some sticklers for precision recommend recalibrating before every flight, but, in practice, you need to do so only if you move more than 50 miles from your last flight or are in a location roughly 1,000 feet higher. The drone's "memory" of magnetic North may be off a bit if you've changed your locale by that much. DJI has programmed the drone to suggest recalibration after a particular period of time has passed since the last update.

IMU Normal

Inside your drone is a compact self-contained module called the Inertial Measurement Unit (IMU), which uses an accelerometer, barometer, gyroscope, and thermometer to provide the information that is necessary to keep your drone stable and level during its flight. From time to time it may need to be calibrated using this entry.

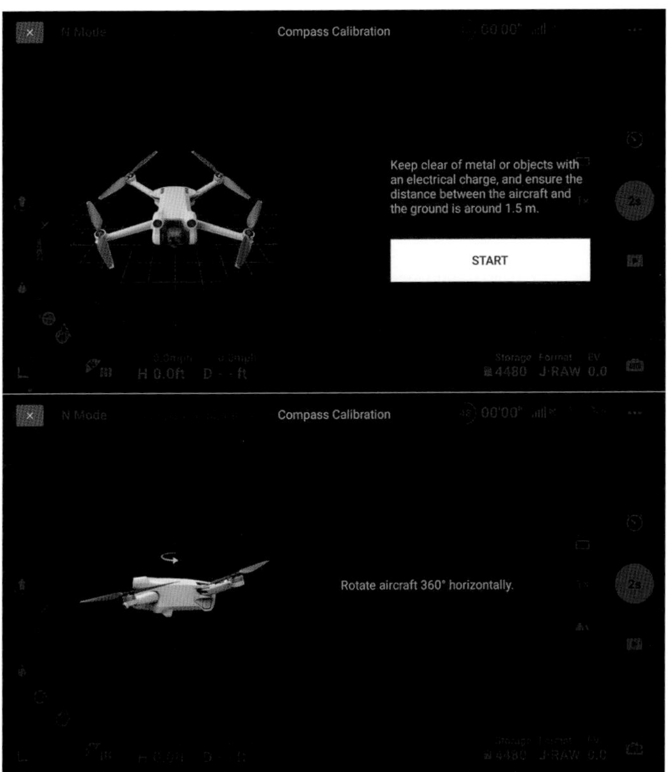

Figure 9.3 Compass calibration.

The IMU contains four essential components that measure the drone's temperature, angular velocity, external forces, and the attitude (tilts and rotation) of your drone:

- **Thermometer.** Your drone is rated to be operated in temperatures ranging from 32 to 104 degrees F (0 to 40 degrees C), although flight time may be drastically reduced (by 75 percent or more) at low temperatures. Operating the aircraft generates heat from the batteries. The IMU's thermometer tracks temperatures.

- **Accelerometer.** Accelerometers measure a drone's change of velocity in a single direction, as when you fly forward or backward, or ascend or descend.

- **Barometer.** This component measures atmospheric pressure as a way to determine your drone's altitude.

- **Gyroscope.** Accelerometers can't measure twisting or rotational movement, so a gyroscope (a tiny spinning disk inside your drone) is used to measure angular velocity along the x, y, and z axes (pitch, roll, and yaw).

You won't need to recalibrate the IMU often, but you will want to do so if the app gives you a notice that calibration is needed, if you see the drone is leaning to one side while hovering, or when you're flying in a new location (as I recommended for compass calibration). If you've had a minor crash, it's a good idea to calibrate, even if there appears to be no damage to the drone.

Recalibrating your drone's IMU is easy. All you need is a flat, level surface on which to rest the drone, avoiding proximity to metal, concrete, or electronic devices that can interfere with the components' readings. You should have at least 50 percent battery power. The process will take from 5 to 10 minutes. With the gimbal cover removed, access the IMU Normal entry to view the screen shown at upper left in Figure 9.4. Once you start, you'll be prompted to place the aircraft on the flat surface in the orientations shown in the figure.

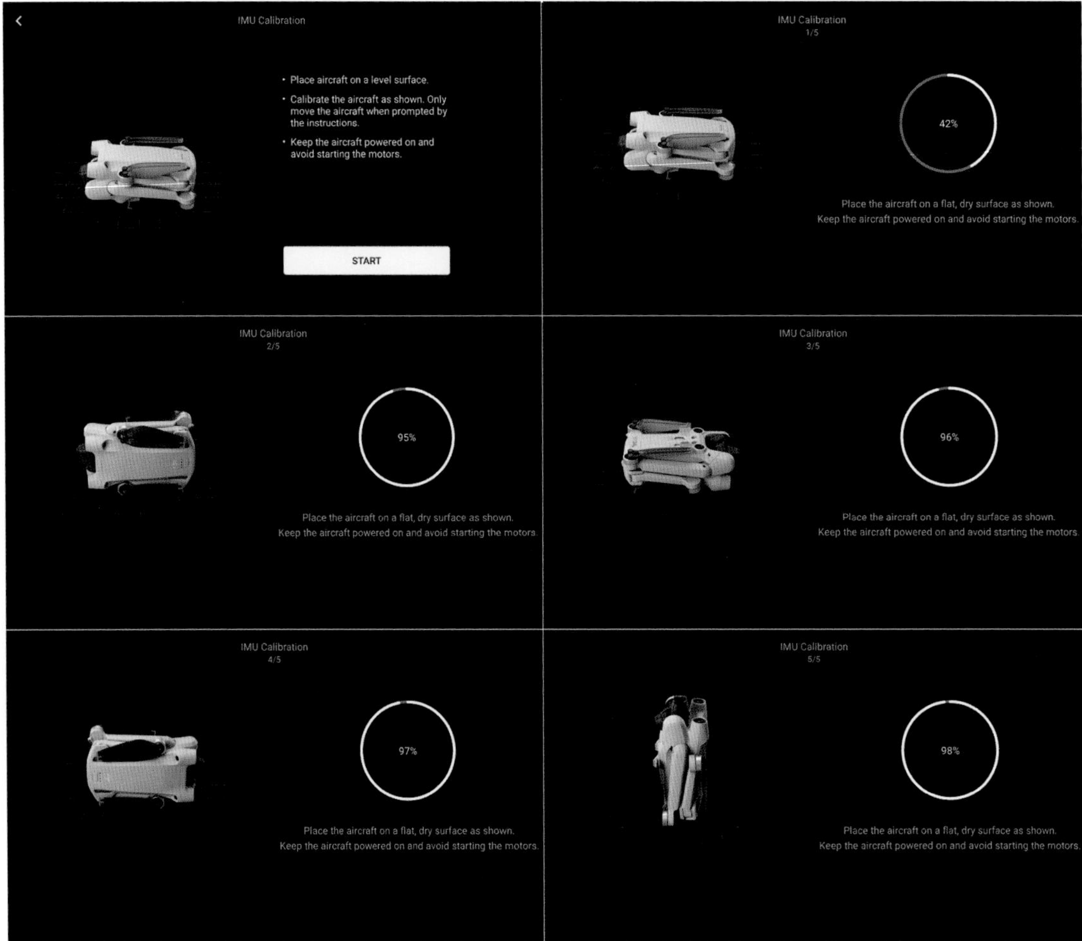

Figure 9.4 IMU calibration.

Battery Info

This entry gives you a great deal of useful battery status information, including the amount of charge remaining in the three individual cells inside each Intelligent Flight Battery and the current voltage and temperature. The latter can be useful for spotting overheating, which can occur when the drone is operated vigorously. You can also see the battery serial number and cycle count. (See Figure 9.5.) If you have lots of batteries, you may want to track them so their usage can be spread evenly. If your batteries are stored with the correct charge, roughly 60 percent, and at normal temperatures, they should each be good for at least 200 discharge/charge cycles.

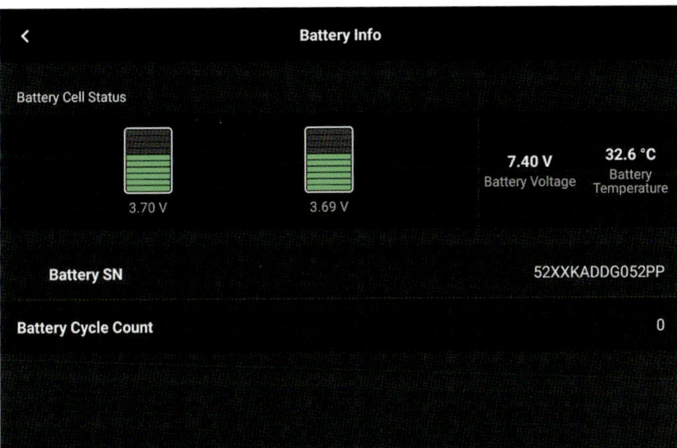

Figure 9.5 Battery status.

Unlock GEO Zone

I described geofencing and DJI's system of GEO Zones in Chapter 4. You must obtain an unlocking license for each zone using the DJI web page (https://dji.com/flysafe). You can then view and activate your licenses using this entry.

Find My Drone

With any luck, you'll never have to use this feature, but, if the next-to-worst thing happens (a crash that causes harm to the drone, a person, or property is the worst), you may lose track of exactly where your drone is located. Your misfortune might be caused by flying the drone to the limits of its battery capacity, forcing a landing when the battery reaches a critical low point. The drone may have lost both its GNSS signal and connection to your remote. There may have been a malfunction of the drone itself, or a flyaway in which the aircraft takes off for parts unknown for a variety of reasons.

If the drone is still powered up and has a GPS signal, this Find My Drone entry may be your first line of defense. The screen shown in Figure 9.6 appears showing the last known location of the drone (a blue triangle) and you, the operator (a blue dot). You can tap the box seen at lower right in the figure to prompt the aircraft to begin flashing its lights and emitting a beeping sound. On the right side of the screen is a "stacks" icon you can use to select the map layers you want visible.

Figure 9.6 Find My
Drone.

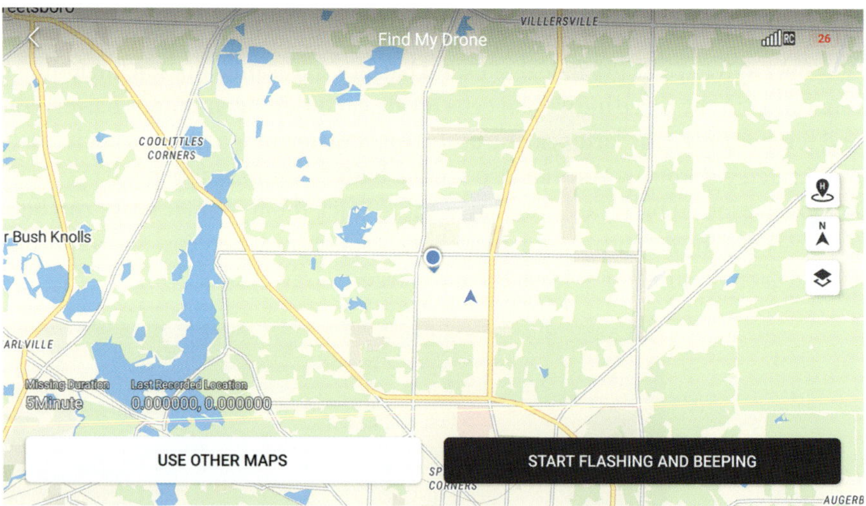

Advanced Safety Settings

The Advanced Safety Settings entry has three parts, shown in Figure 9.7, which specify how the drone behaves when the remote signal is lost and provides emergency propeller stop instructions.

- **Signal Lost.** In practice, your drone will not often lose its signal from the remote controller when you have a clear visual line of sight (VLOS) with the aircraft. It can happen if you wander too far, but it's more common to lose the signal because of some interference, particularly from buildings that block the drone's reception. This entry enables you to tell the drone what to do when the signal is lost and not quickly restored.

  You can select RTH, the default, in which case the drone will backtrack and return following the procedures I outlined in Chapter 4. If you choose Descent, the aircraft will reduce its altitude, which is often sufficient to restore the connection between it and your controller. You can also opt to have the drone hover in place. When that happens, if the signal isn't restored quickly,

Figure 9.7 Advanced
Safety Settings.

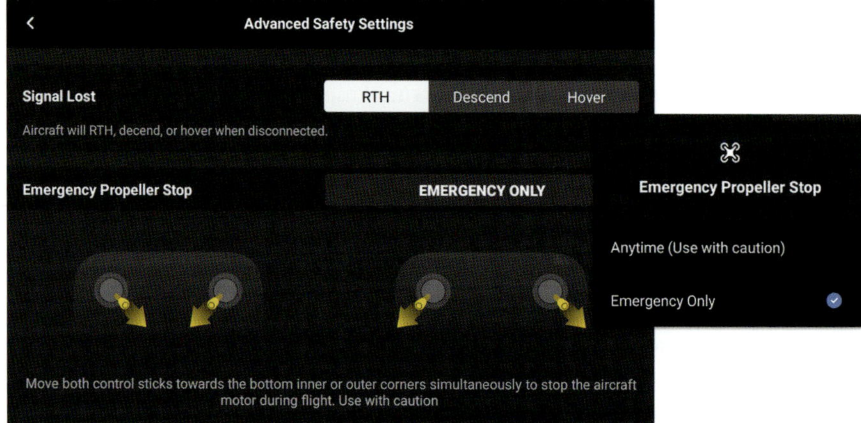

you'll want to move yourself (and the controller) in the direction you think the drone is located, which often may be all you need to reestablish the connection. **Note:** Failsafe RTH is disabled if you have selected Descend or Hover as the Signal Lost behavior.

- **Emergency Propeller Stop.** There is no function to access here; it's for your information only. The screen displays an illustration showing how to stop the propellers in an emergency using the Combination Stick Command (CSC). That command is invoked by pulling the right control stick down and diagonally to the right, and the left control stick down and to the left. You can also pull the left and right sticks down and to the left and right (respectively). As you can imagine, the drone will crash, which may be your best-case scenario in the event of an impending collision that will cause property damage or injury.

  Note: An important option within this entry is the setting that specifies *when* the Emergency Propeller Stop function can be invoked. Emergency Only is displayed by default, and the CSC sequence will stop the propellers *only* if the drone is in a collision or is rolling out of control after one of the motors stalls, or the aircraft is ascending or descending very quickly. Tap on the Emergency Only label and the screen shown at right in Figure 9.7 appears, and you can select Anytime (Use with Caution). In that case, the drone's motors will stop *at any time the sticks are used (even accidentally) to issue the CSC command during flight.*

  It may be possible to regain control of the aircraft by repeating the CSC command to restart the motors, but you may not have sufficient time to do this before the drone crashes.

Control Menu

The Control tab in the System Settings menu contains a dozen entries you can use to fine-tune the operation of your Mini 3 or Mini 3 Pro. As with all the menu tabs described in this chapter, only a portion is displayed on the screen of your controller at one time. You'll need to scroll down to see all the options shown in Figure 9.8.

Units

This entry is a simple region-centric option that allows you to specify how distances and speeds are displayed on the controller's screen when using DJI Fly. You can select either of two metric representations—meters or kilometers—for distance/speeds, or the Imperial system of feet and miles, which are *officially* used in the USA, Liberia, and Myanmar, but linger on for some measurements in Great Britain (where the Imperial system originated) and a few former Commonwealth nations, including Canada and India. You'll choose the system that is most comfortable for you.

Subject Scanning (Mini 3 Pro Only)

As described in Chapter 7, subject scanning is a feature that allows the drone to identify and mark potential video subjects with a green highlight box. You can tap the box to lock in that subject for focus/tracking, or draw a square around it on your controller's screen to define your own subject.

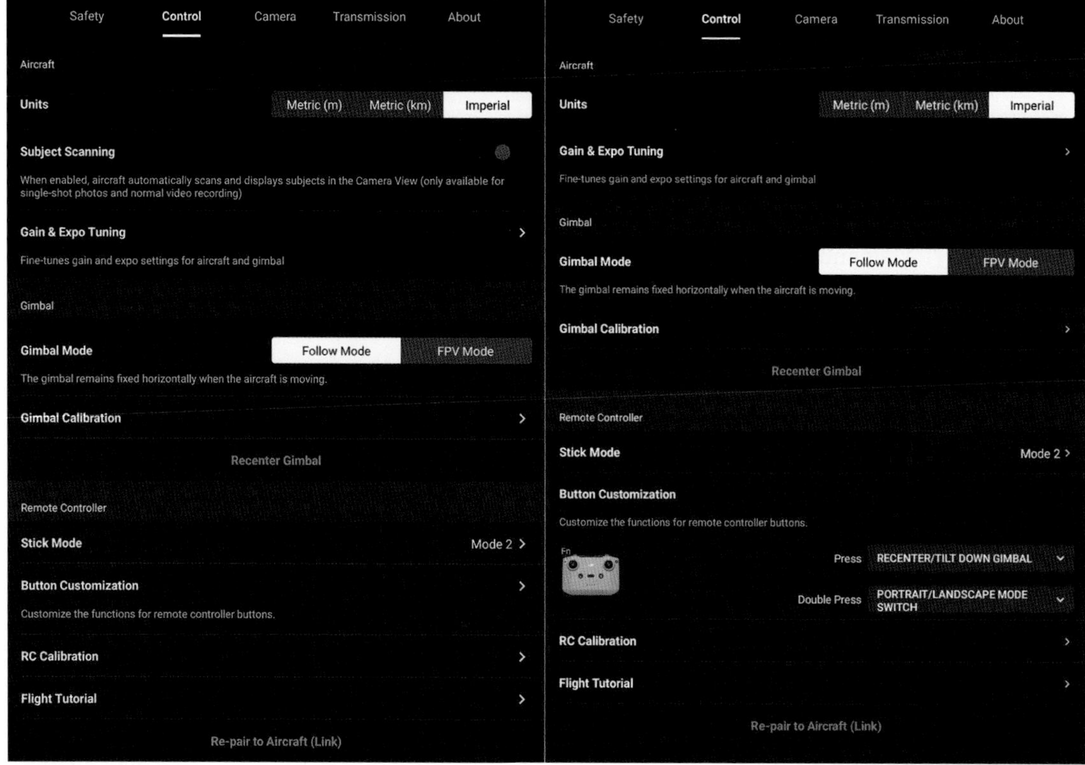

Figure 9.8 Control menu tab.

Gain & Expo Tuning

This entry (shown in Figure 9.9) is an advanced tool for changing the sensitivity of the drone's response to control movements (Gain) and the exponential curves (Expo) that determine the range in which your adjustments are applied. Ordinarily, recreational flyers won't ever need to make any changes here, but as you gain experience you may want to fine-tune your drone's response when capturing cinematic video or high-performance flight in Sport mode. You have separate options for the aircraft itself and for the gimbal. **Note:** The separate Advanced Gimbal Settings adjustments available with earlier versions of DJI Fly have been integrated into the Gain & Expo Tuning settings.

- **Maximum Horizontal Speed.** This option sets the fastest horizontal speed available when pushing the control stick, from 2.2 to 22.4 miles per hour. Slower speeds give you more precise control, while faster speeds are more responsive.

- **Maximum Ascent Speed.** This setting specifies the fastest ascent speed available from 2.2 to 6.7 miles per hour. As with the horizontal speed adjustment, slower speeds give you more precise control, while faster speeds are more responsive.

- **Maximum Descent Speed.** This setting is the reverse of the ascent speed adjustment, with the same 2.2 to 6.7 mph range available.

- **Maximum Angular Velocity.** This setting controls how quickly the drone rotates when the yaw stick (the left stick in Mode 2) is pressed left or right. The default is 40 degrees per second in Normal mode, with slower movement in Cine mode contrasted with a faster response in Sport mode.

- **Yaw Smoothness.** This determines how smoothly the aircraft rotates using the velocity specified above. The available range is from 0 to 100, and a little goes a long way, as Cine mode uses a value of just 8.

- **Brake Sensitivity.** This setting controls how quickly the aircraft brakes when you release the pitch control stick. The range is 10 to 150, with a default value of 100.

- **Expo.** The exponential curves setting requires a little explanation. Check out the graph midway down in Figure 9.9, which has red, blue, and green lines representing pitch/roll, yaw, and up/down motion, respectively. Straight lines from lower left to upper right in the graph would represent the same amount of adjustment from each end of the control stick's movement from either extreme to the midpoint.

But instead of that unchanging response, the exponential curves are steeper at the extremes, meaning the response is much faster, then tapering off to neutral in the middle. As a result, when a stick is pressed to its furthest point (far left/right or top/bottom), the change is quick, while in the areas toward the middle, where most flight adjustments take place, are slower. That gives you more precise control around the neutral position in the center, where most of your actual flight adjustments take place. A mere finger twitch won't send your drone far off course, but when you need to make large adjustments, the aircraft will respond immediately. You can make adjustments from 0.1 to 0.9, and can see from the table that only relatively small changes to the curves are needed.

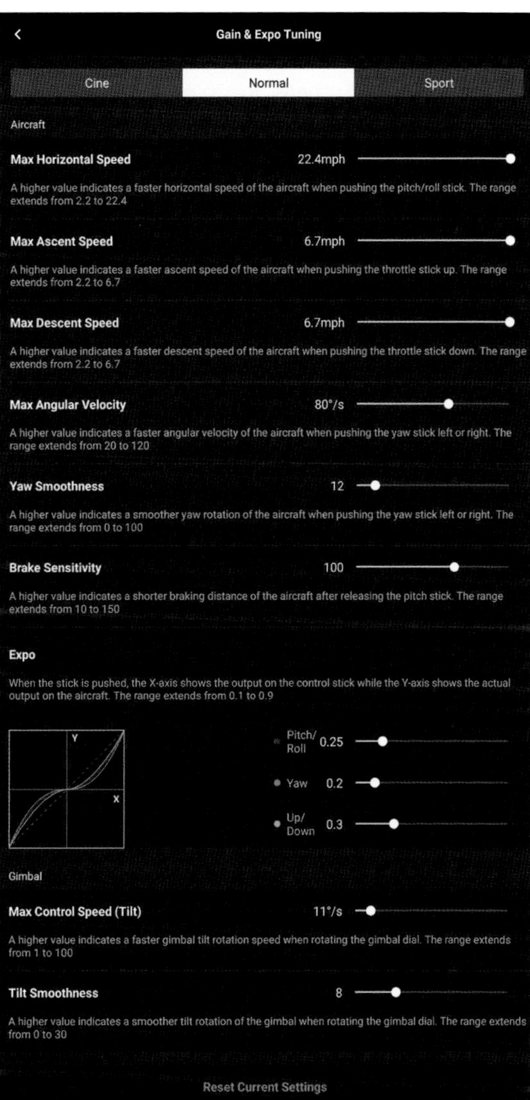

Figure 9.9 Gain & Expo Tuning.

- **Maximum Control Speed (Tilt).** This is the first of two gimbal adjustments. Here you can change the number of degrees per second the gimbal will move when rotating the gimbal dial. Select from 1 (for slow gimbal movement) to 100 (extremely fast) tilts. Keep in mind that, by default, the gimbal can only be tilted 90 degrees from horizontal, unless you activate Allow Upward Gimbal Rotation, as described shortly.

- **Tilt Smoothness.** This setting determines the smoothness of the gimbal's rotation when using the gimbal dial. You can choose values from 0 to 30. Coordinate this setting with the speed control above to produce the combination of speed and smoothness you need for your video.

- **Reset Current Settings.** Returns all the Gain and Expo settings to their defaults.

Gimbal Mode

Your drone defaults to Follow mode, in which the gimbal remains horizontal as the drone rolls slightly right or left during a turn, or tilts up or down when moving forward or backward. FPV (first-person view) mode locks the gimbal in the straight-ahead position, allowing the camera to tilt along with the drone, providing the perspective of what you'd see in an aircraft performing those maneuvers. I provided an example illustration in Chapter 4. FPV mode is used most for special effects, including MasterShots (with the Mini 3 Pro) or drone racing.

Gimbal Calibration

If your gimbal isn't providing the correct orientation, you can calibrate it using this entry. In the first screen, shown in Figure 9.10, upper left, you'll be asked to place the aircraft on a flat, level surface and choose to use Auto or Manual calibration. When you select Auto, you'll be prompted to position the drone in various orientations, including on its side, upside down, and facing in different directions (see Figure 9.10, upper right), until calibration is complete (see Figure 9.10, lower left). You can also perform a manual calibration, as seen in Figure 9.10, lower right.

Recenter Gimbal

There are times when you want to return the gimbal/camera view to the default centered position. You can do it from this menu entry if you like. A better solution is to define a button to perform the task, such as a double press of the Fn button on the RC-N1 remote controller. I'll show you how to customize buttons shortly.

Stick Mode

Those piloting DJI drones and those from many other manufacturers generally use what is called Stick Mode 2, which makes the left stick control up and down motion (throttle) and horizontal rotation (yaw), while the right stick controls forward/backward movement (tilt) and side-to-side movement (roll). You can select from two other modes if you happen to prefer them or have been using them with other aircraft, or create your own custom configuration. (See Figure 9.11.)

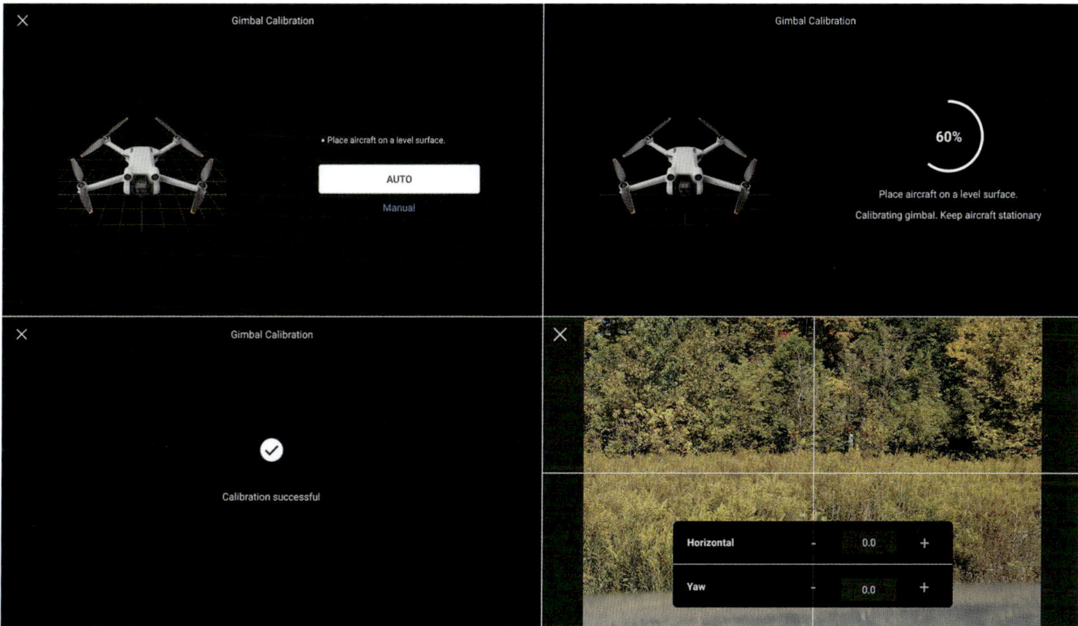

Figure 9.10 Gimbal calibration.

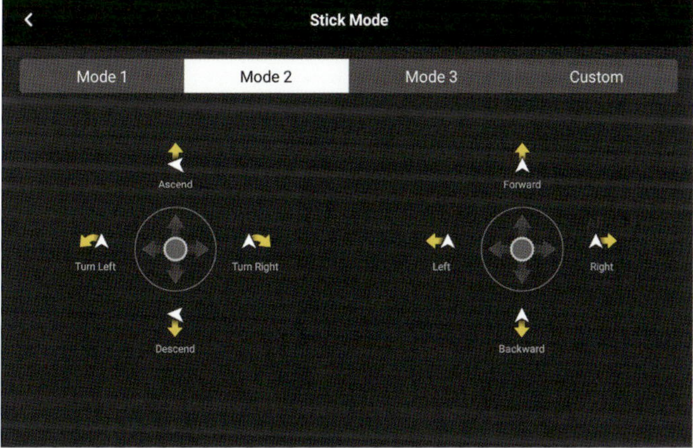

Figure 9.11 Stick Mode.

Those who have previously used weight shift aircraft (such as ultralights) may have the altitude control on the right and prefer to retain that orientation. Mode 1 does that: pressing the left stick forward and back moves the aircraft forward and back; pressing the right stick forward and back increases/decreases the altitude. Keep in mind that you will quickly develop muscle memory for any mode you settle on, and if you don't select Mode 2, you may not be able to use other folks' drones comfortably.

Button Customization

You can create custom definitions for a variety of buttons on your radio remote, with the behaviors and available buttons varying depending on which controller you are using. The DJI RC-N1 and RC-N2 have only a single Fn button that can be customized for either a single press or a double press. The DJI RC and RC 2 include both C1 and C2 buttons on the back of the unit with a variety of behaviors available.

The DJI RC Pro has three custom buttons, C1, C2, and C3 and a 5D "joystick" that can be tilted in multiple directions like the control sticks, or pressed inward as if it were a button. While the RC Pro has two dials, only the right dial can be programmed. You can specify a behavior for spinning the dial or for spinning the dial while custom buttons C1, C2, or C3 are depressed.

Figure 9.12 shows the main Button Customization screen for the DJI RC Pro, while a typical definition screen is shown in Figure 9.13. There are three column headings at the top of the definition screen: Control, Camera, and Other. When you highlight each in turn the available definitions appear.

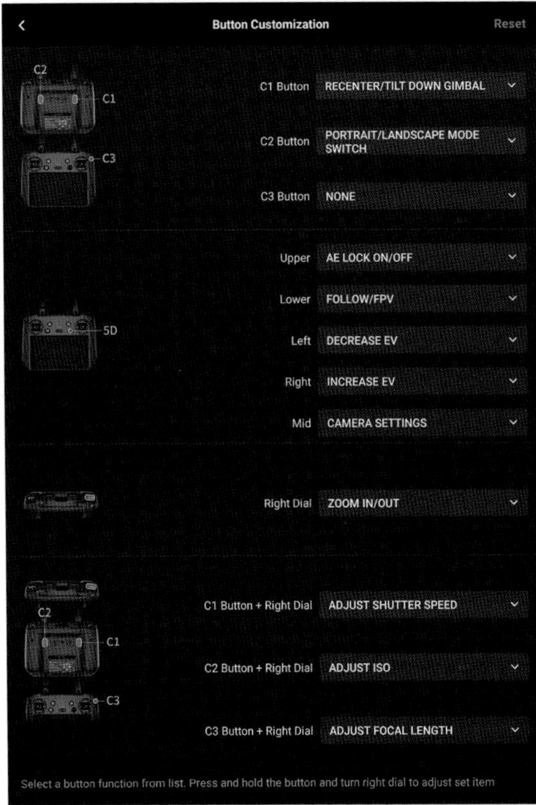

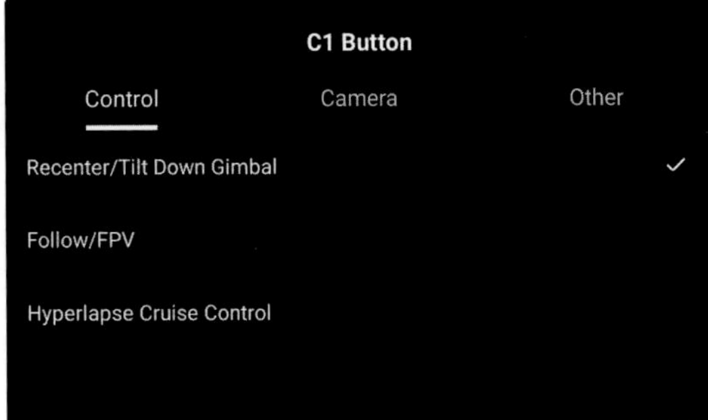

Figure 9.12 Define a custom button.

Figure 9.13 Choose the button's behavior.

RC Calibration

It's important that your remote is calibrated such that when your dial(s) are rotated to their far left/ right positions, or either control stick is in its neutral center point, or pushed to their extremes at right, left, up, or down, the controller "knows" that position accurately. This entry allows you to rotate your dials and manipulate the sticks while the controller "observes" what you've done and sets itself to reflect the positions accurately during flight. Figure 9.14 shows the screens for the DJI RC Pro.

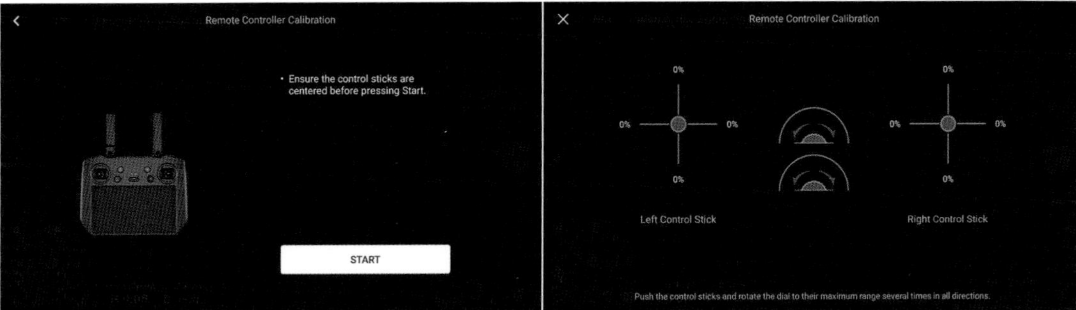

Figure 9.14 RC calibration.

Flight Tutorial

The DJI Fly app has some tutorials available in Camera View, in addition to the Academy videos accessible from the initial screen of the application. You can view pre-flight check screens, seen at top and bottom in Figure 9.15 before tapping the Start Tutorial panel (at lower right in the figure) to view the full tutorial. I recommend this as a review if you haven't completed reading this book.

Re-pair to Aircraft (Link)

If you use multiple remote controls with a single aircraft or use the same remote with other DJI drones, you may sometimes need to re-pair/bind the remote and your drone by following the prompts this command supplies. Although there is a method of re-pairing by simultaneously pressing the RC-N1's Fn, Shutter/Record button, and Photo/Video toggle buttons, the function is carried out so infrequently that few will remember the combination when needed. This entry, highlighted in blue at the bottom of the Control menu tab, is easy to access.

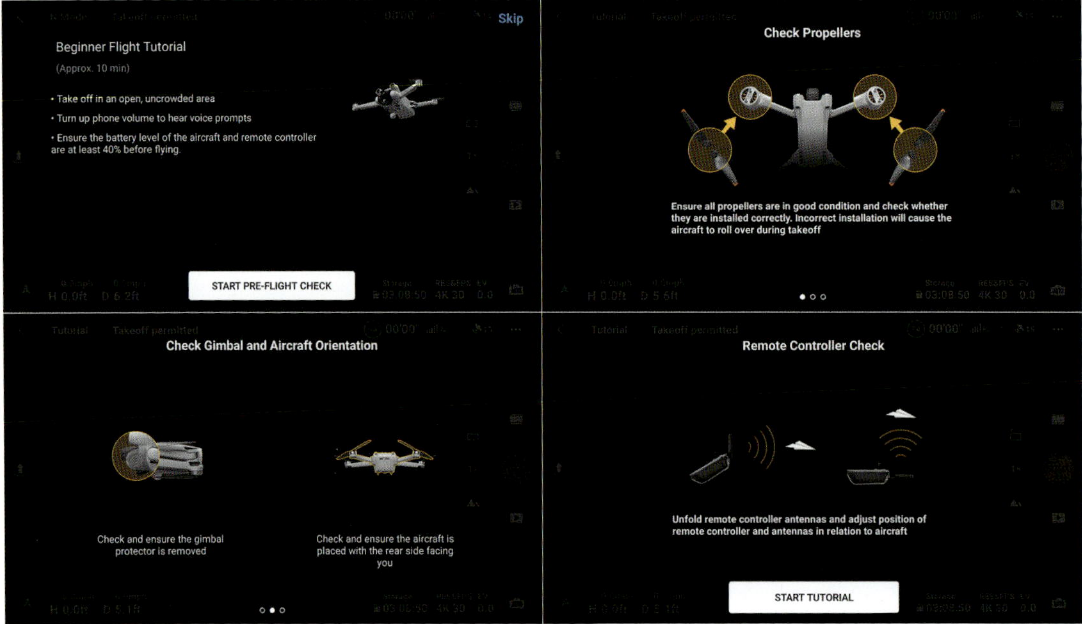

Figure 9.15 Flight tutorial.

Camera Menu

The Camera menu tab includes entries that allow you to make photographic- and video-oriented adjustments to the drone and its storage. The available entries vary, depending on the shooting mode you are in. The options in Still photo mode for the Mini 3 Pro and Mini 3 are shown at left and right in Figure 9.16. In Video mode, the available entries are similar, except those in the Photo section of the Mini 3 Pro menu are replaced by the Video entries seen in Figure 9.17. I explained how to use the Mini 3 Pro's video format, color, coding format, and video subtitles entries in Chapter 8 and will not repeat that information here.

Format (Mini 3 Pro Only)

Don't confuse this File Format entry with the Format command in the Storage area of the Camera menu tab, which erases internal or external storage and creates a fresh file system for new data (as I'll explain shortly). This command allows you to choose between capturing JPEG (only) images, or saving your drone's shots in both JPEG and RAW formats. The Mini 3 Pro does not offer an option to save *only* RAW images.

As I noted in Chapter 6, JPEG is a compact, compressed image file format that discards some information in order to maximize your available storage capacity. RAW files, which for DJI drones is actually Adobe Digital Negative (DNG) format, is useful when you want to have access to all the information captured by the camera before the camera's internal logic has converted it to JPEG. RAW format preserves your *settings* information, but can be manipulated in an image editor to fine-tune an image. I explained this option in more detail in Chapter 6.

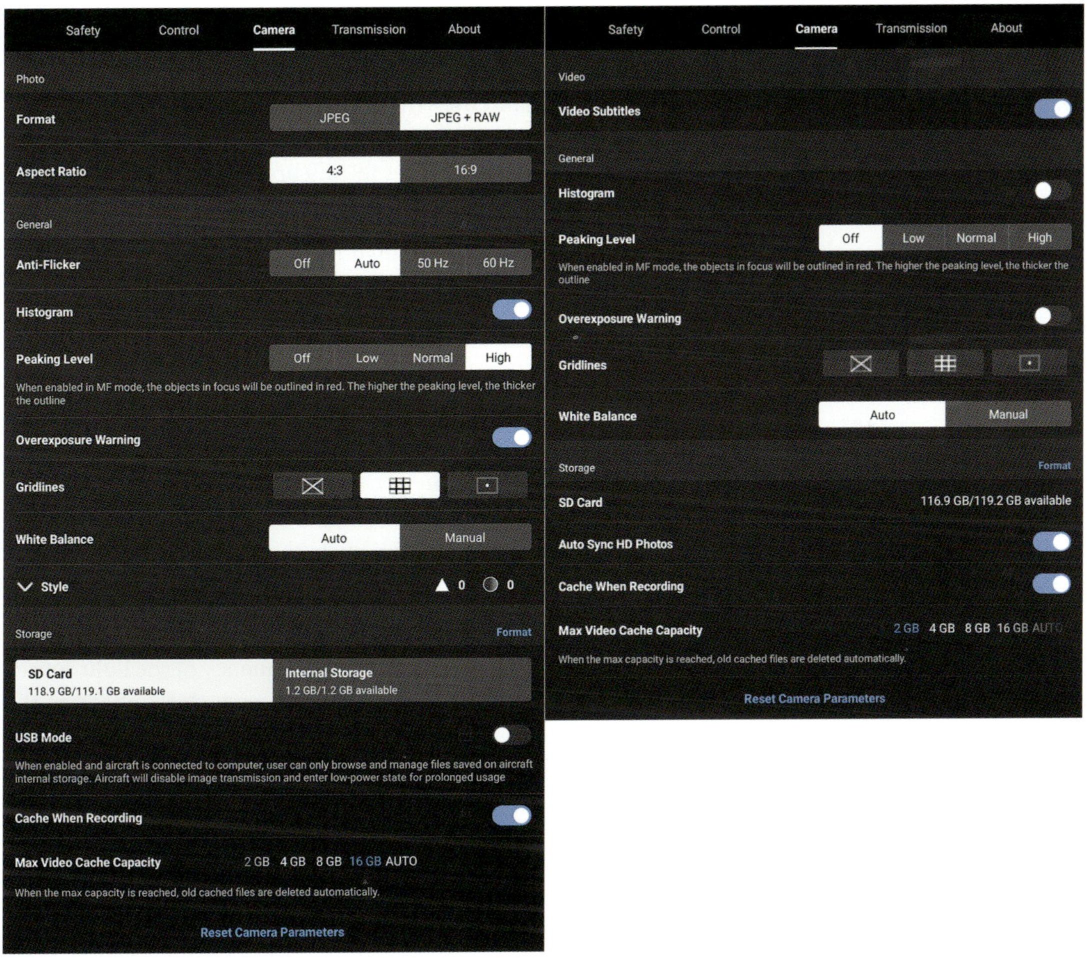

Figure 9.16 Camera menu.

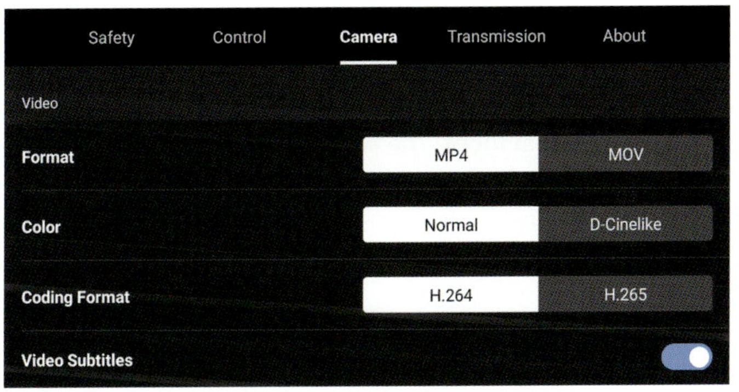

Figure 9.17 The Mini 3 Pro video-oriented commands, explained in Chapter 8.

Aspect Ratio (Mini 3 Pro Only)

In Photo mode, the Mini 3 Pro and Mini 3 capture images using a 4:3 aspect ratio by default. The Mini 3 Pro has the additional capability of switching to the same 16:9 proportions used for video. If you're preparing a presentation that will mix stills and video and want to standardize on one aspect ratio, you can use this entry to force the drone to capture images in 16:9 proportions in still photography mode as well.

DJI Fly is smart enough that in Photo mode, if you have specified the 4:3 aspect ratio, the image will display on your remote controller's screen in 4:3 proportions, and if you've selected 16:9, that cropping is what you'll see instead. Of course, in Video modes, the display is always seen with the 16:9 crop.

Anti-Flicker (Mini 3 Pro Only)

Those who shoot with conventional still cameras probably have noticed that shots they take in certain gymnasiums or arenas have inconsistent exposure, wildly varying color, or banding. The reason is that certain types of artificial lighting actually have a blinking cycle that is imperceptible to the eye, but which the camera can capture.

You'll encounter the same effect with your drone when capturing aerial stills or videos in which that kind of artificial lighting is seen. This setting, when enabled, detects the frequency of the light source that is blinking, and tries to sync capture at the moment when the flicker has the least effect on the final image or frame. You may have to experiment when encountering a new light source; while Auto will work most of the time, you can also select the 60 Hz and 50 Hz frequencies encountered in the United States and elsewhere (respectively). When not shooting under artificial light, you can safely leave the setting Off.

Histogram/Peaking Level/Overexposure Warning

I explained the use of these three evaluation tools in detail in Chapter 5 and will not duplicate that information here. All three apply equally to still photo and video modes.

- **Histogram.** The live histograms your Mini 3 or Mini 3 Pro can display on the screen while you shoot can be useful in determining the correct exposure for your still images and video. You can enable/disable the histogram here.
- **Peaking Level.** When using manual focus, the color highlighting offered by your drone's Focus Peaking can provide the visual cues you need to judge correct focus. Choose Off, Low, Normal, or High levels of edge highlighting.
- **Overexposure Warning.** The "zebra" stripes produced by this tool can show you which areas of your image will be overexposed.

Gridlines

Markers superimposed on your frame (and which don't appear in your finished image) can help in composing or aligning your image. You can have your choice of Rule of Thirds, X, and Crosshair, or combine any two or all three, as shown in Figure 9.18.

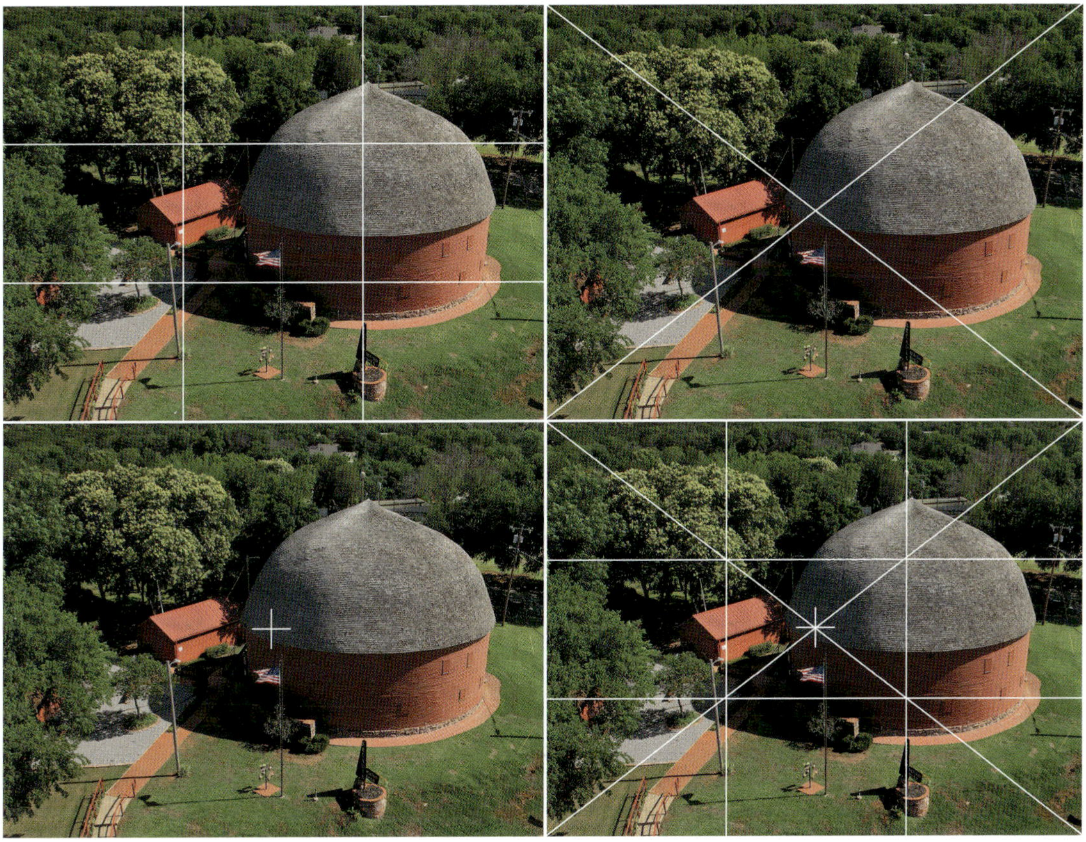

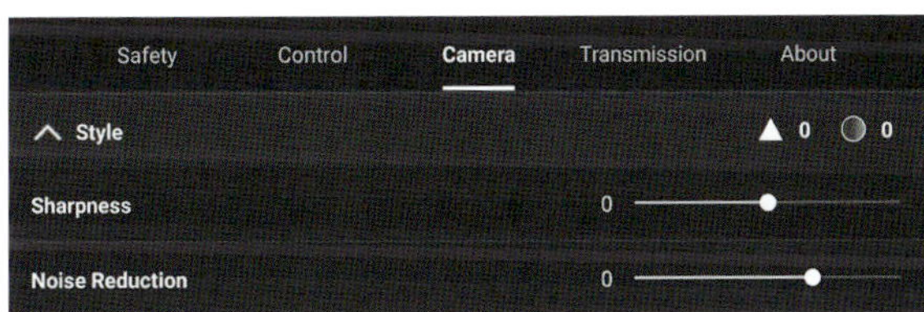

Figure 9.18 Available markers include Rule of Thirds (upper left), X (upper right), Crosshair (lower left), or a combination (lower right).

White Balance

You can choose an appropriate white balance for your stills and video. Choose Auto to let the drone calculate an appropriate balance or select Manual and use a slider to specify color balance on the Kelvin scale from 2,000 to 10,000.

Style (Mini 3 Pro Only)

When you click on this entry, two sliders appear that let you increase or decrease the amount of sharpness and/or noise reduction applied to your images as they are saved to storage. (See Figure 9.19.) While it's usually a better idea to make these adjustments in your editing software, if you want to tweak all the files you capture slightly, you can dial in some changes here.

Figure 9.19 Adjust sharpness and noise reduction applied by the Mini 3 Pro.

Format

The Storage area of the Camera menu tab displays the total amount of space available and amount remaining for storage on both the microSD card in the drone (if present), and, in the case of the Mini 3 Pro, the aircraft's own minuscule 1.2GB internal memory. (The Mini 3 has no internal storage at all.) If you're using the Mini 3 Pro, click on the blue-highlighted Format label and the screen shown in Figure 9.20 appears. You can choose either SD Card or Internal Storage and tap Format to reformat the media. Note that when you reformat a card (or insert a new card), the drone's file number system reverts back to zero.

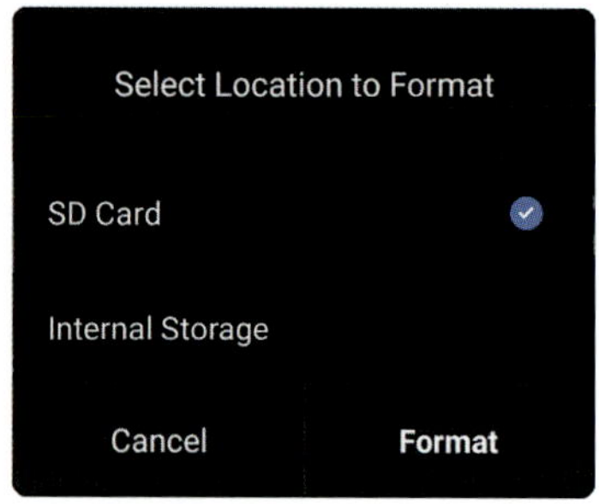

Figure 9.20 Choose the Mini 3 Pro location to format.

USB Mode (Mini 3 Pro Only)

This is a power-saving mode you can use when you've connected the Mini 3 Pro to your computer using a USB cable and want to be able to view and manage files stored on the aircraft's storage. The drone disconnects from the remote controller and functions, basically, as a disk drive in a reduced power state. This feature can be especially handy if you want to transfer images from the aircraft to your computer without inflicting a significant drain on its battery. Remember to disable USB mode when you're ready to resume flights.

Auto Sync HD Photos (Mini 3 Only)

Those flying the DJI Mini 3 will need to activate this setting in order to enable automatic transfer of HD photos to your mobile device when using the RC-N1 remote controller. (The DJI RC does not support this function.)

Cache When Recording

Your drone stores any still photos or videos you capture on the aircraft's media during flight, and you can transfer those full-resolution files to your controller or computer for viewing, sharing, or post-processing. If you can also activate this feature, the drone will create a low-resolution version of the video clips to transmit to your remote control for viewing any time, even while the drone is still in the air. You can enable or disable that feature here. It's useful to be able to review your shots quickly without needing to download the large original file. Unless my memory card is starting to fill up, I leave this capability turned on.

Max Video Cache Capacity

You can specify how much of the available on-board storage of your drone to dedicate to storage of cached videos, from 2GB to 16GB, or allow the app to select an appropriate amount for you. If you are directing storage to an installed microSD card that's reasonably large, say, 128GB, you can be generous. But if you anticipate using most of your available storage for video on a single flight, limiting caching or turning it off completely may be a good idea.

Reset Camera Parameters

Use this to reset all camera settings to their factory defaults.

Transmission Menu

The Transmission menu tab (see Figure 9.21) contains four or three entries (for the Mini 3 Pro and Mini 3, respectively) that control certain features of your remote control's operation, including any live-streaming platforms you use, HDMI output (Mini 3 Pro only), radio frequencies used, and channel selection mode.

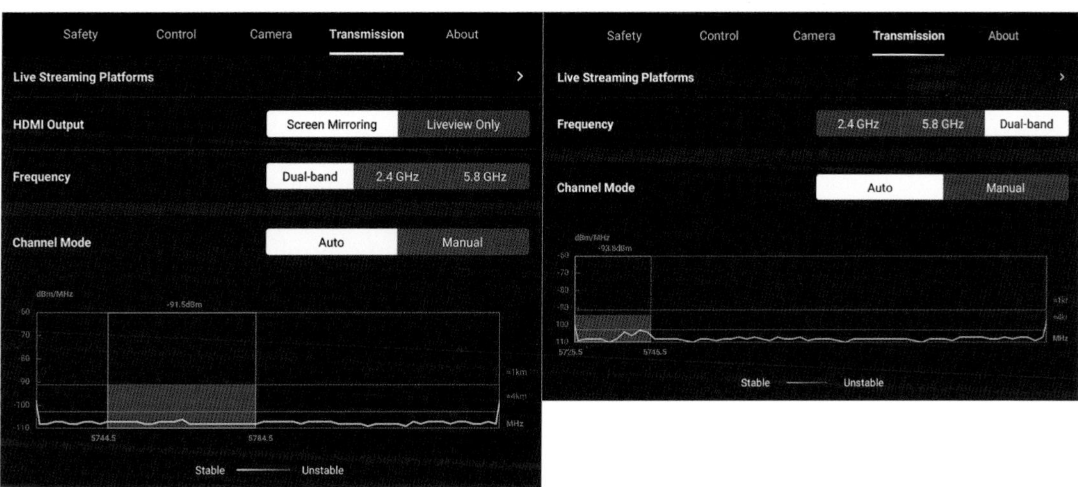

Figure 9.21 Transmission menu tab.

Live-Streaming Platforms

Believe it or not, you can actually live stream what your drone is seeing to your social media platform, including YouTube, using RTMP (Real-Time Messaging Protocol). You'll need to retrieve your streaming "key" (not password) and fill it in, along with the social media URL, in the RTMP Address field shown in Figure 9.22. Choose your resolution and bit rate, and if your internet connection can handle it, you'll soon be sharing your exploits with admirers worldwide (as well as potential bad actors and the FAA, so be careful about where, when, and what you stream).

HDMI Output (Mini 3 Pro Only)

If you have a controller that offers HDMI output to a monitor or recording device, this menu option appears allowing you to choose Screen Mirroring, which is basically a screenshot that displays everything on your screen including information overlays. Or, you can select "clean" output by opting for live view only, so only the actual scene being captured will be displayed and/or recorded on the external device.

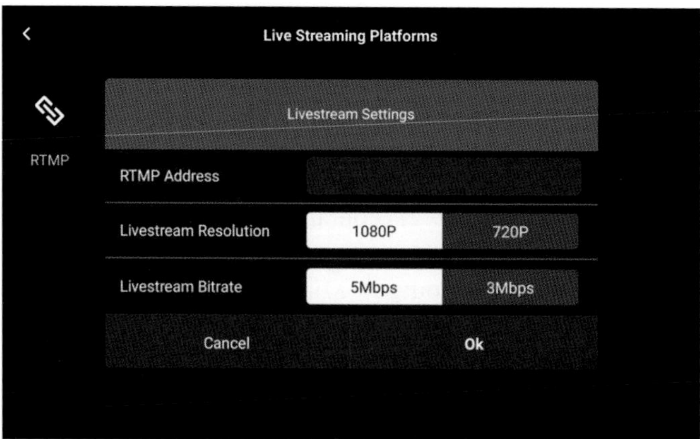

Frequency/Channel Mode

Your drone can transmit its data to your remote control using two different radio frequencies, 2.4GHz or 5.8GHz, or it can access both as required. Each frequency band has its own set of advantages. In either case, you should keep in mind that the orientation of your controller's antennas can also be important. It may be necessary to move around until the signal strength displayed on your screen becomes stronger. The graph at the bottom shows the relative signal strength for the current band.

You can select the following parameters:

- **Frequency.** You can enable either 2.4GHz or 5.8GHz bands, or both:
  - **Dual Band.** If you choose Dual Band, your aircraft and controller will seek out the best connection for you, and will switch from a weakening signal at one frequency to a stronger signal on the other band automatically.
  - **2.4GHz.** The drone will operate only using this band. This frequency can cover a longer distance and is less directional, but cannot carry as much information as 5.8GHz. Many other devices, including Wi-Fi, garage door openers, security cameras, and baby monitors use this frequency, so interference can be a problem. In areas where competing devices aren't a problem, especially rural areas, 2.4GHz can be extremely reliable.
  - **5.8GHz.** The drone will use only this band, which can carry larger amounts of data, but doesn't travel as far. Its range can be limited by interference with trees, concrete, and steel. Nevertheless, because there are fewer devices competing for its wavelength, it is often the best choice in urban areas and modest distances. If you have problems getting a strong link to your drone with 2.4GHz, you can switch to this frequency.
- **Channel Mode.** You can select Auto switching or choose to select the band manually.
  - **Auto.** This option is available only if 2.4GHz or 5.8GHz are selected under Frequency, and disabled if Dual Band is enabled.
  - **Manual.** When this option is selected, Dual Band disappears from the Frequency entry and you can then select 2.4GHz or 5.8GHz manually by tapping that setting.

About Menu

This menu tab provides basic information about your drone and its software, including its name (which you can edit), model number, version number of the DJI Fly app, your aircraft and remote control's firmware, and FlySafe Data. You can check for updates for the latter two, and install them from this screen. Also shown are the serial numbers of the currently installed battery, your Remote ID, Flight Controller, Remote Controller, and Camera. (See Figure 9.23.)

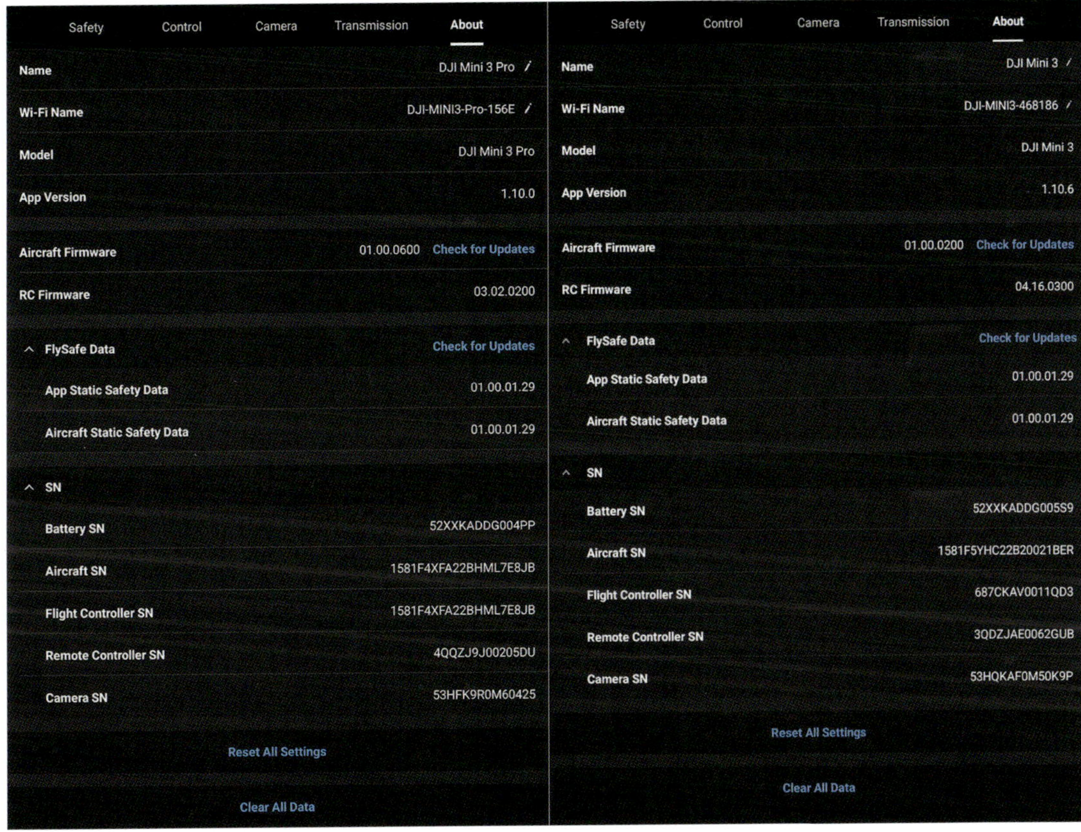

Figure 9.23 About menu tab.

DJI Fly Main Screen

By this time you've probably worked with the DJI Fly app enough that you've explored all the features available from the main screen. Here's a recap of their functions (labeled in Figure 9.24):

1. **Fly Spots.** Connects you to DJI FindSpot, where you can check GEO Zones, restrictions, regulations, and other information about specific locations using a useful, searchable map.

2. **Academy.** This gives you access to a treasure trove of videos you can view right on your controller screen, including a beginner guide and vast course library on features, flight safety, and creative ideas.

3. **Album.** Your videos and still photos are accessible from your personal library.

4. **SkyPixel.** DJI touts this web resource as the largest aerial photography community in the world. It's a rich resource with tools, forums, and galleries for sharing your best work.

5. **Profile.** Provides a link to your DJI Profile, where you'll find tabs for Device Management, the DJI Forum, DJI Store, Find My Drone utility, and Settings. It also displays the total number of hours of flight time, distance, and number of flights.

    Your flight records synchronize to your DJI account automatically when your controller is connected to Wi-Fi. You can actually view information about individual flights, including date, distance, altitude, and duration.

6. **Connection Guide/Go Fly.** Tap Connection Guide to connect your controller to your aircraft. If the drone has already been connected, the label Go Fly will appear instead. Tap to switch to Camera View.

When your aircraft is connected, before take-off you can tap the Takeoff Permitted label at the top edge of the screen to produce a Flight Checklist screen with any applicable warnings, as shown in Figure 9.25. You can set the Maximum Altitude and Maximum Distance from this screen, and adjust your storage location.

Figure 9.24 DJI app main screen.

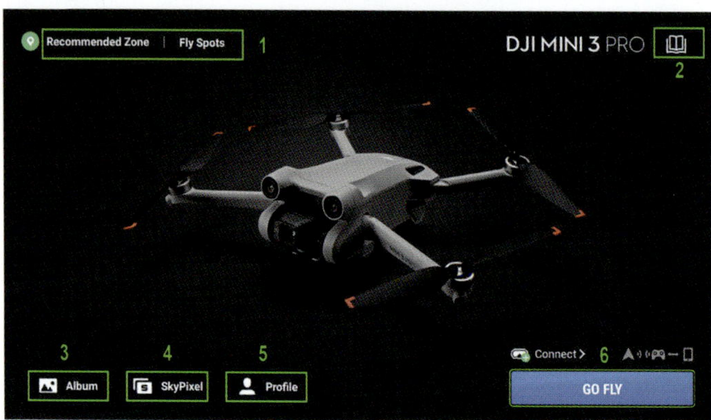

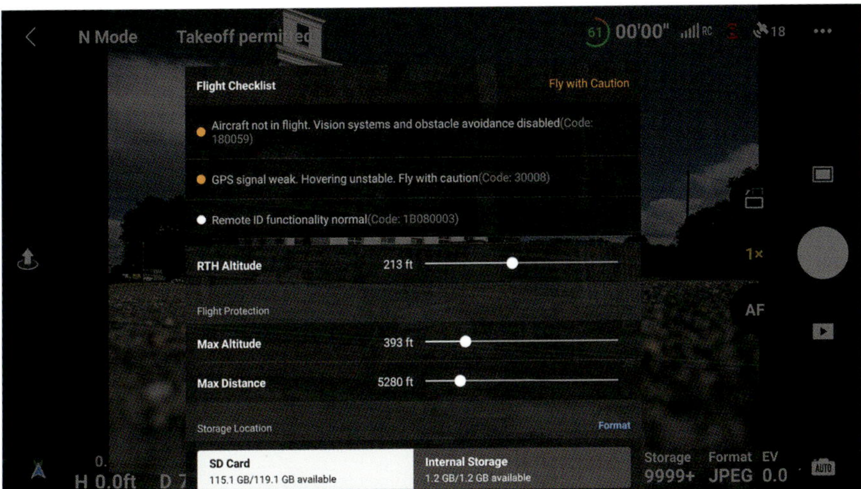

Figure 9.25 DJI Flight Checklist.

Next Up

Congratulations! By finishing this book, you've graduated from your DJI Mini 3/Mini 3 Pro boot camp, having familiarized yourself with all the basics, sent your drone aloft successfully, and at least dabbled with many of your quadcopter's most exciting features. You're now free to explore all the amazing photography your aircraft is capable of. However, as with any avocation, there's a lot more to learn and discover—particularly if you're thinking of taking the next step and qualifying for your Part 107 certification. There are plenty of more advanced online and printed courses and tutorials to help you on your journey, and I hope you'll return to this book from time to time when you want a refresher or need to expand what you already know.

Index